I0801878

# MICK WALKER'S JAPANESE PRODUCTION RACING MOTORCYCLES

REDLINE BOOKS

This book is dedicated to the memory of my son Gary Walker, whose life and developing skills on the track were cruelly cut short by the sport he loved so much.



British Library Cataloguing in Publication Data

A catalogue record for this book is available from the British Library

ISBN: 0 9544357 0 2

Designed and published in 2003 by
Redline Books
2 Carlton Terrace, Low Fell, Tyne & Wear, NE9 6DE
www.redlinebooks.co.uk

Printed in Italy by Printer Trento.

# Contents

# Introduction

One of several Mick Walker Racing teamsters was Tom Tunstall, later to graduate to British and European championship level (on various machines). Tom is seen racing his Honda RS125 at a British 125cc championship meeting in 1997.

Frame builders Tigcraft produced this Mini Mono special for the 2002 British Supermono Championship. Ridden by Mark George, this diminutive Yamaha 425cc motocross liquid-cooled single-cylinder ohc engined bike, put many larger models to shame. Besides Rotax and BMW the other contenders in the class were powered by Japanese Suzuki and Yamaha engines of up to 800cc.

Japanese Production Racing Motorcycles is the sixth in a series of books that ultimately will cover the world's racing motorcycles from the dawn of the combustion engine to the present day. Volume five covered Japanese Grand Prix Racing Motorcycles; it being necessary to split the Japanese content into two volumes due to the sheer scale of material involved.

My own involvement with Japanese motorcycles began during the early 1960s, when I owned a Honda CB92 Benly SuperSport. This machine convinced me that not only were the Japanese capable of building excellent machines, but with bikes such as the CB92 they had already surpassed existing European and British designs in many areas.

As Grand Prix Racing Motorcycles in this series explains, the Japanese did not, as many had thought, suddenly become proficient in the design and development of motorcycles when they first appeared in Europe at the end of the 1950s. Instead, the Japanese had been interested, involved even, with motorcycles since the beginning of the 20th century.

True, early Japanese motorcycles copied Western design - a trend that continued for several years after the end of the Second World War. But soon they were to prove that they were very much their own men, by designing a succession of highly innovative machinery, not only to the Grand Prix world's benefit but the paying 'over-the-counter' customer too.

In years gone by, the British, Italians and to a lesser extent the Germans, had offered privateers the chance to own replicas of works machinery, or specially built limited batch production models intended solely for fast road work or clubman type events. But from the mid 1960s Japan has led the world in this area.

Rhodesian Nobby Clark, regarded by many as the world's number one race mechanic, at various times he worked for Honda, Yamaha, MV Agusta and Cagiva. Nobby is pictured here at Daytona Speedway in March 2002.

# Mick Walker Racing

*The first rider to benefit from the Mick Walker Racing team support was Darren North who rode this 1993 updated Honda RS250 in the 1995 British Championship series. Darren (in the foreground) is seen here dicing with Yamaha-mounted Max Vincent, at the Snetterton round that year.*

*14-year-old Ollie Bridewell with a smiling Mick Walker at Mallory Park in March 2000. The bike is a 2000 model year Honda RS125.*

Mick Walker Racing was formed shortly after the author's son Gary's tragic death following a freak start-line accident at Brands Hatch on the 4th September 1994. The purpose of the team has been to train, help and act as a mentor for young British racing talent. Since then, some thirty riders have benifitted. Riders who have progressed and become well known in the road racing world include; James Toseland, Mark Heckles, Darren North, Dean Johnson, Guy Etherington, Tom Tunstall, Chris Burns, Michael Gavin, Djon Compton, Darren Wnoukoski, Robin King, Barry Rudd, Ollie Bridewell and Steven Neate.

*The 1999 British Superclub champion Barry Rudd (extreme right) with his friends and supporters at Oulton Park that year. Mick Walker is centre rear with baseball cap. The machine is a 1995 (updated) Honda CBR600.*

*14-year-old Steven Neate joined the MW squad for 2002 and is definitely a star in the making. He is seen here on the Mick Walker Racing/M Price Honda RS125 at Cadwell Park, 30th June 2002.*

*Guy Etherington (Mick Walker Racing Honda RS125) at Cadwell Park on his way to winning the New Era club championship, 1998.*

*Gary Walker (centre) pictured with George Roberts of sponsors Youngs Motors in Spring 1994, and Mick Walker (right). The bike is a 1993 RS250 Honda.*

*Mick Walker (rear left) with the Neate family at Snetterton, June 2002. Father John was a top line racer in his own right.*

*Brands Hatch 2nd May 1983 and a jubilant Barry Sheene with the Transatlantic Trophy depicting the three circuits used for the Britain v America team races.*

Honda, Kawasaki, Suzuki and Yamaha, plus Bridgestone and Tohatsu have all built and sold racing motorcycles which the public could buy. At first these were restricted to the smaller displacement engine sizes, but mirroring the developments made with larger machinery for the road rider, so the Japanese industry responded by offering bigger and bigger racers. Today this means the likes of Suzuki's GSX-R1000, Honda's VTR1000SP and Yamaha's R1, plus of course other machinery right down to the superb built-for-purpose Honda RS125 single.

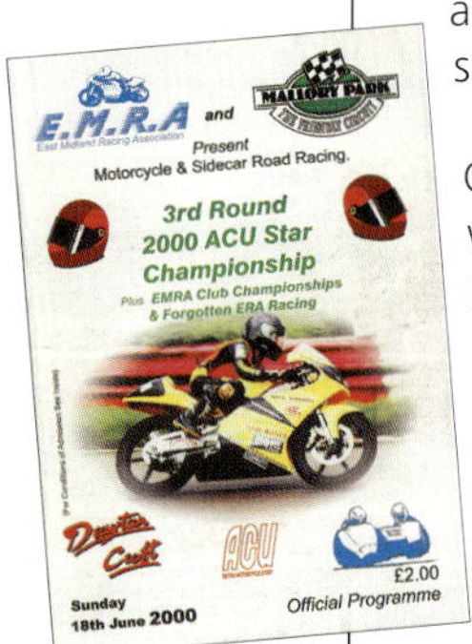

Today the early production racers such as the Honda CR110 and CR93 are highly prized by enthusiasts and collectors alike - recognised for what they are - jewel-like masterpieces of a golden era in motorcycle racing, the 1960s.

What is amazing, as readers of this book will soon discover, is the sheer range which the Japanese have produced, everything from a 50cc twin to 1-litre plus superbikes. With the four-strokes there have been 2,3,4 and 5 valves-per-cylinder, whilst two-stroke development has encompassed piston-port, rotary, disc-valve, reed-valve, mechanically and electrically operated power valves and much more.

As with the earlier volumes in this series I would like to put on record the various good people who have assisted me in its preparation. This includes the companies themselves, marque specialists, existing and former riders, engineers, tuners - the list is almost endless.

*The 1987 Honda endurance squad at Le Mans with its works-supported RVF v-four (left and right) and NR oval piston model (centre).*

Once again, Doug Jackson provided several rare photographs from his collection, Barry Hickmott gave information on Bridgestone, Tohatsu and Kawasaki, Dave Simmonds' widow Julie kindly loaned me the family photograph collection, Alan Horner (Ian Lougher photographs), Richard Tracey (Yamaha) and Don Leeson (Suzuki) were also vital. Many people provided information and or photographs. Amongst these were Rod Scivyer, Andrew French, Tommy Robb, Hugh Anderson, Roy Everett, Barry Sheene, James Arnold, Terry Grotefeld, Phil Read, Kent Andersson, Kork Ballington, Terry Naughtin, Bob Hansen, Bob Blakeley, Roy Francis, Tony Collison, Martin Jones, Dave Pearce, Ron Pladdys, Christopher Marshall, John Kirkby, Nobby Clark, Dara Brady, Rick Brett, Dave Evans, Mike Kirby, Peter Hillaby, Ian Lougher, Martyn Harris, Nick Nicholls and Jim Parker.

After completing this book I was left asking, What next? If one clear answer seems to emerge, it is that the two-stroke is on the way out - seen as no longer environmentally friendly. SuperSport and  are the buzz words and the four-stroke is rapidly making a come back in all forms of competition, a feature which I believe can only speed up over the next few years. The two-stroke dominated from the mid 1960s until the beginning of the 1990s and has been in decline ever since.

All that is left is to wish you, the reader, as much pleasure as I have had in compiling Japanese Production Racing Motorcycles. It has also made me realise just how much the racing fraternity have to thank the Japanese for producing and selling such a vast range of machinery over such a long period. Long may this continue.

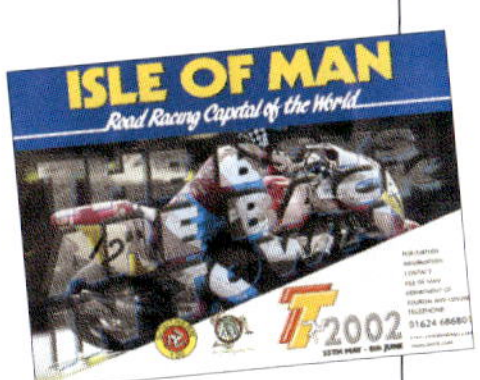


Mick Walker
Wisbech, Cambridgeshire
October 2003

*Goodwood Festival of Speed, June 1999. Left to right, George Beale, Luigi Taveri, Allan Robinson and Mick Walker.*

# Bridgestone

# 1

*1966 Bridgestone 175cc Dual Twin, a disc valve twin cylinder with a particularly advanced specification.*

Today Bridgestone is one of the biggest and most successful tyre companies on the planet; but duing the 1960s the company looked set to challenge the likes of Honda, Suzuki and Yamaha as a major motorcycle manufacturer. Equally, its racing bikes appeared to offer a serious challenge too. So what happened? Read on for the full story.

The Bridgestone Tire Co. Ltd. was established back in 1931, by company founder Shojiro Ishibashi. He adopted for its corporate name the literal translation of his name, 'stone bridge'. Bridgestone then proceeded to become the major tyre producer in Japan - besides being its oldest.

Bridgestone was also a major producer of pedal cycles. So perhaps it was an obvious step when the Tokyo-based concern moved into the field of powered 2-wheelers in 1952. At this stage 'powered' meant little more than a clip-on engine on a pedal cycle. The engine was a two-stroke - as were all subsequent Bridgestone designs. But in case one is given the impression that this first Bridgestone was lacking interest, it should be noted that the frame was of cast aluminium, as were all pedal cycles produced by the company at that time. Called the BS Motor, rather than Bridgestone, the engine was manufactured by the Prince car company, which then had close trading links with Bridgestone. The BS Motor was unique in that it was mounted to the rear wheel upside-down, with the spark plug at the bottom. It was also highly unusual in that the first few examples manufactured had no piston rings! This latter feature was soon altered, following a catalogue of engine seizures from overheating.

The first complete Bridgestone, a moped, appeared in 1958. This was followed in April 1960 by the marque's first motorcycle, the 49cc fan-cooled Champion 2. This became the Model 3 the following year, with a 3-speed gearbox.

*With a maximum speed of over 100mph, the stock 350GTR certainly had performance. Add aluminium cylinders, rotary disc-valves, 6-speeds and a dry racing-type clutch and you had an excellent basis for a competitive circuit racer.*

By 1964, Bridgestone's annual turnover amounted to in excess of 200 million US dollars, and besides occupying tenth spot in the world tyre sales league, it was beginning to enjoy a healthy profit from its two-wheel activities. The group had more than 10,000 employees within its Japanese plants and sales offices in New York, Singapore, Hamburg, Tehran, Bangkok and Beirut. Bridgestone's two modern factories, in Ageo (Saitama Pref.) and Aashi (Saga Pref.) had a yearly production capacity of 240,000 motorcycles and 600,000 bicycles.

It is perhaps to be expected that the 'big four' domestic motorcycle marques, Honda, Suzuki, Yamaha and Kawasaki, all major users of Bridgestone tyres, mounted a joint campaign to limit Bridgestone's two-wheel expansion. They also requested that the company concentrate its efforts in this field on the export, rather than the home market. 1964 was also the year of the highly successful 90cc Sports - this being Bridgestone's first model to feature disc-valve induction.

At the end of that year, Bridgestone displayed its latest and largest motorcycle to date, the 5-speed BS125. This was a 125cc rotary valve two-stroke twin with such advanced features as a disc front brake and pump-type lubrication. The BS125 was to act as a forerunner to the 174cc (50 x 45mm) Dual Twin of 1965 and the 345cc (61 x 59mm) GTR, which was introduced two years later.

All three of Bridgestone's twins came with a specification which would have been more at home on a Grand Prix circuit than on the street. Besides the twin rotary disc induction and auto oiling system there were hard-chrome-plated aluminium cylinders, a dry clutch and, in the case of the larger model, a 6-speed gearbox.

Realising that it would need to publicize these new models, the Bridgestone management decided to authorize a racing programme. This was considerably assisted by an inflow of technology and personnel from the former Tohatsu factory during late 1964, and as outlined in the companion volume Japanese Grand Prix Racing Motorcycles (Redline Books) Bridgestone used the twin cylinder 50cc Tohatsu as the basis for the Grand Prix challenge, but with various modifications, including liquid cooling.

At the same time the newly set-up Bridgestone race shop produced a race kit for its 90 Sports, thus enabling the factory to contest the popular 90cc Japanese clubmans racing class.

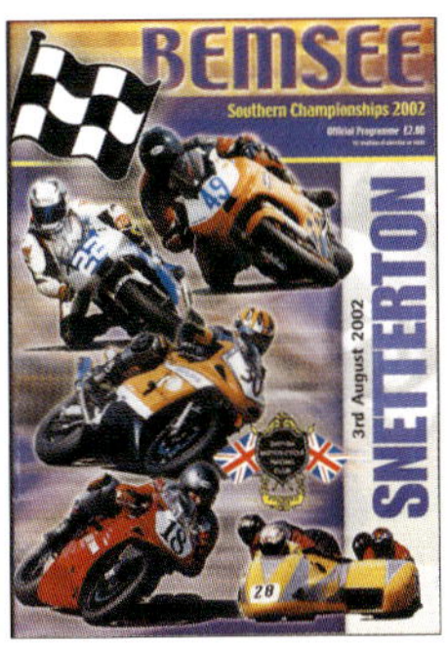

Florida rider Mike Kirby racing his home-tuned Brigestone Dual twin, circa 1991.

The first real test for the new racers came on the 13th March 1966, when Bridgestone took part in no less than three categories at the inaugural meeting, staged over the new 3.7 mile Fisco circuit. In the novice races, Bridgestone won the 50 and 90cc classes and also the Experts 50cc event.

Both the 175 Dual Twin and 350 GTR had been designed very much with the American market in mind, and although both models were subsequently exported to Europe, numbers were much smaller; for example a mere 33 examples of the GTR were sold in Great Britain.

At the time of its launch, the 350 GTR was the most advanced two-stroke street bike ever to reach series production. Even Suzuki's T20 Super Six couldn't boast disc valve induction. A conventional piston-ported two-stroke employs the rise and fall of the piston to control the flow of incoming exhaust gases through ports in the cylinder walls. However, the weakness of this set-up is that it inevitably gives symmetrical port timing in highly tuned engines and the side effects can be poor running and spitting back through the carburettors, particularly at low rpm.

In contrast, by offering asymmetrical timing, rotary disc valves - basically thin discs mounted on the crankshaft - solved the problem. The man to harness this technology successfully was the East German two-stroke guru Walter Kaaden. He then saw his work stolen by the Japanese via Ernst Degner's defection to Suzuki in 1961.

Other important design features of the GTR included Bridgestone's Jet Lube positive oiling (driven by a pump found under the offside (right) carburettor), a choice of right or left hand gearchange, rubber-mounted engine, a dry clutch, horizontally split crankcases, a duplex frame, 2LS front drum brake and full-width aluminium hubs.

In standard form and with full silencing the engine put out 37bhp at 7500rpm. Weighing in (dry) at 330lb (150kg), maximum speed approached 100mph. But its potential as a racing machine was considerable. For example Welsh dealer/sponsor Wyn Richards (who ran a dealership in Cardiff) got together with two-stroke specialist George Todd (of BSA Bantam fame). The result of their work was the Altair racer which produced a very healthy 60bhp (at 110,000rpm). The tuned GTR motor was mounted in a purpose-built frame constructed by specialist Jim Lee, with MP (Metal Profile) front forks and a Seeley double-sided drum front stopper. Raced in 1969, replicas were subsequently offered for £625 in 1970, but few were sold.

Another British Bridgestone effort was an interesting air-cooled 124cc (42 x 45mm) model based around the 174cc Dual Twin disc-valve engine. This was constructed by TSR (Terry Shepherd Racing). Terry Shepherd, the former Norton and MV Agusta works rider was also a talented engineer. Based in Liverpool, he was responsible for many interesting two-stroke racers and besides the Bridgestone he also tuned Kawasaki, Suzuki, Yamaha and other engines. The TSR Bridgestone revved to 12,000rpm and was claimed to produce 22bhp and 110mph. Built in early 1969, it was scheduled to go into limited production, but this never came about.

In the early 1970s many of the top two-stroke tuners were based in Holland, and it was in this country that a new private Bridgestone effort had its origins. Ridden by such stars as Henk Van Kessel (later 50cc world champion) and Jos Schurgers, a pair of race kitted, production-based Dual Twins, sleeved down to 125cc, were campaigned from 1972 until the end

*The Bridgestone 100 Sport with a top speed of 72mph made an excellent basis...*

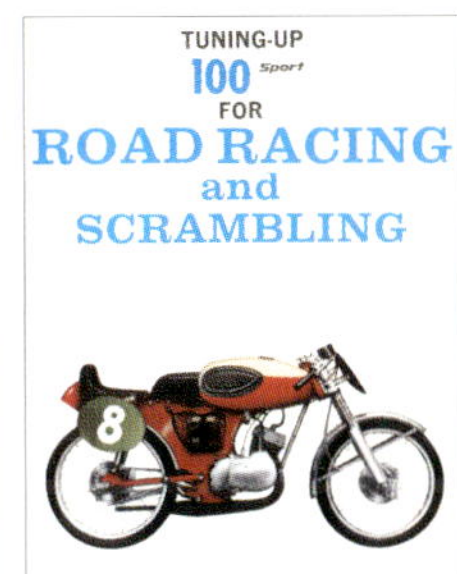


*...for the 100cc Bridgestone racing conversion for Japanese domestic events.*

*Mike Kirby of Longwood, Florida, with his father built this very competitive racer out of a Dual Twin street bike. Specification includes extensive porting, 22mm carbs, special rotary valves and almost 30bhp.*

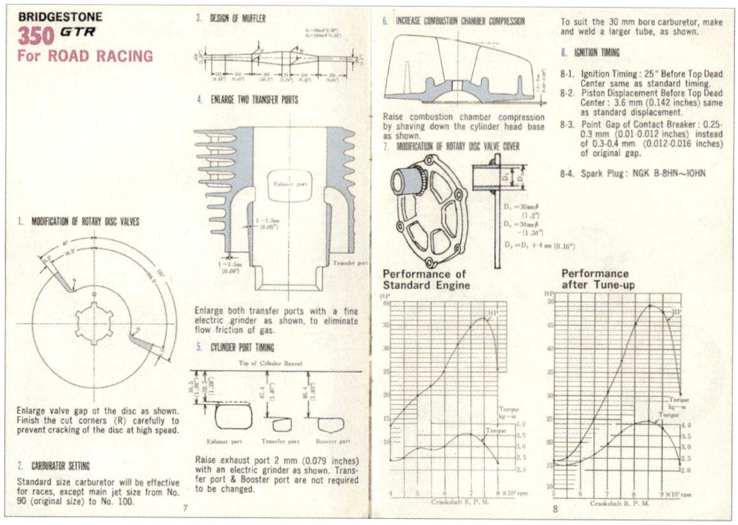

BRIDGESTONE
350 GTR
For ROAD RACING

1. MODIFICATION OF ROTARY DISC VALVES

Enlarge valve gap of the disc as shown. Finish the cut corners (R) carefully to prevent cracking of the disc at high speed.

2. CARBURATOR SETTING

Standard size carburetor will be effective for races, except main jet size from No. 90 (original size) to No. 100.

3. DESIGN OF MUFFLER

4. ENLARGE TWO TRANSFER PORTS

Enlarge both transfer ports with a fine electric grinder as shown, to eliminate flow friction of gas.

5. CYLINDER PORT TIMING

Raise exhaust port 2 mm (0.079 inches) with an electric grinder as shown. Transfer port & Booster port are not required to be changed.

7

6. INCREASE COMBUSTION CHAMBER COMPRESSION

Raise combustion chamber compression by shaving down the cylinder head base as shown.

7. MODIFICATION OF ROTARY DISC VALVE COVER

To suit the 30 mm bore carburetor, make and weld a larger tube, as shown.

8. IGNITION TIMING

8-1. Ignition Timing : 25° Before Top Dead Center same as standard timing.
8-2. Piston Displacement Before Top Dead Center : 3.6 mm (0.142 inches) same as standard displacement.
8-3. Point Gap of Contact Breaker : 0.25-0.3 mm (0.01-0.012 inches) instead of 0.3-0.4 mm (0.012-0.016 inches) of original gap.
8-4. Spark Plug : NGK B-8HN~IOHN

Performance of Standard Engine

Performance after Tune-up

8

*Bridgestone tuning literature for the 350GTR, showing modification of disc valves, carb settings, cylinder port timing, changes to combustion chamber compression and ignition timing.*

of 1975. The results obtained were truly exceptional, with 1973 as the highlight when Schurgers not only finished 3rd in the world championships series, but also made history by becoming the first rider to use Bridgestone power to win a Grand Prix - the Belgian. This victory on what is, after all, a 'speed' circuit, proved that the Bridgestone-engined bike, now known as the 'Condor' had considerable potential remaining a force until as late as 1980.

The basis of these Dutch Bridgestones was a pair of cylinder barrels and heads from the Van Veen Kreidler 50. With liquid-cooling and an increase in capacity to give the machines a full 125cc engine size, these 'Flying Dutchmen' certainly surprised even the best of the works team with their efforts.

In the USA, father and son team of Bill and Mike Kirby of Longwood, Florida have been responsible for keeping the Bridgestone racing name alive for the last 16 years. The basis of their machine is a 1960s 175 Dual

*Standard GTR with factory racing conversion.*

*Riders eye view of the Kirby Bridgestone Dual Twin racer.*

*This 350GTR is one of the limited batch of Altair racers. Built in Cardiff by Wyn Richards and George Todd, the engine was tuned to give 60bhp. Going on sale in 1969 it sported a purpose-built Jim Lee frame.*

Twin. With a displacement of 177cc the bike has been carefully developed into a race winner. For example during 1990 and 1991 rider Mike was the AHRMA (American Historic Racing Motorcycle Association) 200 GP national champion.

The list of modifications is extensive;

- Porting by WKR (Woody Kyle Racing)
- 22mm carburettors (stock 17mm)
- Special rotary valves
- 26-29bhp at 10,600rpm (rear wheel reading)
- Kawasaki AIR seat
- Yamaha TZ fairing
- Yamaha TZ750 screen
- Aluminium wheel rims
- Special fuel tank
- Expansion chamber exhaust, with end cans
- Front fork rubber gaiters

As for Bridgestone themselves, rumour has it that Honda, Suzuki and Yamaha all put pressure on them regarding original equipment tyre contracts - in other words, if Bridgestone didn't stop their racing effort and making motorcycles in general, the 'big three' would place their business elsewhere... Whatever the real truth of this might be, Bridgestone decided to concentrate on its core activity of tyre production and quit the motorcycle manufacturing side of their business in 1968.

There is certainly no doubt that their rivals were worried, and they had every reason to be, because Bridgestone built some of the most sophisticated machines of the era - and top quality ones too.

# Honda - the classic years

# 2

*CR110 50cc Enduro, Snetterton 1964.*

Soichiro Honda's interest in speed and racing did not stop at the factory special. He also took an active interest in providing sports machinery for the 'boys'.

Honda correctly perceived that machines such as the British Norton International and BSA Gold Star, together with the Italian Gilera Saturno, had won considerable acclaim for their respective marques, even though they were production sportsters, rather than works racers.

As early as 1959, there were a couple of Hondas which could be presented as 'SuperSport' machines—the CB92 sports roadster and clubmans racing CR71. The latter was based firmly on the production CS71 with its sohc 247cc (54 x 54mm) engine and four-speed gearbox. In the CR71, the compression ratio was increased to 9.5:1 and the maximum power output raised to 24 bhp at 8800rpm. It retained the crankshaft-mounted clutch with its characteristic cable entry and lift mechanism cover.

*British serviceman Chris Profit-White in action on his Honda CR71 at the RASC training circuit at Sambawang, Singapore, 1960. He won both the 250 and the 350cc events.*

The CR71 cycle parts differed considerably from the stock version and closely followed the original RC141 125 works twin of the same year, notably in the leading-link front forks and twin-leading-shoe front brake. The wheels were 18in., in place of the 16 in. type fitted to the CS71 tourer.

When delivered, the CR71 came complete with all road-going equipment, including lights and silencers (in much the same way as the Italian Formula 2-3 racers of the period), and in this trim was capable of 95 mph. However, by the simple expedient of removing the silencers and fitting a pair of optional open megaphones, the maximum velocity could be raised to a genuine 100mph.

*As early as 1961, two Hondas existed which could be presented as 'SuperSport' machines, the CB92 sports roadster and the pukka racing CR71. The latter machine, shown here was based around the series production CS71 with a sohc twin cylinder engine and 4-speed gearbox.*

# The Chis-Honda CB92

*Currently owned by enthusiast John Pitt of Marlow, Bucks, the bike still sports Bill Ivy's home-made seat and the combination of an alloy front and steel rear wheel rims!*

The Saga of the Chis-Honda CB92 began in 1961, following delivery of an early batch of machines by the Japanese company, via their British importers at the time, Hondis Ltd, to Kent's first Honda dealership, Chisholms of Maidstone.

Don and Bill Chisholm employed two mechanics at the time, Bill Ivy and Roy Francis. A CB92 was put on the road and once run in fitted with one of Honda's race kits for the model, plus a home-made thinner copper head gasket to enable the compression ratio to be raised. Bill Ivy knocked up a rather crude home-brewed seat, fitted 'Ace' handlebars and changed the brake and gear pedals to opposite sides (to match British taste at the time) - and set off to the local Brands Hatch circuit to test their handywork.

It soon became apparent that however good the rest of the bike might have been, the suspension, in the shape of the leading link front fork and Japanese-made rear shocks were simply not up to the job. Looking round for an improvement, the Chisholm brothers had in stock a blown-up MV Agusta 175. So the front telescopic front forks, together with the rear shock absorbers were removed and utilized on the race kitted CB92. It was also necessary to cast a special top fork crown to enable the MV forks to fit the Honda, and this was carried out by the brothers themselves. A clamp half way down the nearside fork leg took care of the front brake anchor arm.

Thus equipped, the handling of the machine was, as Roy Francis described it, transformed. This enabled Bill Ivy to achieve a series of excellent top six place finishes at Brands Hatch during 1961 and 1962, plus a notable 'get-off' when running at the front of the field with EMC rider Rex Avery and Derek Minter (witnessed by the author, who actually saw the crash).

But with Bill moving to Frank Sheene's (Barry's father) Bultaco, Don and Bill Chisholm then promoted Roy Francis to the Chis-Honda CB92 ride, in place of Roy's existing standard-forked CB92 racer.

Roy well remembers the 19th April 1964 - because when challenging for the lead at Cadwell Park's 'Boys Day' on the second lap he fell off at the infamous Barn Corner with its adverse camber (which is still there today!).

When Bill Ivy returned to the Chis-Honda squad upon the arrival of the CR93 production racer in 1964, Roy Francis's routine was in his own words, 'to warm up my own machine (the Chis CB92) early, park it in the assembly area and then get Bill's ready. As he (Bill) was riding in several classes I had his trust to make sure the Chis-Honda was ready for action.'

Roy Francis ends by saying, 'Happy days, little did we realise what the future held for this Maidstone group of enthusiasts. Bill Ivy went on to become 125cc World Champion, Don and Bill Chisholm in 1975 sold their business to Roy Francis and Paul Smart, Roy and Paul sold out to the GK Group in 1988 and returned to motorcyling as a hobby, tending their respective race machines of yesteryear.

The Chis-Honda CB92 has survived and is now owned by enthusiast John Pitt, of Marlow, Bucks.

*Roy Francis in action on the Chis-Honda CB92 at Thruxton, circa 1964.*

*The CB92 in its original guise. The 124.7cc chain-driven sohc twin produced 15bhp at 10,500rpm in standard trim.*

Originally, all the CR71 production was intended for domestic consumption and Far Eastern markets, such as Hong Kong, Malaysia and Singapore. At least one such CR71 reached Britain in the early 1960s, when it was brought home from Singapore by British serviceman/racer Chris Profit-White. The Honda team also brought over a small number for course learning for their 1959 TT debut.

Compared with the very limited number of CR71s produced, the CB92 could be labelled a series production machine, being mass-produced from 1959 until the end of 1964. I owned one of these superb little bikes when stationed in Aden (now South Yemen) during 1963-4, and soon found

*Oulton Park, Cheshire, May 1962 and a CB92 leads an MV Agusta 125 single. The MV had originally cost a small fortune, the Honda a lot less - plus a degree of tuning.*

*One of the first CB92s imported into Great Britain is seen here in 1961 with Mick Matthews in the saddle. In the background is Ron Pladdys' Ducati 175 Formula 3.*

that it could match the vast majority of 350s in fact, my home-tuned CB92 actually blew-off a Norton 88 with an engine capacity four times its own size!

From personal experience, the only three things with which I could find fault were the lack of another gear (four were standard), a camshaft which ran directly in the head without any bearings, and the front end which could be skittish at very slow speeds on tight bends. Otherwise, it was a fantastic motorcycle. Its 124.7cc (44 x 41mm) chain-driven sohc engine produced 15bhp at 10,500rpm in standard trim. With the factory race kit and megaphones, this could be bumped up to almost 20bhp and over 85mph. Needless to say, many examples reached the racetrack. Several of these were raced quite successfully during 1960-2, even in international events. One particular example was taken by its owner, Londoner Tom Jackson, to compete in Soviet Russia, while another was mounted in a Cotton frame to create a very interesting and competitive special. In Australia, as early as February 1960, eight converted CB92s appeared in a field of 21 in the 125cc class of the Victorian TT at Fisherman's Bend, Melbourne, with Alan Osbourne bringing one of them home second, ahead of Len Tinker's MV Agusta production racer.

*With the factory race kit and meggaphones, the power output of the CB92 could be bumped up to almost 20bhp and over 85mph.*

*Programme cover for the BMCRC Barawanath Trophy Meeting at Silverstone on the 19th September 1964. The bike is a race kitted CB92 with dolphin fairing.*

Superbly restored CB92 seen at Daytona Bike week, March 2002.

By 1961, the CB92 had been joined by the CB72. This was a completely redesigned CS71 with a much improved engine, including a 180-degree crankshaft, twin carburettors and five-speed box. Also, its tubular frame, telescopic forks and full width, twin-leading-shoe brakes at both front and rear were much improved over the early machine - as was the performance. Its output of 24bhp, albeit at the higher engine speed of 9000rpm, matched that of the limited-run CR71 production racer. Once again, the CB72 soon found a special niche with competition minded riders, being widely race-kitted for open events and also used to great effect in sports production races around the world during the early 1960s.

In Britain, the CB72 was a class winner in both the Thruxton 500-mile and Silverstone 1000-km races, two of the toughest events in the world.

CB92 powered Cotton special in the Brands Hatch paddock, circa 1963.

# Rod Scivyer British Champion

*Rod Scivyer at Snetterton, Norfolk, Summer 1964, his first season with the bike.*

Rod Scivyer ordered his CR93 in late 1963 through Jim Pink Motorcycles of Wallingford, Berkshire. And it was delivered direct from Japan just in time for the start of the 1964 season.

Whilst running in the engine a piston broke up - due to a ring groove being machined too deeply. This virtually destroyed the engine - cylinder head, barrels, crankshaft etc all needed rebuilding!

But thanks to the good offices of Alf Briggs at Honda UK, these parts were supplied free of charge, which allowed Rod to begin the season without the need to take out a mortgage. Rod recalls that the bike cost 'as near as I can recall, £540, without the alloy fairing, I made do with a much cheaper Bill Jakeman fibre-glass product.'

The CR93 was run in standard tune throughout the 1964 season, at the end of which Rod finished 6th in the British Championship.

For the 1966 season more radical modifications were carried out in the closed season. The valve gear was extensively lightened and Terry valve springs substituted for the standard components. As Rod says, 'As long as the head was stripped and rebuilt every two race meetings this enabled us to maintain 500rpm more than the standard rev limit.' An Italian Oldani front brake was also fitted.

Other modifications included removing the magneto and replacing it with coil ignition, using two Wipac 'pencil' coils and a small 6 volt battery. This saved a considerable amount of weight, but the much reduced flywheel effect made things somewhat critical when leaving the startline or negotiating slow corners. One major improvement was the removal of problems caused by small pieces of valve spring finding their way down the cam-drive tunnel and embedding themselves into the ignition coils of the flywheel mounted magneto!

By now Bill Ivy had departed the British domestic scene (having signed a works Yamaha contract), so as Rod says ,'I ended up British Champion for 1966 , winning the first seven events and sewing up the championship by the end of the first half of the season.'

His last season with the CR93 came in 1967. 'It was an uphill struggle as the advent of the water-cooled Bultaco with its increased reliability over the '66 model, and its vast weight advantage, meant that I failed to win a single British Championship event.' Nevertheless, due to the CR93's amazing reliability record and his consistent riding, Scivyer finished runner-up.

Rod remembers, 'Apart from the initial problems during running-in, the bike only let me down on three occassions in four years and during a three year period I finished in the first six at every race meeting I contested,' which must be some sort of record.

*In 1965 Rod Scivyer finished runner up behind Bill Ivy in the British Championship. The following year, he went one better and won the title. The picture shows him at Castle Combe in 1965.*

## 1963 CR93

| | |
|---|---|
| Engine: | Air-cooled dohc parallel twin, 8-valves, with inclined cylinders, unit construction and horizontally-split crankcases. Gear driven cams |
| Capacity: | 124.8cc |
| Bore: | 43mm |
| Stroke: | 43mm |
| Comp ratio: | 10.2:1 |
| Carburation: | 2 x Keihin 22mm |
| Ignition: | Energy transfer magneto |
| Gearbox: | Five speeds |
| Clutch: | Dry, multi-plate |
| Frame: | Steel, spine-type construction. Engine employed as stressed-member |
| Suspension: | Front exposed spring, telescopic fork rear swinging arm, twin shock |
| Brakes: | Front single sided 2LS drum or double sided 5LS drum rear single sided |
| Tyres: | 18 inch front and rear |
| Dry weight: | 279lb (127kg) |
| Max power: | 20bhp @ 11,500rpm |
| Max speed: | 102mph |

*Jim Curry with his CR93 at Brands Hatch in 1964. Before the Honda, Jim like many other 125 stars rode a dohc Ducati Grand Prix single.*

*This factory fresh CR93 of the 1st series with the double sided SLS front brake is seen here in spring 1963.*

# Andrew French

*Leading Derek Woodman (works MZ) Brands Hatch International, 1965, it remained this way to the flag.*

Born into a motorcycling family, Andrew French's father Hes (Roger) was a contempary of Stan Hailwood, George Collett and other famous grass track racers of the inter-war period. Affectionately known as 'Froggy' French, he won many Southern area ACU championships at circuits such as Donington Park, Syston and Oxford.

Andrew French left school in 1962 and began selling secondhand motorcycles from a garage at his parents' home. When King's Motors decided to quit a small scooter shop in Park End Street, Oxford in early 1963, Andrew took over the lease and began selling scooters and lightweight motorcycles.

At this time, he became aquainted with Jim and Barbara Pink of Wallingford, who were then Honda agents. Andrew French travelled over to their establishment many times to obtain spares and struck up a friendship with Jim, a veteran racer. He had just begun racing a Honda CR110, and had an old 3-speed Itom for sale. Andrew managed to do a deal and took his new purchase to the Snetterton 50cc Enduo. The Itom blew up after 2 hours! Then came another, this time a 4-speeder in a Simmonds frame. Andrew commented, 'Much quicker. I had varying degrees of success on this bike and decided to go up a class to 125cc.'

Rod Scivyer, who lived reasonably close to Andrew in Oxford, had been racing a CB92 and had recently taken delivery of new CR93. As Andrew says, 'This machine looked so beautiful and sounded unbelivieble, I knew this just had to be the bike for me.' Early in 1964, he bought a CR93, unfortunately without its fairing, from Richard Wyler, the American film and TV star. But it was no fairy-tale. 'When lying 4th and lapping a slower rider I crashed,' The rider about to be lapped looked behind, panicked and cut across in front, causing all three (including another rider who Andrew was dicing with) to go down.

He then raced the CR93 through 1964 and 1965 mainly at national and international level against the likes of Bill Ivy, Chris Vincent, Tommy Robb, Derek Chalterton, Grant Gibson, Ron Pladdys, Phil Horsham, Terry Grotefeld, Gary Dickinson, Roy Francis and his friend Rod Scivyer. No wins but many top place finishes, including various fastest laps.

Highlights included beating Luigi Taveri on a factory Honda at the 1965 Mallory Park Post TT and Derek Woodman on his works MZ at the Brands Hatch GP circuit, also in 1965.

But a serious accident at Paddock Bend, Brands Hatch in late 1965 meant that the CR93 was sold in the spring of 1966. Andrew explains, 'An impending marriage meant that I had to bow down to my responsibilities and put my energies into the business of selling motorcycles and subsequently cars and a Toyota dealership.'

Now retired, Andrew has never been without a motorcycle of some description and has just restored a couple of Ducati 350s to parade at various meetings.

But as he says, 'The Honda CR93 was a most endearing motorcycle, the fantastic noise, handling and braking. It looked fast standing still. Although I also raced an Aermacchi at the same time, nothing could compare to the Honda. I fully understand the requirement to reduce noise levels these days,but the current race spectator can have no idea of the thrill generated by half a dozen or more CR93s all accelerating off the line or on full chat past the pits at Mallory Park, where the sound used to reverberate off the corrugated steel walls.'

*Andrew French doing what would now be described as a 'stoppy', Little Rissington road races, 1964 with his CR93.*

# Ron Pladdys CR93 racer and specials builder

*Ron Pladdys at Southbank Brands Hatch, 1965, on his original CR93, with dual front brake.*

*Ron Pladdys (right) with Jim Curry and his wife Daphne, at Brands Hatch after Jim had won the Golden Sash award, 1965.*

Ron Pladdys was born in Coventry on the 10th March 1939; his father being a coppersmith and his brothers, Dick and Jack toolmakers.

Ron's first motorcycle was a Villiers-powered James Captain of 1955 vintage, which he raced at Honeyborne Airfield near Stratford-upon-Avon in 1957 at the age of 18. This was followed in 1958 by a 350cc BSA Gold Star.

By 1960 he had progressed to a Ducati 175 Silverstone Super, which was used mainly in 200cc events - this he part exchanged for another Ducati, a genuine 175 Formula III from Kings of Manchester later that year. Ron recalls riding

*Ron Paddys (65) 182cc CR93 leads Bill Ivy, Cotton, at the international meeting, Cadwell Park, September 1965.*

the Formula III at Brands Hatch in October that year for the first time, finishing third. 'It was the loveliest bike to ride and to look at."

Then in 1961, the 200cc class was dropped, except for some very minor events - plus races in Scotland and Ireland, so, as Ron says, 'We soon found we needed a full 250cc machine to compete.'

In 1962 an NSU Sportmax Special was purchased from Doug Beasley, but although it was very quick he was unable to get to grips with it. So in 1963 he obtained a Aermacchi, which was fast enough - for the first time he was able to keep up with the opposition.

Then came the big break. When deciding to compete in two classes, Ron bought a Honda CR93 from Geoff Monty, recalling, 'At a practice day at Silverstone on the CR93 I found that I was lapping only a few seconds slower than on the Aermacchi.'

*The very special 3-cylinder CR93-based 250cc racer built by the Pladdys brothers Dick, Jack and Ron.*

The Pladdys family's firm, Burnsall Engineering, had had some previous success in boring out engines so Ron considered obtaining another CR93 and increasing the displacement as much as possible. 'We went to see Fron Purslow who had a relatively new CR93 for sale. We struck a deal and paid him a cheque there and then, which he accepted without hesitation, he was very trusting, wasn't he?'

Bringing the bike back to Coventry, the Pladdys brothers made a start on increasing the capacity to 182cc, which they believed to be the maximum possible. But they encountered two problems, there were no pistons or rings available. Ron's brothers Dick and Jack made suitable pistons from RR58 aluminium alloy cold compresed material which was provided by Redditch specialists, High Duty Alloys, The Pladdys brothers were told it was an off-cut from the main spar of Concorde.

The rings proved much more difficult, in the end they had to settle for ones from an agricultural engine, which did not have an oil control ring.

The conversion was finished late one Saturday night, and the bikes were loaded into the van for a meeting at Perton Airfield (near Wolverhampton) on the Sunday. The 182 fired first time and seemed okay, finishing first in both 250cc races.

The 182 was campained until the end of 1965, not only scoring victories at several mainland events, but also finishing 10th in the 1964 Manx Grand Prix, followed by a 6th place the following year. But with the increasing speed of the Yamaha TD1Bs and later the TD1Cs, the 182 was sold to Ralph Varden of Stratford-upon-Avon, who sponsored a number of riders including Jim Curry. Finally, in 1969, disillusioned by 2-strokes and a Drixton 350cc Aermacchi, Ron Pladdys retired from competitive riding.

*Manx Grand Prix action, circa 1965, Ron Pladdys with his (overbored) 182cc CR93. He came home 6th in the lightweight (250cc) race, averaging 84.60mph in a field of 96 starters and 53 finishers.*

In mid-1969 Ralph Varden contacted Burnsall Engineering (jointly owned by Dick, Jack and Ron Pladdys) to enquire if they could improve the performance of the 182. Various configurations were discussed as they previously had considered building a full 250cc based on a CR93 - the obvious solution was to combine two engine to produce a four, but by far the best proposition would be a three cylinder as this would be only two-and-a-half inches wider than the standard CR93 engine.Ralph Varden financed this project, which was successfully constructed.

A few years ago Ron Pladdys was fortunate enough to obtain the Ralph Varden three cylinder Honda and he still owns and parades it today.

*Mid 1970s, Dick Pladdys working on Roy Garnett's 182cc CR93 in the Manx Grand Prix paddock.*

*Honda twins on the start line. Andrew French (19) is alongside Bill Ivy (4), Snetterton national road races, Summer 1965. Number 2 is another CR93 and 28 a CB92-based machine.*

The first indication of a totally new breed of Honda came at the Tokyo Show in late October 1961. It was here that the company, already Japan's largest two-wheel concern, displayed a prototype of what was to emerge later as the CR110, a 49cc over-the-counter racer. This original prototype boasted an output of 8.9bhp at an amazing 14,000rpm and a five-speed gearbox. At the show, it was referred to simply as the Honda Cub Racer.

Almost six months were to pass before Honda introduced the larger CR93. This was produced in two forms and went on sale in Japan in May 1962. In its 'standard' form, the 124.8cc double-knocker, five-speed twin came complete with full road-going equipment—head and tail lights, a horn, a pair of large silencers and even a rear-view mirror—and in this trim, a top speed of 84mph was claimed. In its more well-known, at least to British eyes, stripped racing guise, the speed was increased to 96mph, and fitted with a fairing, 102mph was the figure. The 'square' 43 x 43mm bore and stroke dimensions gave the racing version 20bhp, while the 'street' model gave 16.5bhp, at 11,500rpm.

*Nearside view of the twin cam CR93 power unit.*

*CR93 engine showing dry clutch, engine breather, exhaust camshaft driven rev-counter and Keihan carburettors.*

*Snetterton 1964, one of the CR93s to be supplied with the single-sided 2LS front brake instead of the works type double-sided SLS component.*

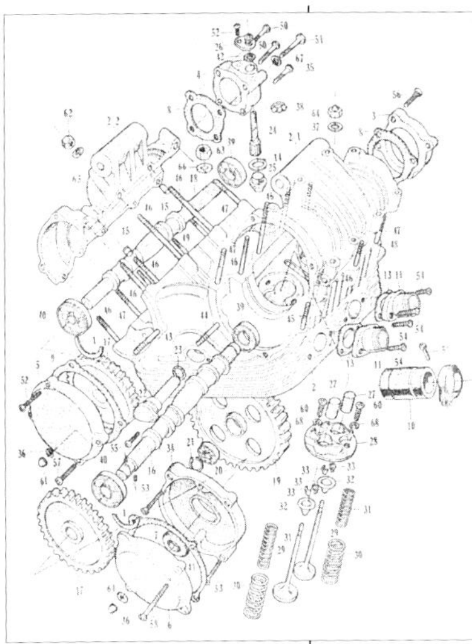

*CR93 cylinder head showing gear driven camshafts, valve springs, bearings and rev-counter drive pinion...*

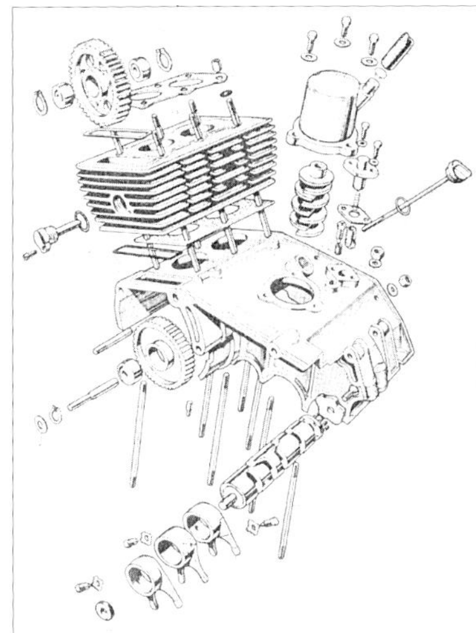

*...the cylinder barrel and crankcase details. Note also large baffled crankcase breather, selector forks and drum, plus engine oil dipstick.*

The CR93 was designed by a Honda back-room boy by the name of Suzuki... no relation to the rival Japanese manufacturer. It shared the four-valves-per-cylinder technology of the works racers. A conventional roller big-end, 360 degree crankshaft (both pistons rise and fall together) drove the five-speed, unit-construction gearbox by helical spur gears. There was a surprisingly large primary reduction of 3.7:1. The standard Honda technique of wet-sump lubrication (with a scavenge pump) was employed.

Producing maximum power at 11,500rpm, the engine was still mechanically safe at 13,000rpm. Within these limits - and provided the oil was changed after every race - it would give long life with reliability. The CR93 would rev beyond its redline, but with a greatly increasing likelihood of mechanical failure.

When the CR93 went on sale in Britain in early 1963, it cost £609, but was later reduced to £504. However, it remained on the British market for only two seasons.

Generally, the CR93 was an easy bike to ride and was very easy to bump into life. There was absolutely no power below 5800rpm. Then the power surged in suddenly, as if one had released a cut-out button. It was entirely free from vibration and would run straight up to the safe 13,000 peak. A change at this speed brought the revs down to around 9500. Therefore, it was extremely easy to keep smack in the powerband, which was just as well because of the lack of urge and the severe 'megaphonitis' when out of it. The shallow-taper megaphones emitted a superb mellow howl, which was not too sharp, but carried over a long distance.

Other interesting features of the design included a compression ratio of 10.2:1, 22mm bore Keihin carbs, energy transfer magneto ignition, spine-type frame (with the engine assembly as a structural member), a light-alloy 2.2-gallon fuel tank and a dry weight of 127kg (279lb).

Some 40 CR93s found their way to Britain, and riders such as Bill Ivy, Chris Vincent, Rod Scivyer and Derek Chatterton used them to score victory after victory for several years. In fact, the CR93 ruled the British 125cc short-circuit scene until the appearance of Austin Hockley and his Terry Beckett-tuned Granby Yamaha YASI in 1970.

*Steve Murray with his brand new CR93 at Oulton Park in 1963. This photograph shows the bike as it left the factory.*

*Another Oulton Park shot from the same 1963 meeting, with Tommy Robb (2) and Steve Murray (9) disputing positions.*

# Team Hansen

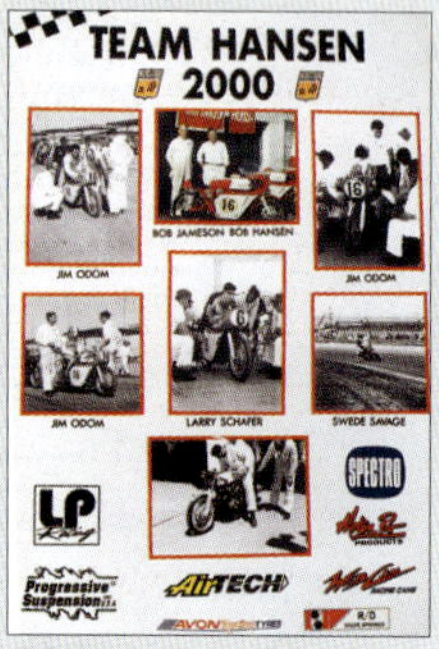


Bob Hansen is very much a piece of American Honda history. It was Bob who largely put the Japanese marque on the Stateside racing map. Cycle World recently said 'Long-time Britbike campaigner Dick Mann herds the Hansen-prepared Honda CB750 through Daytona's infield. The 1970 win was the first for the Japanese brand in the 200-miler.'

What this really meant was that Honda had entrusted Bob Hansen with the bike with which veteran Dick Mann re-wrote the history books by becoming the first to pilot a Japanese bike to victory in America's number one road race.

But for Hansen and Honda, it wasn't the first time the two had worked together, far from it in fact. First, after quitting racing himself (he rode the likes of Ariel and Indian) Bob had become one of the original American Honda dealers. Then he suggested a local parts department, Honda were impressed enough to allow Bob to sign up and recruit new dealers himself. Then in March 1966, after sponsoring a team of riders on Matchless G50s, he progressed to Honda's five-hundred class 450 twin. At Daytona Jim Odom, Swede Savage and Larry Schaffer all rode CR450s.

The story of why the machines arrived in the States and Bob Hansen's influence on first Honda, and later Kawasaki, is of considerable historic interest.

Essentially, Soichiro Honda wanted to publicise the company's new 450 twin in America. At that time, as mentioned above, Bob Hansen was running the midwest region Parts and Service School for the Honda Corporation from his Eaton Lane, Racine, Wisconsin premises. And Team Hansen had a trio Matchless G50s in the equipe's traditional orange and white livery for Daytona in March 1967. Then in December 1966, Mr Honda contacted Bob and suggested that he run three Hondas instead. Bob agreed, sending paint chips of his team colours to Japan for paint matching.

Some two months later he received by air 3 machines, one of which had been tested at Suzuka, Japan. During the testing, cracks were found in the frame which were repaired. However, this resulted in gussets being added, which set the Hansen machines apart.

The reason these 450s were painted in Bob's colours, was that Honda wanted the world to think that Bob had built them at his dealership. Infact, they had been built in the works race shop in Japan by the very same men who were responsible for the Grand Prix bikes ridden at that time by the likes of Redman and Hailwood. Terry Naughtin, explaining, 'We feel that this was just in case they did not perform well and that people would not realize it was in fact a factory effort.' Besides the bikes Honda also shipped spares totalling US $66,655; from cylinder heads to gears, control cables to bodywork.

The Cycle World report of the pre-race period for the 1967 Daytona had this to say, 'Team Hansen turned up with three of the most beautiful orange and white Honda 450s imaginable, one being ridden by young amateur, Jim Odom, in his first road race. The sound of the Honda on its 132.8mph qualifying lap was incredible as Jim broke the existing amateur record by over five mph.'

In the Amateur 100 Miler 18 year old Odom showed his qualifying performance was no fluke, by leading the race for most of the first eight laps. Then, as Cycle World describes, 'The jolly game came to an end and Jim grounded the very low Honda exhaust pipes coming out of the infield and all but totalled the beautiful Honda - the end of a brilliant ride.'

*Left to right Brent L Hensley, Bob Hansen and Terry Naughtin, pictured with the Bob Hansen Trophy at De Land, Florida, 1st March 2002. Hensley was the first winner of the award in 2000.*

So it was left to Swede Savage and Larry Schaffer (who finished 10th and 12th respectively in the 200 Miler) to uphold Honda's honour. After Daytona, the three 450s were disposed of by Honda. One went to the son of Canadian Honda parts distributor, Mike Manley, who rode the 450 to the Canadian Championship in 1968. This bike was tuned by the company's service manager, Tom Faulds. Another bike was kept at the service school and dismantled over time, with components going in all directions. As for Jim Odom's machine, it is now owned by an American enthusiast. Finally. Swede Savage's motorcycle was restored and is now owned by Bob Hansen, it looks like it will end its days as part of the AMA Museum.

*One of Team Hansen-Honda CR450s at Daytona in March 1967.*

After the 450, Honda was going to build a new 750cc twin on similar lines for both production and racing. However, with his close connections with the factory, Bob Hansen told Mr Honda that instead it should be a 750n four cylinder. The result was the CB750 street bike of 1969, followed by the racing only CR750 in 1970. And of course, Bob Mann won the Daytona 200 that year riding one of the new CR750s. As a further point of interest, the original prototype CR750 was fitted with a drum front brake; but by the time the bikes appeared at Daytona in March 1970 all of them sported dual discs up front.

During the early 1970s Bob Hansen was asked to run the Kawasaki factory-backed effort in the States, which meant the fearsome KR750 triple (see chapter 4 Kawasaki - The Classic years).

Among the many motorcycles which Bob Hansen has been involved with down the years - including the Ariel Red Hunter, Indian Scout, Matchless G50, Honda CR750 and Kawasaki KR750, his personal favourite is the CR450. So bringing the team back together in the year 2000 made Bob a happy man, 'It's like racing in 1967 all over again.' And Team Hansen Race Director is no less enthusiastic, 'I treasure the opportunity to share this experience with him.'

*One of the Team Hansen CR450 machines specification includes specially blueprinted dohc parallel twin, 5-speed gearbox, 4LS front brake, oil cooler and hydraulic steering damper.*

## 1963 CR110

| | |
|---|---|
| Engine: | Air-cooled dohc single, with 35 degree inclined cylinder, 4-valves, unit construction and vertically-split crankcases.Gear driven cams |
| Capacity: | 49cc |
| Bore: | 40.4mm |
| Stroke: | 39mm |
| Comp ratio: | 10.3:1 |
| Carburation: | Keihin 26mm |
| Ignition: | Magneto* |
| Gearbox: | Eight speeds |
| Clutch: | Dry, multi-plate |
| Frame: | Steel, spine-type construction. Engine employed as stressed-member |
| Suspension: | Front exposed spring, telescopic fork rear swinging arm, twin shock |
| Brakes: | Full-width drums front and rear 5LS operation |
| Tyres: | 18inch front and rear |
| Dry weight: | N/A |
| Max power: | 8.5bhp @ 13,500rpm |
| Max speed: | 90mph. |

*Several machines modified by their owners to battery/coil

*Frenchman Bruno Gridel with his CR110 during the early 1980s.*

*The CR110 49cc (40.4 x 39mm) dohc single was officially launched in July 1962. Together with the 125cc CR93, 250cc CR72 and 305cc CR77, this was a purpose-built road racing motorcycle of the first order.*

*Like the CR93, the CR110 was offered with full road-going equipement for the Japanese home market, or as a pukka racer for export.*

Other notable achievements by the CR93 included capturing the British National speed record for the 125 and 175cc classes in the standing-start quarter mile and kilometre at Chelveston airfield, Bedford, on 7th November 1965, with rider Jack Terry. Another was an over-bored 182 cc model used in 250cc races with considerable success by Jim Curry and Ron. When this was outclassed by the ever improving Yamahas, Pladdys built a 249.2cc (49.6 x 43mm) three-cylinder model. This unique bike achieved a number of victories and proved its reliability by finishing in the gruelling Isle of Man Lightweight TT.

The only real change during the CR93's production life concerned its front brake. Some examples were fitted with a production-based, single-sided, two-leading-shoe type, while others came with the pukka works double-sided, single-leading-shoe front stopper.

Without doubt, the CR93 was the most successful of Honda's over-the-counter racers.

Next came the single-cylinder CR11O 'fifty'. This was officially announced in July 1962. Like its bigger brother, the CR110 was offered with full road going equipment for the domestic market, or as a pukka racer for export.

*Dave Simmonds with the CR110 he rode to 6th place in the 1966 50cc Isle of Man TT. Simmonds completed the 2-lap 75.46 mile event in 1 hour, 41 minutes and 50 seconds at an average speed of 66.70mph. The CR110 was clocked through the Motor Cycle News speed trap on the drop down to Creg-Na-Baa at 82.4mph.*

*Hughie McIver's CR110 photographed at Mallory Park; circa 1984. Bottom section of the fairing removed to show engine and nickel-plated frame.*

*The 49cc engine developed 8.5bhp and 3.55ft/Ib of torque on a compression ratio of 10.3:1.*

The most significant difference between the production model and the prototype exhibited at the 1961 Tokyo Show was that it had eight instead of five speeds. This was a direct result of Honda's Grand Prix experiences, which had shown that at least eight gears were needed to extract the maximum advantage from the dohc four-valve engine.

Like the CR93, the CR110 was the work of Honda engineer Suzuki. It was introduced into Britain for the 1963 season. Relatively few (21 to be exact) were imported that year, when they sold for £330, but they were even scarcer 12 months later, when their production was discontinued.

Revving to 13,500 peak power speed, and to 15,000 for occasional drastic use, the 49cc (40.4 x 39mm) 'egg-cup' racer developed 8.5bhp and 3.55lb/ft of torque on a compression ratio of 10.3:1. Ball and needle-roller bearings were used in profusion, the gear-train to the overhead camshaft mechanism being a case in point. Roller-bearing big-end and mains were featured, the crankpin being formed integrally with the drive-side flywheel.

Using a cross-over, all-indirect, eight-speed gearbox, the CR110 had its clutch on the offside, gear-driven directly from the engine shaft. The multiplate, oil-bath clutch was hydraulically operated. A wet sump, integrated with the transmission, stored oil for pressurized distribution from the clutch-driven plunger pump.

*It was all-important to be flat on the tank of the CR110 to acheive maximum performance. Also it was a bike best suited to someone of small build and light weight.*

*Another period CR93, Snetterton late 1963. It is interesting that the original fairing, shown here, was in aluminium. This bike has non-original chromed meggaphones and Girling rear shocks.*

A 26mm Kelhin carburettor was controlled by a neat and unusual push-pull, twin-cable arrangement with the throttle wire wrapped round a pulley on the instrument. A single 10mm spark plug was fired by a crankshaft-mounted magneto. However, several machines were modified to battery/coil ignition to improve starting.

The cylinder was inclined 35 degrees forward, and like the CR93, the engine unit was installed in a spine-type frame with the motor functioning as a structural member. Besides ensuring that the engine itself was mechanically sound at all times, there were two other areas of special preparation. One was making absolutely sure that the oil was changed between races and on cold days pre-warmed before being added to the sump. The other was checking rear-chain tension, which was critical. If too light, or loose, it would impair gearchanging.

*J. Kiddie (78) leads D.P. Warren (84) during the 1965 125cc Isle of man TT, both rode CR93s. Warren came home 22nd, Kiddie 25th.*

As for the gear ratios themselves, they were very close, as little as 800rpm apart on some changes. No power at all was produced below 8000rpm, and not much until 11,000. Above that, it flowed in with increasing gusto up to the recommended 13,500rpm. Once again, to exceed this would be to invite reducing the level of mechanical reliability.

*CR110 with non-standard inlet cover mounted contact breaker points.*

Roy Francis, a mechanic for Chisholm's of Maidstone winning the 1964 Brands Hatch Stars of Tomorrow award on the company's CR93 normally raced by Bill Ivy. Roy had instructions from Bill 'Don't bother coming back if you don't win!' Later Roy was able to purchase the Chris-Honda CR93 from Don and Bill Chisholm in a dismantled state at the end of the 1970s...

The first British owner to take delivery of a CR110 in 1963 was Val Knapp of Dorking, but the list of riders to race one of the all-conquering Honda 50s reads like a 'who's who' of the class - Bill Ivy, Dave Simmonds, Brian Kettle, George Ashton, Charlie Mates and Jim Pink. Perhaps the bike's most noteworthy achievement was Chris Walpole's tremendous second spot in the 1963 50cc TT.

Like the CR93, Honda also offered the CR11O on the home market in full road-going trim. In this guise, its top speed was restricted to 62mph, whereas the full racing version was good for well over 80mph.

After the 125 and 50cc models, the 250 CR72 and 305 CR77 production racers were planned. However, even though several pre-production models were raced by various riders, including Tommy Robb (who debuted the 305 in the 1963 West German Grand Prix at Hockenheim), Luigi Taveri, Bruce Beale, Ralph Bryans and Bill Smith, they were never officially offered for sale to the general public in the UK. The CR72 pumped out 41bhp at 12,500rpm, and the larger CR77 47bhp at the same engine speed. Both employed the same bore and stroke dimensions as their CB72/77 road-going brothers - even though the racers used double overhead camshafts and six-speed gearboxes.

...Roy carried out a restoration and was to take part (seen here) in the final Bill Ivy Memorial Trophy meeting, held at Brands Hatch in 1999, 30 years after Bill's death whilst racing the Jawa V4 2-stroke at the East German Grand Prix in July 1969.

## 1963 CR72

| | |
|---|---|
| Engine: | Air-cooled dohc parallel twin, 8-valves, with inclined cylinders, unit construction and horizontally-split crankcases. Gear driven cams |
| Capacity: | 247cc |
| Bore: | 54mm |
| Stroke: | 54mm |
| Comp ratio: | N/A |
| Carburation: | 2 x Keihin |
| Ignition: | Magneto |
| Gearbox: | Six speeds |
| Clutch: | Dry, multi-plate |
| Frame: | Steel, spine-type construction. Engine employed as a stressed-member |
| Suspension: | Front enclosed spring, telescopic fork rear swinging arm, twin shock |
| Brakes: | Front double sided 2LS drum, rear single sided 5LS drum |
| Tyres: | 18 inch front and rear |
| Dry weight: | N/A |
| Max power: | 41bhp @ 12,500rpm |
| Max speed: | 129mph |

*Honda CB72 mounted Derek Minter has time to stick his tongue out at the photographer on his way to a class victory in the 1962 Thruxton 500 miler, he was partnered by Bill Smith. Look at the marks and massive hole on the underside of the silencer!*

*This CB72 has been for more radically modified. Not only has the bottom end of the engine had various covers and electrical components removed, but there are a pair of British Amal Concentric Mark 1 carbs fitted, whilst the ignition coil has been relocated just in front of the battery.*

The bikes had four-valve heads with the cylinder block in two pieces, bolted together on the centre line to allow the central timing gear-train to be inserted before the whole assembly was fitted. The cylinder head was in one piece, however, and the power taken from the left-hand end of the crankshaft, which had the pins located at 180 degrees for better balance.

At the 1963 TT, the factory showed that it had been in some difficulty over the frame design, as there were three versions, all based on their well known spine-type construction in which the engine acted as a frame member. The first model incorporated duplex downtubes, so relieving the engine of dynamic road loads. The second model retained these tubes and had duplex tubes substituted for the vertical portion of the spine tube at the rear. This permitted a redesign of the rear fork, which was carried between gusset plates on the downtubes. While this set-up was the most rigid of the three, none of them was particularly clean or attractive to the eye.

In the 1963 Lightweight TT, three of the new CR72s took part, ridden by Kunimitsu Takahashi, Luigi Taveri, and Chester dealer/racer Bill Smith. First it was Takahashi's turn to go out with engine trouble, then Taveri's bike was hit by serious misfiring problems, after which he went out with engine trouble. This left Smith, who eventually came through to finish third at an average speed of 91.12mph.

*Barry Lawton (son of former racer and Southampton dealer/importer Syd) with his 247cc CB72 twin during the 1962 Thruxton 500 mile race. He was partnered by P. Bugden.*

*Bill Smith took his CR72 to a superb 3rd position at the 250cc TT on the 10th June 1962, finishing in front of Japanese works Yamaha star Takehiko Hasagawa on a disc valve RD56 twin.*

There was only one of the new 305 cc CR77s in the Junior race, ridden by Tommy Robb. This was timed at 134mph, the second fastest machine in the race - only team captain Redman was faster on a four-cylinder model. Perhaps most interesting of all, Honda's 305 production racer was faster than Hailwood's MV four and the Gilera fours of Read and Hartle. Unfortunately, Tommy Robb was soon to be sidelined after dropping the new twin.

However, development continued throughout 1963, with a number of excellent results being obtained both in the Grand Prix and short-circuit meetings. Everyone fully expected, after what was generally accepted as an outstanding year with their 250 and 305 twin-cylinder prototypes, that Honda would offer them for sale in 1964. This was not to be the case, however, and in January 1964 the company announced that it had decided not to produce any more of the twins that year.

*The CR72 without its streamlining. Its 247cc (54 x 54mm) dohc twin cylinder engine featured 4-valves-per-cylinder and a 6-speed-gearbox.*

From time to time several works Honda riders rode the CR72/77 production racers, including Tommy Robb, Luigi Taveri and seen here, Ralph Bryans (on a two-fifty CR72).

Particularly disappointed was Chester racer and Honda dealer Bill Smith, who in addition to having taken several orders for 250s and 305s, had already sold his G50 Matchless to a Swiss rider and was planning to organise a Honda team consisting of himself, John Hartle and Australian Jack Ahearn. Later, in a letter published in *Motor Cycling* on 22nd January 1966, Smith said that he thought Honda's decision not to offer the machines for sale was because of the very high cost of spare parts. But the more likely reasons, in the light of experiences with the only twins to escape to Britain, were poor engine reliability and high-speed handling.

In October 1964, the racing world was amazed when Londoner Dave Simmonds said that he'd got hold of a CR77, for these prototypes were supposed never to have been offered for sale, and were only raced by works or semi-works 'approved' riders (such as Bill Smith). Yet Simmonds had acquired one and had had it shipped to London.

A CB72 being ridden in the Lincoln Motorcycle Club's race meeting at Cadwell Park in the summer of 1966. Virtually a standard roadster - even the kickstart lever is in place.

*During the 1963 Singapore 250cc Grand Prix, Nobby Wales keeps his CB72 (104) ahead of Doug Curran's Ducati Diana (40). In the background is NG Yeng Guan and his Ducati Formula 3.*

The story began when he had gone out to Japan to race Tohatsu's machine in the local Grand Prix at Suzuka in 1963. There he met an import-export agent who dealt with motorcycles, and Simmonds asked to be informed if he ever got hold of any ex-works machines. Six months later, in the middle of the 1964 TT week, a letter arrived out of the blue, offering a 250cc, six-speed, dohc, ex-factory Honda twin complete. As the price was reasonable, Dave Simmonds agreed to buy it. Then, when the bike was already on the ship, a cable came to say that a mistake had been made and that the machine sent was actually one of the near-identical 305cc models.

What had happened was that the bike originally offered to Simmonds had been shipped to America. The exporter offered to send him a conversion kit— the bikes were the same except for the cylinder barrels and pistons—or, alternatively, he said he could now supply a complete 250 as well. Eventually, after mortgaging all the family resources, Simmonds got both bikes.

It was never established quite how this private exporter got the bikes, but it is believed that they came from a small number sold to the Japanese works riders at 'special' prices as part payment for their services.

Dave Simmonds raced both the 250 and 305 Hondas for a couple of seasons before gaining a works ride with Kawasaki for 1967 (see Chapter 8). His first outing on one of the Hondas came at Oulton Park in October 1964 when he rode the 305 to fifth place in the 350cc race. It was the first time that he had ever raced a machine over 250cc, and he rode without a fairing, there being no time to fit one!

*Factory rider Luigi Taveri guns his CR72 production twin away from the start of the 1962cc TT, 10th June 1963.*

*Englishman Dave Simmonds (seated on the bike) created a minor sensation when he imported a pair of CR72/77 production racers direct from Japan. The less-than-perfect handling of the larger machine was cured by employing a Norton Featherbed frame. Also in the picture are his father (left) and brother Mike (right).*

During 1965 - his first full season with the 305 - it broke six crankshafts. At first, Simmonds thought that this was due to the material not being strong enough. The team even had stronger replacement parts made, but they kept breaking. Then it was realized that the crankcase was distorted, so the bearings were out of alignment. This was putting stress on the crankshafts and causing them to break.

After checking, it was decided that nothing could be done with the old crankcase, so the Japanese exporter was contacted in the hope that he could find a new crankcase. To Dave's Simmonds' surprise, he said that he had one and that they could have it for nothing! The reason for this generosity was discovered when it arrived - there was a large hole right through the bottom! obviously, a con-rod had broken and smashed its way out through the bottom, as well as gouging chunks out of the top. Fortunately, they managed to get it repaired, and as all the work was done by friends, it did not cost too much.

*Dave Simmonds at Ballaugh Bridge with his CR77 during the 1966 Junior TT in which he finished 7th. The Honda was timed by the Motor Cycle News speed trap at 123.8mph. This compared with Giacomo Agostini's MV 3 cylinder at 144mph, Heinz Rossner's MZ twin at 132.4mph and Alberto Pagani's works Aermacchi single at 129mph.*

*Dave Simmonds Honda-Norton 305cc race winner, Castle Combe, Saturday 10th September 1966, at Tower Corner.*

The other major problem with the 305 was its navigation, or lack of it. To remedy this, a Norton frame was fitted, which largely cured the problem, even though it added to the overall weight. At long last, 1966 saw the 305 both reliable and with decent handling.

On the 250, Simmonds won the ACU Star (British Championship) in 1965, but the following year three problems cropped up with the Honda - a faulty magneto and broken clutch and cylinder-head studs. To effect a cure, the magneto was thrown away and the machine fitted with coil ignition, whilst clutch and cylinder studs of Simmonds' own design were fitted.

All these modifications seemed to work well, especially the coil ignition. In Dave Simmonds' opinion, this was better than the original magneto - it took no power to drive it, was no heavier and made starting very much easier. A 12 volt system was used with a Japanese battery and some Tohatsu bits and pieces, together with the original Honda contact breaker.

*A brand new CB72 Dream in an American dealer's showroom, circa 1961. With its advanced specification it was light years ahead of most European machines of the same era. And like the CB92, could easily be race kitted for the circuit.*

# Roll your own - race kitted CB twin cylinder models

Many people successfully converted their road-based Honda twins for serious circuit use. This trend began as soon as the first CB92s arrived in Europe during the early 1960s. Earlier in this chapter the most famous converted CB92, certainly as regards the UK, the Chis-Honda raced by Bill Ivy and Roy Francis is reviewed.

But it was the 305CB77, the later CB350 and the CB450 that really got things going in this sector, a situation which continues to the present day, with converted CB350s ruling the roost in classic racing events. The following are just a small selection of the genre:

*De Land, a former US Naval air base was the scene for this picture of Tim Mings (left) with his sponsor/mechanic in early March 2002. The bike is a 1962 CB77 RC181 replica. This features goodies such as sand cast CR31 carburettors, 5-speed, 4LS front brake and many other tasty details.*

*Former Honda works star and world champion Luigi Taveri riding Dumfries enthusiast Doug Curran's very special CB77 at Knockhill, 21st June 1992. The bike was the subjest of a considerable amount of engine tuning coupled with development of cycle parts, including the suspension and braking. The cosmetics also received the Curran treatment so the machine was a working replica of a 1960 works Honda.*

*During 1964 ace special builder Len Harfield of LCH fame, purchased a written off CB77 with less than 100 miles on the clock. The frame and forks were trashed, but the engine unit and wheel hubs survived. So Len set to and manufactured his own frame and so came about the last LCH special, the LCH CB77. After a test session at Castle Combe, Len was so impressed that he decided to do some work on the engine. First the crankshaft weight was reduced by a third, Hepolite liners and piston kit were purchased to increase capacity to 348cc, the cylinder head re-ported, a pair of American cams were reprofiled to the same opening as his dohc 125 racer, Nimonic 80b valves fitted, together with $^{13}/_{32}$inch Amal GP2 . Initially the machine misfired at about 11,000rpm so a Luminition electronic ignition was fitted which cured the problem. Len also managed to obtain one of the new rare pukka Honda 5-speed gear clusters.*

*This CB450 was converted in 1969 by the Swiss racer/engineer Olhmar Drixl. The engine size was increased to 462cc, whilst the frame was one of Drixl's well known Drixton's, with Ceriani GP front forks and an Italian 4LS drum front stopper. This photograph was taken on the 1st July 1984 at Donington Park where it was being ridden by Mark Linton (son of Aermacchi specialist Dick Linton).*

*Classic racer Dennis Murfin riding what many would view as the ulimate CB77 at a CRMC meeting, Cadwell Park 18th August 1985. The overbored 305cc engine was mounted in an ex Dave Simmonds CR72 chassic. It performed as well as it looked.*

*Probably the most impressive of all the production based CB twin racers - and the biggest flop was the Lyster CB450 of 1969. Colin Lyster was nothing if not innovative. From manufacturing early disc brakes to putting wings on a TT bike, Rhodesian Lyster did it. He also built this CB450 with a special 8-valve cylinder head, in one of his Bianchi-inspired chassis. The idea was funded by American Harry Glah of Philadelphia and called the Revolution. But no production version followed and Lyster later emigrated to Canada.*

A Yoshimura tuned CB750 of the type campaigned in the early 1970s.

By the time Simmonds signed to ride for Kawasaki, Honda had stopped their policy of letting existing works riders use the CR72 and CR77 models at non-championship meetings, so the twins effectively disappeared from sight at the end of 1966. Therefore, it came as something of a surprise when, at the Tokyo Show in October 1968, Honda displayed a brand new 350 cc production racer, the CYB350RSC. This was claimed to produce 53bhp at 10,000rpm, and was based around the CB350 roadster.

Instead of the specialised dohc and four valves of the CR models, the newcomer only featured sohc and two valves per cylinder. However, whilst undergoing its test programme at Honda's Suzuka circuit, it had proved capable of well over 120mph and, therefore, capable of offering a viable challenge to the British singles and Aermacchis that had been the mainstay of the class for so long.

The RSC was intended mainly as a conversion kit to fit the existing CB350 roadster. Included in the kit were a modified cylinder head with enlarged and polished ports, higher-compression pistons and a polished and lightened crankshaft assembly. Carburation was by two butterfly-valve Keihin carbs and ignition by flywheel magneto.

*The CB750 four-cylinder was a good choice for long distance endurance events, thanks to its excellent reliability. Here's one in action during the 1970 Barcelona 24 hour race.*

*Dave Degens riding the CB750-powered French Japauto, which he shared with Bernard Sailler in the 1976 Bol' d Or. Japauto was a motorcycle dealership based in Paris, and had won the event in 1972 and 1973 - again with Honda power*

The five-speed gearbox had close ratios, and there were five rear-wheel sprockets included in the kit, from 30 to 35 teeth. The specification was completed by Ferodo brake linings, Dunlop racing tyres and alloy rims, a fibreglass tank, fairing and seat, clip-on bars, rearset foot controls, a 19,000rpm tacho and a pair of long, tapered, matt black megaphones.

The advent of the dohc torsion-bar Honda CB450 'Black Bomber' gave rise to a number of interesting racing versions - on both sides of the Atlantic. The first appeared at Daytona in March 1967 when Zenya Nakajima, service director of American Honda, and Bob Hansen, of Wisconsin, got together to encourage the parent company to develop a number of special bits for the CB450. Early in 1967, Honda agreed to help, and this came in time to enter a trio of Hansen 450s at Daytona. Ridden in the 200-miler by Swede Savage and Harry Schaffer, the 450s came home tenth and twelfth - an extremely good first-time showing. Then in the Amateur 100-miler, Jim Odom broke the existing lap record by over 5mph before crashing out.

*Last of the single cam CB750s, the F, being put through its paces at Mallory Park, circa 1977.*

One of the specially constructed factory-built Formula 1 racers used by Honda Britian during the late 1970s and ridden by a variety of riders, including Phil Read, (seen here in the 1978 Isle of Man TT), Tom Herron, Charlie Williams and Mick Grant.

Meanwhile, in Europe, three men took the 450 route: Marly Drixl, Fritz Egli and Colin Lyster. Swiss special-builder Drixl's first effort appeared in 1969, but for 1970 he enlarged the engine from 450 to 500cc. With a special crankshaft, con-rods, pistons, camshafts and 38mm Dell'Orto carburettors, the engine revved to 9800rpm and drove through a close-ratio, five-speed gear cluster. The complete bike weighed 130kg (286 lb).

The most successful Drixl-Honda rider was the Australian Terry Dennehy, who scored a number of excellent leaderboard placings in the Grands Prix during 1969 and 1970, including a fourth at Imola in 1969. Fellow Swiss special-builder Fritz Egli also constructed a full 500 twin. This was ridden by Florian Burki, who made an appearance at Brands Hatch in October 1970.

South African Colin Lyster had been a racer in the Continental 'circus' who switched to manufacturing disc brakes and frames during the late 1960s. He had also been involved in the aborted Lynton project (see Mick Walker's British Racing Motorcycles, the first book in this series). Lyster's Honda offering was a 450 with a towering cambox housing a completely redesigned dohc arrangement and eight valves. Called 'Revolution', it was projected as both a racer and a SuperSports roadster and was funded by Harry Glah of Philadelphia. The racing prototype appeared in 1969, but the project died the following year.

Built very much with Europe in mind the four cylinder CB400F arrived in 1974. The version sold in the UK (seen here in the Production TT that year) had a displacement of 408.6cc (51 x50mm), whilst the Japanese home market machine had a smaller engine size of 398.8cc.

*The late Dick Aldous, known as The Flying Farmer with the Spooner sponsored Honda CB500 four he shared with fellow racer Gordon Russell in 1976. Norfolk farmer Dick had by then been racing 22 seasons, after taking up the sport in 1955.*

Like the 450 twin, Honda's CB750 four created quite a stir when it had been launched at the end of the 1960s. Unlike the situation with the smaller bike, however, the factory decided to take an official interest. This led it to build a small number of special bikes for the Daytona 200 in 1970. Riders were to be Ralph Bryans, Tommy Robb and the American star Dick Mann. The last was the fastest of the Honda qualifiers at 152.67mph - five short of Gene Romero's new record of over 157mph on a Triumph triple.

During practice, the Hondas had been troubled by oiling and cam chain problems. After watching the race-kitted CB750s in action, puffing smoke with every gearchange, no one expected them to go the distance. Robb was destined to drop out early in the race with machine troubles, while Bryans' machine was destroyed after it caught fire in spectacular fashion. This left only one Honda circulating, with that wily campaigner Mann aboard. Throughout the race, everything but a Honda led, but slowly the favourite runners dropped out, and by the end it was Dick Mann and the machine everybody had forgotten about, the Honda 750 four!

*Former Honda and Yamaha star Tommy Robb with the Honda CB250 the Ulsterman used during a Production TT in the early 1970s. The bike was owned by the Worcester dealer John Skellern.*

*The same CB500 four as Bill Smith rode in the 1973 TT, on the British mainland after the event, being ridden by Charlie Williams (in production trim).*

*Deb Lower's 1963 CB77 with full race kit fitted. De Land, Florida races, 1st March 2002.*

The CB750 was also successful in the period 1969 - 71 in production sports machine events - until the Italians took over the class for the next few years with bikes such as the Laverda SFC, Ducati SS Desmo and Moto Guzzi Le Mans. Then in 1976 Honda got back into the sport with the 750-based 941 RCB machine, which dominated European long distance events that year.

*A CB500 four racing in the Isle of Man Production TT during the mid 1970s. Like its bigger brother, its reliability was a major plus, whilst speed and handling were only marginal.*

For 1977, Honda made a return to road racing at the lower end of the scale when it introduced the MT-125R for sale to private customers, via its normal dealer outlets. This machine was powered by a highly-tuned version of the single-cylinder CR125 Elsinore two-stroke motocross engine, giving 25bhp at 10,500rpm. It featured lots of magnesium and aluminium, seven intake ports, CDI ignition, a 34mm Mikuni carb and a six-speed transmission with ratios matched to the engine and to road racing's needs. The single downtube, twin-cradle frame was made from chrome-moly steel, and standard equipment included a hydraulic front disc brake, tacho, racing tyres and dolphin fairing. Dry weight was 70kg (154lb). Honda claimed a maximum speed of 115mph.

The machine had been under development for three years prior to its release. It was to remain in production until well into the 1980s, by which time it was substantially more powerful (around 32bhp), featured water-cooling for the cylinder barrel and head, and sported a rear disc brake.

*Tony Rutter with the Mocheck-entered CB400F at Silverstone in 1975.*

*Bill Smith is seen here having his Yoshimura tuned CB500 four being fuelled ready for the 1973 Senior TT. A few days earlier rider and bike had taken part in the 500cc Production TT. It was then stripped of all its road kit and fitted with an open 4-into-1 exhaust.*

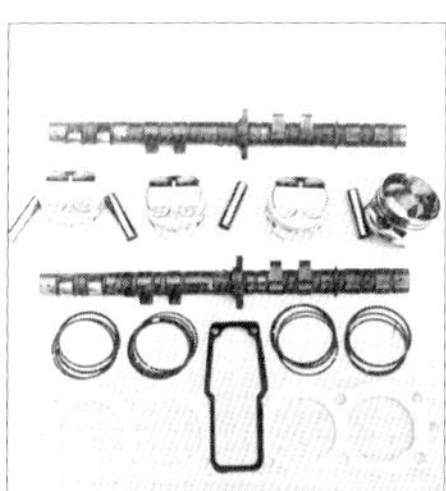

*With the introduction of the new CB900 in 1979 Honda offered this RSC (Racing Service Centre) Formula 1 kit, for road or track use. Charlie Williams used it on the F1 machine he took to 2nd place in the 1979 Formula 1 TT.*

Also in 1977, Honda had made a successful return to the Isle of Man TT, Phil Read taking his works-prepared four-cylinder 750 to victory in the TT Formula I and setting the fastest lap at 101.74 mph. In addition the company saw its machines take the F2 (Alan Jackson) and F3 (John Kidson) events. As these races constituted the newly-introduced 'World Championship' in each category, Honda could be doubly satisfied. The following year, Read lost his title in sensational fashion to Mike Hailwood on a Ducati V-twin, but Jackson retained his F2 title, and Bill Smith was the new F3 champion on his Honda.

Right at the end of the 1970s, the company introduced the CB900, and as Honda entered the new decade, it was to garner yet more success with this larger-capacity model from the four-cylinder line.

Later still came the CBR1100 to carry on the tradition. But for many, the 1960s and 1970s were the most exciting times in what is now talked of as the 'classic era'.

*German-entered CB500 four as raced in the Barcelona 24 Hours during 1973.*

# 500 Classic Honda

The five-hundred Classic Honda currently owned by Harry Copnall and his son Mike, began life as a standard CB450 roadster first registered in 1972. It was first constructed for its new life as a race bike in 1990, by the respected and renowned Honda engine tuner, David Gawthorpe, as one of his team bikes.

The machine was purchased by the Copnalls in 1995, at this time still with the original 450 engine with the torsion bar valve arrangement. A new full size 500cc engine was fitted for the 1998 season, proving far more competitive than the 450cc unit. In 1999 the Copnall equipe fitted a new Nova close ratio gearbox - the original Honda component too fragile for the extra bhp. The frame and front forks were stock 450.

Several engine improvements that were carried out, including a much modified and gas flowed head, torsion bar valve gear replaced by conventional springs, re-profiled cams, cylinders bored to full 500cc to accommodate race type pistons, and heavy duty 6-spring clutch fitted.

*Harry Copnall (standing) with his son Mike at Rockingham, at a CRMC meeting in 2002 - after Mike and the 500 Honda twin won their class at the same venue - perhaps the first 500 classic Honda to win on the new circuit.*

*One of the pukka works specials for Formula 1 racing. Production based, in this case was a rather loose phrase.*

## 1977 MT125R

| | |
|---|---|
| Engine: | Air-cooled single cylinder 2-stroke, with piston-port induction |
| Capacity: | 124cc |
| Bore: | 54mm |
| Stroke: | 54mm |
| Comp ratio: | 8:1 |
| Carburation: | Mikuni 28mm |
| Ignition: | CD1 |
| Gearbox: | Six-speed |
| Clutch: | Wet, multi-plate |
| Frame: | Steel, single downtube, twin cradle |
| Suspension: | Front telescopic fork; rear steel swinging with twin shock absorbers |
| Brakes: | Front hydraulically operated single disc with 2-piston caliper; rear aluminium full width drum |
| Tyres: | 18 inch front and rear |
| Dry weight: | 154lb |
| Max power: | 25bhp at 10,500rpm |
| Max speed: | 115mph |

*A line-up of 19 brand new MT125 single cylinder 2-stroke racers awaiting delivery at Honda GB's Chiswick, London headquarters in 1977. All but the nearest bike has a box on the seat containing the spares kit included in the purchase price.*

*The air-cooled MT125 engine. It was a more highly tuned version of the already successful CR125 Elsinore motocross engine. Featuring seven intake ports, CD1 ignition, a 34mm Mikuni carb and 6-speed gearbox, it produced 25bhp at10,500rpm.*

# Honda UK MT125 Championship

*The original MT125R from 1977 used an air-cooled engine based on an existing motocross unit. Weighing in at 154lb (70kg) dry, Honda claimed a maximum speed of 115mph.*

The UK's MT125 Championship series was the brainchild of the then Honda UK chief Gerald Davidson, himself a former racer. Gerald visualised a one-machine formula with identical specification for every motorcycle, each of which was to be sponsored by one of Honda's dealerships.

Its concept was to re-vitalise 125cc racing which, with the withdrawal of much factory interest, had gone into decline. One major difference with the Honda series. was that with each machine precisely the same as the next, racing would be intensely close. Only rider skill would separate winners from losers - and here was the centre of attraction.

A lot of money was poured into the MT125 Championship, £1000 for the overall winner, with £200 for the victor of each round, more than was paid out at many of the major racing events at that time.

By 1979 the first prize had risen from £1000 to £1250 with the second finisher winning £750, third £450, fourth £300, fifth £250, sixth £175, seventh £125, eight £75,ninth £50 and tenth £25. Total prize money was £11,235.

In its first year (1977), the series saw many 125cc lap records falling, including some set by works riders Phil Read and Bill Ivy.

Clive Horton, winner of the first championship in 1977, was sponsored by Manchester dealers, Forsters. Bernard Murray, backed by another Manchester dealership, Derek Johnson Motorcycles, came second.

Then, during 1978, the improved MT125III proved faster still. Outright lap records were beaten and, with a season's experience behind them, both riders and dealers were even more focussed than before.

The series gained even more public recognition and Cadwell Park and Scarborough were added to the list of famous venues like Brands Hatch, Mallory Park, Oulton Park and Snetterton.

With many of the bigger names committed to Grand Prix action, the championship became a two-man battle between out-of-retirement Rod Scivyer (Hartford Motorcycles) and Dave Hunter (Granby Motors).

After the final round at Brands Hatch in October 1978, Rod Scivyer found himself richer by £2000 - half for the outright title, the other half for winning five of the nine rounds. Dave Hunter was runner-up, with the 1977 champion, Clive Horton third, even though he missed several rounds due to 125cc World Championship duties. It is also worth noting that Bernard Murray not only finished fourth in the MT championship, but also took the British 125cc title with his single, and Leigh Notman came third in the same series on his MT125III.

Into 1979 and although Scarborough was not included in the MT125 fixture list, Donington Park appeared for the first time.

So that entrants and riders were able to make the fullest and best use of their MT125s, Honda UK provided a van at each meeting in the series, giving a comprehensive parts service. Additionally, a complete spare machine was taken to every circuit to provide under normal circumstances the possibility of putting a machine back into full racing specification should a major incident occur. All this made the Honda MT125 series one of the most successful one-man race championships ever staged.

*Clive Horton, the 1977 Honda UK MT125 Champion, entered by Manchester dealer Fosters.*

# MT125 RIII/W 1979

| | |
|---|---|
| Engine | Liquid-cooled single-cylinder 2-stroke, with vertical cylinder |
| Bore | 56mm |
| Stroke | 50mm |
| Capacity | 123cc |
| Comp ratio | 7.6:1 |
| Ignition | CDI Ignition coil |
| Carburation | N/A |
| Gearbox | 6-speed |
| Clutch | Wet, multi-plate |
| Final Drive | Chain |
| Frame | Semi-double cradle, steel construction |
| Suspension | Front; telescopic forks, 82mm travel Rear; steel swinging arm, twin shocks, 70mm travel |
| Wheels | Wire, with alloy rims, 18inch front and rear |
| Tyres | 2.50 x 18 front and rear |
| Brakes | Front; single hydraulically operated solid disc with 2-piston caliper Rear; SLS drum |
| Dry weight | N/A |
| Max power | N/A |
| Max speed | N/A |

*Left to right: Bob Blackely (team owner), Tony Smith, Chuck Downs and Art Blight with the 1977 MT125 which was raced by Englishman Tony Smith at Daytona on the 5th March 2002.*

# Honda - the modern years

3

*The author's late son Gary with his 1993 RS250 at Donington Park British Supercup (the national championship series) May 1994. 1993 was the first year of the new series RS model with Elf-inspired single sided swinging arm. Unfortunately the 1993 bike suffered from piston problems and wrong internal ratios in the gearbox, hampering the rider's progress out of slower corners.*

In the companion volume *Japanese Grand Prix Motorcycles* (Redline Books) what connects the classic and modern eras was Honda's last gasp effort to build a competitive four-stroke 500 Grand Prix bike, the oval piston NR. However in this volume the connection is the large displacement air-cooled four cylinder models for the likes of endurance and Formula 1 events, as the 1970s merged into the 1980s.

## Endurance Racing

As outlined in the previous chapter, Honda had begun their entry into the large capacity market with the mould-breaking CB750 during the late 1960s. Subsequently the original single overhead cam four cylinder found its way onto the the race curcuits, both in production sportster events and open class racing. As the design was updated first by dohc and soon afterwards with increases in capacity the name Honda began to appear as a race winner. During the late 1970s Honda's top model (if one discounts the CBX six cylinder) was the twin cam 900. But as far as endurance racing was concerned the progress was earlier and for bigger displacement.

First in 1972 came the French Japauto which not only sported a 950cc big bore version of the seven-fifty motor, specially prepared by HRSC (Honda Racing Service Corporation), but also a British Dresda frame; the whole assembly weighing in at only 375lb (170kg). This historic effort won the legendary Bol d' Or 24 hour endurance race - a first for Honda.

*American star Mike Baldwin with one of the very tricky four cylinder Hondas (basically a specially prepared CB750/900 street bikes) in the Daytona Superbike race, March 1981.*

HONDA COLLECTION HALL

A year on and Japauto won the Bol d' Or again, this time with a 969cc engine. Then Kawasaki joined the field, winning with the Godier and Genoud 903cc Z1 engine, a feat they repeated, albeit with a new chassis the following year.

Then in 1976 Honda introduced a new machine, at first displacing 941, then 997 and finally 998cc took over. This in many ways was the forerunner to all the air-cooled dohc Honda fours which followed - for either road or racing.

*The 1981 CB1100R with 1062cc (70 x 69mm) air-cooled four engine with dohc and 4-valves-per-cylinder. Although based on the series production CB900 of the period there were many other differences besides the increase in bore size from 64.5 to 70mm.*

The works bikes, coded RCB, featured gear instead of chain driven cams, giving the machines an unusual and distinctive whine - and provided a convenient countershaft so that the alternator (needed for the after dark periods of 24 hour endurance racing) could be mounted atop the gearbox. Another major innovation to the cylinder head, besides the double overhead cams, was 4-valves-per-cylinder.

Another major area of development was the exhaust system. It had to be a compromise between noise levels, ground clearance and of course, power output and mid-low torque requirements.

The ignition system of the RCB endurance machinery was self-powered using a tiny generator, driven by one of the camshafts, to supply a fully transistorized circuit.

Although at first glance the chassis and suspension seem quite conventional, there were, nontheless, noticeable innovations around the remainder of the motorcycle. For a start the wheels were of a new design, with alloy rims and hubs, joined by five sets of spokes (from 1976 Honda fitted steel-spoked Comstar wheels, as later used on a number of their production roadsters) which were riveted. An experimental 'long life' final drive chain was also developed, together with eccentric adjustment for the chain located in the swinging arm pivot (from 1977).

By 1978 Honda came up with yet more development, with the engine now being capable of revving to 11,500rpm and putting out a highly impressive 140bhp. With this Honda continued to dominate the endurance world as it had done in 1976 and 1977.

*An AHM Special Projects Honda of the type used by Mike Baldwin, Freddie Spencer and Roberto Pietri at Daytona in 1981; including hydraulic dry clutch and wet sump lubrication.*

Joey Dunlop with his Honda Formula 1 bike in 1981. Specification included anti-dive front forks, Lockheed brakes, Koni rear shocks, braced aluminium swinging arm, special frame and equally special engine.

## CB1100R

Many of the developments pioneered in the endurance races were passed onto the Formula 1 racers, and perhaps more importantly into a new breed of production-based racers, headed by the mighty CB1100R which arrived at the end of 1980.

At its launch Honda made no bones about it; the CB1100R was strictly a limited production model, with only 1100 examples of the original batch made for the 1981 model year.

The CB1100R's 1062cc (70 x 69mm) engine was based largely on the CB900, but with lessons clearly learned from the factory's endurance racing and Formula 1 programmes.

Pistons were semi-forged, whilst the gudgeon pin diameter had been increased from 15 to 17mm, the five plain main bearings and the quartet of plain big-ends were a different material although remaining the same size.

The silent type Morse chain had been increased from 1 to 1.25 inches in width whilst the exhaust ports had been reshaped, the valve timing altered and the valve springs made 0.1mm larger in diameter. A small generator, on the lines of the CBX six, and the brushes were moved so the outer casing could be chamfered for additional ground clearance. The clutch springs were stronger

Ron Haslam putting one of the works HER Formula 1 through its paces in 1981.

Frenchman Bernard Fau, a member of the 1982 Honda World Endurance team.

*Joey Dunlop leads Ron Haslam at Spa Francorchamps, Belgium during a round of the 1981 World Formula 1 championship with their air-cooled 998cc four cylinder models, with twin shock rear suspension.*

whilst remachining in the gearbox had been improved for racing use. The 13 tier oil cooler was similar to the CB900F's but twice the depth, and the spring on the oil pressure release valve was heavier. Carburettor size at 33mm was 1mm larger than the 900. The detachable lower right-hand frame tube of the CB900F had been deleted to improve rigidity, if not ease of engine removal. Also in an attempt to cope with the extra performance, the steering head stem was of a larger diameter. And even though the front forks had the same 37mm tubes, they were given a balanced pipe between the two, for adjusting the air spring preload, whilst their travel was reduced by 20mm to 140mm.

The CB1100R also benefitted from development and attention to detail by its design team, examples being; an aluminium fuel tank (from the 1982 model year) with a large flow fuel tap, multi-adjustable clip-on handlebars and a clutch lever designed to provide superior leverage.

Honda sources claimed 120bhp at 9000rpm and a stock CB1100R achieved a maximum speed (prone) of 148.21mph in a 1982 road test. By then attention had also been given to reducing the bike's weight by the adoption of a smaller battery, single instead of double-skinned exhaust system, an alloy tank (already mentioned) and a new lighter fairing. Also for 1982 the front fork diameter was increased to 39mm and TRAC (Torque Re Action Control).

*Wayne Gardner being challenged by Ron Haslam as they race along Cooper Straight at Brands Hatch 25th October 1981; both rode CBR1100Rs.*

*The CB1100R debuted in Great Britain at the Earls Court Show towards the end of 1980. Honda never made any bones about it - the CB1100R was a limited production (only 1,100 were made in 1981) street class racer. A total of 100 bikes were imported into the UK that year.*

*Besides the limited production over-the-counter customer CBR1100R, Honda also campaigned an even more specialised motorcycle. This was built by HER (Honda Endurance Racing), with a Honda frame playing a major role. A small number of bikes, based loosely around the existing road-going CB900 were constructed for both endurance and Formula 1 world championships. This is the F1 model.*

Finally in 1983 (the final year of production) a box section swinging-arm replaced the 42mm tubular assembly used previously. This was necessary because of developments in tyre technology which meant that the latest slick tyres could not be used. Dry weight of the 1983 CB1100R was 233kg.

Although by then Honda was begining to use its Pro-Link single shock rear suspension system on more machines, the CB1100R stuck with the twin shock set-up for its entire life. Its also worth noting that Honda issued a safety warning saying that the CB1100R needed to run on 40 grade oil and that an oil pressure relief valve set to operate at a high level meant there was a risk of blowing oil seals unless the engine was warmed up thoroughly before any hard use.

Proof of just how effective the CB1100R was on the track is to mention that Ron Haslam literally blew off the opposition in the Motor Cycle News/ Shell Oils British Streetbike championship series in 1981 and 1982.

As for production numbers, it is believed that 1050 CB1100Rs (1981) were built followed by 1500 RCs (1982) and finally another 1500 RDs in 1983. Of these around 400 came to the UK.

*Bol d'Or 24 hours, France, 1982. This CB900-based machine was ridden by Alastair Copland and Michael Hunt. It finished 24th after electrical problems during the night. Entered by Peter Darvill they completed 1974 miles at an average speed of 82.33mph.*

*Joey Dunlop on a RS500 triple, Cadwell Park, April 1984.*

## RS500

The development and use by the factory backed riders, including Freddie Spencer of the three cylinder NS500 two-stroke, is fully outlined in Japanese Grand Prix Racing Motorcycles (Redline Books). What is less known is the model's subsequent success with privateers for many years after the production version, the RS500.

Developing the triple Honda not only employed an engine layout largely forgotten since the mid 1950s and the days of the German DKW 350 V3, but also, except for Yamaha's TZ750, it made use of reed valve induction in road racing. Previously tarmac racers had either the choice of the long-running, but far from perfect piston-port or rotary -disc valves.

The big advantage which the reed valve gave was flexibility and thus superior low  and mid range engine torque. And it was no doubt this characteristic which had made its use so widespread during the early 1980s in motocross engines.

Designer Shinichi Miyakoshi ruled out an inline three because, in his opinion, the frontal area would have been too great, instead he favoured a vee configuration. Even so Miyakoshi still mounted all three pistons on a single crankshaft, with the two outer cylinders mounted vertically like a parallel twin whilst the central cylinder pointed forward and downwards. Thus Miyakoshi's design was only very slightly wider than a twin and was hardly any bigger than a two-fifty. All three connecting rods were attached to the same crank in a manner which was to become a Honda trademark.

The single crankshaft was not only more compact but also reduced friction as a two crank engine would have needed four additional bearings.

*Eero Hyvarinen from Finland zooms his production RS500 around Devils Elbow, Mallory Park in 1984.*

*Finland's number one in the early 1980s, Eero Hyvarinen.*

# RS500 Technical details

These photographs show the main technical features of Honda's RS500 3-cylinder 2-stroke, it was virtually replica of Freddie Spencer's 1983 500cc World Championship winning NS500. The RS500 was probably the nearest any Japanese manufacturer got to offering customers a pure-bred Grand Prix bike. Introduced during the the early 1980s, it was effectively to replace Suzuki's RG500 as the top privateer bike in international events. Production finally came to an end in 1989.

*Small neat ignition unit and dry clutch. The works bikes had a slightly modified clutch with smaller, lighter plates thus reducing rotating weight.*

*A full range of jets, slides, needles etc were available, even though the RS500 was a much easier bike to set up than the Suzuki RG500 and normally only required main jet changes. Note the magnesium carb body and reed-valve assembly.*

*Close-up of the later specification ATAC cylinder, this was really a work of art with little the private tuner could do to improve it. By this time the Honda triple had reached its final development and thus maximum power output potential.*

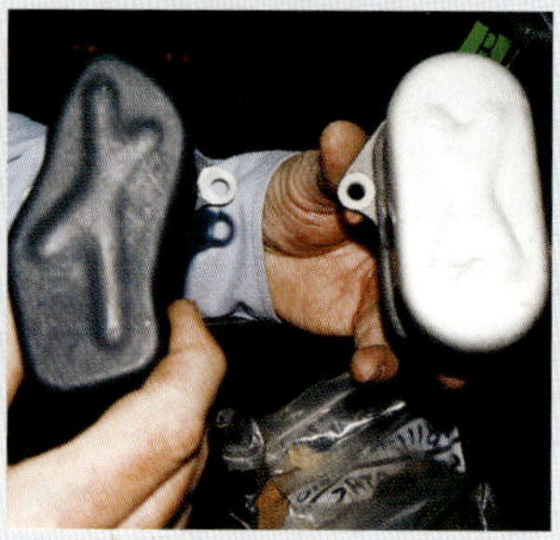

*ATAC chambers fitted to improve performance. A factory kit was available which included all parts including new cylinders and pipes. It was an expensive modification for a privateer. Very much cutting edge technology for its era, initially ATAC was only available for the top two cylinders, apart from the works NS500s which had it on all three.*

*Top cylinders with special extra short spark splugs which were revolutionary at the time, these were particularly necessary on the bottom cylinder which was hard up against the lower radiator.*

*The barrel on the left is one of the later ATAC type. The one on the right demonstrates a privateer's work to achieve the later spec using an earlier non-ATAC barrel. You can just see where the exhaust port has been machined off and a flange fitted to accommodate the ATAC mechanism. This together with a bit of clever porting work has transformed the earlier cylinder to the latest spec.*

*Early RS500 crankshaft with 18mm gudgeon pin and small-end bearing. These pistons were prone to cracking around the skirt, one of the very few weaknesses of the triple. Honda modified the later crank with a 16mm pin and small-end bearing to cure the problem. There were other minor improvements to the seals and bearing housings being changed to aluminium components. The cranks were a work of art.*

*Two early cylinders modified to take ATAC chambers. The ATAC system was mechanically operated by a centrifugal drive system; unlike the Suzuki power-valve equivalent which was driven via a trigger box in the ignition system requiring a battery. This proved more troublesome than Honda's simple and effective method.*

*The serious privateer had a full selection of gear ratios together with three gearbox shafts, to provide an infinite range of gearing. This together with engine sprockets made the RS package hard to beat. Note the gears on the right are all spark eroded and are in fact works or NS type. The standard RS gears were solid.*

*Early production RS500, circa 1984. Features include aluminium box section frame, rising rate monoshock rear suspension, 16 inch front, 18 inch rear Comstar wheels, crossover expansion chambers.*

The vee of the cylinders was 110 degrees - a wide angle - with the trio of carburettors nestling between and operating via the 4 - petal reeds feeding into the crankcase at the base of each cylinder.

The bore and stroke were 62.6 x 54mm, the stroke being considerably .shorter than usually found on two stoke engines. This helped reduce piston speed and meant the engine could rev cleanly through to 11,500rpm.

A total loss battery ignition system was driven off the nearside of the crankshaft, as was the water pump. And because the 34mm Keihin carburettors were fitted at the front of the power unit, the radiator had to be in two sections. Actually there was one large radiator above the carbs, with a smaller v-shaped component at their base.

A little known fact is that on the original works prototype NS500 the cylinder walls were chrome plated (owing to the motocross heritage of the NS programme). However after experiencing a number of piston seizures it was decided to use Nikasil coating instead which largely cured the problem.

*Ron Haslam on a NS500 provided by Honda GB leads Barry Sheene (7) Kevin Wretton (46) and Steven Henshaw (227) on Suzuki RG500s, Brands Hatch Powerbike meeting, 23rd October 1983.*

*For 1983 Honda seemed to be in a dilemma because they produced four cylinder bikes with both the traditional across-the-frame (shown) and v-four configurations. Joey Dunlop monowheels at Cadwell Park in April 1983 on an aluminium-framed model...*

Also early works bikes had steel frames which were soon ditched in favour of an aluminium box assembly, this was later refined to a beam frame identical to that of the works bikes.

The ignition was changed, the heavy battery pack being axed in favour of a special valve which Honda in the vogue of the time named ATAC (Automatic Torque Amplification Control). This was in reality Honda's response to Yamaha's power-valve system, being in effect a way of giving variable exhaust timing. In fact Honda later switched to this type themselves.

*...whilst team mate Wayne Gardner does the same, but with the 1982-type steel chassis and across-the-frame 998cc four cylinder engine.*

*Future world 500cc champion, Wayne Gardner on a 498cc RS triple at Cadwell Park, 1984.*

*Besides its full works-backed Grand Prix effort in 1982 and 1983 with the three cylinder NS500 2-stroke, Honda also built small batches of the RS production replica. This one is being ridden by Chris Guy at Cadwell Park, 1984.*

As early as 1982 works rider Ron Haslam had been testing a production version of the RS500 a replica of the 1982 factory bikes. To be honest it was, unlike many so called replicas, a damned fine copy. The main difference was one of weight - 275lb (125kg) dry - due to less magnesium components and no carbon fibre. Even so it retained the aluminium chassis with a power output of 120bhp at 11,500rpm, it was only 5bhp down on the pukka works model.

At first, thanks to a higher price and the proven RG500 Suzuki, the RS did not find many buyers. However, with Spencer's 1983 world title, the position changed drastically, so the demand was for the Honda with the Suzuki now being left out in the cold. Production continued for the remainder of the 1980s finally coming to an end late in 1989.

In 1989 Simon Buckmaster came a creditable 12th in the 500cc World Series riding an RS500 for team Katayama. Although by this time the bike was wildly outclassed it had demonstrated its prowess for at least 6 years. By this time an over-the-counter beam frame RS500 with ATAC was not far removed from the earlier works bikes.

During the life of the NS and RS500s much experimenting with wheels and tyres took place - earlier bikes were fitted with Comstar wheels with 18inch rear and 16inch front, towards the end they tended to have 17inch front and rear. The Comstar wheels had been replaced with magnesium of Honda's own make or supplied as original equipment and stamped Honda.

*Probably the last of the production RS500 triples made in late 1989. Delta box aluminium frame, revised exhaust, 3-spoke 17 inch wheels.*

*Freddie Spencer at the 1998 Isle of Man TT. The machine he paraded was an RS500 painted in a similar style as the one he took his first championship win on in 1983. It should be pointed out that Honda are very pro-Isle of Man TT. This stems from the fact that it was at this venue that they scored their first international success. It was Freddie's first visit to the Island.*

*In 1983 Joey Dunlop turned up at the Isle of Man TT with the brand new RS850R 859cc V4 and promptly won the F1 event. However, if one compared the bike Dunlop used a couple of months earlier at Cadwell Park with this new liquid-cooled V4, it becomes obvious that the RS850R was far more closely related to the factory's GP machinery of the same year in the chassis department.*

## RS850R

During the early 1980s Honda created a trio of new innovations - liquid-cooling, its Pro-Link monoshock rear suspension and a new range of 90 degree V4 engines.

With the arrival of the RS850R in 1983, all three features were embodied in a single motorcycle. Not only this, but the same machine was amazingly successful that year winning the World (Joey Dunlop) British (Wayne Gardner), and Isle of Man (Joey Dunlop) TT Formula 1 titles.

The RS850R was a liquid-cooled 859cc, 16-valve, 90 degree dohc V4 race bike, with the engine based loosley on the VF750 roadster unit, but with the cylinders bored out from 70 to 75mm. With the stroke remaining at 48.6mm this added up to ultra short-stroke dimensions. Another major change was a move from chain to gear driven camshafts. With a quartet of magnesium-bodied 32mm Keihin CV carburettors, an 11.5:1 compression ratio and Kotusan-Denki CDI ignition the RS850R put out an impressive 132bhp at 11,500rpm, giving a maximum speed of just over 170mph. The transmission was courtesy of a 15-plate all-metal wet clutch, 5-speed close ratio gearbox and a final drive chain.

There is no doubting that Honda really went to town in creating the RS850R, with the 'production' label being stretched to its very limit. In reality this works special was just as much a one-off as any multi-million pound Grand Prix effort.

*Roger Marshall on another of the works RS850R V4s at Greeba Castle during the 1983 Formula 1 TT.*

For example such exotic material as titanium and magnesium were used in its construction - the former being used for components such as the the valves and American-made connecting rods, as well as a host of bolts and fasteners, whilst magnesium was employed for many of the engine's outer covers.

The frame of the RS850R was a full double-cradle tubular steel creation, with an aluminium swinging-arm, using a Pro-Link rising rate system and a single Showa-made shock absorber. Front suspension, in the shape of 41.3mm telescopic forks with adjustable damping and hydraulic anti-dive came from the same source.

But it is all very well to have a blisteringly quick bike with excellent handling, if it can't stop. So here Honda provided a pair of 310mm semi-floating discs at the front with 4-piston Nissin calipers, the pistons being of two different sizes on each caliper, whilst at the rear a single 210mm solid disc with a 2-piston Nissin caliper.

At that time 16inch front wheels were very much in vogue, with an 18inch at the rear; both of the company's riveted Comstar variety. Tyres were Dunlop KR108, a 3.50 section at the front and a 3.85 rear.

At the end of 1983 the rules for TT F1 racing changed from a maximum of 1000 to 750cc. This saw the arrival of the RS750R. But although the power at 132bhp remained unchanged, it was at the higher 12,000rpm rev limit and was much more difficult to ride thanks to a 'cammier' power delivery. Also maximum speed was down to 165mph. A noticable difference was the use of 18inch wheels front and rear.

## RVF750

Then for 1985 came the new RVF 750, which in effect was the forerunner of the production RC30 (which is described later in this chapter). The 1985 RVF had an additional 3bhp, but its biggest gain was that torque levels were back to those of the 1983 RS850R with maximum power being developed at 11,000rpm. Chassis-wise, not only was there the all-alloy frame in Delta-box pioneered on the 1984 RS750R, but the use of a 17inch wheel at the front. Another improvement was a revised cooling system, with two large radiators in place of the RS750Rs three. The exhaust system was new, the 4-into-2-into-1 design comprising no less than 16 different sections. The wheels were 3-spoke magnesium affairs.

For 1986 the RVF was developed further, featuring for the first time the single-sided swinging-arm which had been pioneered in a joint venture by Honda and the French-based Elf endurance squad of the early 1980s. The single sided swinging-arm saved time in the pits for tyre changes and general maintenance. A further increase in power output came from the use of the new swinging-arm because of the ability to use round exhaust pipes where they pass behind the engine, rarther than the oval ones previously needed to clear the swinging-arm.

1987 was the final round of the Formula 1 world championships, prior to the introduction of the new SuperBike formula in 1988.

*This factory entered Honda RS850R V4 ridden by Christian Sarron, Raymond Roche and Guy Bertain contested the Le Mans 24 hour endurance race in May 1983.*

*The first Honda single cylinder 2-stroke road racer, the MT125 debuted towards the end of 1976. This employed an air-cooled piston-port engine based on the CR motocross unit. By 1982 when this photograph was taken it had been replaced by the liquid-cooled RS125RW. Although still a motocross-derived engine, it now featured reed-valve induction. There was also a disc brake at both front and rear and a full duplex frame. (still of steel construction)*

## RS125RW

As laid out in the previous chapter Honda had entered the world of 2-stroke road racing motorcycles with its air-cooled single cylinder MT125 production racer during the late 1970s. With an engine based on an existing motocross unit, its purpose was to provide a cheap, single model race series. In Britain, this proved a tremendous success. However, once let loose, the limitations of the MT125's performance became apparent when matched against full blown Grand Prix-type machines such as the Derbi or Morbidelli twins.

*The 1988 RS125 Series production begins.*

However, Honda didn't give up. This was partly due to seeing how rivals Yamaha had benefited from their continued support of racing at club and national level with the liquid-cooled TZ models (see Chapters 9 and 10).

First produced in 1976, the air-cooled, piston-port induction MT125 single ran through little changed until 1981, when it was replaced by the liquid-cooled RS125RW. Like the earlier machine it, used a motocross-derived power unit. However, there was now reed-valve induction into the base of the cylinder, almost universal practice with reed-valve engines at the time.

With an output of 30bhp at 11,300rpm the RS125RW was to prove a competitive little bike, even though it was still not up to the pace of the very fastest Grand Prix class twins from the leading European factories.

However, as the 1980s progressed, and with pressure from Japanese companies, the FIM took the decision to limit the 125cc class to single cylinder machines, with a maximum of 6-speeds from the 1988 racing season.

*1989 RS125 little changed from 1988 version.*

*The 1992 RS125 Cosmetically very similar to the 1991 bike, but with work done in porting to increase low and mid-range power. Primary drive gears and drum in gear change mechanism strengthened.*

*1990 RS125. This bike brought in several innovations, notably 6-spoke magnesium wheels and a straight exhaust pipe before it joined the aluminium end can (silencer), uprated chassis, front forks given compression damping and improved cylinder porting.*

## RS125

In 1987, the Italian, Ezio Gianola rode what was in effect the prototype of the new RS125 which would put Honda in number one spot in the following year's new 125cc world championship formula for single cylinder bikes. It also placed the Japanese company in a dominant position as the number one supplier of 125cc racing machines to the paying customer.

1987 also marked a major change in Honda forsaking the previously used 56 x 50.6mm bore and stroke dimensions in favour of the virtually square 54 x 54.4mm ones. The smaller bore allowed Honda to use a thicker cylinder wall.

And so it was after a successful year by Gianola (including a runner up spot at a wet French Grand Prix at Le Man), Honda introduced its new RS125 customer racer. This not only employed the 54 x 54.4mm bore and stroke, but reed-valve induction directly into the crankcase. However, unlike many 2-strokes at that time there was no form of mechanical or electronic exhaust valve system.

*1991. Carburettor size increased to 38mm, port timing, crankcases and ignition upgraded, new exhaust, upgraded suspension. Shown with, and without streamlining.*

*The 1994 RS125 with...*

*...and without fairing. That year saw the introduction of a wider rear wheel rim and fully floating front brake disc.*

The frame, similar to the company's existing RS250 twin was in aluminium. The rear suspension was not a sophisticated state-of-the-art rising-rate design, but instead the long horizontally mounted monoshock layout as employed by Yamaha on its TS250/350 racers during the 1970s.

Braking was taken care of by a single disc on both the front and the rear wheels, whilst the 31mm diameter front forks were non-adjustable. Weighing in at 152lb (69kg), the 1988 production RS125 put out 36bhp at 12,000rpm and could reach 125mph. As outlined in the RS125 Evolution boxed section within this chapter, the model has been the subject of constant

*The 1995 model RS125 saw a major update of the series, with balancer shaft, cassette-type gearbox, rising rate rear suspension and inverted front forks.*

*The 1997 RS125 with its fairing removed. This is Tom Tunstall's British Championship series bike. Note tape on the radiator. The engine will perform best between 50 and 60 degrees.*

development to both the engine and the chassis. But probably 1995 was the really big leap forward with the engine given a balancer shaft, a cassette-type gearbox, rising rate monoshock rear suspension and inverted front forks. Also the 1997 onwards model has been designed to run on unleaded fuel, with new cylinder-head, exhaust and ignition.

At all levels of the sport the Honda single has proved itself a most competitive little bike. Only at the extremes of International competition has it been surpassed from time to time by the Italian Aprilia. However without the benefit of full works support (and a large amount of money), the RS125 remains the first choice for privateers wishing to race in the highly competitive 125cc class.

*The new RS125R appeared in 1987 in response to the FIM's decision to ban anything other than singles for international 125cc racing. The formula, as it surely was, also limited the number of gears to six. The RS125 was a sophisticated piece of kit with an aluminium beam-type frame, aluminium swinging arm, horizontal single shock, conventional telescopic front forks, 17 inch wheels front and rear disc brakes and a liquid-cooled reed-valve engine.*

# RS125 Evolution

1987 Prototype machine campaigned by Ezio Gianola in the Grand Prix series against the Garelli and MBA twin-cylinder machines; the twins being outlawed by the FIM from the end of 1987, to create a new 125 single cylinder formula for the class.

1988 Production version of the RS125 put on sale. Based on the 1987 works prototype, this empolyed reed-valve induction straight into the crankcase. Bore and stroke dimensions were shared with the exisiting RS250, 54 x 54.5mm. 36mm flat-slide Keihin carburettor, 6-speeds, wet clutch, CDI ignition. Conventional telescopic front forks, monoshock (non rising rate), single front and rear discs, wire wheels 17inch rims. 36bhp@12,000rpm, 152Ib (69kg) dry weight.

1989 Unchanged.

1990 Minor engine change, including considerable work on the cylinder porting. Chassis updated by bracing swinging-arm. Wheels now 6-spoke magnesium instead of previous wire type. Front forks given compression damping.

1991 Carburettor size increased from 36 to 38mm. Port timing, crankcases, exhaust and ignition upgraded. Power output 39bhp. Uprated front and rear suspension with increased adjustment. Dry weight reduced to 150Ib (68kg)

1992 Work done on porting to increase low and mid-range power. Primary drive gears and drum in gear-change mechanism strengthened, thicker rear brake disc.

1993 Detail work on cylinder and exhaust, plus new ignition box gave an additional 2bhp, making 41bhp in total.

1994 Rear wheel with wider rim, fully floating front disc brake.

1995 Major update: Balancer shaft, cassette-type gearbox, rising rate monoshock rear suspension, inverted front forks. Dry weight 156Ib (71kg).

1996 New seat base.

1997 Engine designed to run on unleaded fuel, new cylinder barrel, head, exhaust and ignition.

1998 Detail improvements.

1999 Detail improvements.

2000 Detail improvements.

2001 Detail improvements.

2002 Detail improvements.

*1998 RS125, little changed from previous year.*

*Joey Dunlop on his way to victory on his Honda GB-backed RS125 in the Ultra-Lightweight/Singles Isle of Man TT, 7th June 2000. Sadly he was to be fatally injured on the same bike a few weeks later at Tallin, Estonia.*

Guy Ethrington (1) leads a pack of RS125s at the start of the 125GP class at Mallory Park New Era Superclub, 3rd May 1998.

## RS250

The RS125's bigger brother, the RS250 was a somewhat later addition to the Honda racing family. Whereas the 125 single had really begun with the air-cooled piston-port MT back in the mid 1970s, it was to be almost another decade before serious thought was given to creating a challenger for Yamaha's quarter litre TZ twin.

And the emergence of just such a machine for the 1984 season came as a direct result of the successes gained by the three-cylinder NS500 Grand Prix bike. Remember that Honda had poured millions of yen into the failed NR project and the NS 2-stroke had come along to save Honda's corporate blushes. And by 1983, the NS project had built a 2-stroke on which to expand.

Really the first effect of the NS500 Grand Prix on production models, was the NS400, a road-going race replica which was to be marketed on a world-wide basis during the mid 1980s and followed the Japan-only MVX250 triple modelled on the factory NS500 of 1982.

Following on from the triples came another roadster, but this time a twin, coded NS250, which was first reported by the press in January 1984. At the same time Honda had decided to offer an over-the-counter customer racer, as a direct competitor to the existing Yamaha TZ, which had dominated this category for the previous decade. And so came the RS250R, based on the NS250 street bike - to maximize

The first RS250 based on an existing sports roadster went on sale in 1984. The 248cc (56 x 50.6mm) 90-degree v-twin produced 66bhp @ 11,500rpm. It needed more development.

*A 1992 RS250. That year the engine was modified to increase flow through the unit, with the exhaust port opening earlier and new reed valve assemblies. Visually a major change was the arrival of inverted front forks.*

profits and speed up production. That this policy was risky to say the least would soon be realized. There is no doubt that Honda screwed up, no one seemed to consider that the Yamaha TZ had drifted away from series production models over the years and was by 1984 a highly specialised, fully developed motorcycle. But either Honda didn't realise the gap between production roadsters and production racers, or were over confident in their ability to bridge the gap.

The RS250R was a 90 degree v-twin displacing 248cc (56 x 50.6mm). The reed-valve induction was fed via the base of each cylinder and was controlled by the inlet skirt of the respective piston. As the Honda development team chose to use the stock crankcase they were saddled from the start with a much too bulky and heavy engine unit. And even in carburettor size the team must have known that they were behind the game, with the TZ boasting 38mm Mikunis, the new Honda had only 34mm Keihins. A square section aluminium frame was employed, the team hoping to make up some of the weight disadvantage created by their engine.

The ATAC (Automatic Torque Amplification Control) which had been used on the NS500 triple, was also to be found on the production RS250R, with a mechanical linkage to open and close the chambers.

At the time of its launch in the spring of 1984, Honda claimed that with 66bhp at 11,500rpm and a dry weight of 220lb (100kg) their bike was a match for the 1984 Yamaha TZ250L. Well on paper it was, but sadly, as soon as the Honda got onto the circuit, it quite simply didn't perform. 'Slow and unreliable' is how Colin Mackellar summed it up in his book *Honda Grand Prix Racers* (Crowood).

As the 1984 race season got under way, so the failings of the new Honda v-twin were revealed. This lack of any success spurred Honda engineers into sorting out what had become an embarrassment. A prototype of what was to emerge as the new 1985 model RS250 was debuted at the British Grand Prix at Silverstone in August 1985.

The new bike, as it most surely was, used a twin-beam spar alloy frame and a heavily revised engine which Honda sources claimed put out 70bhp at 12,500rpm.

Although the 1984 power unit was used as a starting point, the 1985 machine featured smaller lighter crankcases, the vertical (rear) cylinder turned 180 degrees, revised

*Another competitor to use an RS250 in the 1985 Junior TT was Gary Padgett from Batley, West Yorkshire.*

*Joey Dunlop winning the Junior TT on his RS250 in June 1985. He is seen here at Ballaugh Bridge.*

*Top clubman Ian Kimberley racing at Oulton Park circa 1993, on one of the ex Honda Britain team RS250s from the early 1990s. The bike is either 1990 or 1991.*

# RS250 Evolution

1984 First RS250,(based on exisiting sports roadster) offered for sale as a competitor to Yamaha's long running TZ model. 90 degree v-twin 56 x 50.6mm with nearside (left) cylinder vertical and the (right) cylinder horizontal. Reed valve induction via base of cylinder barrel. 34mm Keihin carbs. Square section aluminium frame, 66bhp at 11,500rpm, 220Ib (100kg).

1985 Redesigned engine with smaller crankcases, the vertical cylinder turned 180 degrees, ATAC exhaust valve system as standard and revised porting, new twin-spar beam frame.

1986 Carburettor size increased to 38mm, new exhaust pipes, front wheel diameter decreased from 18 to 17inch. Twin instead of single disc front brake.

1987 Complete redesign. New bore and stroke dimensions of 54 x 54.5mm, crankcase mounted reeds, casette gearbox, round slide carburettors (still 38mm), the twin exhaust pipes now exited on the offside (right hand) of the bike. Hollow-spoke magnesium wheels replaced previous Comstar type. 17inch front, 18inch rear wheels. 39mm telescopic (non adjustable) front forks.

1988 The ATAC exhausts were axed in favour of power valve system. Cylinder and port timing changed to match new variable height exhaust. Bridge on exhaust port widened (to prevent previously experienced piston ring breakage). TRAC anti-dive system discarded - new 41mm diameter front forks, with dump and rebound damping adjustments 71bhp, dry weight 226Ib (103kg).

1989 Unchanged.

1990 Major update. Frame totally redesgned, with detachable sub-frame, steering head angle changed,. Front brake disc diameter increased to 296mm, 17inch wheels front and rear, revised suspension both front and rear. Engine lighter and more compact. Changes to transfer port timing, with all port openings slightly later, revised exhaust system, piston skirt lengthened to provide better support. Small battery previously fitted in 1988 (but not 1989) to drive power valve mechanism return. In 1989 electrical power was taken from the generator.

1991 Engine saw changes to piston and cylinder porting to increase component reliability. Reed valve blocks widened to increase air-flow, carb size/type unchanged. Primary gear ratio decreased by adding a single tooth to the primary drive gear. Steering head angle changed to quicken reponse, new magnesium wheels. Dry weight 220Ib (100kg).

1992 Engine modified to increase flow through the unit, exhaust port opening earlier, new reed valve assembly. Inverted front forks.

1993 Major redesign, taking technology developed on previous year's works NSR model. Engine changed from 90 to 75 degree v-twin, balancer shaft fitted. Revised gearshift mechanism, cooling system capacity increased. Adoption of single sided swinging-arm, originally developed by French Elf concern in endurance events - allowing quicker wheel changes and more freedom for dimensions of expansion chambers/exhaust pipes. Dry weight 227.5Ib (103kg).

1994 Revised cylinder and heads to regain lost power due to regulations which permitted low-lead 100 octane racing fuel at international level. Internal gear ratios changed to provide more acceleration out of slow corners.

1995 Minor cosmetic changes only.

1996 No changes.

1997 Engine converted to run on unleaded fuel - new cylinder barrels, heads, ignition and exhaust system.

1998 No changes.

1999 No changes.

2000 No changes.

2001 No changes.

2002 Discontinued.

*For 1997 the engine of the RS250 was converted to run on unleaded fuel - this meant new cylinder barrels, heads, ignition and exhaust system, although the end can-silencers remained unchanged.*

*For 1995 there were cosmetic changes only. Compare components such as seat and front brake disc inners to the previous year's bike.*

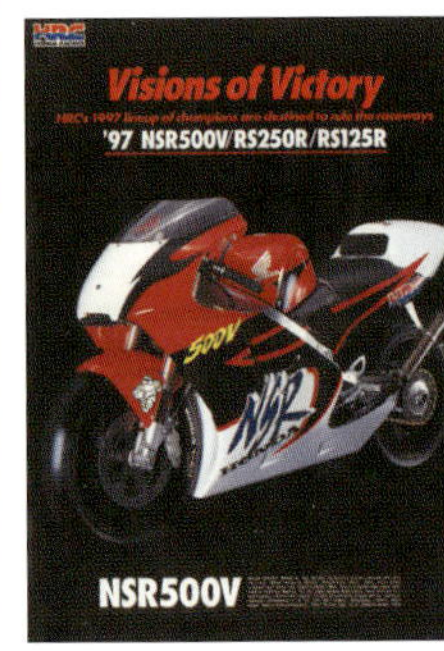


porting, ATAC exhausts as standard and the new alloy twin-spar beam frame. There were now 36mm carburettors and the dry weight had been reduced to 198lb (90kg).

The fact that this time, the engineering team had got things much better was demonstrated by some excellent results.Joey Dunlop took an RS250 to victory in the Isle of Man TT, the Italian Massimo Matteoni won the 250cc European Championship title and the likes of Jacques Cornu and Alan Carter scored world championship points.

With Yamaha struggling with the TZ250 in 1985 (partly due to using too small reed blocks on the crankcase's induction system), Honda received a lot of interest from would-be buyers of the 1986 RS. The changes were kept to a minimum with larger 38mm carburettors, the front wheel decreased in diameter from 18 to 17inch and the addition of an extra disc up front to improve braking performance. But lack of real development meant that Yamaha resumed their number one spot in the production 250 racer war of 1986.

Again Honda sprang into action, the result being in effect a Spencer replica for 1987. The engine had the 54 x 54.5mm of the works model, displacing 249cc; there were now crankcase reed-valves and a cassette type gearbox (on the original RS250 the crankcases had to be split to carry out work on the gearbox). And the flat-side Keihin carburettors gave way to larger 38mm round-slide instruments from the same manufacturer. Both of the twin exhaust pipes exited on the offside (right) of the bike. Hollow spoked magnesium wheels replaced the road-based Comstar components; wheel sizes being 17inch front, 18inch rear.

A major source of problems that year centered around the poor performance of the inadaquately damped 39mm front forks. In fact the whole suspension both front and rear was not up to standard (many customers were forced into buying aftermarket suspension, including 41mm front forks from specialists such as the Swedish Öhlins concern, .

Another problem was that due to differing lengths of the inlet tract caused by new crankcase mounted reeds, the two cylinders now required individual jetting. Yet another glitch that year was constant ignition failure,

*For 1994 there were revised cylinders and heads and the internal gear ratios were changed.*

John Creith, QUB Honda RS250, Aberdare Park, 1998.

caused through what one well known rider described as 'god-awful vibration levels over 12,000rpm'. One of the few real successes of the 1987 RS250 was the British championship title, won by the consistent Gary Cowan.

Although many of the faults of the '87 bike were rectified for the 1988 model, the RS still struggled, due to the performances of Yamaha and the emergence of a new challenger in the shape of Aprilia. The changes for 1988 are listed in the RS250 Evolution box, as is the lack of progress made for the 1989 model. The consensus is that Honda had enough on its plate with the works NSR500 Grand Prix model, so it conveniently shelved development of its RS250 over-the-counter racers.

But at last in 1990 the design was given the update it so badly needed. As described in the Evolution section, this was truly a major update, with braking, frame, wheel size, suspension and engine all coming in for major surgery.

There were further significant improvements in 1991, whilst inverted front forks arrived in 1992.

Again 1993 saw a major reshaping of the RS250, taking several leaps in technology from the previous year's works NSR model. For example the engine's v-twin configuration switched from 90 to 75 degrees and there was the single sided swinging-arm, originally developed in conjunction with the French Elf concern. However nothing is perfect and the 1993 RS250 was to suffer from a batch of under-par pistons and lack of engine torque, not helped by incorrect internal gear ratios, which hampered forward progress out of slow corners. Another weakness, which was never fully cured, was a tendency to eat its dry clutch rather too rapidly.

*The outstanding British 250cc rider of 1995 was without doubt the newcomer Chris Walker (no relation to the author, although a close friend). He put up some tremendous performances that year on a 1995 Padgett RS250.*

1994 saw revised cylinders, pistons and heads not only to put right the problems of the previous year, but to allow the use of low-lead 100 octane fuel at international level (most non-international riders still tended to use the high octane aviation fuel Avgas). There were also changes to the internal gear ratios, thus sorting out another 1994 model failing.

From then until the present, development of the RS250 has stagnated. This is for two reasons, firstly from the 1994 model year the bike has proved the best combination of performance, reliability, running costs and purchase price of the class (the others being Yamaha and Aprilia). Secondly, Honda, together with the other manufacturers seemed to have lost interest in their 250 (and 125) over-the-counter racers. Instead, the author feels, Honda has switched its efforts from pure bred racers to supporting the new 1000 4-stroke Moto GP effort and the advancment of SuperSport (600s in particular) as this helps showroon sales, truly sad.

Everyone I speak to is of the same opinion, the 250 and 125s provide 'real racing' with some fantastic battles all the way down the field. This applies equally to GPs, nationals or club events. In fact it seems only a matter of time before the lightweight 2-stroke 125 and 250s join their 50, 80 and 350cc brothers who have already been axed.

*Launched in mid-1980s, the NSR500V was a 100 degree v-twin with computer controlled rotating exhaust valves. Coded AR (Active Radical), this combustion system is so named because an explosion is produced by active radicals - highly reactive fragmented molecules left over in a cylinder after combustion - which cause the incoming mixture to ignite spontaneously. In conventional engines this causes pinking or knocking.*

# NSR500V

The NSR500V (500cc, v-twin) was Honda's way of providing a customer 500 Grand Prix bike for privateer teams. This had arisen on two counts, the need for the world's number one factory to be seen leading the way in helping swell the grids - and the progress made by Aprilia's 400cc v-twin raced by Loris Reggiani. The NSR500V was conceived and designed in 1994/5 and raced in prototype form by Tadayuki Okada during 1996.

When it was announced in December 1995 that that Honda would be building a batch of twenty machines, this came as something of a surpise because there were not enough places on the grid of a Grand Prix to accommodate that number. However, several were actually sold to wealthy racers/collectors at a reputed price of around £75,000 pounds sterling.

The priorities of the NSR-V project were to use as much of the technology gathered through their NSR500 four cylinder model and other racing programmes, but balance high performance with a 'reasonable price', whilst reducing running costs and providing a more useable power band, rather than concentrating on all-out performance, cornering speeds were improved by reducing weight and concentration of mass.

The NSR500V was a liquid-cooled 499cc (68 x 68.8mm) 110-degree v-twin 2-stroke with a single crankshaft, reed-valve induction and two Keihin PJ40 carburettors; Honda claimed 125bhp plus.

Actually, many insiders originally thought that a 375cc 3-cylinder machine would appear, and when asked, the project leader, Shiguru Hattori said, 'We studied various forms of 500cc class machines, considering the balance between performance and cost, its layout and specification together with our abilities to develop and deliver it. The conclusion we reached was for a v-twin, especially since the lap times between the 500 v-fours and 250 v-twins were much reduced by the mid 1990s. We looked way beyond production costs. We actually did a comparison strip-down of the v-twin engine and a v-four, two crank engine that a privateer might use and discovered it took half the time to strip and rebuild the v-twin. In real terms that meant a small team could afford to employ one less mechanic and of course, there was half the maintainance expenses in parts for a v-twin.'

Another reason for the v-twin 500 was to obtain more technical knowledge with an extremely favourable power to weight ratio rather than producing machines with a more moderate power to weight ratio,. 'We were sure the v-twin was the way forward for the privateer - and also a way to ensure a full 500cc grid.'

*Technical drawing of the NSR500V showing the 110 degree angle of the cylinders, and details such as the ignition rotor and fuel system. The NSR500V gave privateers the chance of at least taking part in a 500GP. On certain circuits its lighter weight and greater manoeuvrability could be a distinct advantage over the pukka factory four cylinder models.*

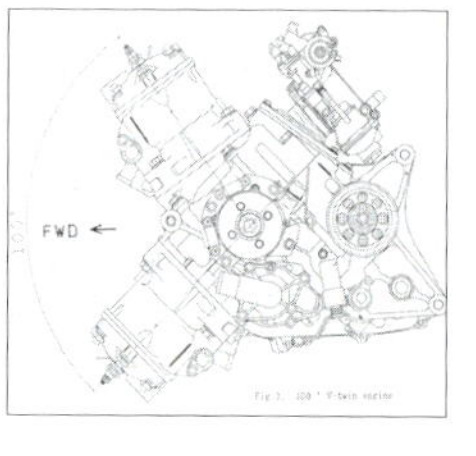

*At works level Honda campaigned the RVF750 v-four in the world endurance championship series. The bike shown here is being ridden by Frenchman Gerard Coudray, circa 1987.*

# V4 4-stroke

It has to be said, the V4 4-stroke Honda didn't get off to the best of starts. It was 1982 when the world's biggest bike builder launched the VF750S. This was an attempt to offer a luxury sports/tourer, with shaft final drive; it was also the world's first mass-produced v-four street bike.

Unfortunately, this revolutionary motorcycle was compromised by awful styling, an equally awful riding position and, to cap all, mechanical glitches and unsure handling. Its launch wasn't helped by much adverse press comment, typified by one journalist who said that the 750 was met with all the enthusiasm one accords cold porridge!

The following year, 1983, Honda introduced the VF750F, a sports version, which looked the business and out-sold every other 750 that year. But again the V4 didn't deliver, this time it was its appalling lack of reliability, notably the much publicised cams and chains string of warranty claims.

But, as revealed earlier, this is in stark contrast to the pukka racing RS850R Formula 1 bike which Honda campaigned in 1983, which won the World, British and Isle of Man TTF1 later that same year.

The big difference was that the RS racer featured gear-driven cams, the VF750S and VF750F chain-driven cams. And following the example of the successful RS850R, Honda launched its VFR750 street bike in 1985. It was this model which, together with the RS850R's successor, the RVF750, pointed the way ahead for Honda's V4 concept.

*The Rothmans Honda RVF750 team of J.L.Battistini, J.M.Mattioli and D.Sarron, pictured at Le Mans in 1987.*

*1991, left to right; Naill Mackenzie, Carl Fogarty, Phillip McCallan and Alan Carter. At that time each of the four was riding for Honda Britain in various racing classes. The bike is VFR750R (RC30) in Honda Britain colours.*

*Miniature v-four, the NC30 (sold in some markets as the VFR400). Its 399cc V4 dohc engine was mated to a slick shifting 6-speed gearbox. It also proved an excellent, although an expensive 400 SuperSport racing option, compared to the more common Kawasaki ZXR400 or Yamaha FZ400RR.*

## RC30/45

The VFR was an all-rounder not a racer. So for the latter purpose the company decided to offer the RC30 (RC standing for Racing Corporation). The RC30 was not simply a road-going Racer Replica in the mould of Suzuki's GSX-R750 or Kawasaki's ZXR750, instead it was a proper race bike which could legally be ridden on the public highway as well as winning races. And win races the new RC30 certainly did, including the first two World SuperBike championship titles in 1988 and 1989.

Built from 1988 through to 1992, the RC30 was in fact a WSB special. The 748cc (70 x 48.6mm) liquid-cooled 90-degree v-four could produce 135bhp at 11,000rpm with the full factory race kit. In as delivered road legal guise the power output was 112bhp - complete with silencing. Even detuned like this it could still top 150mph.

After the RC30 came the RC45. Much of the RC45, which ran from 1994 through to 1998, aped the RC30, including the engine size, aluminium frame and single-sided swinging-arm. Yet it was very much a case of attempting to improve on an existing successful design. Attention was given to updating the formula, together with weight reduction, the latter saving 8.7lb (4kg) - total weight being 416.75lb (189kg) against 408lb (185kg) for the RC30).The RC30 was built in RJ, RK, and RL series but in truth the original design was so good, its 'updates' were minimal, with very little changes made throughout its production life.

A feature carried over from the RC30 was the lightweight titanium connecting rods, but the ones on the RC45 were now attached to low-friction slipper pistons with three rings replacing the RC30's two, which operated in new powder-metal composite cylinder liners. Some 3.3lb (1.5kg) was saved through this alone (the RC30s being manufactured in steel). Another major change was that of programmed fuel injection, a first on a production Honda motorcycle. This was borrowed from the company's hi-tech ultra expensive, limited production oval piston NR750 Superbike.

# VFR750R (RC30)

From its debut in 1985, the forerunner of the production RC30, the works RVF750, dominated TTF1, with 6 wins from 6 races in 1985, 5 wins from 8 races in 1986; the World Endurance Championship with 4 wins from 6 races in 1985; 6 wins from 6 races in 1986, and victories in the gruelling 1986 Bol d'Or and 1987 Le Mans 24 hours event.

Then came the new WSB (World SuperBike) series from 1988. Honda responded by producing a special, the VFR750R (RC30), a low production high quality sports/racing motorcyle in sufficient numbers to allow the racing version to compete in the new series.

The RC30 really was intended for competition, so its liquid-cooled 748cc (70 x 48.6mm) 16-valve dohc 90 degree V4 was very much a production version of the works VFR750 power unit.

Compared to the roadgoing VFR750, the major modifications for both the RVF and RC30 were made in the interests of reduced size and weight. Since the engine's size was the key factor in determining the machine's overall layout, the cylinder heads were totally re-engineered to be as compact as possible which achieved significant improvements in weight distribution and handling.

To reduce head size, Honda engineers designed new 3-piece pressed-up camshafts, with the smallest possible cam drive gears that could be used. Greatly improved high rpm was achieved via major reductions in friction and inertia, and their accompanying power losses.

The unitised gear trains minimised engine height by using additional reduction gears to drive the cams, and featured Hondas unique split-tooth gears held between special steel plates to maintain precise gear backlash for lower noise and greater efficiency at high racing speeds and temperatures.

Fed by a quartet of 35mm Keihin racing type carburettors, the inlet ports were arrow-straight. The valves operated directly by cam lobes via 0.6mm thick ultra-lightweight buckets, thus allowing valve stem diameter to be minimized for maximum breathing efficiency. This was further enhanced by a specially designed lightweight 4-into-1 exhaust system. Sparks were provided by a newly conceived entirely computerized and programmed CDI.

Lightweight forged pistons were connected to the RVF-type crankshaft by lightweight titanium connecting rods, weighing in at a mere 240grams.

To reduce rear wheel hop during downward changes, was a one way clutch. This permitted a number of plates to slip momentarily when back loaded. Likewise, on the RC30, missed changes and jumping out of gear under hard acceleration had been all but eliminated by the use of under-cut-shift dogs in the close ratio 6-speed transmission.

A pair of fan-assisted, lightweight U-shaped aluminium radiators provided no less than 23,000kcal/h of cooling capacity to maintain optimum engine temperature, assisted by the water-cooled oil cooler positioned under the spin oil filter.

Very similar to works RVF, the RC30's frame was of aluminium extruded triple-box main spar tubing with shell-cast components being specially formed for increased thickness and strength at key stress points, and where stress was minimal, thinner walls for reduced weight.

At the rear was a cast aluminium Pro-Arm monostrut, in place of a conventional double-sided swinging-arm. This design, claimed Honda, 'combines rigidity with a compact simpilcity and narrow form.' The front forks, with 43mm diameter stanchions were of conventional telescopic design and multi-adjustable.

The brakes, too, took their design from the RVF, with a pair of 310mm fully-floating front discs which bit onto 4-piston opposed calipers, with a single solid 220mm disc with a 2-piston caliper at the rear.

A comprehensive race kit was available from HRC, this included a full racing exhaust system, carburettor tuning parts and much more. With this fitted, power went up from the standard 122bhp, to 135bhp. And its worth as a racer is shown by the fact that the American Fred Merkel took the first two World SuperBike championship titles on a RC30 in 1988 and 1989. Add to that countless other victories all around the world, making the RC30 one of the greatest of all true production racers which could be bought over-the-counter. To many it was and still is, superior to its successor, the RC45.

# VFR750R (RC30) 1988

| | |
|---|---|
| Capacity | 748cc |
| Engine | Liquid-cooled 16 valve dohc 90 degree V4 |
| Bore | 70mm |
| Stroke | 48.6mm |
| Comp ratio | 11:1 |
| Ignition | CDI with computerised electronic advance |
| Carburation | 4 x Keihin 35mm |
| Gearbox | 6-speed |
| Clutch | Wet, multi-plate |
| Final Drive | Chain |
| Frame | Aluminium, extruded triple-box main spar tubing and shell-cast components. |
| Suspension | Front: fully adjustable 43mm cartridge-type telescopic fork. Rear: Pro-Link with remote hydraulic pre-load adjuster, and Pro-Arm swinging arm. |
| Wheels | Front: 17inch U-section 6-spoke aluminium<br>Rear: 18inch U-section 8-spoke aluminium |
| Tyres | Front: 120/70 V17<br>Rear: 170/60 VR18 |
| Brakes | Front: 2 x 310mm floating discs with opposed 4-piston calipers<br>Rear: single 220mm single disc and 2-piston caliper |
| Dry weight | 408Ib |
| Max power | 112bhp @ 11,000rpm (standard production) |
| Max speed | 150mph+ |

*To many the RC30 was the best 4-stroke SuperBike of its era. 'RC' stood for Racing Corporation. The American Fred Merkel won the World SuperBike championship on an RC30 during 1988 and 1989.*

*Arron Slight (left) and Carl Fogarty rode for Castrol Honda in the 1996 World SuperBike championship series, but even Foggy couldn't repeat his1995 Ducati first place on the RC45.*

*The new RC45 made its debut, in prototype guise at the Japanese Suzuka 8 hours in the hands of Eddie Lawson and Satoshi Tsujimoto. It went on sale the following year, replacing the long running RC30.*

There were also improvements to both the 6-speed gearbox and NR-derived hydraulic clutch, the cooling system (now with two radiators instead of one) and a revised 4-into-1 exhaust.

Also new was the inverted front fork assembly (the RC30 featuring conventional teles), whilst a massive, cast aluminium single sided swinging arm was still employed, but in modified form. This was necessary because the RC45 had been redesigned to hold a fatter 190 section rear tyre than that found on the RC30. The fairing was another area of change, with the RC45's upper cowling incorporating a pair of slit-shaped ducts to provide a maximum flow of cool, dense air into the fuel-injection's massive 1.5 gallon (7 litre) airbox.

*New Zealander Arron Slight an important member of the mid 1990s Castrol Honda RC45 WSB squad.*

Honda claimed 120bhp at 12,000rpm for the standard RC45 in full road legal guise. On paper this was a considerable improvement, and at £17,780 in 1994, it was virtually double the price of the lighter and faster FireBlade. Neither could it match its older brother's WSB record, as even the signing of Carl Fogarty couldn't bring a world title. Eventually, the Grand Prix star, John Kocinski, was drafted into the the Neil Tuxworth-managed, British-based Castrol Honda World SuperBike squad, and the RC45 won its one and only world title in 1997. But from then on, Ducati dominated WSB, resulting in the RC45 being ditched in favour of the new VTR SP-1 996cc v-twin from the 2000 model year onwards.

## RVF750 (RC45) 1995

| | |
|---|---|
| Engine | Liquid-cooled 16 valve dohc 90 degree V4 |
| Capacity | 749cc |
| Bore | 72mm |
| Stroke | 48mm |
| Comp ratio | 11.5:1 |
| Ignition | Electronic digital |
| Carburation | Electronic direct fuel injection |
| Gearbox | 6-speed |
| Clutch | Wet, multi-plate |
| Final Drive | Chain |
| Frame | Aluminium Delta-box construction |
| Suspension | Front: fully adjustable 41mm inverted cartridge-type telescopic fork.<br>Rear: Pro-Link Pro-Arm, fully adjustable, with remote reservoir damper, 130mm of travel. |
| Wheels | 6-spoke U-section cast aluminium |
| Tyres | Front: 130/70 ZR16<br>Rear: 190/50ZR17 |
| Brakes | Front: 2 x 310mm discs with 4-piston calipers<br>Rear: single 220mm single disc with dual-piston caliper |
| Dry weight | 417lb (189kg) |
| Max power | 120bhp @ 12,000rpm (standard production) |
| Max speed | 160mph+ |

*Seventeen-year-old James Toseland was signed up for the 1998 season to contest the World SuperSport series (he is seen here in January that year on Aaron Slight's RVF(RC45) SuperBike at Alexandra Palace, London.*

Formula TT, Isle of Man 3rd June 2000, the legendary Joey Dunlop winning on his Honda Britain VTR SP v-twin. Joey's time was 1 hour, 52 minutes, 15.3 seconds, an average speed of 120,99mph.

# VTR SP-1(RC51)

The racing version of the Honda 996cc v-twin, the VTR SP-1 (RC51 in the USA) was a major step forward over the old RC45. The standard production SP-1 could exceed 170mph and weighed 440lb (200kg). But compared with Colin Edwards' 2000 World SuperBike winning machine it was but a pale replica. The WSB factory racer putting out another 50bhp and weighing an amazing 84lb (38kg) less. As for maximum speed, Edwards' world championship winner could reach a staggering 190mph on optimum gearing. And so, for the first time, Honda had a machine which could equal Ducati's all-conquering 996cc v-twin. And although Troy Bayliss regained the World SuperBike title for the Italian marque in 2001, Honda and Colin Edwards snatched it back in 2002, after a season-long battle with Bayliss. In fact the turning point came at Brands Hatch in early August when his Ducati challenger collided with team-mate Ruben Zeus. The injuries sustained meant that Australian Bayliss was off par at crucial part of the season, which very much played into Edwards' and Honda's hands.

The 2000 World SuperBike champion, American Colin Edwards with his Castrol Honda VTR SP v-twin. It was Honda's fourth World SuperBike title and their first with a v-twin.

*Lester Harris (right) looks at one of his Honda Britain riders with a VTR SP, Silverstone, August 2001.*

During the closed season of 2002-2003 there was considerable controversy as to whether Honda would defend their World SuperBike crown, now that Valentino Rossi had taken the new five cylinder Moto GP Honda to its debut year World Champion title in that sector of the sport.

Many observers felt that the whole purpose of the Moto GP formula was to upstage and replace SuperBikes. But by winning both titles in 2002, Honda had given themselves a dilemma. What would they do next? They decided to withdraw, but before this Honda had at last proved it could build a premier league SuperBike contender in the VTR SP-1(RC51).

*Edwards with the Castrol Honda VTR SP during the Spanish round of thge 2002 World SuperBike championship series*

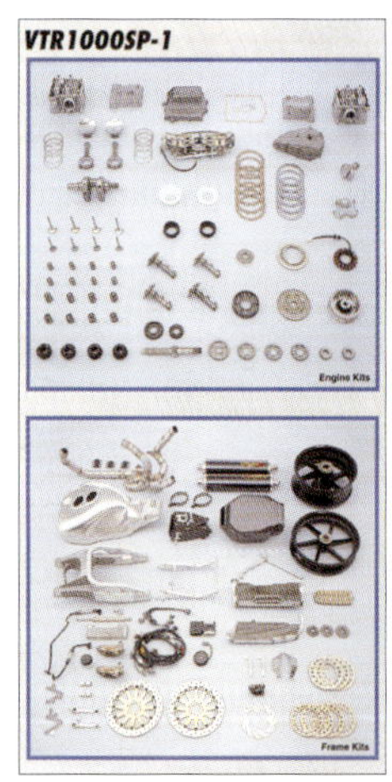


*The engine and frame kit for the 2001 VTR1000SP-1.*

*The CBR600F was launched in late summer 1986, going on sale the following spring, as the FII model. It featured an across-the-frame liquid - cooled dohc 16-valve engine, with 6-speeds, 3-spoke 17 inch alloy wheels and fully enclosed bodywork. Scottish rider John Campbell is seen here with his CBR600 at Oulton Park on Easter Monday 1988. His is pictured right, with his other bike a Suzuki GSX-R750.*

# CBR600F

Honda's CBR600 has dominated the SuperSport 600 class since it entered production in early 1987. Rivals have, from time to time, been faster or lighter, but the CBRs excellent all-round ability has seen it remain at, or near the top of, both the sales chart and the race track results year after year.

The CBR600F's huge success has been thanks to Honda's ability to keep it competitive, with a series of updates over the years, adding to the original design's great all-round performance. Even for a company the size of Honda, the CBR's success had been phenomenal. Actually, the first CBR fours were the 400 and the 250, which went on sale on the Japanese home market in 1986, By the summer of that year, rumours had reached the West that 600 and 1000 versions would soon follow. The 250 four was the highest-revving road bike produced up to that time, with a redline peaking at 17,000rpm and a maximum power of 45bhp being produced at 14,500rpm. The 400 version of the motor put at 59bhp at 12,500rpm and featured an engine canted forward at an angle of 35 degrees and fed by a quartet of down draught Keihin VG02 carbs. A 6-speed gearbox was built in unit with the engine, which was mounted in a racing-style steel box-section frame.

A bodyshell similar to the Massimo Tamburini-styled Ducati Paso (which had been launched at the Milan Show in late 1985) was claimed to provide, as Honda described, the aerodynamics of an arrow! Other details of the CBR400 included 3-spoke alloy wheels, triple disc brakes, a 4-into-1 exhaust, and a dry weight of 363lb (164kg)

With the launch of the new CBR400F (and CBR1000F) for the 1987 model year, Honda had taken, for them, a contoversial path. It seemed to have committed its future to the v-configuration and turned its back on the design which had made its name, the across-the-frame four. As previously outlined, at the begining of the 1980s, Honda had introduced the VF750 v-four, followed by the VF1000, VF 500 and VF400, plus the VT250 v-twin.

But Honda was no doubt heavily influenced by the arrival of Kawasaki's hugely significant and succesful GPZ600R (see chapter 5). So in hindsight, Honda's philosophy at the time seemed to have been, 'If you can't beat them, join them only do it better!'

The first CBR600F, the FH, went on sale in early 1987 and, in addition to the aerodynamic body work, was notable for its use of 17inch wheels, both for front and rear, which were, at the time, seen as a fashion whim, yet today are acknowledged as the best size, for both series production street bikes and pukka racers.

The 598cc (63x48mm) ran an 11:1 compression ratio and had a 6-speed gearbox, electric start, transistorized ignition with electronic advance, four 32mm Keihin CV carbs, 3 spoke aluminium wheels, 37mm air-assisted front forks with TRAC anti-drive and Pro-Link monoshock rear suspension. Dry weight came in at 400lb (182kg). There was also a lightweight, aluminium oil cooler and radiator, with a power output of 85bhp at 11,000rpm this, the first of the CBRB600 family could reach 140mph. One feature of the bike which was soon quietly dumped was the TRAC anti-drive, followed soon afterwards by the front fork air-pressure adjustment.

The first major update came in 1989, with the power output increased to 93bhp, as a result of a substantial number of engine modifications (see CBR600 Evolution box). In 1991 came even more power (98.6bhp) and perhaps even more importantly, the balance of the machine received its first major redesign, with many new cycle parts. At the same time, the bodywork was totally restyled.

In 1995, a mechanical revision included larger carbs (36mm) and the introduction of a ram air system. Power was now up to 100bhp. Another major revision occured in 1997, including a power boost to 105bhp, new wheels, brakes, revised suspension and detailed changes including ignition, exhaust and a new air-induction system.

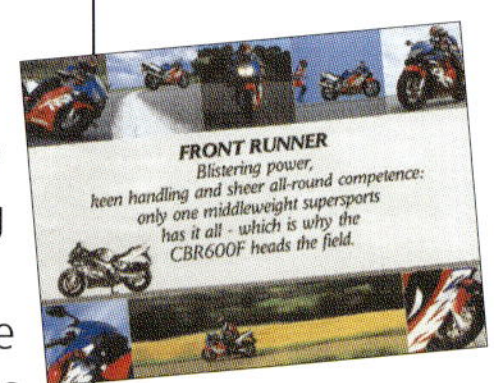


In 1999, Honda introduced what amounted to a new motorcycle. The engine featured shorter cylinder dimensions of 67x42mm. There was improved cooling, new cylinders, lighter moving internal components, larger carbs (36.5mm), and a new ignition system. The biggest development was the adoption, for the first time on the CBR600, of an aluminium frame. The picture was completed by new bodywork and exhaust, the latter in stainless steel.

Finally, in 2001, fuel injection replaced carburettors, power output went up to 109bhp, and there was a new fairing with larger air-inlet ducts, a modified ECU (Electronic Control Unit), and a redesigned cylinder head and cam cover. The CBR was also made available in two guises; the standard 'F' and a new 'F Sport', the latter intended larger for competition use.

Since then the CBR has been updated again (2003) with the 115bhp RR version and weight reduced to 169kg.

*Silkolene Honda Britain postcard showing the 1991 Irishman Philip McCallan aboard his Honda CBR. For 1991 the CBR600 was given a major update, with more engine tuning, larger carbs, revised transmission, new exhaust system, new 6-spoke wheels and modified frame (still steel construction) Power output was 98.6bhp.*

A 1992 CBR600, largely unchanged from the 1991 version.

## FireBlade

At the beginning of the 1990s Honda introduced its CBR900RR FireBlade. This rewrote the rules for the large capacity Japanese sports/racing motorcycle and in the process put all of its rivals at a distinct disadvantage, with its combination of extreme lightness and powerful motor.

Honda,s engineering team, led by Todeo Baba, came up with an 893cc liquid-cooled, 16-valve dohc across-the-frame four, which in its original 1992 'N' guise developed 122bhp at 10,500rpm giving a maximum speed of 165mph. This combined with an extremely low weight of 411.15lb (186.5kg), saw the 'Blade' not only lavished with press accolades and repeatedly winning 'Bike of the Year' awards from journals throughout the world, but getting off to a flying start with racing successes, which included victory in the gruelling Isle of Man TT.

Only its sub-900cc engine size was questioned, but even this, in later years, was rectified with increases first to 918cc then to 929cc!

Its technical specification, for what after all was essentially a series production roadster, was truly impressive and also helps explain why the power-to weight ratio was so good. Todeo Baba and his team set out to create a performance motorcycle with no compromise in the quest for minimum weight. Flat-topped, ultra light-weight slipper pistons allowed high rigidity and equally lightweight connecting rods and crankshaft, thus minimizing inertia and providing extremely crisp engine response. Another weight-saving measure was the fitment of a magnesium, instead of aluminium, cylinder head cover (from 1994 onwards).

# CBR900RR FireBlade 2000

| | |
|---|---|
| Engine | Liquid-cooled, across-the-frame, dohc 4-cylinder, with 16 valves |
| Capacity | 929cc |
| Bore | 74mm |
| Stroke | 54mm |
| Comp ratio | 11.3:1 |
| Ignition | Computer-controlled digital transistorized, with electronic advance |
| Carburation | Electronic fuel injection |
| Gearbox | 6-speed |
| Clutch | Wet, multi-plate |
| Final Drive | Chain |
| Frame | Aluminium construction with triple-box spars and multi-point diamond configuration |
| Suspension | Front: inverted telescopic forks<br>Rear: Honda Pro-Link monoshock, aluminium swinging-arm |
| Wheels | 17inch hollow-section triple spoke, aluminium |
| Tyres | Front: 120/70 ZR 17<br>Rear: 190/50 ZR 17 |
| Brakes | Front: 2 x 330mm floating discs with 4-piston calipers<br>Rear: single 220mmm solid disc with 2-piston caliper |
| Dry weight | 374.7Ib (170kg) |
| Max power | 152bhp at 11,000rpm |
| Max speed | 170mph |

*During a very wet Production TT staged on the 9th June 2000, Richard Quayle rode like a true 'rain master' to clinch runner up spot on his Bullock Vimto Fireblade, at an average speed of 96.73mph.*

# CBR600F Development

1986 CBR600F launched late summer. Across-the-frame four cylinder engine configuration, liquid-cooled, 16-valves, dohc, aluminium head and barrel, horizontally split crankcases, six-speeds, steel frame, 17inch 3-spoke alloy wheels, fully enclosed bodywork.

1987 First production version, the FII goes on sale.

1989 First update. Power increased from 85bhp to 93bhp, as a result of a host of engine modifications, including higher 11.1:1 compression ratio.

1991 Major revision. Engine given 15 per cent larger cylinder head ports, bigger 34mm carburettors and airbox, larger and lighter valves with narrower included angle, strengthened (and lighter) crankshaft, lighter pistons, compression ratio upped to 11.3:1. Clutch reduced in diameter from 138mm (5.4in) to 125mm (4.9in), number of plates increased from six to nine. Relocation of gearbox mainshaft meant new, more compact crankcases. New exhaust system. Power output increased to 98.6bhp. New cycle parts including 6-spoke wheels, modified frame (still steel construction) and swinging arm, revised suspension and braking. Restyled bodywork and graphics.

1995 Mechanical revision including higher compression (now 12:1) larger carburettors (36mm) and introduction of ram-air system, power boosted to 100bhp.

1997 Major update including 105bhp at 12,000rpm, torque increased to 6.7kg (14.8Ib) at 10,500rpm, new wheels and brakes, revised suspension, revised bodywork. Smaller detail changes including ignition, exhaust and air-induction system.

1999 Virtually a new bike. Almost every component was changed, including engine - now 67 x 42mm, compared to 65 x 45.2mm. Maximum rpm increased to 14,600rpm. Cooling efficiency increased by 17 percent, as a result of increased radiator area and revised coolant channels in the cylinder block. Cylinders have aluminium liners coated in graphite and ceramics for improved heat transfer and reduced friction, while other internal losses minimized by changes to valves, pistons and bearings. Carburettor size increased to 36.5mm. New ignition system. All-new twin-spar aluminium frame and new bodywork. Stainless steel exhaust, with aluminium/stainless steel muffler.

2001 Fuel injection replaces carburettors. Revised bodywork, including fairing. Larger air-inlet ports for airbox. New instrument console, modified electronic control unit (ECU). Cylinder head and cam cover redesign to accommodate camshaft pulsar and coolant temperature sensor needed for fuel injection system. 109bhp at 12,500rpm. In addition to CBR600F a new 'F' Sport model also marketed.

2003 New RR version arrives with track oriented specification including higher revving engine producing 115bhp, and weight reduced to 169kg. Power delivery and fuel injection combine to ensure racer type performance, but not under 6000rpm. Existing F model continued for street use.

*The Scotsman Jim Moodie with the Castrol Honda backed CBR600 during the Junior TT in the Isle Man, 7th June 2000. He finished 6th, with an average speed of 117.71mph.*

*Darren Wnunoski (24) and Mick Corrigan (21) lead a group of riders, all CBR mounted, National SuperSport 600, Snetterton, 1998, By then the CBR600 had larger 36mm carbs and forced ram-air (1995) and even more power and improved suspension.Power output in standard guise was 105bhp@12,000rpm.*

The FireBlade's 16-valves were operated directly by twin camshafts, resulting in a compact, low friction valve train that only required adjustment every 16,000miles (normal road use). Originally, a bank of four 38mm diameter flat slide carburettors, assisted by a single-port induction system, provided the engine with its diet of fuel. However, later an electronically controlled PGM-F1 fuel injection system took over, providing even more precise throttle response. The ignition system was computer-controlled and digitally transitorized, with electronic advance. A cartridge-type liquid-cooled oil cooler ensured lubricant temperatures were kept strictly under control for stable output and maximum engine life.

The FireBlade's chassis also played a vital role in the bike's success, as during its life the frame has seen a steady evolution which has kept Honda at the very forefront of motorcycle technology.

For example, the 1997 V series frame was based on twin main spars of extruded aluminium, weighing in at a mere 23lb (10.5kg). Featuring a semi-floating rubber engine mount to combat engine vibes, it supported a high-rigidity aluminium swinging-arm designed using in-depth computer analysis and rigorous track testing. Up to the introduction of the 2000 model year, when the FireBlade became Honda's first large four cylinder production sports bike to come equipped as standard with inverted front forks (43mm), the front suspension consisted of a special version of the conventional telescopic front fork, with massive 45mm stanchions. At the rear was a refined version of Hondas patented Pro-Link system, with a remote reservoir single shock absorber.

# CBR600F 2001

| | |
|---|---|
| Engine | Liquid-cooled, across-the-frame, dohc. 4-cylinder, with 16-valves. |
| Capacity | 599cc |
| Bore | 67mm |
| Stroke | 42.5mm |
| Comp ratio | 12:1 |
| Ignition | Electronic |
| Carburation | Fuel injection |
| Gearbox | 6-speed |
| Clutch | Wet, multi-plate |
| Final Drive | Chain |
| Frame | Twin-spar aluminium main frame |
| Suspension | Front: telescopic fork<br>Rear: square section swinging-arm, with rising rate single shock absorber |
| Wheels | 17inch aluminium 3-spoke, front and rear |
| Tyres | Front: 120/70 ZR17<br>Rear: 180/55 ZR17 |
| Brakes | Front: 2 x 296mm discs, with 4-piston calipers<br>Rear: single 220mm disc, with 2-piston caliper |
| Dry weight | 374.8Ib (170kg) |
| Max power | 109bhp at 12,500rpm |
| Max speed | 155mph |

*2001, British Junior Supershocks Campionship, Brands Hatch, CBR600F Sport, fully race prepared.*

*Rick Ellis on his Holbeach Tyres/Mike Smith Tuning CBR600 taking off at the Mountain section, Cadwell Park New Era Superclub, 29th June 2002.*

Honda was the first manufacturer to use the combination of 16inch front and 17inch rear wheels on a production roadster, this ensuring razor sharp reactions and sure-footed handling in a single package. However, from the 2000 model year, Honda switched to 17inch rubber for both wheels, a move it made, according to Honda, because of the difficulty in obtaining supplies of high performance 16inch tyres, both for road and racing use.

Braking has been another area where the FireBlade has seen changes during its life. At first, there were twin 296mm discs up front, but over the years size has increased to 310mm and finally 330mm. It is worth noting that these are all of the floating variety and feature 4-piston calipers. At the rear, a single solid 220mm disc with 2-piston caliper has remained a constant fitment. In any case, even early 'Blades were capable of putting in brick-wall-like stopping figures.

Although it was largely conceived as a street bike, the FireBlade has had considerable track success, having not only won the British Production Powerbike Championship, but also several Isle of Man TTs. By the end of 1998 Honda had sold more than 14,000 FireBlades in the UK alone and by the end of 2001 this figure had comfortably exeeded 20,000. This success has been largely due to its combination of being as light as a 600 with the power of a 1100.

*Colin Edwards looking tense during an official Team Castrol Honda photo-shoot in early 2002.*

# CB900RR FireBlade Development

1992 Lauched with 893cc 16-valve liquid-cooled dohc across-the-frame 4-cylinder engine and a 6-speed gearbox. Aluminium frame, with 24 degree streering head angle, 4-into-1 exhaust, 122bhp and 165mph.

1994 New fairing, new 'fox-eye'headlamps, modified suspension, including revalved, fully adjustable front forks. Engine given magnesium cylinder head cover in place of aluminium original. Electronic speedomoter, redesigned warning lights.

1996 Major changes introduced. Engine size increased to 918.5cc, by increasing cylinder bore, compression raised from 11 to 11.1:1, the big ends, crankshaft and clutch all strengthened, a new slimmer alternator reduced engine width by 9.5mm, modified gear change with three new ratios, 3D ignition mapping, curved aluminium radiator, silencer muffler increased from five to six litres. The chassis was given thinner wall frame rails, with cross-bracing to swinging-arm and pivot plate made by reinforced open casting, lighter final drive chain. Rear suspension given increased damping control and lighter internals. Front forks modified, including reducing internal component weight and wider range of adjustment. Bodywork given improved aerodynamic lower fairing, top portion unchanged. Front mudguard redesigned to provide down-force at speed. Riding position modified.

1998 Engine size, bore and stroke dimensions left unchanged, but some 80 percent of internal components modified, crankshaft, connecting rods and camshafts left unchanged. Power output increased to 128bhp, combustion chambers intake and exhaust ports reprofiled to reduce airflow resistance. 38mm carburettors retained, but vacuum piston size changed to produce sharper throttle response. Clutch plates reduced from 10 to 8, top gear ratio increased for higher maximum speed. Radiator capacity increased by seven percent, silencer larger, but lighter. Small changes made to frame to increase strength and reduce weight. Combined with engine changes, weight dropped 7lb (3kg). Steering head angle modified to provide more responsive steering, with fork offset reduced from 35mm to 30mm and a 5mm increase in trail. New braced swinging-arm, modified front suspension, also fork legs moved apart by 10mm to increase torsional rigidity. Front brakes, new opposed, 4-piston calipers and floating discs increased in diameter from 296mm to 310mm. Wider and higher fairing, with new headlamp shape. New 28mm thick, one-piece electronic instument panel, with centralised rev-counter.

2000 Radical updates introduced. New bore and stroke dimensions of 74 x 54mm, giving a capacity of 929cc. Computed-controlled fuel injection (PGM-Fi), Honda Variable Intake Exhaust Control (H-VIX), higher compression ratio (11.3:1), bigger diameter valves (incorporating a narrower angle), forged in place of cast pistons , new hollow camshafts (20 percent lighter). Semi-pivotless frame with longer swinging-arm. Inverted 43mm cartridge type front forks. Larger 330mm front brake discs, front wheel diameter increased from 16inch to 17inch. Smaller battery, but with 10 percent increase in output.

At the time of its launch in 1992, machines such as the Suzuki GSX-R1100 and Yamaha FZR 1000 EXUP reigned supreme in Open 1300cc class production racing and in the showroom too. Both bikes had been brilliant machines in their day - hugely powerful and extremely rapid. But with one fell swoop, the FireBlade destroyed them both. After riding the Honda, the GSX-R and EXUP felt like something from a bygone age - rather like cumbersome dinosaurs. A new era in high performance large displacement motorcycles for both fast road and racing had arrived. Things would never be the same for the across-the-frame Japanese four cylinder motorcycle.

# Padgett's

*Clive Padgett (far left) with the Padgett racing team and rider Jay Vincent, Sachenring, German Grand Prix, 2000.*

Padgett's of Batley is probably the best known of all British based companies to have specialised in Japanese over-the-counter racing machinery. But how many readers know much of the West Yorkshire firm's history?

In February 1958 in a small premises in Wellington Street, Batley young Peter Padgett had taken a lease and the plunge into business with capital of £300. Peter was fresh out of his apprenticeship with Leeds dealership Watson and Cairns and keen to make his mark.

Bithplace of the new company was an old furniture manufacturing unit in which the traditional props of woodturning machinery and French polishing were soon replaced by a stock of new and used British motorcycles and the smell of the bike world.

His first official agency, Matchless arrived in 1959 and was quickly followed by all the other major British marques of the era, including BSA, Triumph, Norton, AJS and Velocette.

Soon Peter's reputation was spreading outside his West Yorkshire base and with his sales success came a racing career, which also saw Padgett's stocking Italian Aermacchi racers, supplied via British importer and former racer, Bill Webster.

Then in December 1961, the Japanese invasion began. Yamaha and Honda, together with Suzuki steadily began to make inroads into the European market, including Great Britain. In fact Padgett's (Peter was now assisted by his younger brother Don) became the third Yamaha racing agency behind Monty & Ward and Ted Broad.

The first Yamaha racer stocked and sold by the Padgett Brothers was the TD1A, some of which Peter and Don used successfully themselves

Soon Padgett Yamaha became a buzz word in the race paddocks. This use of a dealers name on a machine broke new ground, certainly as regards Japanese bikes. In fact until this time advertising was not allowed on racing machines. Peter and Don argued successfully that it was their expertise which was making the machines successful, so why not allow them to prefix the Japanese marque with their company name? Eventually, even the 'ametuer' Manx Grand Prix gave in.

But before this was a now famous incident which centred on the Manx Grand Prix where the word Padgett had to be removed from their machines. They responded by replacing the Padgett's decals with a question mark on the side of the fairing!

Padgett's also began sponsoring other riders on Yamaha machinery, particularly after the introduction of the TD2/TR2 series at the begining of 1969.

In the early 1970s Padgett's were stocking machines from all four Japanese producers. The introduction to Kawasaki came when they began buying Kawasaki racers from Nottingham-based importers Agrati Sales.

Using up and coming privateer Mick Grant as their rider in the 1972 Senior TT with an HIR air-cooled triple, Mick finished third behind the two MV's of Agostini and Pagani. The factory was suprised by this success - and the reliability of the bike. Peter Padgett commented, 'We lowered the compression ratio and got them more reliable. They simply couldn't believe that our machines would do six laps of the TT course.'

Don's affection for the Isle of Man saw him eventually settle there - and establish the Douglas branch of the family business. The next generation of the Padgett family saw Clive begin on the British short circuits, before going on to the GP trail. He was soon showing his worth and recorded several excellent performances on his 250 and 350TZ Yamahas scoring points in the World Championship series. Sdaly this talented rider's career was brought to a premature end with an accident at St Joris in Belgium, whilst competing at an international event on closed roads. The subsequent arm

*Steve Hislop with the Padgett's Honda RS250, Lightweight TT circa 1992. The photograph is inscribed 'To Clive Thanks for all the support' Steve Hislop.*

injury meant that he was unable to resume his world championship career.

However it is worth noting that he became British Champion at only 18 and the youngest ever King of Brands at 19 years of age, taking the title from no less than Barry Sheene.

Then Clive switched his attention to helping younger brother Gary who had watched and learned avidly from the exploits of his older brother. Sadly Gary's career was to be short. And after winning TT races and exciting everyone who saw him ride, Gary was to die in a road accident near his home in 1987.

On the business front, the Padgett's had expanded greatly during the 1970s and 1980s. An endless list of names had raced for the company, including the likes of Terry Grotefeld, John Cooper, Stuart Graham, Phil Read, Jon Ekerold, Peter McKindley, Dennis Ireland, Phil Mellor and Mark Phillips - plus of course Mick Grant. There was also success on three wheels with the likes of Dennis and Julia Bingham and Dave Molyneux.

Padgett's also became racing distributors for Honda and Suzuki as well as Yamaha. Suzuki appointed Padgett's the sole supplier of RG500 Mark 10, 11 and 12 engines after the company ceased producing complete bikes. These were fitted into Harris and Spondon chassis to offer customers complete machines.

Into the 1990s Padgett's became major suppliers of Honda RS and Yamaha TZ racing machinery and spares. They were also heavily involved during the early 1990s with the Suzuki RGV250 for SuperSports events, including race kit components.

From the mid 1990s the Padgett Grand Prix Racing team was formed and headed by Clive Padgett. This saw rider Jay Vincent racing in GPs aboard Hondas with considerable success, quite often being the leading British rider in his class.

Today, almost half a century after Peter Padgett made his first steps in the motorcycle business world, Padgett's can look back with great pride. Some of their remarkable acheivements include:

British Champions 27 times.

TT and Grand Prix winners.

European Champions.

Longest established Yamaha franchise in UK.

First Honda HRC Service Shop outside Japan.

# Kawasaki - the classic years

# 4

*Gary Nixon, Daytona 1976 on his works KR750. He finished second in the 200 miler, an impressive result considering earlier setbacks for the American Kawasaki team at the same venue.*

Shozo Kawasaki founded a shipyard in 1878 at Tsukiji, Tokyo, to construct ocean-going ships and was thus a true pioneer; someone who contributed greatly to Japan's rapid growth towards transferring itself from a feudal nation little known to the West, into an industrial giant.

Then only three years later, due to the huge success of his initial venture, the Kawasaki Hyogo Shipyard was formed in 1881, at Higashide-cho, Hyogo, and five years later the two yards were combined. A decade later, 1896, Kawasaki Dockyard was incorporated as a company, with Kojiro Matsukata as its first president and its base being Kobe. So in reality Kawasaki's international reputation was founded on sea-going successes.

Expansion continued apace, with the first major diversification coming in 1906, with the establishment of bridge girders. The following year, production of marine steam turbines began at the dockyard. During the First World War (which Japan fought on the side of the allies - Great Britain, France the USA and Italy) more muscle was put on with a major new steel manufacturing facility. Then in 1918 an aviation division was established at the Hyogo works, a decade and a half after the Wright Brother's historic first flight, not only to build airframes, but engines too. At first Kawasaki's aircraft were largely licence-built versions of Western designs, notably from France and Britain. However, with the arrival of the German designer Dipl. Ing. Richard Vogt, Kawasaki began turning out innovative designs of its own.

*One of the very first A1-R racing machines built - and of the type used at the Japanese GP Junior 250cc class at Fisco in late 1966. Note unpainted seat back, square section oil tank and paint job compared with later versions.*

*One of the very first customer A1-Rs built. Note different paint job on fuel tank compared to factory prototypes.*

During the inter-war period, each division of Kawasaki's growing industrial empire became prominent within its own sphere and played a major role in Japan's growing international influence. Dates of notable importance include; 1919 - the marine freight division split off to form Kawasaki Kisen Kaisha Ltd (K-Line); 1928 - the Hyogo Works split off to become Kawasaki Rolling Stock Manufacturing Co Ltd; 1937 - the aviation division split off to form Kawasaki Aircraft Co Ltd.

Although Dipl. Ing. Vogt returned to Germany during the mid-1930s (to join Blohm and Voss), the man he left behind was the talented Tokeo Doi. It was this talented young Japanese engineer who went on to create many of his country's best aircraft during the succeeding years; including the Ki10 (Japan's last Army fighter biplane), the Ki32 light bomber, the Ki45 heavy fighter, the Ki48 medium bomber and Kawasaki's most famous product of the Second World War, the Ki61 Hein (Swallow).

*During late spring of 1966 Kawasaki launched its new 247cc A1 Samuria. Producing 31bhp@8,000rpm, it featured disc valves and a unit construction five-speed gearbox. In full road trim it could reach 100mph, making it ideal for fast road or clubmans-type racing events.*

# Meguro

As outlined in the companion volume Mick Walker's Japanese Grand Prix Racing Motorcycles (Redline Books), Nazaro Shimazu designed and built the first motorcycle engine ever made in Japan. This was fitted into an imported Triumph frame and the year was 1908. From these humble beginnings grew what was ultimately to become the largest motorcycle industry in the world.

But foreign machines from Great Britain, Europe and notably the USA subsequently flooding into Japan almost killed off the fledgling domestic industry. In 1922 the government introduced the Military Subsidy Law which gave them the powers to assist 'makers and owners of machines suitable for military use as long as they were manufactured in Japan'. In effect this was a way of getting around complaints of restrictive trade practices. It also had the effect of introducing several major firms to the motorcycle.

One of the first of these was the Murato Iron Works who produced a blatant copy of the existing Harley Davidson v-twin, at the time one of the most popular of the imported machines - and also as it happened - comprising the entire fleet of the Japanese Imperial Army's motorcycle inventory. Two complete examples of the motorcycle were despatched to government officials - but both were returned in due course 'without comment'. The youthful founders of the company, Hobuji Murato and Takaji Suzuki (no relation to the founder of the later famous marque - Suzuki being as common a name as Smith in the UK), then had to consider what was wrong with their proposal.

Murato and Suzuki came up with a fresh approach, rather than try and build a complete motorcycle they would concentrate on one aspect of it, and master this before venturing further. They chose (like Albion, Burman and Sturmey Archer in Britain) transmissions as their specialist field. Thus, in 1928, they founded Meguro Seisakusho 'to design and manufacture gearboxes for the motorcycle trade'

This time their business idea proved a winner, even though in the Western world an economic recession was about to rear its ugly head. But in Japan this had the effect of spurring the government on to even greater import restrictions (which benefited domestic industry) and, at the same time a military expansion policy was being introduced which dictated the need for motorised transport. So with these measures the 1930s became a decade where tariffs and growth went hand-in-hand within the Japanese economy.

And at the start of the decade Meguro benefited from a deal with the American Harley Davidson concern, who needed cash (they were badly effected by the New York Wall Street crash of October 1929). The result was a batch of drawings and tooling for production by the Rikuo marque - who then purchased gearboxes for their machines from Meguro. Rikuo and Maguro both learned from the deal. The most important part was not the motorcycle itself - which in any case was obsolete, but the vital heat treatment data for the steel material specifications - and a visit from senior HD technical officials. This resulted in the Japanese learning techniques on modern mass production, including the various requirements and technology to build motorcycles in quantity and still retain high standards. And it was this input from the Americans which really helped the Japanese build good quality machines efficiently.

*An A1-R on display at the London Earls Court Show, held between 16th and the 23rd September 1967. British imports of Kawasaki racing machines at that time were handled by Northamptonshire dealer and race entrant Peter Chapman.*

At Meguro the desire to build their own motorcycle had never gone away, so in 1935 Murato and Suzuki decided to have another stab at doing everything themselves. The result was to be the Z97, a twin port ohv single, based on the Velocette MSS. But production quantities at that time were small compared to Western countries of the same era.

Japan entered the Second World War with the infamous attack on Pearl Harbour in December 1941. It was not until 1948 that Meguro were able to restart production of motorcycles again. The Z97 five hundred was now joined by 350 and 250 ohv singles and a 125 commuter machine. Then in the mid 1950s came more modern designs and Meguro's entry into road racing. On the series production front this period saw the Z500 - with a single port ohv single engine mounted in a modern spring frame and equipped with telescopic front forks. At around the same time Meguro wheeled out its first twin, named the Senior. This was clearly based on the typical British pre-unit ohv vertical twin; many of these bikes went to the Japanese Government for police duties. Together with an updated lightweight line, Meguro were for several years number two in the Japanese sales league, only outsold by Honda (which at this time only built lightweights up to 250cc).

This level of sales success enabled Meguro to take part officially in the famous Asama races, which were staged during the 1950s. During their best year, 1957, the winning Meguro machines featured single cylinder overhead camshaft engines of 499cc. This was almost, but not quite, a Japanese Manx Norton, except the cammy Meguro put out around 30bhp compared with the Norton's 50bhp.

At this time the whole Japanese motorcycle industry, including, of course, Meguro, benefited greatly from even more stringent tariff controls on foreign goods - and foreign currency control. What this meant was from 1955 onward the Japanese motorcycle buyer had no option but to buy a home-made product. However, conversely, domestic bike producers didn't have to pay import duty if they imported a foreign machine which they wished to study. So companies such as Meguro and Honda did just that. This was to result in the early Honda racers being modelled on NSU, whilst in 1959 Meguro launched the 500cc K1 twin with the engine and gearbox modelled on the British BSA A7/A10 series. The cycle parts were entirely of Japanese design and benefited from components such as full-width aluminium brake hubs, and a deluxe specification, which even included 12volt electrics and flashing indicators.

However, in case the reader has formed the opinion that Meguro simply copied other manufacturers' engines this is not quite true. They built, in conjunction with Kawasaki many engines entirely of Japanese creation. There were both 2 and 4 stroke. A particularly neat example was the 164cc ohv Ranger. Of full unit construction, it could rival any Western design of the period and , after the Kawasaki takeover, to be built, as the SG250, versions of it continued until as late as 1969.

As laid out in the main section, from the late 1950s Meguro and Kawasaki began to work more closely and in 1960 Meguro became affiliated to Kawasaki Aircraft (there was no separate 'motors' division then). This link was reinforced in 1961 when there was a further increase in corporate co-operation, with the two partners working as a team. In 1962 Meguro changed its name to Kawasaki Meguro and this operation was merged with the Kawasaki parent company in 1963. The rest is history.

*Kawasaki's first over-the-counter production racing motorcycle was the 90SS (89cc). Here M. Mithuhashi leads American Gary Nixon (76 Yamaha) during the Junior race at the 1966 Japanese Grand Prix.*

*Meguro was one of the pioneers of the Japanese motorcylce industry. Having been set up in the 1920s it became a transmission specialist, before offering a Velocette MSS copy in 1937. Their K1 five-hundred twin modelled on the BSA A series of 1959 is shown here. Meguro merged with Kawasaki in the early 1960s.*

With its liquid-cooled engine (a licence-built German Daimler Benz DB601), long tapered nose and wings of high aspect ratio, the Ki61 was unique amongst Japanese fighters of the period. Unlike designs such as the Zero, it was the first Nipponese aircraft to incorporate armour protection and self-sealing tanks which had been shown to be indispensable following early war reports from Europe.

When the war finally ended in August 1945, Kawasaki, unlike many rival companies, found its engineering skills in such demand that only one of its many facilities was standing idle. But, this too, soon found an outlet for its mechanical expertise - by manufacturing engine and gearbox assemblies for the rapidly expanding domestic motorcycle industry. Although the word Kawasaki didn't at that time appear on any motorcycle's fuel tank, it was certainly deeply involved in Japan's growth as a provider of powered two-wheelers during the late 1940s and the entire decade of the 1950s. This was a boom time for both large and small manufacturers alike. But towards the end of the 1950s the industry began to rationalise into bigger operations, with only the fittest ultimately surviving.

One of these was Meguro a mature company which had been established back in 1924; its original purpose being to produce components for the automobile and motorcycle industries. By the beginning of the 1930s it had begun specialising in transmissions. Meguro made the transition to the ranks of a motorcycle producer during 1937, when it began building a five-hundred ohv single. Together with Asahi, Cabton and Rikuo, Meguro supplied motorcycles to the Japanese armed forces throughout the years of war.

After the end of the conflict Meguro constructed a number of models with a distinct British flavour. But with its 651cc Senior of the late 1950s the engine (built by Kawasaki) was a dead ringer for BSA's A10 Golden Flash.

*The American rider Frank Scurria, seen here (left) in hat, pictured at Brands Hatch during the summer of 1967. He rode both the A1-R and the larger displacement 350cc A7-R.*

With the launch in September 1968 of the new H1 Mach III triple roadster, and subsequent H1-R racer in December 1969, Kawasaki built new A1-RA (250) and A7-RA (350) machines using cycle parts from the triple. An A7-RA is shown, Note the many changes to the original A7-R, such as brakes, frame, front forks and bodywork.

In 1959 Kawasaki gave the first serious signs that it was considering an entry into the motorcycle field in a more serious way, by opening a new research and development centre. Then came an entirely new assembly plant in Akashi, which was completed in 1960 - and the same year Meguro became officially affiliated to Kawasaki Aircraft. This link was strengthened further the following year, when in early 1961 Kawasaki and Meguro effectively merged, with a single corporate headquarters in Tokyo. Then in mid-1961, Kawasaki Auto Sales was incorporated, with its first model to carry a Kawasaki badge, the 125cc B8 single cylinder 2-stroke commuter bike.

The same year, Meguro changed its name to Kawasaki Meguro and the company merged with Kawasaki in 1963. Thus the transformation of the corporate giant into a motorcycle manufacturer was complete.

As for racing, Kawasaki was able to link up with Meguro's success (the latter having tasted victory in the 500cc class of the 1957 Asama races). But unlike the 1950s effort which had seen the use of a British styled overhead camshaft single cylinder-engined bike, the newly created Kawasaki motorcycle marque looked to the 2-stroke and the smaller classes on which to base its fledgling efforts.

In fact, Kawasaki's first forays into motorcycle sport were directed to motocross, rather than road racing. And this policy immediately bore fruit, with the newly created company winning the 1963 Japanese 125cc National Motocross Championship, with its famous 'Red Tank' model. This resulted in a production version, the B8M which ran from October 1963 until the end of 1964. The 125cc engine used piston port induction and a 4-speed gearbox in unit with the engine, which itself was based around the existing B8 roadster (built from 1962 through to 1966).

Rear view of the same machine. The frame was clearly based on the H1-R triple. The rear suspension chamber pipes are swept upwards. Some A7-RAs had straight tail pipes, as did the 250 A1-RA. The 'A' version of the disc valve twins were only offered for a short period as they couldn't match the Yamaha RD/TR series.

Side mounted 26mm carburettor of A1-R with remote float chamber. Kickstart shaft and inclination of cylinders evident in this offside view of the engine.

*In this factory studio shot of an A1-R, the round oil tank can be seen clearly. Note long thin tail pipes for the expansion chambers and exposed chrome springs on the front and rear suspension.*

In their successful attempt to create a competitive motocrosser, the power output had been raised to around 12bhp, whilst the running gear had been suitably upgraded for its new role, including hi-level exhaust, strengthened frame and telescopic front forks, a sprung front mudguard, braced handlebars and lightweight components such as mudguards. Weight, compared to the roadster, had been reduced by some 25 per cent.

It is also worth saying that at that time Kawasaki saw Japan and the USA as its two main markets and a series of off-road bikes were to be developed during the remainder of the 1960s with the American market very much in mind. These were to be mainly trail bikes, but motocross models were also built, not just in 125cc engine size, but also 85, 90, 120, 175 and 250cc displacements.

Kawasaki approached road racing from two directions. The first, as outlined in the companion voume on Grand Prix machines, at the cutting edge of technology was all its specialist works machinery (which created both twins and fours in the 125cc category) and over-the-counter production racers. Of course, it's these particular bikes that we are primarily interested in here.

At that time 'Junior' class racing for production-based bikes was very popular in Japan. And as the 90cc class was buoyant this was seen by many as an ideal way of setting out on a racing career, Kawasaki being a leading supporter. Effectively there were two such basic engines from Kawasaki, the 85cc J series and the 90cc G series - all using disc valve induction and 4-speeds. In fact the J was the first Kawasaki production model to feature a rotary disc valve. On both the J and the G the cylinder was inclined slightly forward. The J1, when it arrived in November 1964, represented several technical advances for Kawasaki - including the aforementioned disc valve - and oil pump lubrication. The first of the G series began production in July 1966 and the exact capacity was 89.9cc (47 x 51.8mm). In standard form the engine put out 10.5bhp at 8000rpm and with the factory race kit, this went up another 2bhp - or 4bhp when the 'racing only' expansion chamber exhaust was fitted.

Just how seriously the company viewed the 90cc Junior class is best illustrated by the fact that it scored its first major success in this class, when a works-supported 90SS, ridden by M Mithuhashi narrowly beat the American star Gary Nixon riding a Yamaha in the Support race at Fisco, the scene of the 1966 Japanese Grand Prix.

Perhaps more importantly, Mithuhashi, together with other members of the works Kawasaki team also contested the 250cc Junior race at the same meeting but with brand new disc valve twins.

During the late spring of 1966 Kawasaki had launched its new 250A1. This was to become known as the Samurai and almost overnight it proved big in the USA. The A1 was for its day, an advanced design, featuring disc inlet valves, with side mounted carburettors - although this had the disadvantage of additional width and complexity. However, Kawasaki engineers partly solved this by mounting the generator behind the cylinders rather than on the crankshaft end. Thus both sides of the power unit looked very much the same - as each carburettor was hidden beneath an aluminium casing and controlled by a pair of cables.

With slightly long-stroke dimensions of 53 x 56mm, the engine displaced 247cc - and like other Japanese twin cylinder designs (except Tohatsu) featured horizontally split crankcases. The crankshaft had its pins at 180 degrees and was supported by four ball race main bearings with an oil seal between the two centre ones and a single one at the crank end. The crankshaft assembly was pressed and featured full circle flywheels with the rims of the outer section of the wheels chamfered to improve gas flow through the disc valve controlled inlet tract into the crankcase and up under the piston crown.

The pair of outer crank flywheels were integral with their mainshafts, whilst the offside inner wheel was similar and its shaft extended to the rearside inner wheel to which it was keyed. The correct balance factor was achieved by a series of metal plugs pressed into holes in the flywheel sides. The crank assembly was held in place by the main bearings, one of which was located by a circlip to a groove in one of the bearing housings, these items being given to all the mains and located to the crankcase.

*Japanese GP 250cc Junior race, November 1966. 22 and 26 are Kawasaki riders Murakami and Mithuhashi respectively. The result was a dead heat between another Kawasaki ridden by Kanaya (leading here with number obscured) and the American Gary Nixon (76 Yamaha).*

*Art Baumann (71) was Kawasaki's leading rider in the States during the late 1960s. He is seen here at Daytona in March 1969 on one of the twins. Baumann's machine sports Italian Ceriani front forks.*

The silicon aluminium pistons featured a pair of rings each. Aluminium was also used for the heads and barrels. Which featured reborable cast-iron liners. The pistons were supported by needle races at both small and big ends. A pump was employed to supply lubricating oil to the engine and its output varied according to the throttle opening as well as engine revolutions. The pump was located on the nearside disc valve cover and driven from the crankshaft by a pair of gears. The generator specified to the initial batch of A1 street bikes was a permanent magnet alternator and the complete assembly was mounted on top of the crankcase, just aft of the cylinder barrels, under a massive cover. On the roadster this cover also carried the air filtration system, complete with its trunking and filter element. Drive to the generator was via the geared primary drive, with a pinion on the end of the armature shaft meshing with the clutch drum. It is worth pointing out that the three gear wheels were all marked for correct mesh alignment as the ignition cam and points were housed in the end of the generator remote from the drive. Coil ignition was employed and the generator ran at half engine speed so the ignition cam had twin lobes to open each set of points the required number of times. To assist correct timing one pair could be moved on the points backplate, which itself could be turned to adjust the other.

The gearbox was an all-indirect 5-speed cross-over assembly, with the clutch on the offside end of the front shaft and the final drive (gearbox) sprocket on the nearside end of the rear one. A trio of selector forks moved the necessary gears to provide the five ratios and each shaft was supported by a ball race and a needle roller bearing.

*Lincolnshire ace Derek Chatterton, winning at his local Cadwell circuit, on his A-1R disc valve twin.*

*Works supported rider Dave Simmonds with his 250 A1-R at Brands Hatch in August 1967.*

A full cradle frame with duplex front downtubes which extended backwards under the power unit promised good handling. Suspension wise there was a set of 32mm diameter hydraulically damped telescopic front forks up front, whilst at the rear things were taken care of by a conventional twin shock swinging arm layout.

Kawasaki claimed 31bhp at 8000rpm for its production A1 roadster. This figure was impressive and certainly would have been enough to win anything except international Grand Prix-type events up to only a few years previously. And all this from a comprehensively equipped street bike with full silencing! 100mph was possible in the right conditions, but the stock A1's biggest draw was its excellent acceleration, which put many bikes over double its size to shame. Then in December 1965 came the launch of a pukka racing version, the A1-R (Racing). Based on the roadster, this featured extensive changes to both the engine and the running gear.

Not only were there bigger 26mm racing Mikuni carburettors (the standard bike had 22mm instruments) with remote float chambers and a full expansion chamber exhaust system, but there were internal modifications too. The port timing was changed whilst the compression was upped to 8:1 (7:1 on the A1). The actual ratio was taken from the point of exhaust port closure. The cylinders and heads were also given attention to improve output.

The remote floats were mounted forward of the carburettors. In this position they tended to enrich the mixture when accelerating and on climbs, whilst weakening it for the reverse, in other words when the rider was braking or going down a hill. This might have assisted performance and reduced plug fouling, as Kawasaki claimed, unfortunately the down side was the risk of seizure when shutting off on a downhill section (for example coming down the Mountain in the Isle of Man). This combined with inferior oils then available and less sophisticated ignition systems, meant that an A1-R rider always had to ride with his hand hovering over the clutch lever - ready to grab the clutch at the first hint of the engine tightening up. The throttle-controlled oil pump lube system was retained, with a small oil tank centrally mounted below the seat and tank, the petroil mixture being 15:1 ratio. Ignition was by magneto with external coils. The nearside engine outer casing was dispensed with completely, as was the front section on the offside - but the rear portion had to remain as it carried the clutch release mechanism.

*Simmonds again, this time on his way to an excellent 4th in the 1967 Isle of Man (250cc) TT on his A1-R. It should be noted that this is a standard model, rather than the Jim Lee Special he rode earlier that year.*

*Dave Simmonds (right) with his brother Mike. They are pictured relaxing in the Florida Everglades, circa 1969.*

The primary drive gears were altered from the roadster's helical-cut type (for quietness of operation), to the straight-cut variety in the quest for increased performance. The overall gearing was raised and the gearbox given a close ratio cluster, this being needed as the power band was now considerably decreased. Strangely, for a racing machine, the roadster kick start shaft was retained instead of the more usual blanking off procedure. This meant the A1-R's engine could be started with the lever if one was fitted. But usually none was - racers preferring to bump start their bikes - which they had to in actual races anyway during the 1960s.

These changes resulted in the power being increased to 40bhp at 9500rpm and a maximum speed of 125mph. But the A1R had three problems, the first was the arrival, for the 1997 season, of Yamaha's much improved TDIC, the second was the Kawasaki's marginal reliability and the third was that at that time in the West, the 'Big K' brand name didn't sound as familiar as Honda, Suzuki or Yamaha. On the chassis front the same basic layout as the A1 street bike was retained, together with the suspension system - although the front forks had their rubber gaiters removed, and the rear shock their spring covers. In both cases the springs themselves were now chrome-plated.

*New Zealander Ginger Molloy during the 1970 Ulster Grand Prix at Dunrod on his H1-R. He finished the race runner up behind MVs Giacomo Agostini, the same pairing finished 1-2 in that years 500cc World Championship series.*

Both brake assemblies were replaced from the roadsters originally highly polished 180 x 30mm (2LS front) aluminium drums, to purpose-built racing units. At the front was an impressive looking 200mm four leading shoe stopper, with air scoops both front and rear cast into the brake plates on either side. At the rear was a 180mm SLS - which although being the same size as the roadster unit was not the same, featuring an additional 6mm of width (36mm). Both hubs were laced onto 18 inch welled aluminium rims; tyre sections being 3.00 front, 3.25 rear, with a few late A1-Rs having wider 3.50 rear section rubber.

Ron Chandler joined the H1-R set in 1971. He is seen here with his mount, an ex Cliff Carr machine, but modified with British suspension front and rear and twin Pagehiln disc brakes. Aluminium tank is large capacity, needed for longer continental races.

As delivered the A1-R's specifications included a braced front mudguard, dolphin fairing, tachometer, racing tyres, toolkit and spares including sprockets and jets. The fuel tank was aluminium, the auxiliary oil tank a plastic elongated, circular affair. Compared to the production roadster A1's dry weight of 319lb, the stripped-down racing-only A1R came in at 240lb.

In October 1966 a number of A1-Rs were wheeled out for the Junior (250cc) support race at the Japanese Grand Prix these putting on a good show against the mainly Yamaha field.

*Australia rider Brian Flak (of Norton Kneeler fame) pictured with his H1-R in the early 1970s, when he was resident in England.*

Then in December 1966 Kawasaki machines (including the A1-R, but not the 90cc racer) reached Europe going on sale via an Amsterdam-based importer. By late January 1967 *Motor Cycling* was able to report, 'A batch of their 250cc production road racers are at London Docks.' The first A1-R reached Australia at around the same time and was put on show at the Australia Day race meeting at Ballarat, 29th January. It had been flown in a few days earlier, but was not ready to race at the meeting. It made its debut with top Aussie star Dick Reid, winner of no less than three races at Ballarat and promptly showed its potential by winning first time out, in the Victorian TT at the Calder Raceway. Reid took the lead at the halfway stage and finished three seconds ahead of Ron Angel and Alan Osbourne (Yamahas). On the same bike Reid went on to finish runner-up in the 350cc event, narrowly beaten by Ron Toombs (AJS).

*Previously unpublished photograph of an H1-R during the Isle of Man Senior TT in the early 1970s.*

Back in Britain, Wallingford, Berkshire dealer Jim Pink said he would be 'entering' a standard A1 Samurai in the Production TT - if a list of optional extras could be notified to the ACU before their March deadline.

As for the batch of A1-Rs which arrived in the UK, this contained six bikes, with another twelve being reported 'in transit'. One machine had already been earmarked for the Australian, Eric Hinton, at that time resident in Britain and living in Kent. In the USA Kawasaki fielded a works-supported team of five A1-Rs at Daytona in early March. After the race in Florida they were to be shipped back to Japan, where two were subsequently converted for the 350cc class. This was the first indication that Kawasaki was considering building a larger-engined

*Yorkshireman Mick Grant sprang to the publics attention with some excellent rides at the begining of the 1970s. One of the best was when he gained a rostrum position on a Padgett H1-R, by finishing a magnificent 3rd in the 1972 Senior TT, with only the MVs of Agostini and Pagani in front.*

version of the A1-R. The two riders promised these development machines were British, Alan Baker and American Frank Scurria (who raced in Britain during 1966). And 'over 200 A1-Rs had already been sold, *'Cycle World'* were able to report by mid March.

In January 1967 Englishman, Dave Simmonds had been signed to race the 125cc liquid-cooled disc-valve-twin cylinder works Kawasaki. Having already planned to replace his private specially-framed Honda CR72 dohc twin with a Yamaha-powered special, Dave constructed a Jim Lee-framed machine using a specially prepared A1 Samurai engine featuring the larger carburettors, straight-cut primary gears and other components from the A1 production racer. With the engine unit came an A1-R rear hub. The front hub chosen was a 180mm Italian Fontana assembly, whilst the forks were Honda, with a Tohatsu steering damper. Simmonds gave the bike an impressive debut, finishing runner up in the 250cc race at Brands Hatch on Good Friday. Much of the testing of the A1-R production racer had been carried out by former Honda works star Naomi Tanaguchi (who had raced the first Honda machinery in Europe during the early sixties). However, even with all this testing, the new Kawasaki twin was to be blighted by producing power over a very narrow range - the gear ratios not being close enough. As Dave Simmonds commented in April 1967, 'The engine has terrific power, but the ratios are so wide that at Brands and Oulton I was using only three of the five speeds.in any case, first is far too low. With a seven or eight-speed gearbox, it would be a fantastic machine. It definitely gives the 40bhp they claim, but at the moment you can only use it for ten per cent of the time.'

Chris Vincent, who rode a standard A1-R (for sponsor Peter Chapman), found that he was unable to get the gearing low enough even for Oulton Park. 'The sprockets they (Kawasaki) sent are all for very fast circuits. At Oulton, I wasn't getting top gear.'

By the beginning of May Dave Simmonds had received a new, improved A1-R engine, which 'Has a much improved spread of power over my original motor.' He finished the 77.3 mile Spanish 250cc Grand Prix in 7th position. Then at the next round of the world series in Germany, the bike was timed at 128mph; however ultra-high fuel consumption (20 miles-per-gallon) meant that even with a new 4-gallon tank he was going to have to pit for fuel - but he didn't have to - as a piston broke at the halfway stage of the 95-mile long race.

*Cliff Carr aboard his lime green and white H1-R. The bike has Girling rear shocks and Joe Dunphy set-up brakes.*

In the Far East, RAF Serviceman Terry Pallister finished 3rd in the Singapore Grand Prix on a new factory-supported (via the local distributor) A1-R. Dave Simmonds showed how much better his latest bike was by finishing an excellent 3rd at the international Brands Hatch meeting at the end of May. Chris Vincent on the Peter Chapman supported machine was 4th; the race being won by Honda six-mounted Mike Hailwood.

The 250cc disc valve Kawasaki had an excellent Isle of Man TT debut. First Dave Simmonds brought a standard A1 roadster home 6th in its class in the Production race, then he went even better in the Lightweight (250cc) event finishing 4th at an average speed of 92.53mph. Another A1-R was 5th (Bill Smith averaging 89.53mph). However, for much of the race John Cooper had been fourth on yet another A1-R, only to push home 25th after seizing on the final circuit. Cooper also had to make two pit stops during the 6-lap, 226.38 mile long race. Cooper's machine had been lent to him by RAF Sergeant Mick Norman (based in Singapore). Over the measured 1176 yards near the Highlander, Simmonds' and Cooper's machines were identical at 124mph, whilst Bill Smith's clocked 120.4mph.

On Stand 121 of the Earls Court Show in September 1967 the newly appointed British importers C Itoh & Co Ltd of Camomile Street, London EC2, had no less than nine models on display, including the A1-R racer and the brand new 338cc (62 x 56mm) A7 Avenger, heralding the arrival of a 350cc class machine, at least on the roadster front. But the tie-up with

*Another previously unpublished photograph, of John Judge on the RGM (Luton) H1 Mach III production racer. Note non-standard twin disc front brake. Brands Hatch, mid 1970s.*

*A French aluminium monoque-framed Kawasaki triple, using disc brakes front and rear, together with lightweight magnesium wheels, mid 1970s.*

Peter Chapman remained, as it was, the Guilsborough, Northamptonshire dealer who was responsible for marketing the competition bikes - which, of course, included the racing machines. And at £618 the A1-R was the most expensive 250cc racing motorcycle sold in Great Britain at that time. By way of comparison the Bultaco TSS was £525, the Greeves Silverstone £385 and a Vic Camp Ducati £329.

In October Peter Chapman visited Japan and came back full of enthusiasm. He also revealed that he was expecting a new 350 class machine - not a converted roadster but a pukka race bike - a bigger A1-R in fact. Although most of the bigger Japanese factories were cutting back on production, Kawasaki was booming. Chapman reported, 'A new factory is being built which should eventually double the present output of 100,000 units a year.'

When the British short circuit racing season kicked off at the beginning of March 1968, Rex Butcher showed the new 350cc class Kawasaki would be competitive by finishing runner up to John Cooper (Yamaha) in the 350cc Final at the Leicestershire circuit. The following weekend at the Redex Grand National at Brands Hatch, Derek Chatterton finished 3rd in the 350cc race on a '275' Kawasaki - probably an over bored A1-R, whilst a week on at Snetterton, Chatterton went one better by finishing 2nd, to race winner Dan Shorey (Norton); Rex Butcher on another Kawasaki was 3rd.

*Cliff Carr spent a lot of his time racing in the USA, where he made his first Kawasaki contacts. He subsequently brought bikes back to the UK, including this near stock H1-R.*

Then came the larger Kawasaki's first major success, when at Oulton Park, Cheshire, Dave Simmonds took the new machine to victory in the 350cc race; Rex Butcher was 4th on his Kawasaki. Simmonds and Butcher won their respective heats, with Butcher also setting the fastest lap at 87.65mph. At the 'King of Brands' meeting in mid-April, Martin Carney won the 350cc event, Dave Simmonds was 3rd and Derek Chatterton 6th.

Kawasaki made a considerable impact at the international Singapore Grand Prix, run on the tricky 3-mile Upper Thompson road circuit. In the 350cc race the winner was Araoka and local rider Bulldog Kuan, 2nd. Honda's hopes of success were trashed when a 297cc six (publicised as Mike Hailwood's 1967 World Championship winning machine) failed to finish.

Martin Carney was timed at 132.5mph during the Junior TT - riding a prototype built by former racer Terry Shepherd but after being well placed, the engine seized.

*Padgett's of Batley, West Yorkshire have been a leading race entrant of Japanese 2-strokes for over 30 years, as this 1972 H1-R TT shot proves.*

Actually, the story behind the '350' Kawasaki in racing is complex. For starters Kawasaki had already launched the 338cc (62 x 56mm) A7 (known as the Avenger in some markets) in Spring 1967. At first sight the A7 was simply an A1 with the bigger cylinder bores. This was emphasised by Kawasaki's engineering team leaving the compression ratio unaltered (at 7:1), whilst the port timings were only altered slightly. Aside from the extra displacement, the power increase came mainly from larger 28mm carburettors; this pushing output (in full road going trim) to 42bhp at 8000rpm. To cater for

*The H1-B which Motorcycle Mechanic's prepared for production racing with considerable success. The machine has several non-standard features including fairing, tank and seat, alloy wheel trims and an extra disc on the front. Motorcycle Mechanic's editor and old friend of the author Charles Deane is second from the right.*

this, the lubrication for the bottom end of the engine was modified to supply oil to the big-ends and the revised system was given the grand sounding 'Injectolube' title. In the Injectolube system the crankshaft-driven oil pump was retained along with the throttle control but the output was increased by 20 per cent to cope with the additional loading and power. As on the A1, the lubricant was pumped into the inlet tract but in addition it was fed to the outer side of the outside main bearing. The oil flowed through this and was collected by a disc screwed to the crank flywheel and hence flared to lubricate other important areas. This also assisted lubrication of the big-end, there being a hole drilled partway through the crankpin to a cross hole which fed the big-end needle rollers.

The clutch was beefed up with an additional set of plates, and modified springs. To allow the additional plates they were thinner than on the smaller engine. The overall gearing was raised by reducing the size of the rear wheel sprocket by a single tooth.

But strangely none of the racers used, at least in Britain, were of 338cc engine size. Instead Chatterton's machine was simply an A1-R with larger cylinder bores to give 275cc. The 'works' model campaigned by Dave Simmonds was a prototype of the production A7-R which Kawasaki was eventually to sell to private customers. Unlike the A7 Avenger roadster, the A7-R was of 349cc, achieved by increasing the bore size to 63mm, instead of the 62mm found on the roadster. The compression ratio was upped to 7.7:1, with far more radical port timing and larger 29mm carbs. Kawasaki claimed 53bhp at 9500rpm - and a maximum speed of 138mph. The A7-R used the same cycle parts as its smaller, older A1-R brother. But just to confuse things further, the machine used by Martin Carney to give Kawasaki its first British 350cc victory was an A1-R converted to 349cc by Terry Shepherd (former Norton and MV star). Built in conjunction with Peter Chapman, the TSR (Terry Shepherd Research) used entirely different bore and stroke dimensions to the factory - 60.9 x 59.5mm, a 12:1 compression

*An H1-B suitably stripped and modified for 'Proddie' racing; large aluminium tank, twin disc front stopper, fairing, alloy rims and Dunlop TT100 tyres. Note Austin Allegro in background and humble Morris 1000 race transporter. TT mid 1970s.*

*Launched in September 1968 the H1 Mach III formed the basis for the H1-R racer which arrived just over a year later. The 3-cylinders were set across the frame, there was piston port induction and a 5-speed gearbox built in unit with the engine-and fearsome acceleration.*

ratio, 16:1 petroil mixture and a 17 tooth gearbox and 36 tooth rear wheel sprocket pairing. On the TSR 350 the expansion chamber pipes were of a greater diameter than the Kawasaki factory-built version.

Externally the TSR 350 featured packing pieces between the cylinders and crankcases to accommodate the longer stroke and the absence of an oil pump (a simple petrol-oil mixture in place of the oil pump). As Shepherd said, 'Doubtless Kawasaki spent much time developing their automatic lubrication, but I have discarded it on my three-fifty in favour of a petroil mix - 16 to 1 for running in and less oil for racing.' Shepherd went on to reveal in Spring 1968, 'Existing ones (excluding the Simmonds factory model) are merely enlarged two-fifties. Mine has a new crank assembly with different bore and stroke, con-rods and big-end bearings, the barrels being bored out and sleeved to 60.9mm. I've also reshaped the exhaust system to give a wider power band. With the two-fifty class becoming increasingly competitive, it is worth while devoting more attention to the three-fifty category.' He had seen a business opportunity too, the conversion kit transforming an A1-R into a 350. The kit cost £110 (some 20 per cent of the cost for a new A1-R at that time) but it did give the owner a much better chance of success.

In Australia, Dick Reid swept all opposition aside to win the 350cc event on his newly delivered A7-R, another of the pre-production prototype machines similar to the one ridden by Dave Simmonds in Europe. First supplies to over-the-counter customers of the new A7-R began in the summer of 1968 and although produced in much smaller numbers than the A1-R it was nonetheless a competitive bike - until Yamaha launched its all-conquering TR2 for the 1969 model year. Even so the A7-R produced 53bhp at 9500rpm - more than a match for the existing British singles and as much as a good 500cc Manx Norton or Matchless G50.

Overhead view with fuel tank removed to show frame layout, carburettors and top end of the engine.

## H1-R 1970

| | |
|---|---|
| Engine | Air-cooled across-the-frame 3-cylinder two-stroke with piston port induction |
| Capacity | 498cc |
| Bore | 60mm |
| Stroke | 58.8mm |
| Comp ratio | N/A |
| Carburation | 3 x Mikuni 34mm |
| Ignition | Battery/coils |
| Gearbox | Five speeds |
| Clutch | Dry, multi-plate |
| Frame | Steel, duplex twin cradle construction |
| Suspension | Front oil damped telescopic fork |
| | Rear swinging arm, twin shock |
| Brakes | Front double-sided 280mm 2LS drum |
| | Rear single-sided 220mm 5LS drum |
| Tyres | 18 inch front and rear |
| Dry weight | N/A |
| Max power | 72bhp @ 9000rpm |
| Max speed | 140mph |

*Massive four leading shoe front drum, it measured no less than 280mm. It was operated by a pair of cables, with a junction box two thirds of the way up its length then to a single cable to the handlebar.*

*The original 1970 series of the H1-R racers. The crossover exhaust was used to cut down on width.*

*Many H1s were racerised. Typical is this Reads of Leytonstone (London) model, outside the company showrooms in 1970. Changes include tank, seat, handlbars and rearsets, but still not a real racer.*

By 1969 Kawasaki had become well established abroad, particularly in the USA. So it came as little surprise that the two American importers (American Kawasaki; Motors and Eastern American Motorcycle Corp.) combined to form Kawasaki Motors Corporation at Gardena. A couple of months later the new organisation relocated to Santa Ana, still in California. This was followed in April by a major regrouping of the parent companies, with Kawasaki Aircraft Industries, Kawasaki Dockyard and Kawasaki Rolling Stock coming together to form Kawasaki Heavy Industries; this name still used to the present day.

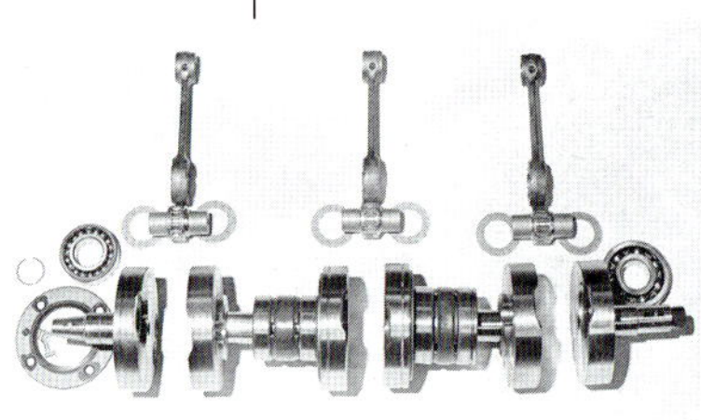

*H1 crankshaft details. This was a pressed together affair, so could use one-piece connecting rods. A total of six main bearings (all ball races) were employed.*

Another vital happening back in September 1968 was the launch of the H1 Mach III (known in Japan as the 500-SS). This was an across-the-frame triple displacing 499cc (60 x 58.8mm). Unlike the earlier Kawasaki disc valve models, the H1 featured piston-port induction. Even so its power-to-weight ratio ensured that it was one of the most talked about sportsters of its generation, with stunning acceleration and a high top speed. However, it suffered (as did many early larger capacity Japanese motorcycles) from a twitchy ride. But this didn't stop big sales and most importantly for this book a racing version which was to appear in time for the 1970 season.

During 1969 the new H1 Mach III established itself as a leading contender for honours in Production Sports machine races all around the globe. Typical of this was the prestigious French Le Mans 24 Hours Bol d' Or classic. This saw Mach IIIs leading for most of the time, only to finally lose

*H1 engine cutaway to show details such as pistons, small end, connecting rod and finning on head and barrel assemblies.*

The late Arthur Bullock astride the Agrati Sales of Nottingham (Kawasaki importers at the time) H1-B getting ready for the start of the 1973 Isle of Man Production TT. Rider is Alex George, later to become a TT winner for Triumph and Honda.

out to a Honda CB750 four. After the first nine hours, a pair of Mach IIIs were a lap ahead of the Honda. But at the finish, the Kawasaki triples were forced to settle for 2nd, 3rd and 4th. However, even this was a superb display of speed and reliability for machines giving away a full one-third in cubic capacity to the winning machines - and the Kawasaki's were air-cooled two-strokes to boot. In the same race, Kawasaki A1 Samurai finished 7th, 13th, 18th and 21st, in the process out distancing several 750s. All in all it had been a 24 hours for Kawasaki fans to remember. *Motor*, the leading Dutch motorcycle journal, carried a front page headline, with the story of how Herbert Spahn and co-rider Rob Norlander had carried off the international 6-hour endurance race at Zandvoort in October 1969. This was Spahn's fifth consecutive victory on his Mach III. Meanwhile in the Isle of Man Production TT, Tony Dunnell had posted the fastest lap in the 500cc class, before retiring at 90.84mph on yet another of Kawasaki's triples.

January 1970 brought the news that the 1969 125cc world champion (Kawasaki) Dave Simmonds would be receiving one of the new H1-R which had been launched at the end of the previous year.

The new H1-R engine was closely related to the H1 Mach III roadster unit. This meant that at its heart was a pressed-up crankshaft, which ran on no less than six main bearings. A quartet of oil seals were fitted, two at the shaft ends and another pair between the inner set of main bearings. The gudgeon pins were offside by 0.5mm towards the inlet side of the pistons (to reduce slap) and were each retained by two circlips. The spring intervals were evenly spaced at 120 degrees, thus providing engine output

*The H2-R 750 triple arrived at the beginning of 1973 - it was a bigger and faster version of the 500H1-R and developed over 100bhp.*

and torque in a very smooth fashion - at least compared to other three cylinder engines. Each of the three cylinder barrels and heads were separate castings, with 2-ring pistons. The bottom half of the H1-R engine was of typical Japanese two-stroke construction, with the main crankcase split horizontally through the centre of the crankshaft and the gear shafts. The two sections were cast in aluminium and held in alignment by two pins. A considerable number of studs joined them together and were screwed into the top section of the crankcase with nuts on the underside whilst the lower section of the crankcase was comprehensively ribbed to provide increased rigidity. The 5-speed gearbox and multi-plate clutch were in unit with the engine. However, on the pukka racing version not only was there a close ratio gear cluster, but the clutch was dry, rather than of wet.

*H2-R, with air-cooled 748cc (71 x 63mm) 3-cylinder engine, 5 speeds, wire wheels, 18 inch tyres, twin 296mm front discs and 239 x 48mm rear drum brakes.*

*Dave Simmonds back in Europe during the 1971 500cc world championship in which the talented Englishman not only finished 4th overall, but gave Kawasaki their first ever Grand Prix victory in the class, at Jarama, Spain.*

The lubrication system followed normal Kawasaki two-stroke practice, which saw oil injected by pump into the inlet tracks from an independent supply. There was also a petroil mixture in the fuel tank at a 20:1 ratio.

A cross-over layout for the exhaust header pipes was employed to reduce the frontal area and to tuck the expansion chambers neatly out of the way. Carburation was taken care of by a trio of 34mm Mikuni instruments. In place of the electronic ignition found on the original version of the Mach III roadster, the H1-R had an alternator, rectifier, battery and a trio of ignition coils. The rectifier and coils were mounted on rubber from a bracket projecting forward from the steering head. Official Kawasaki figures gave the maximum power output as 75bhp at 9000rpm, with the standard final drive gearing of 15/32 and primary drive gearing of 27/65 in the form of straight-cut gears.

The engine unit was housed in a duplex frame of widely-spaced steel tubing with a steering head configuration which owed much to Norton's famous Featherbed design. The front wheel had a massive 280mm diameter 4LS brake assembly, the rear being a single-sided 220mm full-width drum. With fuel consumption under racing conditions of a staggering 11mpg, several owners supplemented the existing 6.2 gallon

*American Kawasaki rider Art Baumann pictured at Daytona during the early 1970s. He was one of the new breed of American racers who were soon to challenge the world.*

*Launched at the Cologne Show in September 1972, the 900Z1 was a significant step in the evolution of the high performance motorcycle for both the street and the race circuit. This Z1 was raced in the 1974 Production TT.*

(28 litre) tank with an additional auxiliary tank, either within the seat moulding or in place of the battery carrier, beneath the rear of the standard tank. The European cost of the H1-R in March 1970 was £1500.

During February 1970 the European launch of an updated 250cc twin took place at the Dutch Amsterdam Show (Kawasaki had established its European parts centre in Holland the previous year). The machine in question was the A1-RA and it differed in several ways from the outgoing A1-R. A significant difference was that it sported many components from the H1-R triple, including the massive 280mm four leading shoe front brake. The engine had, in an attempt to match Yamaha's new TD2, been given a power boost, it now put out 45bhp at 9800rpm, in addition the carburettors had integral float bowls. Unfortunately, only small numbers were actually built, as it simply couldn't match the Yamaha where it counted, out on the race circuit. A similarly updated 350cc A7-RA was also built.

*A Z1B at Brands Hatch in 1973, the rider is taking part in the national Motorcycle Mechanic's sponsored Production Championship series. Recognise anyone in the photograph? Note twin disc conversion.*

*A Z1 rider negotiating Russell's Bend at Snetterton, Norfolk during a Production race, mid 1970s.*

# Daytona Z1 Record efforts

*The American magazine Motorcyclist sponsored a team essentially stock Z1s in a Daytona speed record attempt during March 1973. Riders included Gary Nixon (far left) and Cook Nielson.*

In March 1973, Daytona, Florida was the setting for a series of record breaking attempts. Riding a pair of virtually stock Z1s, a team of riders, including Gary Nixon, Cliff Carr and Cook Neilson ultimately failed, even though one of the bikes set a marginally quicker speed. Both Z1s averaged over 100mph, with the faster of the two setting 109.64mph. Although an improvement, it was not large enough to be accepted as a new 24 hour record. This had been set at 109.23mph by a British team (MLG) with a modified six-hundred BMW R69S flat twin at the notoriously bumpy Monthlery circuit near Paris, France during 1961.

During that same month in 1973, the French-Canadian star Yvon DuHamel set a new lap record for the Daytona tri-oval at a searing 169.19mph. He was riding a specially tuned Yoshimura-prepared Z1 which was reputed to have put out a genuine 124khp. DuHamel also broke the Moto Guzzi held world records for the 10 and 100 kilometre (6 and 60 miles) with speeds of 150.84mph and 141.82mph; he also broke a number of American AMA certified speeds. But plans for the same bike and rider to attack Mike Hailwood's one-hour record of 145.675mph (set on an MV Agusta 500 GP four at Daytona in 1964), were axed when tyre manufacturers Goodyear could not guarantee their rubber would last a full sixty minutes at the speeds envisaged.

*The fastest Z1 was piloted by Cook Nielson (on bike) and Hurley Wilvert, plus the Japanese Masahiro Wada and Englishman Cliff Carr.*

*The 903cc (66 x 66mm) dohc Z1 engine. In standard roadster form it produced 82bhp at 8500rpm and 7.5kg/m of torque at 7000rpm.*

Even though the latest disc valve twins didn't make the grade, it certainly wasn't the case for the new H1-R. The capability of the triple was soon to be demonstrated, at Daytona in March 1970, Rusty Bradley won the 100-miler in convincing fashion. Rusty's average race speed of 100.72mph broke the previous year's class record by over 4mph.

In the main 200 miler, the H1-R proved fast, but displayed its major drawback for long distance events, high fuel consumption hence the constant stops to take on more gas. Even so, the New Zealander Ginger Molloy brought his H1-R home 7th, and it should be remembered that Daytona 200 rules allowed machines with engine sizes of up to 750cc.

On the European Grand Prix scene, a whole host of riders campaigned the three cylinder Kawasaki, including Ginger Molloy, Gyula Marsovsky, Dave Simmonds, Bill Smith, Christian Ravel, Martin Carney and Eric Offenstadt. Of these, Molloy was by far the most successful, finally finishing the year second to Giacomo Agostini and his MV Agusta. Molloy's achievements that year included second places in France, Finland, Ulster and Spain.

Several new names came onto the scene with H1-Rs for 1971, amongst them Ron Chandler who raced the bike which, in 1970, had been ridden by Englishman Cliff Carr (mainly in North America). Although Chandler (a Thames Lighterman) gained some excellent results on the Continental European scene, including a 5th in the West German Grand Prix at Hockenheim and another 5th at the Belgian Grand Prix, he was not so happy on the British short circuits. Here, he found the 150mph potential which had been such a bonus on the ultra fast Grand Prix tracks not so important on the more twisty British tracks such as Brands Hatch, Cadwell Park and Oulton Park. At these venues the Kawasaki's less than perfect handling was a limiting factor. Even at the fastest British tracks,

*Frontal cutaway view of the Z1B power plant, showing central cam-chain, pistons, valves, crankshaft, camshaft and other details.*

Tom Pemberton, a leading contender for class honours in the 500cc Production class of British short circuit racing, seen here winning at Snetterton, circa 1974.

such as Snetterton and Silverstone, the poor road manners proved a handicap. It led Chandler to state in April 1971; 'If I could get a good run on the Norwich Straight (the fastest section of the Snetterton circuit which now no longer exists), the machine would be undergeared as it stands (he had low gearing fitted). I'm sure it would easily top 140mph along there if we could get the handling sorted. It even twitched in a straight line when I really gunned it through the gears.'

Another Pemberton view. The leaders included Tony Rutter on a Honda 400F at Brands Hatch.

*By 1975 the 750 three had been revised with liquid-cooling magnesium, alloy wheels and triple disc brakes, it had a new name too, the KR750.*

This suspect handling was experienced on other H1-Rs, including the model ridden by works-supported Dave Simmonds. In 1970, he had ridden the bike 'as supplied by the factory'. However, for 1971, it had been completely revamped, the three-cylinder engine assembly being grafted into a new, lower and lighter frame designed and constructed at the Birmingham Reynolds Tubing works by Ken Sprayston. How did this perform? Dave Simmonds provided the answer at the end of 1971 'Just great. In fact, I can't see any major way in which the frame could be improved.'

And the results speak for themselves. With the stock frame, Simmonds finished 20th in the 1970 500cc World Championship series; with the Reynolds frame, Dave was 4th - even though he only contested seven of the 11 rounds. He also gave the factory its first Grand Prix victory in the class, when he won the final round of the 1971 series at Jarama, Spain.

The next stage in development of the Kawasaki production based racers came in late 1970, when the Japanese company launched the H2 Mach IV. Going on sale in January 1971 this followed the general layout of the H1, but with a displacement of 748cc (71 x 63mm). With a maximum speed of 126mph in full road going trim, a racing version looked an absolute certainty. But the first racers were factory specials, the over-the-counter H2-R not being available until spring 1973.

The works-supported development machines were mainly seen in North America and it was the fiery French-Canadian Yvon DuHamel who gave the 750 its first major race win at Talladega in 1971, followed by Paul Smart winning the then world record prize of $30,400 US dollars at Ontario.

But, although the bikes showed up well, Daytona was not to be a happy hunting ground for the new, larger triples. The entire team, managed by the well-known Californian, Bob Hansen, was destined to fall by the wayside at the Florida classic in March 1972, even though they had the services of several top line riders, including Englishman Paul Smart. Smart retired after 2 laps, DuHamel seized whilst in the lead and Gary Nixon's gearbox locked up. Even so, Hansen was invited to head Kawasaki

A KR750 on the startline at Brands Hatch for the Easter transatlantic races, rider Art Baumann, circa 1975. Also in the picture is Stan Woods (15) Suzuki TR750.

America's racing challenge the following year. The bikes were the latest version of the 750 H2-R and riders nominated were Yvon DuHamel, Art Baumann, Cliff Carr and Gary Nixon.

Into 1973, and the Team Hansen seven-fifty triples won everything right across America - except Daytona - where once again lady luck deserted them. In the 200 miler, Baumann and DuHamel came off together whilst disputing the lead! Talking to Bob Hansen at Daytona two decades later in March 2002, the ever cheerful Californian, now in his early 80s, confirmed that during his reign as Commander-in-Chief of America's Kawasaki racing operation, 'Things just hadn't gone according to plan at the place it mattered most, Daytona.' And almost as a reminder of the Kawasaki's difficulties Bob now runs a team of Honda 450s in the American historic racing world ... not H2-R triples.

There was also a small number of H2-Rs exported to Europe and Australia. But except for America, the air-cooled 750cc triple never quite made the impact of its 500cc brother.

Meanwhile the H1-R was finding the competition even hotter in the 500cc class. However, Mick Grant finished 3rd in the Senior TT on one of the triples. This was his first success with the marque he became associated with later that decade.

By 1975 both the 500 and 750 triples were works special with water cooling, cast magnesium alloy wheels and triple disc brakes. These machines were provided to selected riders, rather than being sold to privateers, as Kawasaki had done in the past with the H1-R and H2-R models.

*A KR750 on display in late 1976. This photograph shows details such as inverted rear shocks, 7-spoke wheels, front forks, discs and 2-piston calipers.*

For the Isle of Man TT, Mick Grant had both versions of the new liquid-cooled triples on hand. In the Senior (500cc) he won the 6-lap 226.38 mile race at an average speed of 100.27mph and also set the fastest lap in 21 minutes, 59.6 seconds, a speed of 102.93mph. But in the Classic TT (unlimited) after setting a new outright lap record for the famous Mountain circuit in 20 minutes, 36.8 seconds - 109.82mph (previously held for eight years by Mike Hailwood on the works 500 four cylinder Honda), Mick's race ended with a broken final drive chain on lap 3.

But in reality the day of the Kawasaki triples was over, their place effectively taken at Grand Prix level by the brand new inline 2-stroke twins (250 and 350cc); whilst as far as this book is concerned it was very much the beginning of a new era for the massive Japanese corporation, with a brand new four cylinder 4-stroke, in the shape of the 'King' otherwise know as the Z1.

In the Z1, Kawasaki had a motorcycle which established it as a constructor of large capacity, high performance 4-stroke muscle bikes. Launched at the German Cologne Show in September 1972, work on the project actually went back to 1967 - before the H1 Mach III triples had even reached the market place! Initially known under the code NYS (New

*Australian Gregg Hansford (far left of picture) with the KR750 triple on which he won the Canadian round of the 1977 World FIM Formula 750 Championship.*

*Club rider M Hepworth racing his virtually stock Z900 at Carnaby, North Yorkshire, 1st August 1976. Twin 245mm front discs introduced that year. Note non-standard oil cooler.*

York Streak), the Z1's aim was to provide Kawasaki with a big-bore 4-stroke replacement for the then current Meguro-derived W-series parallel twin street bike. However, when it arrived the Z1 did much more than this. It not only put Kawasaki firmly at number one in the sales league in front of Honda for the first time in the 750cc and over sales league, but it also provided the company with an engine which could match the best in the world and form the basis for future development and even racing.

The big Z (or Zee, as the Americans referred to it) was built in two engine sizes: the mainstream Z1 - 903cc (66 x 66mm),and for the Japanese market Z2 - 746 cc (64 x 58mm). The larger 'export' model produced 82bhp at 8500rpm in full road going trim. Both versions weighed in at 507lb (230kg) and featured double overhead camshafts.

*Another production racing shot, this time at Mallory Park in 1976. Bike is fitted with Cernan & McKay 4LS front brake.*

The Z series engines were of the classic across-the-frame four layout - as previously used by the likes of Gilera, Benelli, MV Agusta and Honda, the outer pistons moving together in opposition to the central pair. As was normal Japanese practice, the crankcase split horizontally on the crankshaft and contained the 5-speed gearbox. The crankshaft was an all-caged roller affair with no less than six main bearings supporting it, with the central pair clamped to the upper crankcase half. The crank was pressed together with the mainshafts forged with the webs, and these were shaped to provide the balance factor. With a built-up crankshaft, one-

*Barry Ditchburn with his KR750 well cranked over, Race of the Year, Oulton Park, October 1979.*

*A Kawasaki 1000 taking part in the legendary Barcelona 24 Hours endurance race. Bike details include twin shock frame, 4-into-1 exhaust, cast wheels and Cibie lighting.*

piece rods could be employed. The 3-ring pistons ran in cast-iron liners, with an aluminium cylinder block; the head being in the same material.

The valve seats were cast in the head and manufactured in an extra hard material enabling the engine to run on lead free fuel (one of the very first motorcycle engines to have this feature). The valves (two per cylinder) operated in bronze guides, and this material proved to be one of the very few errors the design team made. Its wear rate being too fast for comfort, in later years it was substituted for iron, this becoming a retro-fit for all Z1 (and Z2 engines). Each valve used duplex coil springs, and valve adjustment was by the shim-set method. Both camshafts ran in four pairs of split plain bearings. The exhaust cam featured an integral skew gear to drive the rev counter.

*Ken Suzuki, Kawasaki's race boss with Kork Ballington (right) and four-cylinder engine, probably Z1000, late 1970s, at the Kawasaki works, Japan.*

The lubrication system was of the wet sump variety, so, unlike the CB750 Honda there was no separate frame-mounted oil tank. With the engine being of full unit construction design, this meant that the gearbox and primary drive (the latter by gears) used the same oil as the engine. On the stock Z1 engine carburation was taken care of by a quartet of 28mm Mikuni VM instruments, whilst the ignition was by coil and battery (12 volt), with two sets of contact breaker points under the offside crankshaft end cover.

*Classic racer Graham Salter's very original 1976 P&M 1170cc four cylinder Kawasaki, Cadwell Park, 5th October 2002.*

*Mick Grant in action during his winning ride in the 1977 Classic TT. Riding his KR750 Grant won at record race and lap speeds - 110.76mph and 112.77mph respectively.*

*Grant wheelies his KR750 over the Mountain at Cadwell Park in 1977.*

As with the triples, the Z1's main drawback for racing was its chassis. Although a duplex cradle frame was used the handling wasn't really up to racing levels. This also applied to the braking system - a single 296mm stainless steel disc and 2-piston caliper up front, with a 200mm SLS full width drum at the rear. But that magnificent engine still ensured that not only did the Z1 receive rave reviews from the press, but more competition-minded souls soon had their Z1s out on the race circuit.

In the USA one of the Z1s grabbed the headlines in early 1973, when with some careful tuning and blue printing and a certain amount of weight saving, some quite astonishing results were achieved (see boxed section within this chapter).

*Mick Grant's KR750 in the Silverstone race paddock, circa 1977.*

*During the late 1970s Kawasaki UK ran a popular one-model series for the KH400 triple. This is a scene from the 1979 round at Cadwell Park, Lincolnshire.*

*March 1979 and the KH400 series rides off at Cadwell Park, with three bikes negotiating the Club Hairpin.*

Then in 1974 Kawasaki went endurance racing at the highest level. Using specially prepared engines mounted in a chassis made by the Swiss specialist Fritz Egli, their top team comprised the French pairing of Georges Godier and Alain Genoud. This team won at Barcelona, Mettet and the Bol d'Or at Le Mans. In the 1000 Kilometre event at the same circuit earlier that year a more standard Z1 was victorious, as was another example at the Dutch Oss circuit. If 1974 was good, 1975 was even better, with Godier and Genoud being World Endurance champions - the first year of the official series. But in 1976 no one could match Honda although Kawasaki finished 2nd and 3rd at the year's biggest event, the French Bol d'Or.

But 1978 was without doubt Kawasaki's year. Not only did Kork Ballington scoop both the 250 and 350cc world championships (see the companion Grand Prix volume) and Mick Grant continue his Isle of Man success, winning the Classic TT at 112.40mph (and a new lap record of 114.33mph), but the American Don Vesco raised the outright world motorcycle speed record to a staggering 318.598mph, using a fully streamlined projectile. This was powered by a pair of turbo-charged and uprated Z1 engines connected by toothed belts, one on each side.

'Pops' Yoshimura was also heavily involved helping various riders on both sides of the Atlantic to success in both road racing and straight line drag (sprinting) events. Many of these drag bikes used a pair of Z1 engines in specially lengthened frames. Another ploy was to use different frames; these included Rickman, Warnell, Seeley, Bimota and Harris to name but a few.

*Probably the most competitive rider of his era, French Canadian Kawasaki star, Yvon DuHamel.*

*A 2-valve Yoshimura - Kawasaki race head, pistons, rings, gudgeon pins, circlips and camshafts.*

In late 1976 Kawasaki introduced its first small four cylinder model, the 652cc (62 x 54mm) Z650. Although an excellent machine, its impact in racing was small. Then in 1979, the four cylinder was downsized further to provide the 498cc (55 x 52.4mm) Z500. This was quickly followed by the 399cc (52 x 47mm) Z400.

Meanwhile the 900 had grown into a 1000. This had been accomplished by the simple expedient of boring the cylinders out by 4mm to 70mm, giving a new displacement of 1015cc. The performance model was the Z1-R, which was not a racer at all, but a sports roadster. Introduced for the 1978 model year it gave 90bhp at 8000rpm. But even so the Z1-R engine, like the original Z1, was soon in demand from speed freaks the world over.

For example, Englishman Nigel Patrick's turbo-charged Maitland Kawasaki was the fastest petrol-burning bike outside the USA during the late 1970s - consuming the standing quarter mile in 9.44 seconds - a terminal speed of 150.46mph (286.78kph).

*Turbo charged Z1-derived drag bike. This projectile could reach 150mph and in a standing start 1/4mile. Shown here doing a 'burn-out' prior to lift off.*

*'Pops' Yoshimura working on a four-cylinder Kawasaki cylinder head in 1978.*

*Monoshock frame kit from Hertford-based specialists Harris, with four-cylinder Z series engine, 1979.*

*A KH400 series bike at Snetterton in 1979; exhaust system modified for greater ground clearance. Note Honda MT125 (204) in background. The scoreboard, for many years a prominent feature of the Norfolk circuit's skyline has long since been demolished.*

But it was the 1980s during which, the production-based Kawasaki really blossomed, with a myriad of hi-tech developments including monoshock rear suspension, electronic fuel injection, modern frame technology, multi-valve, liquid-cooled engines, improved tyre technology and a host of other important developments (see next chapter). Racing itself would also undergo fundamental change and the introduction of the new SuperBike and SuperSport categories would bring racing development much closer to the road rider than ever before.

*One of the Z1s hurtling around the Daytona banking in the Florida sunshine.*

# Kawasaki - the modern years

# 5

*The 1992 Team Green pairing of John Reynolds (3) and Brian Morrison (6).*

The 1970s had been the decade when the Kawasaki name came to the fore, thanks to motorcycles such as the Z1, the KR750 and its KR250/350 inline twin cylinder Grand Prix racers.

From 1975, Kawasaki's racing division had expended vast amounts of time and money on developing specialised machines to contest Grand Prix events. But at the end of 1982, however, the company announced that it was withdrawing from the Grand Prix scene.

Over eight years, Kawasaki engineers had developed several innovations, including Uni-Trak rear suspension, air-adjustable front suspension, and Electro Fushion cylinder bores. However, even though they had been very successful, winning eight world championship titles, the early 1980s had witnessed a worldwide decrease in the sales of standard production roasters. So, Kawasaki's management concluded that campaigning specialised 2-stroke racers, which bore no resemblance to their current large capacity, four cylinder, 4-stroke Superbikes, served no real benefit to future development. So it had been decided to call it a day and the era of the Kawasaki Grand Prix racer - and for that matter any form of road racing Kawasaki 2-stroke was at an end - for the time being.

In taking this decision, Kawasaki amongst the big four Japanese bike builders was unique. It also meant that its engineering staff could be put to work creating a new range of modern high performance 4-strokes, which could not only be used to power a 'next generation street bike range; but also utilised to go racing.' In place of its Grand Prix effort, Kawasaki saw the void being filled by increased participation in endurance racing.

*Kawasaki began the 1980s with its long running across-the-frame 4-cylinder twin shock formula, as demonstrated by this Moriwaki model for Eddie Lawson, at Daytona, 1980.*

*Welshman Keith Ferrel flicks the P&M 1000 Kawasaki through the chicane on home ground at Llandow, 1981.*

*Future 500cc World Champion Wayne Gardner with his 'sit-up-and-beg' Moriwaki 1000cc 4 at Redgate, Donington Park, 1981.*

Honda had forged links with the French Elf concern, which although resulting in much new innovation, didn't greatly assist Honda's track efforts in the short term.

Instead Kawasaki went for a much quicker route to success. This saw them combining their proven four-cylinder Z series air-cooled engines, with the expertise of Frenchman Serge Rosset, boss of the Performance Company.

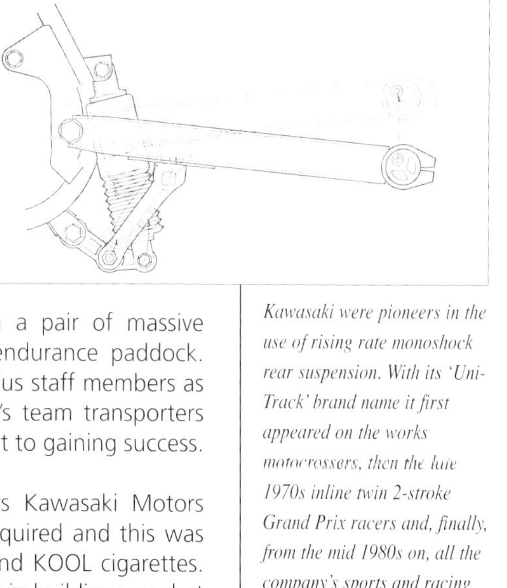

*Kawasaki were pioneers in the use of rising rate monoshock rear suspension. With its 'Uni-Track' brand name it first appeared on the works motocrossers, then the late 1970s inline twin 2-stroke Grand Prix racers and, finally, from the mid 1980s on, all the company's sports and racing motorcycles.*

The FIM had introduced the World Endurance Championship series in 1980, which had been won by Honda. However, with the involvement of Serge Rosset, head of the French Performance Company, all this was set to change. If 'Big H' had dominated in 1980, 'Big K' did so in 1981 and 1982. Soon a pair of massive Performance trucks became a focal point of the endurance paddock. Containing sufficient facilities to feed and sleep 20-plus staff members as well as a truly superbly equipped workshop, Rosset's team transporters were tangible evidence of the man's total commitment to gaining success. Second best was simply not on the agenda.

Even with the backing of the French importers Kawasaki Motors (Japanese owned) additional sponsorship was still required and this was forthcoming from such heavyweights as KVAS oils and KOOL cigarettes. Absolutely no effort (or expense) was spared by Rosset in building up what was, even by Grand Prix standards, one of the most professional and well-structured teams ever seen in motorsport. In contrast to the Honda-Elf avant-garde approach, Kawasaki-Performance bikes were almost conventional in their design and appearance. The Performance-designed chassis was constructed from chrome-moly tubing, bronze-welded, with a cast-alloy substantially ribbed swinging arm for the Uni-Trak rising-rate rocker-arm ATZ single rear shock absorber.

*Jim Wells' P&M Kawasaki endurance racer, Donington Park, April 1982. Specification included air-cooled Z1000 engine, monoshock rear suspension, 3-spoke magnesium wheels with slick tyres and anti-drive front forks.*

*World Endurance round at Donington Park, September 1982. This photograph allows the reader to study the many technical features of the Kawasaki France machine, including full cradle steel frame, box section aluminium swinging arm, eccentric rear chain adjustment, 16 inch front wheel, triple disc brakes and much more.*

At the front of the machine was a pair of Kyaba forks, of similar construction to those used by Kork Ballington's KR500 four cylinder 2-stroke Grand Prix bike; these running in tapered, roller-head bearings. A mechanical anti-dive system (again from the KR500), first seen on a BMW Superbike built in North America in 1976 by Udo Geitl and Todd Schuster, worked by relaying the braking force from the twin 350mm front discs, via a system of pivots and rods, to the fork crowns. It was an effective, although somewhat heavier way of achieving front anti-dive than the hydraulic valving systems used by the other Japanese manufacturers.

Although 18-inch wheels front and rear were occasionally employed, mostly a 16-inch (Campagnolo) and 18 inch (Dymag) were standard. This was at the time when the Japanese industry had its short-lived love affair with 16inch front wheels. Dunlop tyres, 'providing excellent grip and wear properties, both of which are vital in endurance events' were used exclusively by the Rosset team. Chain adjustment was taken care of by eccentric blocks in the rear of the swinging arm and integral with the axle.

With rules stating that engines must be based on the then existing TT Formula 1 - using production-based 4-strokes up to 1000cc, or 600cc 2-strokes - with external engine cases unmodified in any way, the engine chosen was constructed around the Z1000J roadster unit. This air-cooled, across-the-frame four was specifically tuned in France by Performance themselves. They fitted their own camshafts to the 998cc (69.4 x 66mm), 2-valves per cylinder engine, paying particular attention to gas-flowing and porting of the cylinder head. The ports were opened out and oversize valves fitted with twin plug ignition and 34mm smooth-bore Mikuni carburettors.

*Kawasaki France dominated World Endurance racing of the beginning of the eighties, winning the 1981 and 1982 titles. This photograph was taken at the 1982 Bol d'Or.*

*J. C. Chemarin, World Endurance Champion in 1982 on his Kawasaki France machine.*

The crankshaft was welded up to provide additional rigidity, whilst the generator was transferred from its traditional location at the end of the crankshaft, to a fresh home atop the gearbox. Driven by a toothed rubber belt, it charged the battery which was positioned just in front of the rear wheel, beneath the rear shock assembly. All this meant that the width of the power unit was decreased, providing additional ground clearance, once again an endurance racing modification which would find its way through to a new generation of roadsters which Kawasaki was then in the process of designing back in Japan.

Running on a compression ratio of 10.8:1, the Performance Kawasaki reliability put out 135bhp at 10,000rpm. The six-bearing crankshaft, using roller big-ends and plain small-ends, proved more than capable of withstanding a full 24 hours of flat-out action without showing any signs of complaint.

There was a choice of three combinations for the second and third gears in the 5-speed transmission, depending upon the exact circuit and individual rider requirements.

*The 1983 Kawasaki endurance racer pictured at the British Silverstone round that year.*

With an all-French squad of riders, which included the likes of Jacques Cornu and Jean Chemarin, reliable motorcycles and a great support team, it is perhaps little wonder that Kawasaki dominated the early 1980s endurance scene.

Over on the other side of the Atlantic the early 1980s saw the emergence of a new star, Eddie Lawson. Lawson made his international debut when he raced a Yamaha (finishing 33rd) in the 1979 Daytona event.

*The 1983 French Kawasaki endurance effort saw a new bike with an aluminium frame and many other changes. However, it couldn't repeat the success of the previous two years and the title went to Suzuki with the prototype of what was to emerge a few months later as the oil/air-cooled GSXR750.*

*The successful North Leicester Motorcycles team with their 750cc Turbo, 1984. Team boss Stuart Mayhew is on the extreme left, rider Dave Humpstone is seated on the bike.*

Next he rode a Moriwaki-Kawasaki in the 1980 Daytona 200 miler. Even though he was subsequently to retire after 81 miles, he was still impressive enough to gain full Kawasaki backing for his future efforts. During 1981 and 1982 Lawson created something of a sensation riding a series of unfaired air-cooled Kawasakis to victory all over America.

However, by 1983 Lawson had signed for Yamaha, with whom he was eventually to join the European Grand Prix scene and become a multi-World 500cc Champion.

But as with Lawson, Kawasaki themselves were on the move and although they produced a series of air-cooled GPZ models, culminating in the 1983 1100 with digital fuel injection (DF1), which pushed out 120bhp and could top 150mph, the era of the Z1 derived engine was coming to an end. In fact the 1983 GPZ range, incorporating 550 (553cc - 58 x 52.4mm) 750 (738cc 66 x 54mm) and 1100 (1089cc 72.5 x 66mm) versions, together with a 750 Turbo version which went on sale in 1984, were the pinnacle of Kawasaki's series production air-cooled four cylinder models. Each represented class-leading performance for its day: the 550, 61bhp; 750, 86bhp; 1100, 120bhp and 750 Turbo, 112bhp.

Several of these machines were campaigned in production type events during the early 1980s. However, towards the end of 1983 came something which was to have as much effect as the Z1 a decade earlier. This was the arrival of the new GPZ 900R.

Known as the Ninja in the States, the 900R was the first modern Superbike with a liquid-cooled, 16-valve, dohc, across-the-frame four cylinder engine. The GPZ 900R was also the first to combine a lightweight diamond frame, aluminium rear frame section and 16 inch front wheel; and, Kawasaki claimed, the first with a front fork that delivered truly progressive wheel travel combined with the company's rising rate Uni-Trak rear suspension.

*Cutaway view showing the main components of the 750 Turbo powerplant.*

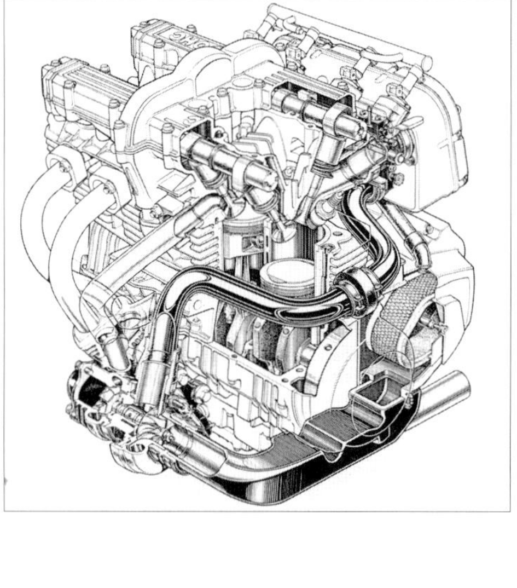

*Details of the turbocharger.*

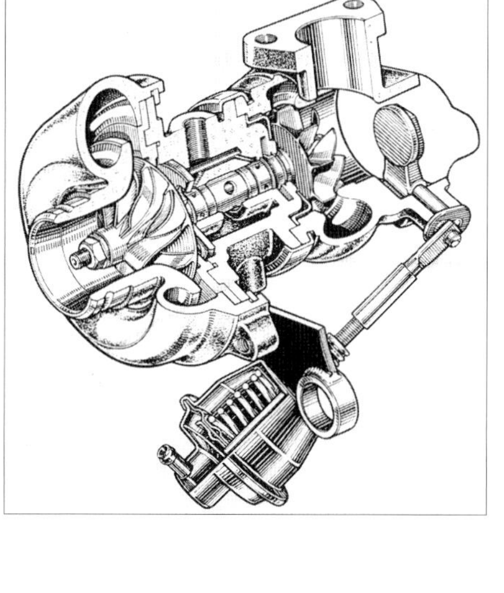

*Kawasaki's GPZ900R was the sensation of 1984. Not only did it usher in a new level of performance and sophistication for the road rider, but it also made a big impact on racing. Clubman Ian Wilson is seen here in winning form at Donington Park.*

As with the Z1, the centrepiece of the newcomer was its engine. Here Kawasaki could look to the fact that this had been the main feature of every large displacement model for over a decade, and that in that time a reputation had been established for power coupled with a high degree of reliability.

As with the Z1 project, the GPZ 900R had a long gestation period, lasting several years, Kawasaki realising by the end of the 1970s that time and technology was fast catching up with the original Z-bike concept. So the company began to examine and test every practical combination of chassis and power train to find the one best suited to a second-generation Superbike. Although several other configurations showed promise, including a V4 and V6 - and an inline six, all were adjudged to offer no significant advantage over an across-the-frame four cylinder for sports bike and racing use. So the proven layout was retained, although virtually every other aspect was re-evaluated. The result was an all-new engine which took Kawasaki - and ultimately the rest of the Japanese motorcycle industry - a giant step forward.

*In 1984 a 16 inch front wheel and anti-dive front forks were hi-tech.*

Although the GPZ 900R's included valve angle had been decreased more than 25 degrees (in comparison to both the 1983 GPZ 750 and 1100 models) to 34.9 degrees, the engine was shorter, top to bottom, than the original Z1, with a reduction of crank centre to the top of the cam cover of 24.5mm. The engine was also 48.26mm (1.9 in) shorter front to back. Including the aluminium radiator, oil cooler, and all other engine components, it was a full 5 kg (11lb) lighter than the Z1. A major factor in this compact design was a basic change in the inline four layout. Liquid cooling meant that the cam chain could be positioned outside the cylinder bank, giving the 900R a wet-liner cooling system that was both compact and highly efficient. This also allowed a more direct combustion path from gearbox to exhaust.

*The GPZ900R engine, liquid-cooling, dohc, 16-valves and a compactness not seen before in an across-the-frame-four-cylinder.*

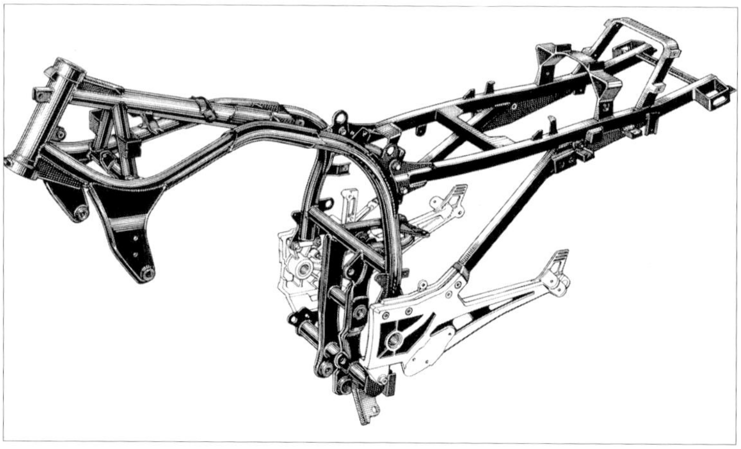

*GPZ900R frame with bolted-on rear sub-frame steel construction, with the engine acting as a stressed member.*

Revving to 10,500rpm, the one-piece crank was supported by five plain bearings which, in addition to driving the clutch, also drove a compact counterbalancer, which virtually eliminated secondary vibration.

At the business end of this 16-valve hi-tech engine, a narrow valve angle (inlet 18.5 degrees and exhaust 16.4 degrees from vertical) allowed shorter ports for increased breathing ability and compact chambers for increased combustion efficiency. But despite the narrow included angle, Kawasaki's engineering team had been able to employ relatively large diameter valves (inlet 29mm, exhaust 24.7mm) which also contributed additional horsepower due to increased breathing efficiency.

With five bearings each, the two hollow (and thus lightweight) camshafts turned in the head itself. Each cam had a quartet of lobes activating two valves, each through dual-finger cam followers. Valve adjustment was carried out by means of a screw and locknut. The cams themselves were driven by a Hy-Vo chain from the nearside of the camshaft, and Kawasaki's newly introduced constant-load automatic tensioner ensured decreased mechanical loss and more consistent chain tension, whilst a 7.94mm chain pitch provided more strength than a conventional chain without any additional weight penalty.

The liquid-cooling system utilised a single aluminium cross-flow radiator, thermostat, electric fan and water pump. Water entered the cylinder liners at the front of the engine, flowed up and back through the head, then back to the radiator. The water pump was gear-driven off the clutch from the same shaft that drove the oil pump. Liquid cooling not

*Geoff Johnson with his 1984 Production TT winning GPZ900R.*

*The top three celebrate after the 1984 Production TT. Winner Geoff Johnson is centre with the champagne, left, Phil Mellor and right, Trevor Nation were runner-up and 3rd respectively.*

only provided more scope for development in the future, but also offered additional benefits such as a decrease in piston/bore clearance and the ability to run a higher compression ratio.

Lubrication was taken care of by a special dual-stage system. In the primary oil loop, lubricant was drawn through the primary filter to the pump then passed via the filter element to the crank, gearbox, cylinder head and other components. In the secondary loop, lubricant was passed from the pump to a four-tier oil cooler, then back to the wet sump.

The oil cooler served a secondary function as a temporary 'storage tank'.Sump oil level was therefore kept to a minimum, whilst a special dam isolated the critical area around the balancer-shaft, primary drive and clutch. This system resulted in a significant rise in mechanical efficiency.

Lubrication was also given an extra boost since the cooler did not restrict oil flow to vital components. To help prevent leakage, oil passed to and from the head via external oil pipes. Other features which contributed to the high level of efficiency and output included a large capacity air box, maintenance-free ignition with electronic timing advancer, Keihin CVK 34mm carburettors and improvements to the exhaust system, which improved both performance and clearance over previous four cylinder Kawasakis.

As well as a hydraulically operated clutch, the 900R featured a 6-speed gearbox - a first for Kawasaki on a large bore machine.

The gearbox shafts were staggered in the vertical plane to save space and reduce mechanical loss, with undercut dogs for third, fourth and fifth gears.

*Geoff Johnson on his way to victory with his GPZ900R in the 1984 Isle of Man Production TT, seen here leaving Ramsey.*

## 1985 GPZ600R

| | |
|---|---|
| Engine | Liquid-cooled, across-the-frame; dohc; 4-cylinder, with 16-valves |
| Capacity | 592cc |
| Bore | 60mm |
| Stroke | 52.4mm |
| Comp ratio | 11:1 |
| Ignition | Electronic |
| Carburation | 4 x Keihin CVK 32mm |
| Gearbox | 6-speed |
| Clutch | Wet, multi-plate |
| Final drive | Chain |
| Frame | Rectangular section steel tubing, with twin downtubes |
| Suspension | Front; 38mm telescopic fork with automatic anti-dive<br>Rear; Square section swinging arm with Uni-Trak rising rate single shock absorber |
| Wheels | 16 inch aluminium 6-spoke, front and rear |
| Tyres | Front; 110/80 V16<br>Rear; 120/80 V16 |
| Brakes | Front; 2 x 280mm discs with 2-piston calipers<br>Rear; single 270mm disc with 2-piston caliper |
| Dry weight | 430lb (195kg) |
| Max power | 75bhp at 10,500rpm |
| Max speed | 135mph |

*A GPZ600R rider taking part in the 1985 Snetterton 6 hour endurance race. The Kawasaki middleweight was single handedly responsible for creating the new 600 SuperSport class.*

*Cutaway GPZ600R engine showing central cam-chain, pistons, crankshaft, generator, radiator and oil cooler.*

*Team Green race boss Alec Wright and the new GPX750R, circa 1987. Wright had previously managed the dirt bike side of Kawasaki's UK effort, before moving to racing during the mid 1980s.*

Another important feature of the new 900 four was its new, high tensile steel frame, which was not only considerably lighter than previous Kawasaki fours, but also lowered the overall centre of gravity, allowing greater lean without sacrificing overall frame strength. In the early stages of development, downtubes were added to determine what stress, it any, they would encounter. Results showed that the downtubes carried virtually no load, so were removed.

There was a box-section, aluminium swinging arm which employed eccentric cam-drive chain adjusters. Braking was looked after by a pair of 280mm front discs, with a single 270mm unit at the rear, all with dual piston calipers.

Other interesting features of this mould-breaking design included AVDS (automatic variable damping system) anti-dive for the front forks, 38mm diameter fork tubes (up 1mm from the GPZ 1100/750 models), 6-spoke alloy wheels, a 4.75gal (22 litre) fuel tank and a dry weight of 503lb (228kg).

In standard form the 908cc (72.5 x 55mm) engine put out 114bhp, with *Motor Cycle News* achieving an impressive 158mph in a 1984 road test.

A trio of GPZ 900Rs filled the rostrum positions, by taking the first three places in the Isle of Man Production TT in June 1984. Headed by race winner Geoff Johnson, the trio (all dealer-entered) finished ahead of the other works-supported teams from rival Japanese manufacturers. Besides Johnson, the other GPZ 900R TT riders were Phil Mellor and Trevor Nation.

The newcomer also did the business in other races for production bikes staged that year, but with the arrival of bikes like the Suzuki GSX-R750 and Honda RC30, the 900R's success came to an end. Even so, in terms of evolution the design is pivotal, pointing as it did to the future of the large displacement 4-stroke.

In 1985 Kawasaki once again stole a march on the opposition - and in the process created what today is the most important class at club and national level, the SuperSport 600 category. The bike? Well, this was the GPZ 600R and it shared numerous features with its bigger brother, being an across-the-frame, 4-stroke, four cylinder with double overhead camshafts, 4-valves per cylinder and liquid-cooling.

The 592cc (60 x 52.4mm) engine, whilst having many similarities with the 900R, was actually more closely linked to the air-cooled GPZ550 power unit, which had proved surprisingly successful in production class racing on both sides of the Atlantic; in America the 550 had been particularly suitable in the Box-Stock category.

Another asset was the 550's exceptional reputation for longevity, with many professional race tuners considering the Kawasaki 550 engine one of the strongest ever built.

The new liquid cooled '600' continued this bullet-proof theme. It also followed the 550's centre cam chain and chain primary drive with an intermediate shaft and crank-end alternator. In creating the 600 engine the engineering team had made it more compact than its predecessor - a full 40mm (1.57in) narrower than the 550.

The five-bearing bottom end was virtually the same as the 550's, however the bore centre of cylinders 2 and 3 had been moved inwards 1mm. The 600 had wet cylinder liners. Coolant entered each jacket through an inlet onto the rear of the cylinders, flowed around the liners, passed through the head and exited via two outlets in the top. The single radiator was aluminium, with a thermostatically controlled fan. Except for the cam-chain location, the head and valve train followed the 900R layout, with the valves operated by cam followers carrying screw-type adjusters.

Strangely, the 600's frame owed nothing to the 900R, the engine simply sitting in the chassis, with rubber engine mounts at the front - in the same fashion as the air-cooled 550. But it was no throwback to an earlier era. Instead, the 600R's chassis featured a double-triangulated

*GPZ600R front end showing AVDS anti-dive, two-piston calipers and drilled solid brake disc.*

*In 1987 Kawasaki UK entered a team of three GPX750s in the Isle of Man TT. Riders left to right: Grant Gooding, Mac McDiarmid and Howard Selby.*

perimeter frame of steel construction and mostly rectangular tubing. Twin downtubes were bolted to the main section near the steering head and swinging arm pivot points, whilst there was a trio of large cross-tubes in the main section to ensure maximum rigidity. An aluminium brace across the downtubes supported the radiator and oil cooler. 16 inch wheels - all the fashion in the mid-1980s - ensured a low seat height (30 inches - 770mm) and with 75bhp (10 more than the 550) at 10,500rpm the GPZ 600 could reach 135mph.

During the first two years of its life, the 600R was not only easily the best selling machine in its class, but also the best to go racing with; rival manufacturers air-cooled fours not being in the same league. However, the entry of the original Honda CBR 600 (coded F) in 1987, changed everything, the Honda putting out 83bhp and 140mph.

Unfortunately for Kawasaki (and also to a large extent Suzuki and Yamaha), since then the Honda has continued to dominate the class, with constant development keeping it at the front.

This is not to say that Kawasaki haven't tried. In fact there has been a succession of models. These have included the GPX 600 (1988) ZZ-R600 (1990) and ZX-6R (1995). It is worth noting that the ZZ-R was the first Kawasaki in the 600-class to feature an aluminium mainframe.

*With the arrival of the GPX750 Kawasaki France came back on to the scene in endurance racing. This is their 1987 squad and GPX750 derived machine.*

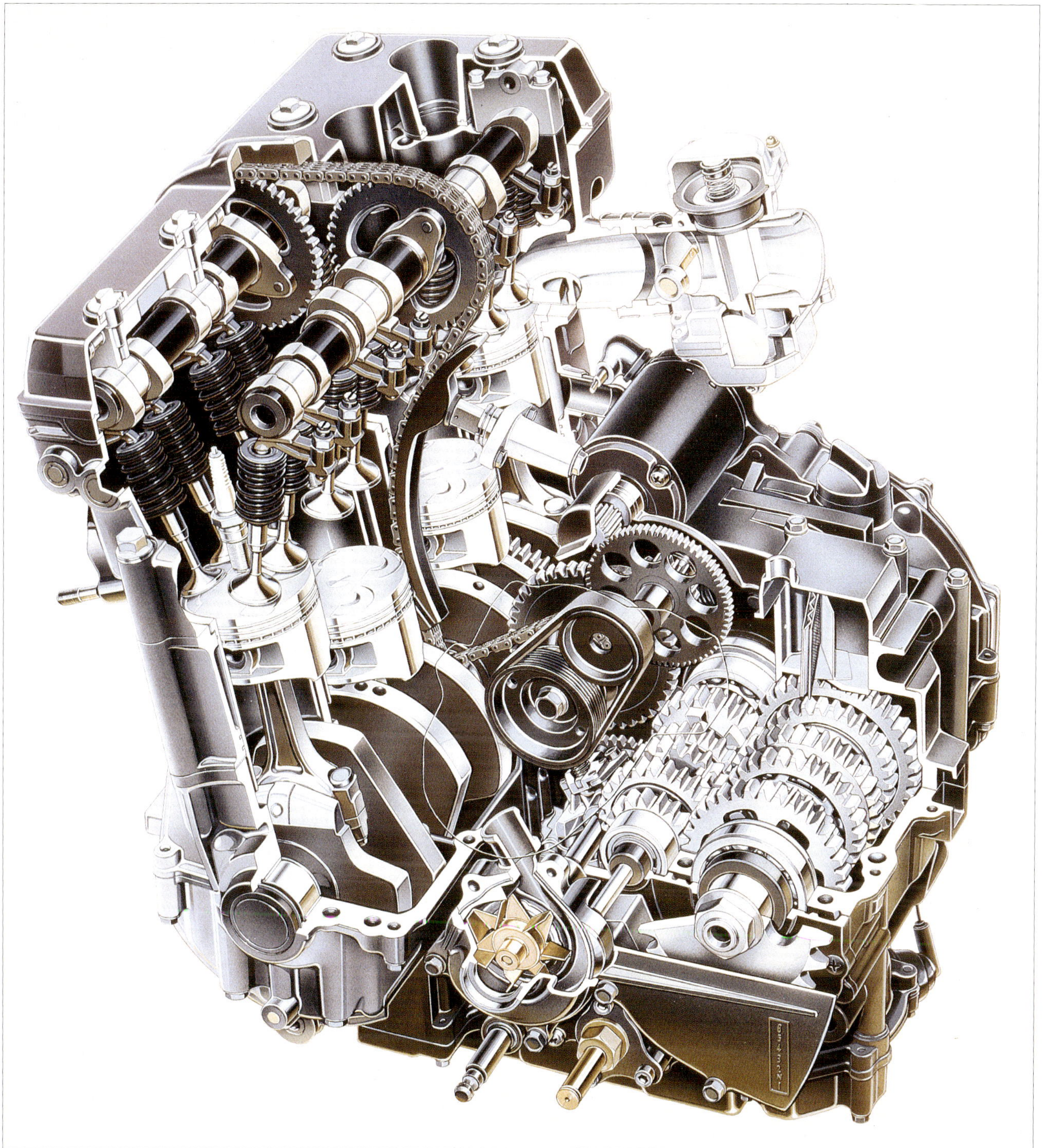

In September 1986 Kawasaki launched its first purpose-built 750cc four-cylinder. Based on the technology already proven in previous Kawasaki engines, the GPX 750 displaced 748cc (68 x 51.5mm). It was also extremely compact, contributing factors included an all-new valve train similar to that introduced the previous year on the high revving dohc GPZ 250R (a SuperSports street bike intended largely for the Japanese domestic market); minimum mass components throughout, including pistons weighing just 165g (6oz) each; a compact new primary drive and gearbox design; and a belt-driven alternator behind the cylinders. The result was a 750 which put out 106bhp at 10,500rpm and 7.8kg/m of torque at 8,500rpm; and all this in full street legal trim with effective silencing.

*The GPX750 was superseded by ZXR750 in late 1989. This is the original ZXR engine of that period. Later (1991) the engine was redesigned to allow the camshaft to be driven from the offside end of the crankshaft rather than the centre.*

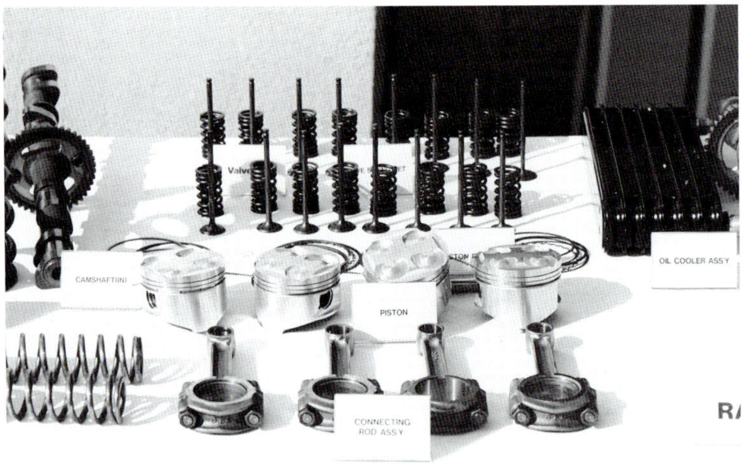


Part of the 1989 ZXR750 race kit, showing connecting rods, pistons, valves, springs, camshaft and oil cooler.

As was the Kawasaki norm by that time, the GPX 750 was liquid-cooled with 16-valves. Running on a compression ratio of 11.2:1; a quartet of Keihin CVK 34mm carburettors and a dry-weight of 195kg (430lb) it was the second lightest machine in its class at the time of its launch. With a maximum speed of 151mph, the GPX was only 1mph slower than the machine which ultimately replaced it in the Kawasaki line, the ZXR 750. The British launch took place at Castle Combe race circuit, where a number of journalists and racers put a group of GPXs through their paces. John Robinson (technical editor of *Performance Bikes* and probably the most experienced tester amongst those present) commented, 'The GPX was the first bike I have actually enjoyed riding around Castle Combe! The circuit is so bumpy that the front wheel can be lifted clear off the ground when you are cranked over. The Kawasaki's suspension was very impressive: I was amazed at the way in which it coped with the surface at high speed. Most machines do not provide sufficient suspension adjustment, but with the GPX, every setting made a discernable difference. The handling itself proved extremely stable; yet it is very fast responding when directional changes are required.'

Also present at the GPX 750 test day was racer Steve Bateman, who had raced at Castle Combe several times on his own Formula 1 Harris-framed Suzuki GSX-R 750. Bateman recorded 1 min 11 secs - better than the existing production lap record, which at that time was held by Dave Hill (Suzuki GSX-R 750).

Three days after the Castle Combe launch, *Performance Bikes* staff man Rupert Paul entered one of the test bikes in the World Record Weekend at Elvington, North Yorkshire. By the end of the event he was the new British national record holder of both the flying start quarter mile (145.86mph) and the flying start kilometre (145.722mph). The speeds were set from the average of runs made in both directions; and a best one-way speed of 149mph was logged. The test bike was entirely stock, with the original road tyres and standard gearing.

The ZXR750 really took off after its update in 1991, when new shorter bore and stroke dimensions of 71 x 47.3mm (formally 68 x 51.5mm) were introduced.

But in actual racing events the GPX 750 was not to achieve much at all, even though a French team took part in events such as the Bol d'Or and Kawasaki UK entered a team of three riders in the 1987 Isle of Man TT.

Instead it was left to its successor, the ZXR 750 to grab all the glory. The prototype of what was to emerge as the ZXR was actually a race-kitted GPX engine in a new chassis which the former Kawasaki GP star Kork Ballington rode in the Japanese Suzuka 8-hour race. Suzuka rules permitted bikes which conformed to Formula 1 regulations - and thus one-off frames. This machine was designated ZXR-7.

The handcrafted perimeter-style chassis was constructed from sheet aluminium folded to shape and then welded top and bottom, which not only resulted in a very rigid structure, but also enabled just the required amount of strength to be designed in at each point to minimise weight. This made the bike very labour intensive to build - only a few were ever made - which probably explains why the British importers were far from pleased when Roger Hurst, riding for Team Green UK, dropped the ZXR-7 he had been loaned for the 1988 Isle of Man TT. Actually, that machine was repaired, but then the same rider wrote it off big-time a few weeks later at Thruxton.

In late 1989 Kawasaki launched its first production ZXR 750 - the H1 - at Estoril circuit in Portugal. Although clearly a development of the GPX 750, it benefited from experience gained from the ongoing Formula 1 and endurance racing programmes.

A major step was replacing the GPX's conventional steel-tube frame with an all-aluminium perimeter assembly. This was manufactured from box-section extrusions rather than sheet, welded to aluminium castings at the steering head and swinging arm pivot. Race-track practice was clearly evident in the distinctively braced, box-section aluminium swinging arm with a bolt-on bracket at the rear to speed chain replacement, plus features such as built-in provisions for fitting a race-stand and steering damper.

Like the works F1 racer, conventional wide-diameter, cartridge style fork stanchions were used, whilst the front brakes featured semi-floating discs with 4-piston calipers - a first for Kawasaki. Yet more track influence

*During the early and mid 1990s the British Phase One endurance team, using ZXR750 machinery, was one of the few private teams able to mix it with the works boys.*

*John Reynolds became a double British Champion in 1992, taking both the National and Supercup titles on his Team Green ZXR750.*

was seen by the use of bottom-link Uni-Trak rear suspension which now featured an eccentric cam in its linkage to alter the ride height settings. The 17-inch wheels were built to take racing rubber, featuring extra wide rims and large hollow hubs and spokes to minimise unsprung weight.

Visually the ZXR750 looked every inch a race bike, too, a feeling heightened by the dramatic twin 'Hoover' tubes which ran from the front of the fairing to the fuel tank. This led, at the time, to much speculation, though in reality they were merely to duct extra-cool air onto the top end of the engine, rather than provide a ram-air effect as on the later ZZ-R 1100 for example. The engine itself was extensively uprated from the GPX, with a new top end which gave superior breathing, a higher compression ratio, bigger 36mm carbs, digital ignition and a 4-2-1 exhaust system.

For those racing in either F1 or the then fledgling SuperBike class, an engine race kit was available, whilst the factory limited its activities to the ZXR-7, which finished runner-up in the Le Mans 24 Hours that year.

In 1990, the production bike incorporated most of the engine components from the previous year's race kit. At the same time, a new cylinder head with larger ports was fitted, together with bigger carbs; a larger capacity curved radiator and a new 4-into-1 exhaust. A useful amount of weight - 5kg (11lb) - was shaved from the chassis, while the braced swinging arm was ditched in favour of a stiffer, neater item based on the factory's latest F1 racer. More track influence was to be seen in the front suspension which gained both spring loaded and damping adjustment, and the rear wheel rim grew still wider.

In that same year, 1990, Kawasaki was placed second and third at the famous French Bol d'Or, a round of the FIM World Endurance Championship with works ZXR-7s, but it was the ZXR 750 that really began to attract attention by the successes it was notching up worldwide. In the WSB (World SuperBike) racing, Rob Phillis riding for the Team Kawasaki Australia, was always up amongst the front runners that year, eventually finishing 4th overall after numerous top five placings, including most significantly wins in Australia and New Zealand. Riding for the American Team Muzzy, Doug Chandler contested just two WSB rounds and really upset the formbook. First the American won his own round (at Leguna Seca) overall to give Kawasaki their first ever WSB victory; and then he repeated his success in Japan. In fact Chandler's real task that year had been to contest the AMA (American Motorcycle Association) SuperBike Championship - securing the title with one round to go in the 8-round series.

*Kawasaki struck gold with the ZXR750 in 1993, when the American Scott Russell won the World SuperBike title. His main rival was Ducati rider Carl Fogarty, and the following year the pair reversed positions in the Championship table.*

*The Scot Brian Morrison became World Endurance Champion for Kawasaki in 1996, riding the new ZX7R, which had replaced the by now ageing ZXR. He was backed by Kawasaki France.*

By now SuperBike racing had really captured the hearts and minds of fans worldwide - and perhaps even more importantly that of the big-time sponsors and television producers. So the manufacturers responded, with Kawasaki launching not one, but two 750 class SuperSport models. Whilst the new ZXR 750 J Series was aimed squarely at the street bike rider, the K Series (coded ZXR 750 R), though fully street-legal, had a more track-biased specification, with a comprehensive race kit available to transform it into a very competitive racer. By using the twin-bike approach, Kawasaki could provide the road rider with a practical sportster, or the circuit racer with a competitive bike at a reasonable price, rather than a very expensive, limited-run bike designed purely for competition.

In fact, this was what WSB was all about. It also had the advantage for spectators who could watch over-the-counter bikes, being raced on the track. This was in stark contrast to the specialised Grand Prix 2-strokes which bore virtually no relationship to the man-in-the-street by this time.

The ZXR 750 in both road and race guises had the factory's F1 racing programme to thank for a series of innovations on the latest models from streamlining, to suspension, to perimeter frames. These comprised rails made from sheet-aluminium pressings welded top and bottom, which in turn were welded to large, hollow-section aluminium castings at the steering head and swinging arm pivots. Using the engine as a stressed member, the resulting frame provided extreme stiffness with the minimum of weight - a full 4kg (8.8lb) lighter than its predecessor. A bolt-on rear section made of square-section aluminium tubing was also featured. The swinging arm also adopted the works racer, welded sheet-aluminium style construction, while use of the upside-down (inverted) front forks complemented the frame's extra rigidity; these were of the cartridge type with 43mm stanchions (41mm on the ZXR 750J).

Not only was the engine designed to allow the camshaft to be driven from the offside end of the crankshaft rather than the centre, but by opting for a shorter stroke design - changed from the original 68 x 51.5mm to 71 x 47.3mm - thus allowing higher revs, the wider bore size brought the benefits of increased combustion and breathing efficiency. Though in different states of tune, both new bikes shared an all-new cylinder head, value train, pistons, crank and oil system. The camshaft drive redesign incorporated a lightweight individual rocker train, and all this allowed Kawasaki's design team to opt for an amazingly compact 20-degree included valve angle. There was a larger 8.7 litre (1.8 gal) air box and a less restrictive 4-into-1 exhaust. Technical differences between the two engines that altered power characteristics included carburettors, cam timing, cam duration and compression ratios.

*The new ZX family had begun with the ZX9R in 1994, then in 1995 the ZX6R made its bow. Heart of the newcomer was a 599cc (66 x 43.8mm) 4 cylinder with a pentroof combustion chamber design.*

Other changes included larger 320mm (previously 310mm) semi-floating discs at the front, and wider rims and tyres, plus F1 works pattern bodywork to the street bike having a dual stepped seat, the K ('R') version a solo hump back. The K model also featured revised cam profiles, flat-slide carburettors, close-ratio gears, uprated suspension and an aluminium fuel tank.

On the World SuperBike scene the revised machine made an instant impact. By the end of 1991, Aussie Rob Phillis was the highest placed non-Ducati rider in the series, with 3rd place in the championship. And in the FIM World Endurance series, the French Kawasaki team started the season on ZXR-7 works specials, but for the important Bol d'Or switched to the ZXR 750R - based bikes and took 1st and 3rd places. By season's end Kawasaki had claimed the top two places in the championship, what a result!

In the USA, Scott Russell won the AMA 750cc SuperSport race series with a perfect score: nine wins in nine races. Further north, in Canada, Steve Crevier won both the National 750cc Production Championship, and the Canadian Superbike title; while down under in Australia, Aaron Slight won both the Pan Pacific Superbike and Australian championships. In the prestigious Japanese TT F1 championship series, Tahahiro Sohwa scooped three rounds outright, and Michael Dowson of Australia another.

*Ian MacPherson (with Terry Rynner) contested the 1997 British SuperBike Championship. Both rode factory-kitted ZX7Rs. Later MacPherson switched to World SuperSport, where he has made a considerable impact on works ZX6Rs.*

For the 1992 model year, the ZXR 750 was virtually unchanged except for colours and graphics - although significantly the race kit included a forerunner of ram-air induction, ducting air from below the steering head to the air box and race victories simply kept on coming. Scott Russell took a big-time victory in the American Daytona 200 - with a new fastest average speed, before going on to win the AMA Superbike crown; but by then veteran Rob Phillis once again had to be content with 3rd place in WSB, but he was still the quickest on a Japanese bike. Team Kawasaki France notched up their second successive victory in the World Endurance series, whilst Britain's John Reynolds totally dominated the UK's 750cc racing, winning both the TT Superbike and televised Super Cup championships, backed by team-mate Brian Morrison. On home territory, Kawasaki scooped both 1st and 2nd places in the All-Japan TT F1 event with Tsukamoto and Kitagawa. Then came Kawasaki's big year, when Scott Russell became the first, and so far the only, Kawasaki rider to win the WSB title (otherwise it's been very much a Ducati and Honda benefit). Russell's factory ZXR 750 set such a blistering pace that even the Ducatis couldn't live with that year. In his championship year he rode in the colours of the American Muzzy-Kawasaki team, managed by the flamboyant Rob Muzzy.

Scott Russell followed up his championship year with another victory in the Daytona 200 in March 1994. But after what was generally agreed to have been one of the most fiercely contested WSB contests ever, against Ducati's new signing, Carl Fogarty, the Team Muzzy-Kawasaki rider had to relinquish his treasured number one plate, though its fate was never certain until the very last round.

After the ZXR 750 had turned in so many major title successes since its arrival five years earlier, the 1995 race season was one of mixed results for Kawasaki. Though the year had begun well with Scott Russell's Daytona victory, his departure to 500cc Grand Prix racing deprived the company of any chance of WSB success, even though Jockhim Schmidt won the German national Pro Superbike title. The second Team Muzzy rider, Aussie Anthony Gobert put up a valiant fight, but it was clear that by now the ageing ZXR had had its day. And so Kawasaki responded with the new ZX-7R for both road and track for the 1996 model year.

At the ZX-R's heart was a heavily revised 748.3cc (73 x 44.7mm) engine. This featured an improved combustion chamber shape, a stronger cylinder block, new direct actuation valve train (shim and bucket) and an increased down draught angle (50 degrees) for the carburettors. These changes, combined with a larger volume, twin ram-air intake system, resulted in superior engine response and improved mid-range power compared to the ZXR. Carburettor sizes of the

*New Zealander Simon Crafer rode the ZX7R in the 1996 World Super Bike championship as part of the American Muzzy-Kawasaki squad.*

Simon Crafer was certainly experienced having ridden in many national championship series and Grand Prix over the years.

R (coded P) street version was 38mm, whilst the RR (coded N) employed 41mm instruments, Keihin flat slide carburettors featured a smooth bore to maximise air flow; the RR's instruments featuring an accelerator pump and fuel enricher.

The lubrication system was also updated and improved, consequently providing increased reliability, particularly under rainy conditions, over the outgoing ZXR. There were also improvements (shared with the ZX-6R six-hundred) to the transmission, resulting in more positive gear changing. A curved radiator reduced the frontal area of the bike, whilst the exhaust system (4-into-2-into-1) had been designed to assist engine torque.

Improvements to the engine also brought the need for a chassis update. So the ZX-7R came with a stronger aluminium frame (on the racing RR version, the rake and trail were adjustable), whilst the suspension was given new inverted 43mm cartridge front forks and a nitrogen gas-charged rear shock; both the front and rear suspension featuring a multitude of adjustments. Although brake disc sizes remained as before, the ZX-7R benefited from the addition of 6-piston calipers up front, rather than the 4-piston assemblies found on the ZXR.

A new 6-inch rear rim for the hollow 3-spoke wheels, was provided to make use of the latest racing tyres. As before, the RR version featured a number of racing features such as a special clutch and a close ratio gear cluster.

Kawasaki again placed Rob Muzzy in charge of its WSB effort. For 1996 the squad had two riders, Gobert and New Zealander, Simon Crafer - both aboard race kitted ZX-7RRs . Crafer had been a consistent top ten finisher in the 1995 WSB series and had ended the year sixth in the points table. Crafer's consistency over Gobert's more flamboyant approach paid off, with the New Zealander finishing 7th in the 1996 championship, with Gobert back in 9th.

The big news in 1997 was that Kawasaki's WSB team would now come under new management, in the shape of the highly experienced German, Harald Eckl; a man with some twenty-two years in the Grand Prix racing world, as both a rider and a team manager. In fact, only Crafer remained from the previous year; Team Muzzy retreated to the States and AMA Superbike racing, whilst Gobert switched to the Grand Prix circuit. Crafer had as his team mate the exciting Japanese newcomer, Akira Yanagawa.

Kawasaki France endurance team at Le Mans, April 1996.

*During 1998 the dynamic Chris Walker joined the British Kawasaki team. He made an instant impact finishing runner-up in the national SuperBike title chase.*

Although Crafer soon left the team - to go back into Grand Prix racing - Yanagawa proved a useful addition to the ranks of World SuperBike and although he didn't challenge the might of Ducati or for that matter, Honda, he often put the ZX-7R at the front of the four cylinder Japanese pack. He chalked up more than one victory, his first coming in the Austrian round at the Osterreichring in August 1997.

But, as with rivals Suzuki and Yamaha, Kawasaki simply couldn't match the really big WSB boys Ducati and Honda; in fact even Honda had to pinch Ducati's v-twin format to become a real force with Colin Edwards in the saddle.

Away from SuperBikes, Kawasaki has always put up an excellent showing in endurance events, where the Japanese factory had provided the championship winning machinery on occasions; whilst in SuperSport 400 and 600 classes Kawasaki has provided a challenge to the likes of Honda, Suzuki and Yamaha.

*John Reynolds ZXR750, circa 1992.*

# Two-Stroke twins

*Standard out-of-the-crate KR1S.*

Green Meanie's first quarter-litre 2-stroke twin was the A1 roadster/A1-R racer of the mid 1960s. With the arrival of the triples later that decade the parallel twins were quietly forgotten, the company concentrating its efforts on large displacement 4-strokes for its production roadsters.

However, things changed in the early 1980s with the arrival of the liquid-cooled Suzuki RG250 Gamma and so Kawasaki took a fresh look as the possibility of producing a high performance 250cc sportster which could also be used for club racing. The result was the KR250 tandem (inline) twin, based loosely around the company's world title winning 250/350 Grand Prix bikes, ridden by the likes of Kork Ballington and Anton Mang.

Unlike the early A1/A1-R and the factory KR inline engined racers, the 1984 KR250 employed reed valve induction for its 249.1cc (54 x 54.4mm) engine. Other features of this attractive little bike were triple disc brakes, cast alloy wheels, a hi-level exhaust system, three-quarter fairing and the company's patented Uni-Trak rear suspension system. Like Suzuki's Gamma, the KR250 used an aluminium main frame and swinging arm. Although a rare sight in Europe, the KR250 sold quite well on the domestic Japanese market. Later in the decade the high performance 250-class became the most important in Japan. This resulted in a surge of new models, including the Honda NSR, Suzuki RGV, Yamaha TZR and Kawasaki KR1. Another reason was the vast numbers of Japanese who had taken up racing. By the late 1980s there some 35,000 licence holders, compared to less than 5,000 in Great Britain!

The first KR1, the B1, arrived in 1988. At its heart was an all-new 249cc (56 x 50.6mm) liquid-cooled parallel twin with crankcase reed valve induction. Running a compression ratio of 7.4:1 the KR1 B1 put out 55bhp.

The KR1 was the closest thing to a race bike that Kawasaki had ever offered customers in a series production roadster. However, although fully street legal, this was very much a track orientated bike. Technical features abounded; exhaust power valves, a cassette-type 6-speed gearbox, box-section aluminium frame and swinging arm, adjustable 41mm stanchion front fork, semi-floating 247mm front discs with dual piston calipers, fully floating rear caliper, wide hollow-spoke wheels and low-profile radial tyres.

There were twin 28mm crescent-slide carburettors, and to keep the engine's low-end and mid-range as flexible as possible there was the newly created KIPS (Kawasaki Integrated Power-valve System). Briefly this was controlled by a miniature computer and servomotors, the KIPS operated with maximum precision to produce power right through to 11,500rpm; but it is true to say that, like other high performance 250 2-strokes, the best power was generated at the top end of the scale.

Factory sources claimed 131mph and a standing start 200 metre (1/8 mile) in 12.5 seconds. The KR1 was an immediate success both in the showroom and race circuit - the latter soon to witness the arrival of the popular SuperSport 400 class (open to 250 2-strokes and 400cc 4-strokes).

The first KR1 to be exported in any numbers was the B2 of 1989. This had several changes compared with the B1; a new frame giving increased rigidity of the steering head and swinging arm pivot, the size of the box-sectioned aluminium beams, front cross beam, and seat rails were increased for additional strength, gussets had been added to strengthen

*Club racer Andy Knowles in the process of enjoying his 40th birthday - by putting in some 44 laps at Mallory Park on the Team Green (British importers bike) KR1S, May 1990...*

... and in the Mallory Park paddock with some of his friends.

the swinging arm, whilst bosses for steering damper and a paddock stand adopted. Performance and power output of the engine remained unchanged.

By the end of 1989 the KR1 was firmly established around the world, no more so than in Great Britain where of the final round of the national SuperSport 400 series held at Brands Hatch, KR1s filled seven of the top ten positions, with John Reynolds setting a new class lap record for the Indy circuit of 50.8 seconds, on his way to clinching his fourth successive victory and being placed 2nd overall in the championship behind fellow KR1 ride Ian McConnachie. If all of this sounds good enough to leave things alone, everyone was caught napping when Kawasaki kept up the pressure on its rivals with an even more potent version, the KR1S, for the 1990 model year.

Although never short of horsepower, the KR1S nonetheless had gained an additional 5bhp, which it developed at the same engine revolutions. This improvement had been achieved by revised porting, a new exhaust system which included different expansion chambers and aluminium (rather than steel) bodied mufflers, and new pistons. Another bonus was that the mufflers and exhaust pipes were no longer a single unit: in the event of damage, the silencers could be replaced separately. The KIPS was retained but with modified porting to boost top end torque without sacrificing middle or bottom end output. The microcomputer-controlled ignition was also modified to provide a faster throttle response throughout the new rev range.

Whilst the wall thickness of the twin spar aluminium frame remained unchanged, the cross section had been modified to provide increased rigidity - the smoother finish being another feature of the KR1S compared to its forerunner. The front cross brace was increased in size, and the cross section of the swinging arm was changed to increase torsional rigidity and welded gussets added to provide extra strength. The length of the swinging arm was increased by 10mm to allow the fitment of a wider tyre (140/60 R18) and the outer diameter of the pivot spindle increased from 17 to 20mm.

Other changes included new chain adjusters, shortened front forks, a nitrogen charged alloy-bodied rear shock with remote reservoir and revised spring rates, larger (300mm) and thicker front brake discs, rear brake given a dual piston caliper, 5-spoke (in place of 3-spoke) alloy wheels, wider and lower profile tyres and revised cosmetics.

Throughout 1990 the KR1S continued to be the machine to beat in the hotly contested SS 400 class. But in 1991 Suzuki uprated its RGV250 v-twin. Sold as the M series, this at last proved the equal of the Kawasaki parallel twin. By 1992 results had swung firmly in Suzuki's favour; to mention nothing of a new breed of very fast four cylinder 400 4-strokes. Almost overnight as it seemed the KR1 and KR1S slipped back down the field to become also rans. Sadly Kawasaki chose not to respond, the result being a rapid decline in numbers sold - and race results.

A competitor working on his KR1S at Cadwell Park, April 1991.

# Suzuki - the classic years

# 6

*18-year-old Guy Etherington with the JBR (Jim Blomley Racing) ex Barry Sheene Heron Suzuki TR750 at Mallory Park, spring 1999...*

*...and in the pits later that year at the Post TT meeting at the same circuit.*

Like rivals Honda and Yamaha, Suzuki built and raced quite a few over-the-counter racers and production-based works machines over the years. The first such effort was the TR50 of 1963. This was very loosely based on the disc-valve RM62 works single of 1962, but as will be revealed, Suzuki missed a golden opportunity to pass on its Grand Prix success to the paying customer.

The 49.48cc (41 x 37.5mm) single-cylinder TR50 used conventional piston-port induction and was claimed to produce 8.5bhp at 11,000rpm. The sandcast crankcases were split horizontally and contained a diminutive crankshaft and six-speed gearbox. One of the most unusual aspects of the whole machine was the ignition system - a half-engine speed magneto running off the top of the clutch primary drive gear, firing twice per revolution and supplying a high-tension coil mounted under the 5.3 litre (1.75 gallon) fuel tank. Another interesting feature was the gearchange shaft, which was splined at both ends, allowing the choice of right- or left-foot gear operation.

The aluminium cylinder barrel was fitted with a cast-iron liner, but unusually no oversize pistons were available. There were a couple of micro-size pistons offered to compensate for wear, but not oversize to enable the owner to rebore in the conventional manner.

The engine was fed by a Mikuni V22 remote-float carburettor with a massive bellmouth. The clutch was a wet multi-plate affair, which was to prove the toughest part in the engine unit.

# 1963 TR50

| | |
|---|---|
| Engine | Air-cooled single cylinder, two-stroke with piston-port induction |
| Capacity | 49.48cc |
| Bore | 41mm |
| Stroke | 37.5mm |
| Comp ratio | 9:1 |
| Carburation | Mikuni V22 |
| Ignition | Magneto |
| Gearbox | Six-speeds |
| Clutch | Wet, multi-plate |
| Frame | Steel, duplex tubular cradle construction |
| Suspension | Front: telescopic fork<br>Rear: swinging arm, twin shock |
| Brakes | Full-width aluminium drums with steel liners front and rear |
| Tyres | 18 inch front and rear |
| Dry weight | N/A |
| Max power | 8.5bhp @ 11,000rpm |
| Max speed | 90 mph |

*The TR50 engine with horizontally split crankcases, alloy head and barrel and duplex frame.*

*The very first production-based racing motorcycle offered by Suzuki was the TR50 in 1963. One of the original batch of machines is shown here. This was, unlike the works model of the era, piston port rather than disc valve. It was both unreliable and under-powered.*

*Much later, in 1967, an improved TR50 appeared. The example seen here at the Isle of Man TT that year still couldn't match the rival Honda and Kreidler machines. However, I can't help thinking it was an attractive little bike. Note large magneto and rev-counter drive to rear of cylinder.*

In fact, within only a few weeks of its release in the spring of 1963, all three of the initial batch of TR50 engines imported into Britain had to be returned to Japan. Owned by Charlie Mates, Paul Latham and Mike Simpson, they had suffered gearbox trouble and piston seizures.

Another problem was the crankshaft, with the motor being prone to con-rod breakage just below the small-end eye if over-revved. This could explain the reason for the transfer-port angle area being well below par, any modest increase in port valve/port area showing a dramatic increase in power - which was obtainable by a skilled two-stroke tuner - over the original 'factory fresh' engine specification. This increase in power was a result of raising peak torque by 1000rpm. The engine could then be revved through to 12,000rpm - but with not only the added risk of con-rod breakage, but also an increased risk of big-end failure.

The cycle parts were a strange mixture of race and road parts, the semi-duplex frame giving an air of being unfinished. The tank and seat, although looking the part, in fact, were manufactured in steel, while the front forks could be identified as being from the Suzuki 50/80 road bike of the era, with only the top yoke manufactured in aluminium. Even the brake hubs appeared to come straight from the production roadster parts bins. There was a cable operated magnetic rev-counter marked up to an optimistic 18,000rpm.

*Aluminium cylinder with shrunk-in iron liner. The piston is of the single ring variety. Matchbox gives an idea of scale.*

All this pointed to a decidedly less than perfect machine, and not surprisingly, the Suzuki never matched its chief rival, Honda's CR110. When looking at the two companies' respective Grand Prix records over the same period, it should have been the other way round!

Much later, 1967 in fact, an improved version of the TR50 appeared. This was imported into Britain in very small numbers, but again it couldn't match the Hondas. The only rider to gain any success with one was Eddie Crooks' runner, Frank Whiteway.

*6-speed gearbox and straight-cut primary drive gears of the 1967 TR50, with another box of matches.*

If the 'fifty' production racer was a distinct flop, Suzuki's next effort was the reverse. In 1966, the company had launched the highly successful T20, a 247cc (54 x 54mm) piston-port twin with quite stunning performance. Right from the start, the T20, or Super Six as it was more commonly known in Britain, dominated the production class at events such as the Brands Hatch 500-mile race. The natural progression from this was undoubtably a pukka racing version. Suzuki responded by building the TR250 and X6. The former was expressly a European machine intended to match Yamaha's TD1C. Unfortunately, although it was an excellent machine, its 1968 launch was too late, as Yamaha was not only fully established, but shortly was to announce the all-conquering TD2. It is worth noting that the TR250 produced 35 bhp at 9000rpm, the TD2 44 at 10,500....

One of the TR250's few successes was victory in the 1968 Manx Grand Prix, ridden by that man Whiteway. Then the TD2 appeared, and along with every other 250, the Suzuki was totally outclassed.

*Future Yamaha World Champion Rod Gould astride a TR50 minus its tank, circa 1967.*

## 1966 X6/T20 Super Six

| | |
|---|---|
| Engine | Air-cooled, piston port, parallel twin, two-stroke |
| Capacity | 247.34cc |
| Bore | 54mm |
| Stroke | 54mm |
| Comp ratio | 7.61:1 |
| Carburation | 2 x Mikuni VM26 (1967 VM27) |
| Ignition | Magneto |
| Gearbox | Six-speeds |
| Clutch | Wet, multi-plate |
| Frame | steel, duplex tubular cradle construction |
| Suspension | Front: telescopic<br>Rear: swinging arm, twin shock |
| Brakes | Front: single-sided 2LS drum<br>Rear: single-sided 5LS drum |
| Tyres | 2.75 x 18 front; 3.00 x 18 rear |
| Dry weight | 260lb (118kg) |
| Max power | 33bhp @ 10,500rpm |
| Max speed | 118mph |

*This photograph shows the American market X6. As described in text, it predated the TR250 by several months and was specially created for America. The X6's debut came at Daytona on the 26th March 1966, with Dick Hammer finishing runner-up in the 250cc. race With a pair of VM26 Mikuni carbs and a 7.61:1 compression ratio, the X6 produced 33bhp at 10,500rpm.*

*The T20 Super Six (so named, because of its 6-speed gearbox) was together with the Italian Ducati Mach 1, the fastest road going 250 of its day. Like the Italian bike it was successfully raced as both a production and open class machine. The three Suzuki factory riders of the Grand Prix bikes rode this trio of T20s at Brands Hatch in the spring of 1966, left to right: Hans Georg Ansheidt, Frank Perris and Hugh Anderson.*

*Several dealers including Crooks, Monty and Thompson built their own racing versions of the standard T20. This is the Thompson version. Specification included lightly tuned engine, a Brealey-Smith seat and fairing, aluminium fuel tank, alloy rims and front mudguard, expansion chambers and Girling rear shocks.*

Across the Atlantic, things were slightly better and Suzuki got into the act quicker, the X6 appearing a couple of years earlier in 1966. Like the TR250 (and the T20 roadster), the X6 shared its square 54 x 54mm bore and stroke and 247.34cc capacity. With a pair of Mikuni VM26 carbs and 7.61:1 compression ratio, the X6 produced 33bhp at 10,500rpm. Besides its special engine bits, which included totally hand-worked pistons, with one 1.5mm piston ring located 4mm down from the top, the porting between the X6 and TR250 was completely different.

The TR250's porting was far more suited to short circuit racing than that of the X6. The TR250's exhaust port was narrower by 4mm, bridged but not T-shaped. The transfer ports were cast vertically in the cylinder and 6mm further to the rear. The TR250's inlet port was narrower by 4mm and far shallower. The result was that the X6 and TR250, although similar externally, were very different. This explains the marked difference in peak power figures of 9500rpm (TR250) and 10,500rpm (X6).

*Ignition on the TR250 was by this Kokusan racing magneto, situated at the nearside end of the crankshaft.*

Also the concepts of the two machines were different; whereas the TR250 was expressly designed as a pukka over-the-counter racer, the X6 was built to demonstrate to the Americans the durability of the standard Suzuki roadster.

*A Crooks TR250 prepared for the Isle of Man with a large main tank in aluminium, together with a small tank incorporated into the seat tail. The little square sticker on the front brake plate denotes these have been fitted with Joe Dunphy-supplied Ferodo linings, circa 1968.*

# 1967 TR250 Crooks Suzuki No 10026

*Now owned by Martyn Harris of Manchester, TR250 No 10026 on display at The Classic Motor Cycle Show Stafford, April 1999.*

TR250 No 10026 was purchased new by Barrow-in-Furness Suzuki dealer/race sponsor Eddie Crooks, from Suzuki GB in early 1968. Frank Whiteway, former Crooks employee and racer remembers assembling it from the delivery crate. It was originally loaned to Welshman Malcolm Uphill, who during the 1968 season acheived some excellent British short circuit results including 4th Brands Hatch, 2nd Croft, 3rd Crystal Palace and 6th Snetterton. But the highlight was probably finishing 5th in a star-studded field at the Ulster Grand Prix that year. In a line-up which included Read and Ivy (Yamaha fours), Robb and Molloy (Bultacos), Cooper and Grotefield (Padgett Yamahas) and Rosner and Braun (MZs), this was an impressive performance. Malcolm Uphill recalls, 'After racing the big 500 Manx Norton we would start the Suzuki by spinning the rear wheel and warm it up, childs play. I thought the TR250 was a great little machine.'

In 1969 Eddie Johnson of Newcastle upon Tyne purchased the TR250 from Eddie Crooks. One of the few changes he made to the bike was to fit a different swinging-arm, replacing the standard T20 Super Six derived item. This swinging-arm remains on the bike to this day. During 1969 Eddie had some good results, including 6th at the Race of the Year at Mallory Park, 3rd in the Scarborough Gold Cup and 8th in the Ulster Grand Prix. But entered as a 254cc, the machine retired in the Junior TT.

Eddie Johnson retired from racing in 1970. The bike was then raced by Cumbrian Peter Berwick, who finished 6th in the North West 200 (128.6mph through the *Motor Cycle News* speed trap) and 9th in the Ulster Grand Prix. Berwick remarked, 'The 6-speed gearbox of the TR250 Suzuki makes it an ideal machine for the long haul races.'

*Martyn Harris has made a magnificent job of restoring the ex Crooks Suzuki TR250.*

*Photograph showing the Kokusan racing magneto and pair of Mikuni VM 29mm carburettors with sand-cast remote float bowls.*

Eddie Johnson then loaned the machine to Jackie Armstrong for 1971 and 1972. Jackie recalls having to rebuild the Suzuki before racing it. He also remembers racing at Scarborough against the latest Yamahas and did very well until a strange misfire started, with each lap it got worse, until it started to shake badly going into the Hairpin. He was then forced to stop to discover that the frame had broken beneath the rear engine mount. The make-do repair weld is still there today.

Jackie Armstrong returned the machine to Eddie Johnson. It then went back to Eddie Crooks, before being purchased by Peter Berwick. Parts of the bike were then used over the years by Berwick and his rider Bob Jackson during the 1980s in classic racing events, before it was sold on again, this time to a collector.

Martyn Harris then came onto the scene, 'I swopped my Yamaha TDIC for the TR250 in the 1990s and stripped it down completely.' But a major rebuild was found necessary as a lot was needed to restore it to original safe working order. For example the brake plates were warped, but after much effort 10026 was finally taken out at the Post TT at Mallory Park in 2002. So enthusiasts were able to share in Martyn's delight when it fired up. And just as his hero, the late great Malcolm Uphill had said, it was possible to start on the stand with one throw of the back wheel.

*Eddie Johnson of Newcastle-upon-Tyne purchased a TR250 No 10026 from Eddie Crooks in early 1969. He fitted a different swinging arm from the T20 Super Six derived item. The machine retains this to the present day.*

*Welshman Malcolm Uphill rode the Crooks Suzuki TR250 No 10026 in the 1968 Ulster Grand Prix (25) and finished 5th. Also in the picture are John Cooper Yamaha TD1C (16) and Dieter Braun (40) works MZ twin.*

*Englishman Ron Grant (American Suzuki team) at Daytona in 1969. The 1969 TR250 was much improved, but never came to the UK.*

*A TR250 with the fairing removed showing details such as the remote float chamber Mikuni carburettors, full cradle duplex frame, exhaust, brakes (a double sided SLS affair at the front) and hydraulic steering damper.*

## 1968 TR250

| | |
|---|---|
| Engine | Air-cooled, piston port, parallel twin, two-stroke |
| Capacity | 247.34cc |
| Bore | 54mm |
| Stroke | 54mm |
| Comp ratio | 7:1.1 |
| Carburation | 2 x Mikuni VM29 |
| Ignition | Kokusun magneto |
| Gearbox | Six-speeds |
| Clutch | Wet, multi-plate |
| Frame | Steel, duplex tubular cradle construction |
| Suspension | Front: telescopic fork<br>Rear: swinging arm, twin shock |
| Brakes | Front: double-sided, 2LS drum<br>Rear: single-sided 5LS drum |
| Tyres | 2.75 x 18 front and rear |
| Dry weight | 253lb (115kg) |
| Max power | 35bhp @ 9000rpm |
| Max speed | 117mph |

*Kings Lynn rider Tony Collison with his beautifully prepared homegrown T20, negotiating the old hairpin at Snetterton, 1971.*

The X6's race debut came at Daytona on 20 March 1966 when Dick Hammer finished second in the 250cc race. Other major placings included Indianapolis where Ron Grant was second and Hammer third, and finally Carlsbad, where Mann came home second, followed by Grant in third and Hammer eighth.

After these initial successes, the X6 was found wanting, and after a poor season in 1967, the American arm of Suzuki switched its efforts to the newer and faster TR250. Unlike Europe, which only took the TR250 in 1968 and 1969, the States also saw the greatly improved 1970 version. This featured a much reworked engine with improved porting, higher 7.03:1 compression ratio and larger Mikuni VM30 carbs. The result was an increase of 6bhp, to 41bhp, at the same 9500rpm engine speed. Maximum speed on optimum gearing went up from 117 to 122mph, and dry weight decreased from 115kg (253lb) to 113kg (248lb). Another improvement was the use of a much larger and more powerful four-leading-shoe front brake of Italian origin.

*Eddie Crooks' racing equipe riders reunited at the Manx Grand Prix Riders Evening, Gloucester, 1998. Left to right, Les Trotter, Eddie Crooks, Malcolm Uphill and Frank Whiteway.*

However, with all these improvements, and riders of the calibre of Grant and Nicolas, Suzuki still could not match Yamaha, and 1970 was the TR250's final year.

In addition to the factory's production-based racers, privateers the world over used the T20 Super Six, and later T250, as bases for their own Suzuki road racers. In Britain, several dealers produced machines both for their own sponsored riders and for sale to the public. Typical of these was that of Harrogate Suzuki specialist Harry Thompson.

*Ulster Grand Prix, 1968. Brian Farmer, Malcolm Uphill's driver and friend with the TR250 now owned by Martyn Harris.*

Thompson had created something of a stir when his rider, Barry Smith, had ridden an almost standard T20 - complete with silencers - into twelfth place in the 1966 Lightweight TT at an average speed of 82.88mph. This success encouraged Thompson to build a full racing version.

To prepare a stock bike for racing, the Yorkshire dealer stripped out the electrics, fitted 11:1 high compression heads, bored out the 24mm Mikuni carburettors by 2mm and blended the inlet ports to suit. In addition, the following components were fitted; Borrani alloy rims, expansion chambers, Dunlop triangular tyres, and cosmetic details such as tank, seat, fairing and mudguards.

*Tony Collison's T20 racer with the fairing off at Jurby Airfield late August 1971. Note period Bedford (Vauxhall) race transport - no motor homes in sight!*

When tested by *Motor Cycling* in the 18th March 1967 issue, the Thompson Suzuki went through the speed trap on the Silverstone club circuit at 102.9mph. Maximum power was claimed to be 33bhp at 8500rpm. But again, sales were restricted by the much faster Yamahas, in this case the TD1C.

*Malcolm Uphill.*

Next on the list of Suzuki production-based racing models came the 500 twin. This was centred around a 492cc piston-ported two-stroke twin with bore and stroke dimensions of 70 x 64mm. In road trim, this offered 46 bhp at 7000rpm. From its overall appearance, the engine was clearly based on the T20/T250, but nevertheless differed from the smaller unit in many details.

The bottom end of the new half-litre twin was almost a carbon copy of the 250, with needle bearings for both the big-end and small-ends, three main bearings and four crankshaft seals. On the roadster, the alternator was situated on the left with the points outside and the helical-geared primary drive on the right. Unlike the smaller engine, the newcomer only used five gears and the gearbox was different.

Top-end details included cylinders and heads in light alloy, the former having replacement cast-iron liners, the cylinder-head gaskets were made of aluminium. The method of changing the heads and barrels differed from the 250 and there were additional bolts to provide extra strength. Each exhaust-pipe attachment ring was held by two bolts, and the exhaust pipes were secured by sliding them into the long and heavily muffled silencer. In standard trim, the 500 could top 110mph.

*Roy Simmonds riding the Vic Bates T250 Hustler (which superseded the T20 Super Six) in the 1971 250cc Production TT; he finished 7th.*

# 1970 TR500 (XR05)

| | |
|---|---|
| Engine | Air-cooled, piston-port, parallel twin, two-stroke |
| Capacity | 492.6cc |
| Bore | 70mm |
| Stroke | 64mm |
| Comp ratio | 7.34:1 |
| Carburation | 2 x Mikuni VM34 SC |
| Ignition | Kokusun magneto |
| Gearbox | Five-speeds |
| Clutch | Wet, multi-plate |
| Frame | Steel, duplex tubular cradle construction |
| Suspension | Front: Ceriani 36mm coil-sprung telescopic fork<br>Rear: swinging arm, twin shock |
| Brakes | Front: Ceriani 9 inch double-sided 2LS drum<br>Rear: Ceriani 8 inch single-sided 2LS drum |
| Tyres | 3.00 x 18 front; 3.50 x 18 rear |
| Dry weight | 298lb (135.5kg) |
| Max power | 70.5bhp @ 8000rpm |
| Max speed | 152mph |

*In 1968 Suzuki introduced its first TR500 (coded XR05). This produced 63.5bhp and could reach 135mph. Specification included Kokusan magneto, Mikuni 32mm carbs, close ratio gears, revised porting, Fontana 4LS front brake and Ceriani front forks. This 1970 version had larger 34mm carbs and 70.5bhp, maximum speed 152mph.*

Ron Grant with his TR500 (XR05) at Daytona in March 1970. He led the 200-miler for several laps before running out of petrol and seizing a piston as he tried to nurse the bike back to the pits.

The first production 500 twins reached Britain in late 1967, having gone on sale in America earlier that year. The Stateside name, Titan, was not used in Britain because the leading customisers of the period, Read Titan of Leytonstone, had already registered the name. Hence the Titan became the Cobra for Britain. In service, it proved itself robust and reliable, these features proving extremely important in its future role as a racing motorcycle.

*Eddie Crooks (extreme left holding bike number 20) at the TT in the early 1970s with a pair of Seeley-framed 500cc Suzuki twins.*

Suzuki realised its potential and in 1968 introduced its first TR500 (code-named XR05). This produced 63.5bhp at 8000rpm and was capable of 135mph. Other changes from the roadster specification included a Kokusan magneto, Mikuni VM32SC carbs, 7.2:1 compression ratio pistons, closer-ratio gears, different porting, Fontana drum brakes (double-sided at the front), a full duplex frame, Ceriani suspension and a dry weight of 135kg (297lb).

At Daytona, on 17th March 1968, works riders Ron Grant and Mitsuo Itoh finished fifth and ninth respectively.

For 1969, more tuning look place, raising the power output to 64.5bhp. Art Baumann responded by taking the TR500 to its first US National Championship victory at Sears Point on 7th September that year.

For 1970, larger VM34 carbs were fitted, the compression bumped up to 7.34:1 and the power boosted to 70.5bhp - still at the 5000rpm bloodline. Ceriani replaced Fontana in the braking department. The maximum speed rose to 152mph. Highlight of the year was Grant's victory

*The air-cooled T350 twin cylinder street bike was built between 1969 and 1973. This 1972 example has a Terry Shepherd water-cooled top end. Note that the carburettors have been removed. It was very much a poor man's TZ.*

# 1972 Seeley-Suzuki TR250

Built by Barrow-in-Furness based Crooks Suzuki in collaboration with Colin Seeley, the chassis of this unique machine was actually a modified Yamsel assembly.

It was built with success in the 1972 Manx Grand Prix in mind. For this event the Crooks team had at its disposal the very experienced Les Trotter. The plan was that Les would win the Manx Grand Prix and on the back of that success the Crooks/Seeley would be built in small numbers for sale to the general public.

However, two problems conspired against this happening. The first was that Les Trotter only managed to come home 7th. This was not helped by the fact that the team needed 6 gallons of fuel to enable the bike to complete the 4-lap 150.92mile race non-stop. But as Les recalled recently, 'The bike was just too top heavy for the first 3-laps.'

The Crooks-Seeley TR250 was also ridden at selected short circuit meetings by Keith Martin, and at the TT and Southern 100 by Roger Sutcliffe.

But what really damaged the project was the announcement at the end of 1972 of the new Yamaha TD3, which produced 44bhp and thus made the TR250 obsolete overnight.

*The 1972 Seeley-Suzuki TR250 as it is today. Except for exhaust, silencers and rear shocks, almost back to original spec; now owned by Dave Evans.*

## 1972 TR750 (XR11)

| | |
|---|---|
| Engine | Water-cooled across-the-frame 3-cylinder two-stroke with piston-port induction |
| Capacity | 738.9cc |
| Bore | 70mm |
| Stroke | 64mm |
| Comp ratio | 7:1 |
| Carburation | 3 x Mikuni VM34SC * |
| Ignition | Nippon-Denso CDI magneto |
| Gearbox | Five-speeds |
| Clutch | Dry, multi-plate |
| Frame | Steel, duplex tubular construction |
| Suspension | Front: telescopic fork<br>Rear: swinging arm, twin shock |
| Brakes | Front: twin hydraulically-operated 270mm discs with twin piston calipers<br>Rear: single hydraulically operated 250mm disc with twin piston caliper |
| Tyres | 3.25 x 18 front; 3.50 x 18 rear |
| Dry weight | 367lb (167kg) |
| Max power | 100bhp @ 8000rpm |
| Max speed | 170mph |

* 32mm instruments used at Daytona only

*Details of Barry Sheene's Suzuki GB TR750 with which he garnered so much success in 1973, ending the season with the coveted MotorCycle News Man of the Year award.*

*Easter 1972 and the American TR750s come to Britain to do battle in the Transatlantic Match races.*

*The Suzuki team at Daytona in 1972 with the new TR750 (XR11) 750 liquid-cooled triples. Left to right, Don Grant, Art Baumann and Jody Nicolas. Baumann qualified fastest at 171.75mph - a new course record - but in the race, tyre and clutch problems sidelined his entire squad.*

Barry Sheene on the 1972 Difazio T500 racer. It featured hub steering and a pair of 10 inch disc brakes with Lockheed calipers. There were also touring and sport versions, manufactured by this Frome, Somerset-based dealer.

in the US Grand Prix with power raised yet again to 71.5bhp, resulting in 2mph extra at the top end. Besides the Stateside team of Nicolas, Baumann, Grant and Pierce, the TR500 made its European debut, culminating in Suzuki taking second place in the manufacturers' class of the 1971 500cc World Championship series. The leading riders were Rob Bron, Jack Findlay and Keith Turner. In addition, Frank Perris, the former Suzuki factory rider, campaigned a Seeley-framed TR500, gaining a third place in the 1971 Senior TT.

The 1971 individual 500cc World Series results were Turner second, Bron third, Findlay fifth and Perris eleventh. Findlay had the honour of scoring Suzuki's first ever 500 Grand Prix win in the 1971 Ulster. His machine was tuned by Daniele Fontana.

Findlay had switched to two-stroke power after many years of riding four-strokes. His choice was between two roadster-based units - Kawasaki's three-cylinder H1-R (see Chapter 8) or the TR500. He chose the Suzuki, 'Because it was lighter, more compact, less complicated and produced peak power at lower rpm.'

In 1972, the TR500 became the TR500II, although the specification remained the same. Then, in 1973, it was changed again, this time to the TK500III, but at least the specification was updated. The most important

Barry Sheene with one of the Suzukis he raced for the British importers, Heron. Here Sheene talks to his mechanic Don McKay (left), whilst team manager Rex White looks on, Spring 1973.

*Barry Sheene cresting Cadwell Park's Mountain aboard his Suzuki Great Britain TR750 with which he garnered so much success in 1973, ending the season with the coveted MotorCycle News Man of the Year Award.*

changes were the addition of watercooling and triple disc brakes. More tuning, including larger 36mm carbs, took the power output up to 73bhp and maximum speed to 157mph. In addition, some of the special works engines had six-speed transmissions for the first time.

Two TR500 riders did well in Europe - Findlay and the Italian Guido Mandracchi.

Suzuki, however, were not the first to watercool their 500 twin. Instead, this honour went to the British Hi-Tac team, run by Peter Inchley and Frank Higley, in late 1971. Hi-Tac used a T500 roadster crankcase assembly, a jacketed, light-alloy cylinder block, 14:1 heads, a close-ratio, five-speed gear cluster, and electronic ignition. Barry Sheene was involved in much of the early testing, the engine being fitted into a Seeley chassis. It is worth remembering that Sheene already had close links with the Japanese marque, having just finished second in the 1971 125cc World Championship

*The 1973 Suzuki Great Britain team, left to right, Don McKay (mechanic), Barry Sheene, Rex White (team manager), Dave Hall (mechanic), and Stan Woods. Numbers 1 and 31 are 500 twins, 3 is a 750 triple.*

series on his ex-works Suzuki twin. The same year, Sheene had ridden a TR500-engined Seeley machine with considerable success.

For the 1972 Daytona 200, Suzuki built the TR750 (XRll) - nicknamed the 'flexy flier'. This 738.9cc (70 x 64mm) watercooled, three-cylinder, piston-port two-stroke was derived directly from its largest production model, the GT750. Like the roadster, the TR750 had a five-speed gearbox. It also had triple hydraulic disc brakes. With 100bhp and over 175mph, the TR750 looked like the toughest opposition to the Hondas, Harleys and Kawasakis. Riders were Grant, Baumann, Nicolas and Perry.

*Barry Sheene and Stan Woods, Spring 1973.*

Baumann qualified at 171.75mph - a new record and the first 170mph arerage around the Daytona speed bowl. There was no doubt that the new Suzukis were the quickest machines at Daytona that year.

Unfortunately, speed is not everything and the team was hit by a series of problems; tyres throwing their treads, clutches which burnt out quickly, and even magneto troubles. The result was that every single TR750 was forced to retire from the race, and a Yamaha TR3, ridden privately by Don Emde, emerged as the winner. It

*Barry Sheene at a very wet Brands Hatch meeting with his TR750 in October 1973.*

*Sheene celebrates his 1973 success with a smile. The stars on his fairing were given to him by the Shell Oil Company, via the author's friend, race chief Keith Callow, in recognition of each of his race victories on the Suzuki that year.*

was not just Suzuki who struck trouble, however, as the Harley and Kawasaki works teams had failed en masse.

Jody Nicolas was to score the TR750's only victory in 1972, when he won at Atlanta on 16th April. The year 1973 saw Sheene rejoin Suzuki GB, with Stan Woods as team-mate. Woods received a brand new TR750, while an ex-American TR750 engine was provided for Sheene for fitting into a Seeley chassis. Early-season results were disappointing, however, with Sheene retiring more often than not.

A number of TR500 III engines had also been provided, and it was with one of these, again fitted into a Seeley frame, that Sheene made his debut in the 500cc World Series at Imatra, Finland. After holding fourth place, he was eventually forced out when a piston seizure resulted in a broken con-rod. After that, things improved, with Sheene taking both the FIMs F750 Cup Series (in effect, the 750 World Championship) and the top British

Hi-Tac Engineering produced water-cooled conversion kits for engines such as the Yamaha TD2/TR2, TD3/TR3 and Suzuki T500. One of these Suzukis is seen here housed in a Seeley chassis at the Isle of Man TT, circa 1973.

MCN Superbike Championship. It was during this period that he had shown the form which was to make him a double world champion.

Meanwhile, Jack Findlay had won the 1973 Senior TT with his TR500III and finished the year in fifth spot in the 500cc championship. The Italian Guido Mandracchi was 14th.

Besides Sheene's success, TR750 riders largely dominated the F750 rounds, with Findlay third, Woods fourth, Mandracchi fifth and Smart seventh.

Across the Atlantic, Emde had brought his TR750 home seventh at Daytona - the highest placed Suzuki - while Smart had won at Dallas, and Perry at Atlanta.

Racing TR750 conversion to reed valve induction by Bernard Hargreaves' Harpowa concern.

*The racing TR750 engine. In this guise the Suzuki triple had 15 degrees of down draught and heat insulating spacers for the carbs. Discarding the street bike GT750's alternator, contact breakers and electric start motor enabled the crankshaft to be shortened at either end. Note the power take-off gear between the middle and offside flywheel assemblies.*

1973 had seen several British dealers offer race-kitted examples of the new GT250 roadster. Among the most successful of these were those built by Geoff Monty and Roy Baldwin. These were intended purely as clubmans-type machines for those new to the sport.

The following year saw the introduction of the new four-cylinder RG500 (XR14). Its story at championship level is recorded in Japanese Grand Prix Racing Motorcyles (Redline Books) but replicas were not released for sale to private customers until two years later in 1976. By then, both the twin-cylinder TR500 and three-cylinder TR750 had been deleted. Their last year of manufacture was 1975, when the TR500 produced 80bhp at 8900 rpm, the six-speed, watercooled engine being capable of propelling the bike at almost 160mph; the TR750, also with six gears, pumped out 116bhp at 8250rpm and 180mph.

It is worth noting that the larger machine was campaigned into 1976 when, as part of the official Suzuki GB team, John Williams won the Classic TT (formally the F750), setting a new lap record at 110.21mph for the class. His team-mate, Barry Sheene also won the MCN Superbike Series. Finally, the third member of the Suzuki GB squad, John Newbold, took third spot in the FIM F750 Cup Series.

*Dutchman Piet Hogervorst and his Crooks-Suzuki T500, circa 1973. Hogervorst rode this and other Suzukis in the important long distance races of the day, such as the Barcelona 24 Hours and Thruxton 500 Mile marathon.*

## 1973 TR500 III (XR05)

| | |
|---|---|
| Engine | Water-cooled, piston-port, parallel twin, two-stroke |
| Capacity | 492.6cc |
| Bore & Stroke | 70 x 64mm |
| Comp ratio | 7:1 |
| Carburation | 2 x Mikuni VM36SS |
| Ignition | Kokusan PEI magneto |
| Gearbox | * Five-speeds |
| Clutch | Dry, multi-plate |
| Frame | Steel, duplex tubular cradle construction |
| Suspension | Front: telescopic fork<br>Rear: swinging arm, twin shock |
| Brakes | Front: twin hydraulically-operated 270mm discs with twin piston calipers<br>Rear: single hydraulically-operated 250mm disc with twin piston caliper |
| Tyres | 3.25 x 18 front; 3.50 x 18 rear |
| Dry weight | 308lb (140kg) |
| Max power | 73bhp @ 8000rpm |
| Max speed | 157mph |

* Six-speeds also available

*Findlay negotiating Ramsey Hairpin during his winning ride on the 500 Suzuki twin during the 1973 Senior TT. His average speed for the 6 lap, 226.8 mile race was 101.5mph.*

*Jack Findlay (centre) with Paul Smart (right) in 1973.*

*The popular Australian Jack Findlay realised a lifetime ambition when he took his TR500 to victory in the 1973 Senior TT. He is pictured here at Quarter Bridge.*

*John Player Grand Prix, Silverstone 1974. Winner Paul Smart set a new lap record of 107.74mph on his Suzuki TR750.*

*Jack Findlay, John Player Grand Prix, Silverstone 1974, finished 5th on his Suzuki TR500.*

## 1974 TR500 III (XR05)

| | |
|---|---|
| Engine | Water-cooled, piston-port, parallel twin, two-stroke |
| Capacity | 492.6cc |
| Bore & Stroke | 70 x 64mm |
| Comp ratio | 7.4:1 |
| Carburation | 2 x Mikuni VM38 SS |
| Ignition | Kokusan PEI magneto |
| Gearbox | Six-speeds |
| Clutch | Dry, multi-plate |
| Frame | steel, duplex tubular cradle construction |
| Suspension | Front: telescopic fork<br>Rear: swinging arm, laid-down twin shock |
| Brakes | Front: twin hydraulically-operated 270mm discs with twin piston calipers<br>Rear: single hydraulically-operated 250mm disc with twin piston caliper |
| Tyres | 3.25 x 18 front; 3.50 x 18 rear |
| Dry weight | 308lb (140kg) |
| Max power | 80bhp @ 8900rpm |
| Max speed | 160mph |

*Gary Nixon was a top star for Suzuki on the other side of the Atlantic in 1974.*

*George Fogarty (father of Carl) with his double disc braked T500 (95) takes the inside line from Honda CB400F-mounted Neil Tuxworth (later to become manager of the Castrol-Honda World SuperBike Team) at Becketts, Silverstone, circa 1976.*

*Paul Smart, Barry Sheene's brother-in-law (Paul being married to Barry's sister Maggie) also rode a TR750...*

With the appearance of the RG500 at privateer level, racing took as big a leap forward in the 500cc category, as it had done in the 250/350 classes when the Yamaha TD/TR twins had appeared a few years earlier. Like the Yamahas, the RG500 was so much faster than anything else on the circuit, that overnight it simply took over the class which for so long had been dominated by the British four stroke singles. With over 100bhp on tap, the output of the production RG500 was double that of either a Manx Norton or Seeley G50! The RG500 soon built up an enviable reputation and was to remain in production throughout the late 1970s and into the 1980s, the RG500's development history is contained in the following chapter.

Besides building its two-strokes, Suzuki also moved into the four-stroke world, in both production roadsters and racing machines.

The debut of the GS750 four came at the end of 1976 and, together with the smaller GS400 twin, it represented the first of the modern Suzuki four-strokes. By the standards of the day (Honda later replied with their equally fast CB750F2), the maximum speed of the GS750 was a revelation. Clocked at a mean two-way speed of 124.3mph, it was the fastest 750cc production roadster on the market at the time of its launch. Acceleration was no less stunning, with 60mph from rest in under four seconds, and 100mph coming up in under 13 seconds. This, together with its safe handling and excellent braking, led several riders to enter it in production races. Later, the improved GS1000, GSX750/1100 and other Suzuki four-stroke models appeared on the scene to retain the factory's lead in both sports machine racing and on the dragstrip.

*... he is seen here on the fearsome 175mph missile, winning the FIM F750 round at Brands Hatch in August 1974.*

## 1975 TR750 (XR11)

| | |
|---|---|
| Engine | Water-cooled, across-the-frame, 3-cylinder, two-stroke with piston-port induction |
| Capacity | 738.9cc |
| Bore & Stroke | 70 x 64mm |
| Comp ratio | 7.4:1 |
| Carburation | 3 x Mikuni VM38 SS |
| Ignition | Nippon-Denso CDI magneto |
| Gearbox | Six-speeds |
| Clutch | Dry, multi-plate |
| Frame | steel, duplex tubular construction |
| Suspension | Front: Kayaba coil-sprung telescopic fork<br>Rear: Kayaba twin shock, with aluminium swinging arm |
| Brakes | Front: twin floating 270mm discs with twin piston calipers<br>Rear: single ventilated 250mm disc with twin piston caliper |
| Tyres | 18 inch front and rear |
| Dry weight | 326lb (148kg) |
| Max power | 116bhp @ 8250rpm |
| Max speed | 180mph |

*The rear end of the 1975 TR750, with massive square section swinging arm and inclined twin rear shock absorbers.*

*Sheene rode a TR750 like this when world championship duties allowed in 1975 and 1976.*

*The Finn Tepi Lansivouri at Chapel Curve during the Formula 750 at Silverstone, August 1976.*

Another area in which the four-strokes from Hamamatsu made their mark was the popular single-cylinder class, first with the 370 and later with the 400 models. These were largely the idea of dealer/race entrant Vic Camp who, for many years, had specialised in Italian Ducati machinery. In 1976, however, Camp had fallen out with the British Ducati importers, Coburn and Hughes, and switched his allegiance to Suzuki. Vic Camp's first clubmans racing effort was the TS250 two-stroke, followed by the SP370 four-stroke. After Camp retired in 1979, the Suzuki single-cylinder racers were continued by fellow North London dealer Alf Hagon, who went on to offer the larger SP400 version, before finally switching his attention to the Honda XBR500 single.

Therefore, Suzuki can claim to have catered for the privateer racer down through the years, although it must be said that some of its offerings were more successful than others - and in many cases, the creator of the 'racer' was not the factory, but a dealer or gifted tuner working from home.

*The GS1000 was top dog in British Production bike racing in 1979. It was a powerful big motorcycle as this Brands Hatch photograph from that year shows.*

# Suzuki - the modern years

# 7

Gary Walker taking part in the British Championship Super Teen series over the Oulton Park Grand Prix circuit, May 1993. The bike is a 1991 RGV250M.

During the late 1970s Suzuki racing most definitely hinged around the famous RG500 square four two-stroke. This trend continued as the 1980s dawned. However, back at the end of 1976 Suzuki had introduced its first modern four-strokes, the GS400 twin and GS750 four. These were air-cooled and even though they were series production roadsters, both engines showed the way forward, with their shorter-stroke and double overhead camshafts. Smooth power delivery and higher engine revolutions were also notable features. All this, combined with engineering standards of design, promised greater durability thanks to ball and roller bearings instead of plain bearings for the built-up crankshaft assemblies, whilst concerns about exhaust and other emissions were looked after by an innovative recycling device. The GS750, with a genuine top speed of 125mph and probably the best handling of any Japanese four cylinder model at that time, meant that Suzuki was being taken seriously in the four-stroke stakes. The 749cc (65 x 56.4mm) engine ran a compression ratio of 8.7:1 and a quartet of 24mm Mikuni carburettors provided 68bhp and 44lb/ft of torque. As *The Motor Cycle* tester said, 'Nothing compared to the thrill of cranking the big Suzy through fast bends. You feel as if you are piloting a responsive fighter aircraft. Squirt it, and the Suzy goes like a jet. Aim it and you have suddenly got an accurate missile on your hands.'

*Heron Suzuki's race boss Rex White (left) talks to privateer Chris Guy. In the foreground is the GS1000 F1 bike ridden by Roger Marshall so successfully during the 1982 season.*

*Nat Woods does a mighty wheelie as he crests the Mountain at Cadwell Park, April 1983 on his GS1000-derived racer.*

If the GS750 was good, what followed was even better, because in November 1977, Suzuki launched the GS1000 which one journalist referred to as, 'A regal combination of smoothness, stability and speed.'

Not only had the dohc, 5-speed engine been increased to 997cc (70 x 64.8mm) but the rest of the machine had been beefed up too. This included larger 34mm carburettors, strengthened frame and swinging arm, a double disc front brake, cast alloy wheels, wider section tyres, electronic ignition (points on the GS750) and stronger clutch. Maximum speed exceeded 130mph.

The combination of a largely bullet-proof engine, good handling (by the standards of the day) and triple disc brakes made it a favourite mount in production machine races. Produced in three variants, E (standard), G

*Rob McElnea rounds Quarter Bridge in the Senior Classic TT of 1983. That year had seen the Classic (1000) and Senior (500) classes combined. McElnea's GS1000 powered him to a new record average speed for the 37.73 mile Isle of Man Mountain circuit of 114.81mph for the 6 lap race.*

# RG500 Evolution

*The first production RG500 was the Mark 1 of 1976. With laid-down twin rear shock absorbers, 35mm forks with no air assistance, 18 inch wire wheels front and rear, steel frame, 56 x 50.5mm bore and stroke and open pipes.*

RG500 MkI - 1976 Distinguishing features include lay down shock absorbers and the facility to put oil in the frame. In practice this was not done and the oil pump in the engine was removed and oil mixed in the fuel. The disc valve covers which were to feed the oil were blanked off. The Mk1 was also designed to incorporate an extra 7th gear but again this was removed. The early Suzuki calipers closely resembled the Lookheed versions of the time. The Mkl also sported open pipes or 'stingers' as they became known. The forks were 35mm and had no air assistance. Wheels were spoked 18inch front and rear. Carburettors were 4 x 34mm Mikuni in magnesium. Bore & Stroke was 56 x 50.5mm. The frame was steel with twin shock rear suspension.

RG500 MkII - 1977 Similar to the MkI, the shock absorbers were now more vertical although still fairly laid forward. The expansion chambers had an integral pre-formed silencer to conform with the noise regulations of the time. The frames no longer had the oil tank facility and the disc valve covers were cast blanked off. The overall appearance was still similar to the MkI with the flip up tail on the seat, not unlike the Kawasaki of the period. Wheels were again spoked, 18inch front and rear.

RG500 MkIII - 1978 Many cosmetic changes to the fairing and seat, with the seat style now going to the pointed tail type which was to become a familiar feature of the marque. The front forks now had pneumatic assistance and the brakes were upgraded. The rear shocks now also had the benefit of undivided gas reservoirs.

RG500 MkIV - 1979 The main change was in the bore and stroke from the previous 56 x 50.5mm to the square 54 x 54mm. This made the bike's power more friendly. There were changes in the expansion chambers and the pressed type silencers were replaced with longer cylindrical steel ends. The forks were upgraded to 37mm and the machine now came with Campagnolo 18inch magnesium wheels as standard.

RG500 MkV - 1980 Very similar to the MkIV but with a braced swinging arm, better expansion chambers and modified cosmetics to fairing and seat. By now a very reliable bike.

RG500 MkVI - 1981 An up-rated version of the successful MkV. The VI had anti-dive fitted to the front forks and modified fairing and improved expansion chambers.

RG500 MkVII - 1982 The main change was the introduction of the stepped engine with its magnesium cases (which often proved fragile and were the subject of some

Frame layout of the 1976 RG500 Mark I, also note air-cooled clutch, side-mounted carbs and rearward facing exhausts for rear cylinders.

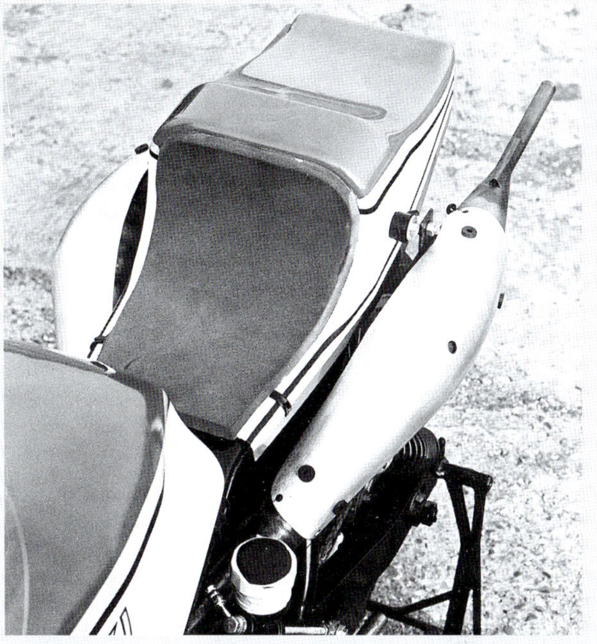

The Mark I exhaust with open pipes or 'stingers' as they were to become known.

1977 RG500 Mark II, with works XR14 magnesium wheels and semi-laid-down rear shocks. For the first time, the expansion chambers have integral pre-formed silencers.

## 1979 RG500 Mark IV

| | |
|---|---|
| Engine | Water-cooled, square-four, 4-cylinder, two-stroke with disc valve induction |
| Capacity | 494.69cc |
| Bore & Stroke | 54 x 54mm |
| Comp ratio | 8.3:1 |
| Carburation | 4 x Mikuni twin-float VM34 |
| Ignition | Nippon-Denso CDI magneto |
| Gearbox | Six-speeds |
| Clutch | Dry, multi-plate |
| Frame | Steel, duplex tubular cradle construction |
| Suspension | Front: Kayaba 37mm, nitrogen-charged telescopic fork<br>Rear: Kayaba shocks with braced aluminium swinging arm |
| Wheels | 18 inch front and rear (Campagnolo) |
| Dry weight | 299lb (136kg) |
| Max power | 110bhp @ 11,000rpm |
| Max speed | 170mph |

*Bill Smith on his RG500 Mark III at Governor's Bridge, on his way to second place in the 1978 Senior TT.*

*Ronnie Russell about to have his first entry on the Hector Neill's RG Mark III during the 1978 Ulster Grand Prix.*

*1978 RG500 Mark III. Many cosmetic changes to the fairing and seat, with new seat style. The front forks features pneumatic assistance and upgraded brakes.*

*A Mark V from 1980. Very similar to the Mark IV, but with a braced swinging arm, revised expansion chambers and modified cosmetics.*

*The Nico Bakker framed Mark X that won the national Dutch title in the late 1980s.*

*The Mark IX was the last of the factory built complete RG500 racers, and at last had an aluminium frame similar to the Grand Prix bikes raced by Mamola and co. Bob McElnea is racing this example at Cadwell Park in 1984.*

*Rear end of the Mark V. The extended exhausts were needed to comply with new FIM noise regulations.*

*The Mark X, XI and XII were not made as complete bikes, Suzuki instead opted to sell an up-rated engine from 1985 until 1988. For example Padgett's, in conjunction with Harris Performance, produced a complete bike, the main drawback was that it reverted to a steel frame and the engine had to be removed even for minor work.*

modification). They also ran two cranks as opposed to four on the previous six machines. Larger 36mm carburettors improved performance. A new more aerodynamic fairing and seat changed the look of the machine and with its departure from twin shocks to mono shock and its up-rated 40mm front forks, the MkVII was a much more sophisticated machine.

RG500 MkVIII - 1983 Very similar in most respects to the MkVII, the VIII had a few minor cosmetic changes and paint-work but was a very similar spec to the previous year's machine.

RG500 MkIX - 1984 The MkIX was Suzuki's last over-the-counter racer and at last had an aluminium box section frame similar to its Grand Prix bikes raced by Mamola & co. The fairing was again uprated and the MkIX looked every part the Grand Prix racer. It had 16inch front and 18inch rear magnesium wheels and a different head stock. By now however, Honda's triple had arrived on the scene and despite its lower price tag the Suzuki could no longer compete.

*The author's brother-in-law Tony Plumridge raced this RG500 - basically a Mark VI with a later seat unit - in classic racing events during the late 1980s and early 1990s with some considerable success.*

*A standard 1982 Mark VII. The main change was the introduction of the stepped engine with its magnesium cases. It also ran two instead of the previous four cranks, whilst there were also larger 36mm carburettors and upgraded suspension - monoshock at the rear, 40mm forks at the front.*

# Suzuki RG500 MkI -XII

| Mk/Year | Bore/Stroke | Carbs | Forks | Suspension | Wheels | BHP | Crankcases | Cranks |
|---|---|---|---|---|---|---|---|---|
| MkI/1976 | 56/50.5 | 34mm Mikuni | 35mm | Twin-shock | 18in wire | 103+ | Alloy | 4 |
| MkII/1977 | 56/50.5 | 34mm Mikuni | 35mm | Twin -shock | 18in wire | 103+ | Alloy | 4 |
| MkIII/1978 | 56/50.5 | 34mm Mikuni | 35mm | Twin-shock | 18in wire | 103+ | Alloy | 4 |
| MkIV/1979 | 54/54 | 34mm Mikuni | 37mm | Twin-shock | 18in Mag | 110+ | Alloy | 4 |
| MkV/1980 | 54/54 | 34mm Mikuni | 37mm | Twin-shock | 18in Mag | 110+ | Alloy | 4 |
| MkVI/1981 | 54/54 | 34mm Mikuni | 37mm | Twin-shock | 18in Mag | 110+ | Alloy | 4 |
| MkVII/1982 | 54/54 | 36mm Mikuni | 40mm | Mono-shock | 18in Mag | 115+ | Mag-stepped | 2 |
| MkVIII/1983 | 54/54 | 36mm Mikuni | 40mm | Mono-shock | 18in Mag | 115+ | Mag-stepped | 2 |
| MkIX/1984 | 54/54 | 38mm Mikuni | 40mm | Mono-shock | 16/18in Mag | 115+ | Mag-stepped | 2 |
| MkX/1985 | 54/54 | 38mm Mikuni | 40mm | Mono-shock | 16/18in Mag | 120+ | Mag-stepped | 2 |
| MkXI/1986 | 54/54 | 38mm Mikuni | 40mm | Mono-shock | 16/18in Mag | 120+ | Mag-stepped | 2 |
| MkXII/1987 | 54/54 | 38mm Mikuni | 40mm | Mono-shock | 16/18in Mag | 120+ | Mag-stepped | 2 |

RG500 MkX - XI & XII 1985 to 1988. Suzuki's alternative to selling complete over-the-counter Grand Prix machines was to supply an up-rated engine with power valves and the complementing expansion chambers via Padgett's of Batley. Padgett's, in conjunction with Harris Performance Products ,produced a complete racing bike which gained some success with privateers. Its main drawback was that they reverted to a steel frame and the engine had to be removed for minor mechanical work. Spondon however, produced a very businesslike beam frame for the engine, which allowed the engine to be dropped and cylinders removed in situ. Few MkX, XI or XIIs remain and it was a changing point in the Grand Prix Circus and the end for many privateers.

*Spondon produced a very business-like aluminium frame for the RG power valve engine (which spanned Mark X, XI and XII - and the years 1985 to 1988). This bike was raced by John Mossey, entered by Martyn Jones.*

*Post TT , Mallory Park, Forgotten Era winner John Mossey with his RG MK XII , Spondon framed Power valve, sponsored by Martyn Jones, early 1990s.*

*Mick Grant leads team mate Graeme Crosby on the final lap of the 1981, at least on the road at the Nook in the Classic TT (1000cc). Crosby won in 1 hour 59 minutes 3.8 seconds for the 6 laps at an average speed of 113.58mph.*

(shaft drive) and S (sport), all produced 87bhp. However, the 'S' featured a small fairing and air-adjustable front forks and rear shocks, giving a wider range of damping in addition to normal multi-position loadings. 1981 saw more powerful GSX1100 and 750 models. Both engines featured the new generation 16-valve TSCC (Twin Swirl Combustion Chamber) cylinder heads, these being the work of engineer Shirasagi. In the interests of the twin swirl arrangement, its designer had abandoned the conventional hemispherical chamber pattern of the 8-valve GS engines, shaping it into a square profile with various angles introduced courtesy of CAD (Computer Aided Design) techniques, to agitate the incoming mixture for more complete combustion. A flat-top piston with four small valves helped the squish effect; Suzuki sources claiming an overall improvement in efficiency of no less than 20 per cent.

Modifications to the double overhead camshafts layout included forked tappets running off the cams to actuate the additional valves, with an incidental advantage by way of screw and nut adjustment for clearance in place of the original time-consuming system of replaceable shims.

*John Newbold discusses the merits of his big Heron Suzuki 4-cylinder 4-stroke racer with his mechanic, circa 1981.*

*Nick Andrews the 1981 Auto 66 1300cc Production Champion with his air-cooled 16 valve Suzuki GSX1100, Carnaby Raceway, East Yorkshire.*

The suspension had also been updated. Already in the vanguard of innovation in this area, through adoption of air assistance at the front, Suzuki refined its system by incorporating isolating valves for each leg of the fork to ensure that, once inflated by a common pressuriser, there would be no danger of a unilateral leak collapsing the entire fork. In addition, variable pre-set damping was introduced in which any of the five settings could be selected by turning a knob at the base of the fork legs. This knob caused a long internal rod to revolve, with different sized holes lining up to regulate damper-oil flow. All very complicated, and guaranteed, of course, to ensure that a GSX1100 racer spent a shade too much time on meticulous pre-race preparation.

*A Suzuki Katana (85) leads at Mallory Park in the British Street Bike National Championships, 1981. Also in the frame are the Honda CB1100Rs of Ron Haslam (2) and Joey Dunlop.*

*Dave Aldana losing his Katana at Daytona in 1981.*

Performance of the 1100's engine (1075cc - 76 x 66mm) equalled any production sports roadster in 1981, with 100bhp at 8700rpm and almost 140mph in full road trim - pure racing versions were soon approaching 150mph and over 110bhp, just by way of a less restrictive exhaust, full fairing and blue-printing the engine.

Meanwhile, although a poor seller, the GSX750 with its notably shorter-stroke 67 x 53mm bore and stroke dimensions was largely overlooked at the time, it did play an important role in the birth of the mould-breaking GSXR750 a few short years later. But before this happened, in Autumn 1981, Suzuki introduced a range of models from 550 to 1100 in a styling exercise which was laid out for the Japanese company by the Target Design Company who had offices in West Germany and Great Britain, and which was headed by one-time BMW designer Jan Fellstrom.

Known under the name Katana these bikes had a unique style, which even today looks futuristic. Although an 1100 was offered, the top performance Katana was the 1000, using an uprated version of the 997cc dohc 16-valve engine; with a power output of 108bhp it could comfortably exceed 140mph. Then for 1983 Suzuki introduced the GSXES series, comprising 550, 750 and 1100 versions. It was this range which bridged the gap between the old and the new, with, for example, the 550 (572cc - 60 x 55mm) model with features such as 'Full Floater' monoshock rear suspension, square tube frame and anti-dive front forks. There was also the GSX1100E in its final form. Its outstanding feature was the engine's power - 124bhp and a torque figure of 17.4 ft/lb. And it was this engine which many used for either drag racing or unlimited (1300cc) class racing.

*Suzuki won the 1983 World Endurance Championship with, what was in effect, the prototype of the forthcoming GSXR750. The French rider Samin is seen here aboard the bike that year.*

But in reality all these machines, many of which had been raced in club, national or even international events during the early 1980s were made obsolete overnight by the first of a new breed of high performance 750s which invented the SuperSport racing category single handedly. And Suzuki were first with the dynamic and exciting GSXR series; the GSXR750 was launched to worldwide acclaim at the international Cologne Show in September 1984.

The GSXR750 series of high performance sports and racing motorcycles was born out of Suzuki's participation in the world of endurance racing at events such as the French Bol d'Or 24 hour during the early 1980s.

The concept of the original GSXR750 was very simply to create the closest possible replica of the 1983 World Endurance Championship winning machine, but at a realistic price. Indeed, to make available to the public a machine, which could, if required, convert dreams of racing into reality was now possible simply by fitting the optional factory performance kit.

The specification underlined the racing background of the GSXR; from the all-new oil/air-cooled 100bhp engine with its 6-speed close ratio gearbox, through to the aluminium tube frame, and even the new Bridgestone endurance tyres. The styling was also pure endurance racer, warts and all. This was a major step forward in the evolution of the modern, high performance sports/racing motorcycle; hence the SuperSport race category.

Right from the start the GSXR was built as a racer first, street bike second. The man who stamped his authority on the project, Tasanobu Fujji, saw to this. His vision was of a bike which could not only achieve a genuine 150mph in standard 'road legal' guise, but also become a pukka race bike with the simple addition of a factory race kit, developed in conjunction with 'Pops' Yoshimura. The kit comprised a serious amount of components, including a ready-to-bolt-on gas-flowed cylinder head, high compression pistons, titanium valve springs, polished carb bellmouths, a dry clutch conversion, polished connecting rods, high lift camshafts and a 4-into-1 exhaust system.

*Roger Marshall (998cc Suzuki) during the Daily Mirror-sponsored Formula 1 race, Donington Park, 18th April 1982.*

# 1985 GSXR750F

| | |
|---|---|
| Engine | Liquid-cooled, across-the-frame, dohc, 4-cylinder, with 16-valves |
| Capacity | 749cc |
| Bore | 70mm |
| Stroke | 48.7mm |
| Comp ratio | 9.8:1 |
| Ignition | Transistorised |
| Carburation | 4 x Mikuni VMSS 29mm |
| Gearbox | 6-speed |
| Clutch | Wet, multi-plate |
| Final drive | Chain |
| Frame | Aluminium, deltabox |
| Suspension | Front: 41mm telescopic fork 4-way adjustable<br>Rear: swinging arm, with single shock |
| Wheels | 16-inch aluminium, 3-spoke front and rear |
| Tyres | 110/80V 18 front; 140/70V 18 rear |
| Brakes | Front: 2 x 300mm discs, with 4-piston calipers<br>Rear: single 220mm disc, with 2-piston calipers |
| Dry Weight | 388lb (176.4kg) |
| Max power | 104.5bhp at 10,500rpm |
| Max speed | 155mph |

*The first major race for the GSX750R in Great Britain was at Brands Hatch on the 5th April 1985. Here Mick Grant (nearest camera) with his GSXR lines up next to the Rothmans Honda pair of Roger Marshall and Roger Burnett. There are two more GSXRs in the frame.*

*The winning style of Mick Grant and the GSXR750 at the Brands Hatch round of the British Super Stock series for production 750s, 5th April 1985.*

*The GSXR750 made a sensational debut at the German Cologne Show in the fall of 1984, going on sale in March 1985. The essence of the design was a real race replica, which could be kitted with factory parts. It proved an instant hit both in the showroom and on the circuit.*

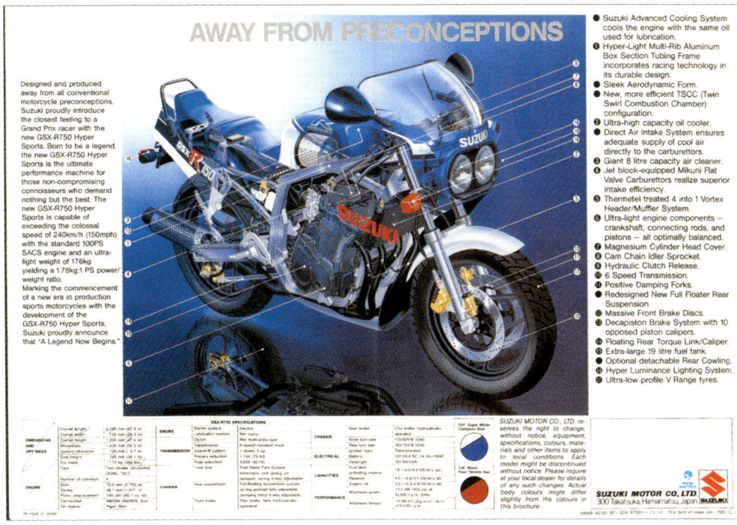


*A ghosted view of the 1985 GSXR showing the main features of this revolutionary motorcycle, which produced over 100bhp and could reach 150mph - more if fitted with the race kit.*

Added to the stock engine, the 1985 GSXR750 ended up with a full 30 extra horses. The result was a 170mph flyer which the likes of Honda's V-four VF750 and Yamaha's 20-valve FZ750 simply couldn't match.

Tasanobu Fujji was Suzuki's head of European-market engine development and as such he was one of a team that had led Suzuki into the 4-stroke market with the launch of the original GS750 back in 1976.

Now, eight years on, the headline grabbing feature of the new GSXR was its use of oil-cooling; this being new in terms of modern motorcycle engineering, but had been used to help control the temperature of aero engines since at least the early 1920s.

*Easter Match Races, Donington Park, 1986 and future Grand Prix star Kevin Schwantz made a big impression on the Motor Cycle Mart, Kidderminster GSXR750.*

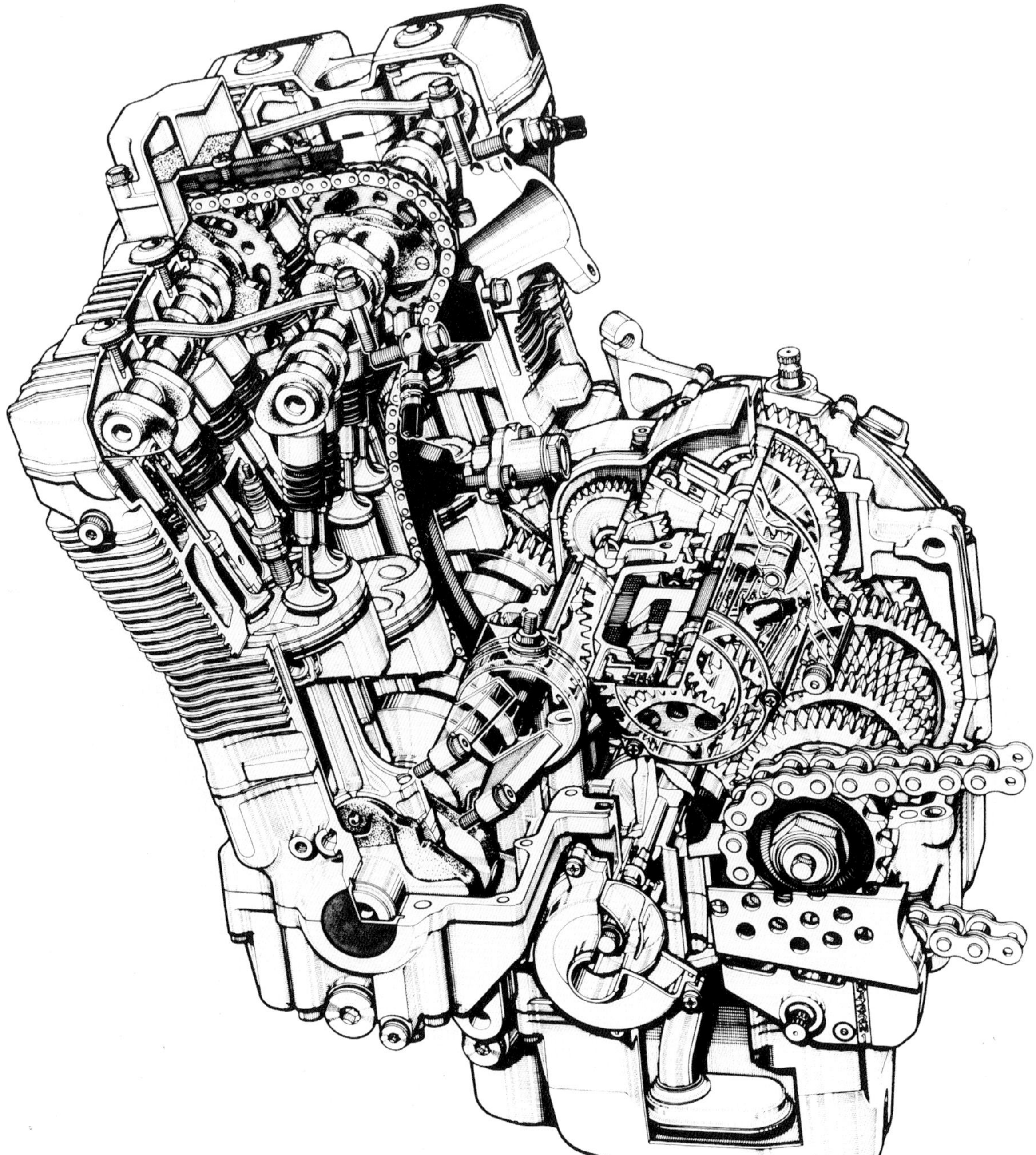

Suzuki engineers first successfully experimented with the idea to cure overheating problems encountered during the development of the XN85 Turbo street bike. Oil jets directed at the underside of the piston crowns prevented the turbo-charged engine from dumping a molten cocktail into the crankcase. The same idea was also employed on the earlier GSX750ES motor to prevent the pistons in the two central cylinders from running hotter than their outside brothers. Whilst it would be accurate to describe the GSX motor as air-cooled with oil assistance, the emphasis was switched the other way around in the GSXR engine.

Oil-cooling came into its own in the new system which employed a second oil pump to concentrate on flushing away engine heat.

*The 1985 GSXR750's engine, 749cc dohc 16 valve, chain driven camshafts, six-speed gearbox and SACS.*

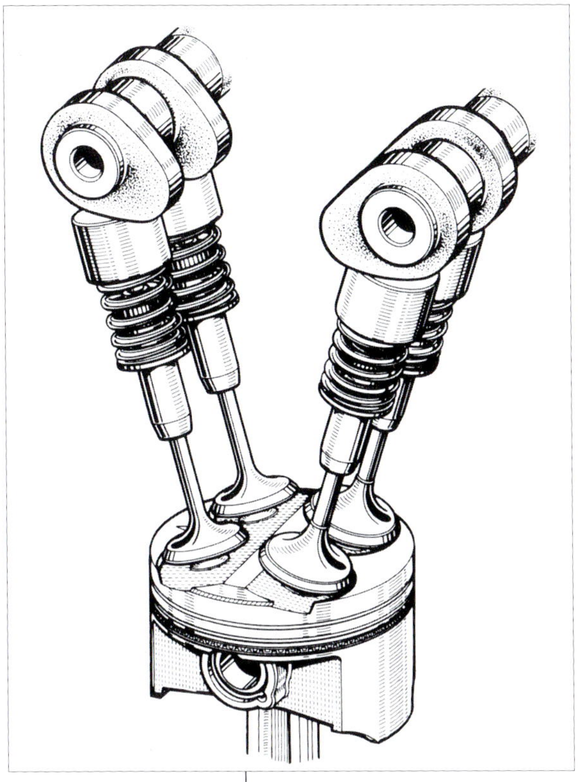

Details of the 1985 GSXR750s 4-valves-per-cylinder layout, showing, cams, pushers, springs, valves and piston.

A sister unit mounted on the same shaft and sharing a common housing handled the lubrication. Each picked up from the sump and pushed oil through the engine at between 20-22 litres per minute. The oil flow rate was in fact very similar to that of a conventionally lubricated engine, but the doubling up of pumps meant a doubling up of the circulation. The 5.5 litres of oil carried in the system was passed through a larger cooler mounted on the front frame tubes.

Heat dissipation was further aided by the employment of a magnesium cylinder head cover and a mass of shallow cylinder fins which gave the engine a distinctive look. All very clever; but why had Suzuki turned to oil- cooling in favour of a water jacket? The answer, claimed Suzuki, was to be found with a measuring tape and a pair of scales. The GSXR was both more compact and a lot lighter than would otherwise have been possible. A prototype bike using water-cooling was found to be appreciably wider and some 11lb (5kg) heavier than the oil-cooled power plant, which weighed

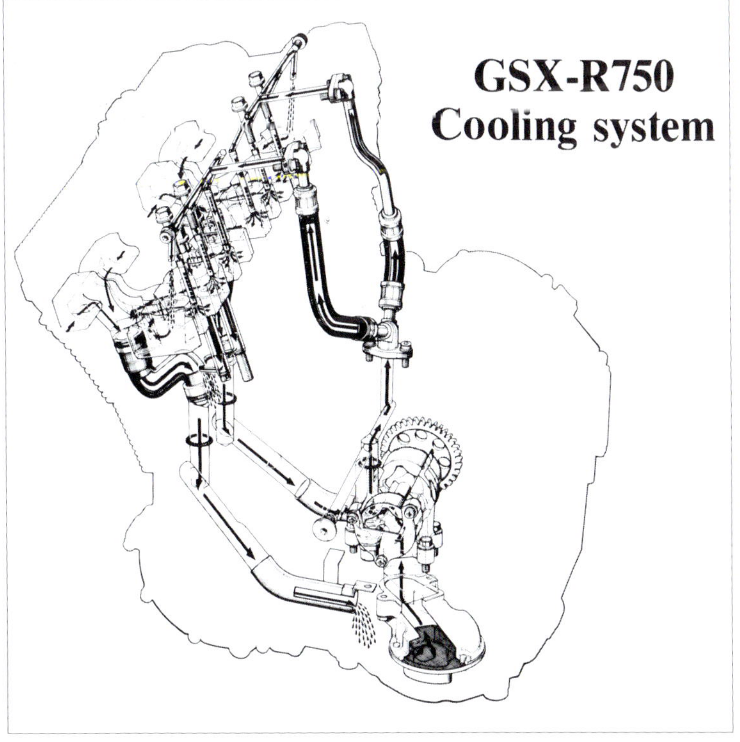


SACS (Suzuki Advanced Cooling System) essentially the lubricating oil was also used for cooling purposes.

# GSXR750 Development

| | |
|---|---|
| 1985 (750F) | Introduced with oil/air-cooled, across-the-frame, four cylinder engine. dohc, 16-valve, 6-speeds, hydraulically operated clutch 104.5bhp, aluminium frame. 1986 (750G). Small increase in power output, 25mm longer swinging arm, radial tyres, modified wheels. |
| 1987 750H) | Stronger front forks, with electronic anti-dive |
| 1988 (750J) | First major update, with 60 per cent stiffer frame, new short-stroke engine dimensions of 73 x 44.7mm. Maximum engine revolutions increased to 13,000rpm; new, semi-flat slide carburettors; maximum power increased to 108bhp. Modified suspension; wheel size decreased to 17-inch. |
| 1989 (750K) | Detail changes only. |
| 1990 (750L) | Engine dimensions reverted to original longer stroke format. Four-into-one exhaust replacing earlier four-into-two layout. Carburettor size increased from 36 to 38mm. Inverted front forks. Power increased to 110bhp, weight also increased, now 436.5lb (198kg). 1991 (750M) Cylinder head modifications, including the adoption of a single rocker arm per valve in place of the original forked single rocker for each pair of valves, thus reducing internal inertia. Power increased to 116bhp. |
| 1992 (750WN) | A major change came with the adoption of water-cooling to supplement the existing oil-cooling system. Power increased to 118bhp and a new frame (24 per cent stiffer than before) adopted. Suspension and braking also improved. Dry weight now 458lb (208kg). |
| 1993 (750WP) | Only detail changes. |

*Riders get under way at the Snetterton 6 hour Endurance race, July 1985. Numbers 31, 32, 36 and 42 are all GSXR750 mounted.*

| | |
|---|---|
| 1994 (750WR) | The WR model had an additional 2bhp, whilst weight decreased to 438.7lb (199kg). There were also 6-piston calipers at the front and an increase in fork tube diameter from 41 to 3mm. Other changes were made to the swinging arm and tyre sizes. |
| 1995 (750WS) | Cosmetic changes only. |
| 1996 (750T) | Major redesign saw not only a brand new styling job (the same as the new GSXR 600), but also a rash of technical updates. The twin cradle frame was replaced by a twin-spar chassis (still in aluminium) based on that of the RGV Gamma Grand Prix 500 bike. There was also a new engine, making the 750T the most compact and light machine in the 750 SuperSport category. Forced air induction was also introduced, with 128bhp and 394lb (179kg), the GSXR shot back to lead its class once again. |
| 1997 (750V) | No changes. |
| 1998 (750W) | Developments included fuel injection, a 50 per cent larger air box, small engine modifications which put power up to 135bhp - and a closer ratio gearbox. |
| 1999 (750X) | Minor changes only. |
| 2000 (750Y) | Given the factory code Project 701, the 2000 year model featured a brand new engine (which was more compact and 11lb/5kg lighter) and a new frame. Overall dry weight was 366lb (166kg). The gearbox employed staggered input and output shafts (reduced engine length) and the fuel injection was given twin butterflies to improve emissions and throttle response. |

*The 1987 GSXR750 Limited Edition.*

*1985 Le Mans 24 Hours and a British based GSXR750 receives attention in the pit.*

in at just 165lb (75kg). The search for power had led Fujji and his team down a more conventional path, with improvements to breathing and combustion coupled with moves to reduce frictional losses in the power chain. The 749cc (70 x 48.7mm) 16-valve dohc four cylinder engine ran a compression ratio of 10.6:1 in standard guise, whilst a bank of four 29mm Mikuni flat slide carbs drew air in a direct path from an enormous air box.

The inlet and exhaust valve heads were larger than in the EF engine, whilst the valve stems were shaved down from 5.5 to 5mm. Higher lift cams and more radical valve timing were exploited, along with the introduction of a new, more efficient version of Suzuki's Twin Swirl Combustion Chamber (TSCC) design and a 4-into-1 exhaust system.

*Parliament Square, Ramsey and Mick Grant with the Heron Suzuki-entered GSXR750 during the Production TT, June 1985.*

*1988 GSXR750J. This was a major redesign in which even the bore and stroke dimensions were changed from the previous 70 x 47.7mm to shorter stroke 73 x 44.7mm. These photographs show the bike with...*

Close attention was paid by Fujji and his team to reducing the weight of the piston and conrod assemblies, allowing the crankshaft journals to be reduced from 36mm to 34mm. Crankshaft and rods weighed in some 4.2lb (2kg) less than their counterparts in the preceding 750 EF engine.

The cam chain took its drive from the centre of the crankshaft and was helped to keep on a path by introduction of an idler sprocket which also cut noise at high rpm. In addition, new materials were specified for the crankshaft bearings to reduce frictional losses in the transfer of power through the hydraulic clutch and 6-speed gearbox. Although Suzuki claimed otherwise, it was soon evident that the original 1985 model year

*... and without its streamlining. It is worth noting that the large aluminium 15-row oil cooler introduced that year improved the cooling efficiency by no less than 48 per cent, compared with outgoing 1987 'H' model.*

*For 1988 the British Suzuki importer Heron selected James Whitham (69) and...*

GSXR750 (coded F) had a power delivery like an on-off switch, as there was little on offer in the sub-7000rpm zone and whirlwind-type performance above this figure; hardly surprising when one considers that the engine's maximum torque of 49.2 ft/lb was produced at 10,000rpm. All this made the GSXR much better as a racer than a street bike.

The chassis was another area in which the development team attempted to out-gun the opposition. Fashioned entirely from case and extruded aluminium, the box section, full cradle frame also incorporated an aluminium swinging arm and an improved version of Suzuki's 'Full Floater' mono-shock rear suspension.

*A 1993 Yoshimura-tuned GSXR750 with its Japanese riders...*

*...and the machine's special racing carburettors.*

Strangely, 18-inch wheels were chosen, at a time when everyone was adopting 16-inch either at the front, or for both wheels, the smaller front being seen as a way of speeding up the steering. And it was to be the handling, or sometimes lack of it, which was to prove the early GSXR's weakest point. Riders, both on the race circuit and the street, complained of high speed weaving, particularly on less-than-perfect road surfaces. But even though it had a flick-switch motor and suspect high speed manners,

*... Phil Mellor to campaign their GSXR750s at national level.*

*Besides its pukka RG500 racer, Suzuki also built, in the mid 1980s, the RG500 Gamma sports roadster. But many of these found their way on to the race circuit where they gave a good account of themselves. Clubman Peter Brett is seen here on a Gamma at Mallory Park in 1986.*

the new GSXR750 not only became the top selling machine in its class, but also established Suzuki as a force to be reckoned with in Super Stock (forerunner of today's SuperSport) and SuperBike racing, in 1985 and again in 1986. In fact works-supported rider Mick Grant won the 1985 British Super Stock title in confident style, in the process showing just what an advance the Suzuki was over the opposition; impressive stuff indeed and in the case of Mick Grant an ideal way to bring down the curtain on a glittering career.

A year after the arrival of the GSXR750 came a larger version of the same formula, the 1100. The actual capacity was 1052cc (76 x 58mm) and, although largely unchanged from the original GSXR, the newcomer was a much more practical roadster, if something of a handful in racing.

Whereas the 750 provided power which was incredibly peaky, the 1100 bigger cubes and reduced compression ratio (10:1) provided a flat torque curve throughout the entire rev range. This added up to respectable grunt from as little as 3000rpm in top, massive mid-range at 5000 and awe-inspiring response by the time the 1100 reached the 750's lift-off point of 7000rpm.

*Manxman Danny Shimmin on his RG500 Gamma follows another rider during the 1986 Isle of Man Production TT.*

*A 1985 RG500 Gamma with tank, seat and fairing lowers removed, exposing the full cradle aluminium frame.*

This only left one small problem - that dreaded high speed weave. And weave they did, as anyone will testify who watched (or rode) those early GSXRs in full-blooded racing action at places like the Isle of Man TT circuit or Scarborough's Oliver's Mount course. Unfortunately several riders paid the ultimate price, losing their lives when one of the GSXRs went out of control. In the Isle of Man it even led to the 1300cc Production class being axed after Phil (Mez) Mellor's fatal accident in the 1988 TT.

The 1986 GSXR1100 could reach a genuine 165mph; the standing quarter in less than 10.8 seconds - a terminal speed of 126mph. Changes from the 750 included 41mm front forks (40mm), 34mm carbs, and maximum torque of 74.5 ft/lb at 8500rpm. The twin front brake discs were increased in diameter from 300 to 310. There was also a slightly longer wheel base, a stronger frame and wider tyres to complement the extra horses and higher top speed.

*In layout, the 1985 Gamma was remarkably like the full-blown RG500 racing engine. The square four, rotary disc induction motor produced 95bhp.*

# Gallina TGA-6

*Factory fresh Gallina TGA6 R1 as it appeared when new in 1991.*

Roberto Gallina, a former works rider for the likes of Benelli, Ducati and Laverda, really made his name as the man who took Suzuki to a pair of 500cc World Championship titles at the begining of the 1980s, with Marco Lucchinelli and Franco Uncini.

Team Gallina had been formed back in 1975 and achieved many triumphs with a succession of top line riders including Virgino Ferrari, Graziano (father of Valetino) Rossi, Loris Reggiani, Sito Pons, Pierfrancesco Chili and Steve Baker.

But it is as a motorcycle constructor and engineer that Roberto Gallina has probably made the greatest impression, founding the Prototype Centre in Rimini to craft many of the most beautiful Italian bikes of the time. Finally, in 1993 Roberto Gallina and his family opened a retail store selling many of the biggest motorcycle marques, backed by a technical division complete with the most modern equipment.

Gallina also produced two special motorcycle models, the TGA4 (750cc four) and TGA6 (800cc single), both for the Japanese market.

The TGA6 single used Suzuki's DR800 engine and was built in both road and racing trim, the latter coded R1.

Actually, Italian race engineer Gaetano Bursi was the first man in Europe to realise the potential of the air-cooled Suzuki DR Big powerplant for single cylinder racing. Bursi had fitted the engine into an aluminium frame fabricated by Diego Golinelli in 1990.

Then a few months later Bursi was headhunted by Bimota in an attempt to sort out its ailing 500 v-twin two-stroke GP racer project. So with no time to continue developing the DR Suzuki-based single the project passed to Roberto Gallina, who had himself been working on a similar device.

At Monza in 1991 Gallina's son Miki won the International Sound of the Singles race in July that year from the best riders and machines from across Europe.

When Alan Cathcart tested Miki Gallina's TGA6R1 racer at the same Monza venue during the summer of 1991 he was in love with the engine, but didn't have the same level of enthusiasm for the frame calling it 'adequate' and the brakes 'rather disappointing'.

However this description of the power and acceleration make interesting reading, 'Out on the track, the straight line performance allows you to out-accelerate most twins, then draft anything bar an eight valve Ducati on top end. The sheer grunt from low down is truly exhilarating, yet unaccompanied by significant vibration - the Suzuki engine, with the chain driven balance shaft, doesn't shake rattle and roll like I'ld expect from a mega-lump single measuring no less than 105 x 90mm, especially when pressed to rev way above its stock 7,000rpm redline.'

But the Gallina racing DR engine was pretty special, not only was there a bonus of a 6 instead of 5-speed gearbox with closer ratios, but the power output had been increased to 72bhp at the rear wheel.

Gallina had retained the standard bore and stroke dimensions of the DR Big engine, but later came up with a 106mm bore piston, giving in the process an increase in capacity from 780 to 794cc.

Both sizes of piston were special two-ring designs. The compression ratio had been raised to 11:1, which initially caused problems with the chain drive to the single overhead cam due to the skimmed cylinder head, until Gallina employed the CNC facilities of his race shop to machine up a half-link  for the single-strand Regina chain which had replaced the stock Morse chain. It also cured the one weak area of the engine, broken camchains.

The crankshaft and connecting rod were modified original Suzuki components, whereas the camshaft was a one-off racing item, giving increased lift and dwell from the standard cam. The new camshaft also offered the invaluable feature of vernier adjustment, permitting the valve timing to be varied for the inlet and exhaust valves individually. Valve sizes were 2mm larger than the original Suzuki components, and these, together with the racing valve springs were specially manufactured. The 4-valve cylinder head had been specially flowed and ported, then given a pair of 40mm Mikuni flat-slide carburettors.

The original twin-plug ignition was retained, but used without battery or generator, only pick-ups and coils, but Gallina varied the curve to move the power further up the scale.

After Alan Cathcart had tested the TGA6 at Monza for the magazine article he bought the bike at he end of the 1991 season. Alan raced the bike successfully during 1992, winning at Mettet, Belgium at an average speed of 155.5kph (over 97mph - at the time the fastest Singles race ever run). He also won at Carole outside Paris, one of the slowest circuits on the calendar that year. After Alan's success in 1992 he received his factory supplied Ducati Supermono for the 1993 season. He then used the Gallina as his spare bike, but the Ducati proved so reliable that.

Gallina stood around in Alan's garage until May 1997, when London racer Chris Lillingston-Price became the new owner.

*Wearing the number 1 plate gained by winning the British and European Supermono Championship titles in 2001, ridden by Mark Lawes.*

*Donington Park 30th March 2002, Mark Lawes number 33 led the pack off the line in the first race of 2002 and went on to win.*

Chris takes up the story, 'I had fun racing it at BMCRC club events - until the last race at Silverstone in September 1997 when the engine destroyed itself. I later discovered that Gallina had been running on Avgas but by using pump fuel I had suffered severe detonation problems and both the piston and head had melted.'

Next came the first meeting between Mark Lawes and Chris. This resulted in Mark, a CNC machinist by trade, developing a new head with an improved downdraft. He also rebuilt the engine with the modified cylinder head and Chris was back on the race circuit by the start of the 1998 season.

Chris explains, 'I definitely had more power than the year before, but during the race I started to lose power and by the end was very disappointed with the performance.'

It transpired that the original Gallina camshaft had worn badly and the inlet valves were only opening half way. Chris Lillingston-Price then acquired a Joy camshaft which 'worked OK but I didn't think it was giving the full potential.'

*Evident in this view are the massive 39mm Keihin flat slide carbs and the aluminium twin-spar chassis.*

During 1999 and 2000 Chris continued to develop the Gallina with Mark Lawes' help.

The cylinder was relined with an aluminium liner and Nicasil plated. Omega supplied a 106mm slipper piston, an Arrow con-rod was also fitted, and an American Megacycle camshaft with special hardened rockers. British company, Reids, manufactured the largest valves the head would accomodate, whilst Mark Lawes converted the ignition timing so that it was now fully adjustable. He also manufactured another cylinder head with even more downdraft. In addition, 39mm Keihin carburettors were fitted. After many hours reading performance-tuning books Mark Hill from MHP constructed an exhaust design to Chris Lillingston-Price's own design.

Currently, the Gallina still uses the original special 6-speed gearbox, which although difficult to select neutral has proved trouble-free in service. The only chassis modification has been the addition of new 5-spoke Marchesini wheels. With these modifications the bike has recorded 83bhp at the rear wheel on the Ascot House dyno.

In 2002, Chris Lillingston-Price raced the Gallina in just three British Supermono championship races. Chris was pleased with the results - two victories and one second.

For 2002 Chris decided that Mark Lawes should race the Gallina in the British Championship. And Mark got off to a great start by winning both races at Donington Park in the first round, which was also the first round of the European Championship. It was therefore decided that he should contest the European series too. After a season long battle with Mark George and the new Tigcraft-formed 420cc bike (see chapter 10) the Gallina was victorious in both championships. Lawes was crowned as both the British and European Champion and to cap it all the same combination of bike and rider won at Daytona in March 2003. Not bad for a 12-year old bike!

*Nearside fairing off shot of the Lillingston-Price Gallina TGA6 R1.*

*Members of the French Suzuki World Endurance squad with their GSXR750, circa 1988.*

Besides those riders already mentioned should be added Roger Marshall, James Whitham and Trevor Nation - all putting in excellent performances on GSXR models.

The first major update came in 1988, when the GSXR750 (coded K) received a new shorter-stroke, higher revving engine. Displacing 748cc (73 x 44.7mm), it was also given larger valves. Meanwhile the double cradle was strengthened with a larger aluminium box-pipe. There were new 'Slingshot' carbs, a DAIS (Direct Air Intake System), a new twin swirl combustion chamber and Nissin 4-pot brake calipers at the front, together with floating brake discs. There was also revised steering and suspension geometry, lower centre of gravity and the adoption of 17-inch wheels (with Michelin radial tyres).

Suzuki claimed the chassis to be 'almost identical to the factory's Formula 1 and World Championship-winning Endurance racers', whilst power was now up to 112bhp at 11,000rpm - with a 13,000rpm redline. The front fork stanchion diameter had been increased to 43mm, whilst the forks now came with 12 rebound and compression damping settings, a shorter swinging arm and 20, instead of 17mm wheel spindles.

*A year after the launch of the GSXR750 came a larger version, the 1100. Displacing 1052cc (76 x 58mm), the bigger GSXR could reach 165mph and the standing start quarter mile in 10.8 seconds - a terminal speed of 126mph. This is the 1989 edition.*

Suzuki engineers had also concentrated upon five features of the engine and its performance:

- Increasing fuel charging efficiency
- Decreasing mechanical loss
- Increasing valve rev limits
- Increasing cooling efficiency
- Increasing engine throttle response

Air intakes at the front of the fairing directed cool air past the hot engine and a thinner, 20 per cent less resistant air filter into a more direct inlet port. New flat slide 30mm Slingshot carbs, much lighter and thinner, featured a half round indexing ridge for an increased, smoother fuel flow.

A 2.5mm increase for the inlet valves and a 1mm increase on the exhaust side, plus longer valve duration ensured more air reached the smoother Twin Swirl Combustion Chamber for increased power.

Mechanical loss and throttle response work together. The less the loss, the better the response. A 4mm shorter stroke, lighter pistons, thinner piston rings and a 10 per cent increase in crankshaft web diameter all played a part to improve both throttle response and improved top end output. But at the same time, superior materials, larger crankpins and journals ensured that reliability wasn't sacrificed. A 13,000rpm redline demanded precise valve timing; this was achieved by employing lighter rocker arms and larger diameter coil valve springs.

The 1988 GSXR was equipped with larger diameter oil pipes which increased flow by 20 per cent whilst a larger oil cooler and improved cylinder head flow meant that cooling capacity shot up by no less than 48 per cent. A cable operated clutch replaced the original hydraulically-operated type.

*A competitor taking part in the Suzuki GSXR750 World Cup Final held at Jerez, Spain in September 1989. Bikes were that year's 'K' series.*

*The 1990 GSXR750L. The 'L' reverted to the long stroke 70 x 48.7mm bore and stroke dimensions. Both the 41mm inverted front fork and remote rear shock became fully adjustable. And there was a wider rear wheel rim than had been used for previous models.*

Again the 1100 was a year behind in the development stakes, the improved version not arriving until the 1989 model year (K series). This saw displacement lifted to 1127cc (78 x 59mm), whilst maximum power rose to 136bhp at 9500rpm. Many of the changes outlined above for the GSXR750 were transferred into the larger bike. The chassis was new and increased rigidity by 25 per cent.

However, even though on paper all these changes appeared impressive, they largely didn't transfer to the road. In fact, the K series was a major disappointment for the development team. For 1990 they were replaced by the L models - and it was to be the smaller engined GSXR model which benefited most from the modifications. *Motor Cycle News* summed it up, 'Yes, less is definitely more with the Suzuki GSXR750L. The gap between the 750 and 1100 we tested last week has narrowed with the new 750L. So much so that in some areas, the 750 nudges ahead.'

The list of changes was long. As well as inverted front forks, there was more gusseting on the frame (using much from the 1100 version), an improved 4-into-1 exhaust, a steering damper, radial flow oil cooler, even larger (38mm) carbs and a remote reservoir rear shock. But the major change was to the engine. Suzuki abandoned the short stroke design of the K and instead adopted the GSXR750 RR (works type racing) dimensions which interestingly were those of the original model launched back in the autumn of 1984.

The problem with the K series short-stroke engine - which also ran big ports and valves was that these didn't work very well with the flow of fuel and air mixture in the mid-range. So, although able to reach a stratospheric 13,000rpm, there was a big gaping mid-range 'hole' in the power delivery.

So it had been a case of returning to the drawing board; the racer RR motor was basically the old design with refinements which enabled it to continue to achieve 13,000rpm and make power - all very clever. These included smaller ports and valves, a 30 per cent more efficient oil cooling system, and stronger connecting rods. Suzuki had learned a lot about the latter components after factory-entered bikes had suffered a spate of broken rods in the endurance racing world. Compared to the K, the GSXR750L produced far more usable power, which was equally important for both the public highway and the race circuit.

A *MotorCycle News* test commented, 'There are no vibes, the clutch is light, the gearbox slick as a Swiss watch and the throttle so easy you find yourself holding it open inadvertently when you're braking.'

However, the 750L did have a problem, its riding position. Even for racing this was severe. Even with wider, further back handlebars, the vast majority of the weight fell on the riders wrists. Quite simply you were forced to adopt a stretched over the tank stance with your legs under your elbows. If you were over 5ft 6 ins tall, this was uncomfortable.

The frame had been stiffened all round with a longer, thicker swinging arm, longer wheelbase, a tad more rake and trail and a massive 5.5inch rear rim - the same size as the 1100, with a 170/16 17inch radial tyre. The result was a motorcycle which at last steered solidly with a good, neutral feel, if a shade heavier than previous GSXRs. Ground clearance had also been improved by tucking the exhaust system (now stainless steel) out of the way. More ground clearance also meant that the GSXR no longer needed rock hard suspension settings to get round corners. The new inverted front forks might have appeared to be a sales gimmick, but actually they worked brilliantly, providing feedback to the rider whether he was braking, cranking hard into a bend, or riding over a poorly surfaced road. As in the past there was a wide range of suspension settings, at both front and rear, to provide the optimum, if one had the expertise, to extract the best. It was also in this era that suspension specialists, for road racing as well as off-road motorcycle sport first really came to the fore; which together with tyres and brakes marked a considerable advancement in track performance, besides the more usual handling and power output figures.

*One of the 1991 factory GSXR750 endurance racers.*

# RG/RGV250 series

*Padgett's of Batley built this RG250 Gamma with a Suzuki liquid-cooled single cylinder 250 motocross engine in 1984.*

*Steve Spray, later to become a British Champion on the Rotary Norton during the late 1980s, began his rise to fame on a RG250 Gamma some five years before. Steve is pictured here with the Suzuki at Cadwell Park in 1985.*

*Steve Spray in action on his RG250 Gamma at Cadwell Park's club circuit Hairpin, circa 1985.*

Although the RGV250 was not the first liquid-cooled production-based Suzuki two-stroke, it is nonetheless the most well-known. It was built in larger numbers and is still current (if one counts its use in modified form to power Aprilia's top selling RS250). The origins of the design can be traced back to 1983 when Suzuki introduced the excellent RG250 parallel twin. Although it never sold in large numbers, the RG250 was, up to that time, the best handling Japanese series production motorcycle. Not only did it pioneer the use of a single shock rising rate rear suspension in Suzuki's range, but it displaced Yamaha LC250 as the top production racer in its class. With 247cc and 49bhp no other sports roadster could touch it.

But the RG was made obsolete overnight by the new RGV250 v-twin. First news of this sensational machine reached Britain in February 1987; with the first examples going on sale in Japan a few months later. The initial version to be exported was the 'K' in the 1989 model year, followed in 1990 by the 'L' which was virtually identical.

Both the K and L version of the RGV250 shared the same 249cc 90 degree v-twin with dual Slingshot carburettors, a new air induction system, a radial flow radiator and AETC (Automatic Exhaust Timing Control) to increase power right across the rev range. The result (with full road-legal silencing) was a power output of 57bhp at 11,000rpm and a top speed of around 130mph.

Made from high quality cast aluminium, the frame was intended to reduce weight, whilst maintaining maximum strength. There was the latest version of Suzuki's 'Full Floater' link-type mono-shock rear suspension, whilst at the front the telescopic forks had massive 41mm stanchions. Braking was taken care of by a pair of 290mm front discs, with a single 210mm assembly at the rear. The system incorporated four pistons for each front disc, reduced to two pistons as the rear. Wheels were of the racing 3-spoke variety, 17-inch at the front 18-inch at the rear. Dry weight was 282lb (128kg). Unfortunately these early RGVs were none too reliable. There were numerous instances of broken or seized power valves, also piston and cylinder seizures.

For the 1991 model year Suzuki engineers virtually redesigned the RGV. What emerged was a much improved machine. Not only was the engine uprated - notably with totally new power valves (the original ones 'borrowed' from Suzuki's motocross division), but there was a crescent-shaped, aluminium alloy swinging arm. This component allowed both expansion chamber exhausts to exit on the offside and also provide a staggering 58 degree banking angle.

Other developments over the earlier RGVs included a coaxially mounted gearshift lever, as well as a needle roller bearing on the shaft for greater strength and revised gear ratios to improve acceleration. The main frame was also substantially improved, and the sub-frame modified for easier maintenance (it was detachable).

The front suspension now employed upside-down forks with a marginally steeper steering head angle. Both wheels were now 17-inch, with wider section rims. Brakes too had been uprated; the front discs now measuring 300mm.

Although the power output remained unchanged, a reprogrammed engine management system provided more usable power characteristics. Suzuki also offered a wide range of 'kit' racing parts; close ratio gears (the gears could be changed without splitting the crankcases), power valve breathers (a revised cover for each cylinder with piping and bottle), full racing exhausts, a racing engine management 'black' box and many more items.

With kit parts and specialised tuning it was possible to obtain around 70bhp; however this level of performance exposed weaknesses, notably piston gremlins, jumping out of second gear (with the standard gears) and a few cases of the pins wearing in the power valve assemblies and allowing the tip of the valve to touch the front/top of the pistons. Even so the RGV250M became the bike to beat in 1991 SuperSport 400 racing series.

Like Yamaha's LC of a decade earlier the RGV allowed a whole crop of new riders to make their names, men like Michael Rutter and James Hayden in the newly launched Super Teen championship in Britain. Even established stars won races on the RGV250M - Jamie Whitham being a prime example. This success continued in 1992 with the 'N' version and the 1993 'P'. The Scot, Callum Ramsey won the Super Teen title in 1992 and Jonathon Peacock made it three in succession when the East Anglian youngster took the crown in 1993. But from then on the very latest 400 four-strokes 4-cylinder models such as the Honda NC30, Kawasaki ZXR and Yamaha FZR took over the class.

However, although it needed constant work between meetings, the RGV was an excellent machine, particularly if the cylinders were not modified. On our own machine we completed over 100 races in 1993 with very little problem, testament, if any were needed, of the tiny v-twin's ability on the race circuit.

It is worth noting that although Suzuki stopped production of the RGV in the late 1990s, it still supplies engines to Aprilia. The Italian company then modifies these to its own specification before fitting them to its RS250 sports/racing machine. The bike had proved itself in a host of one-make series throughout Europe (including Britain), and today forms the two-stroke challenge to the dominant 400 four-stroke in SuperSport events.

*The RG250 Gamma set new standards in performance and especially handling when it was launched in 1983. Its 247cc liquid-cooled parallel twin cylinder 2-stroke engine produced 47bhp. It replaced Yamaha's 250LC as the top 250 Production class runner.*

*The first RGV250 to arrive in Great Britain was the 'K' in 1989, followed by the virtually identical 'L' in 1990. Both used power valves based on the Suzuki motocross design which was to prove a major source of problems. Power output of both versions was 57bhp at 11,000rpm.*

*The much improved RGV250M was introduced for the 1991 model year. Improvements included new power valves, gull-shaped aluminium swinging arm, twin silencers exiting on the offside and inverted front forks.*

*Rookie racer Gary Walker at Pembrey, South Wales, May1992, with his RGV250M, purchased new as a standard street bike in late 1991.*

*Amazing what a year can do. A far more confident Gary Walker with his father Mick at Snetterton in March 1993, for a practice session with the, by now competitive RGV, fully kitted and producing 63-65bhp.*

*Gary Walker leading Doug Cowie (Yamaha FZR400RR) at Mallory Park during the final round of the 1993 British Super Teen Championship, in which Gary's RGV beat the 4 cylinder 4-stroke to claim a rostrum finish.*

Snetterton Esses, KRC (Kent Racing Combine) meeting, 11th September 1993, race winner Gary Walker RGV250M.

Lee Masters with his new RGV250P at Donington Park, British Super Teen series 1993.

Louise Grist RGV Suzuki, Snetterton, Coram Curve 4th April 2003.

*For the 1992 model year (coded WN) the GSXR750 was given a new liquid-cooled engine to reduce heat under severe racing conditions. The bike illustrated is a works endurance racer.*

All-in-all the 750L was the best GSXR yet. In 1991 the GSXRs were coded M, but with very little change, with the exception of a narrower fairing and bodywork and some changes aimed at improving comfort for street use.

At the end if 1991, after seven years of production the GSXR development team, in conjunction with its own programme and the feedback from the endurance racing effort, concluded that the time had come to make a switch to water-cooling.

Since its introduction, the combination of air/oil cooling had served the GSXR range well. It would be true to say that the design never suffered in terms of performance against the competition, having managed to hold its own in the relentless round of annual changes. The system even had some major advantages, such as a greater simplicity in construction, maintenance and weight saving. It was appropriate for its time, and yet when its time was up the Suzuki engineering team had the good sense to realise this.

In laying out the 1992 GSXR750 (coded WN), the Kamamastu works at long last bowed to what many saw as the inevitable and introduced water-cooling (the 1100 remained oil/air cooled for another year). And it was not just water-cooling; the GSXR750 had been redesigned in many other ways, but without losing the structural proportions or characteristics which had so benefited its older brothers.

*German-built DR800 Suzuki single, the BMR Megamono. Note the usual frame construction, circa 1997.*

Even if it appeared very similar to the M version, the chassis had, in fact, been completely redrawn in an all-new 60 x 45mm tubing, forming a continuous double cradle of forged and extruded sections with a detachable offside rail and bolt-on rear sub-frame. The 43mm inverted front forks remained unchanged, as did the link-type rear suspension, with its mono-shock remote reservoir 'cushion' damper. There was however a new swinging arm involving the use of different designs for the off and rear sides. The near side was an

At the end of 1996, both Honda and Suzuki announced Ducati-type V-twins. The Suzuki entry was the 996cc (98 x 66mm) TL1000, with liquid cooling, 4-valves-per-cylinder and 90 degree v-twin layout. The original 'S' version suffered from handling glitches, but the 'R' version introduced from the 1998 model year onwards was much improved. It has proved an excellent choice for Sound of Thunder events, both at club and national levels.

aluminium box-section pipe measuring 71.6 x 38.6mm, whilst the pressed-aluminium rigid one-piece off-side swinging arm was especially shaped to allow the exhaust pipe on that side to be tucked in closer to the centre of the bike. Combined with the new slimline bodywork, this feature allowed a banking angle of no less than 54 degrees.

Revised weight distribution, with the engine being mounted lower down in the chassis and inclined forward at approximately 18 degrees, together with the changes in wheelbase length, trail and rake, resulted in a substantial change in the GSXR's handling characteristics. What didn't alter was the wheels, tyre sizes, or the brakes, which used the standard 310mm disc/4-piston calipers up front and a single opposed piston caliper at the rear.

The same applied to the engine's bore and stroke measurements, though virtually everything else was altered in some way during the change-over to a water-cooled unit. The cooling system itself was served by a large, concave aluminium radiator, used in conjunction with the existing SACS oil-jet system, in which nozzles sprayed the inside walls of the pistons to assist cooling. The main water-cooling circuit also removed heat from the lubricant through a mini-radiator which went around the oil filter base.

Thanks to a total rethink of the internal engine components (lighter pistons and con-rods plus a reduction in the crankshaft length, even though the journals were actually bigger), the liquid-cooled engine was reduced almost by 60mm over the span of its predecessor to a very narrow 433mm. Another major difference from the outgoing oil/air-cooled unit was the camshaft arrangement which now opened and closed the valves by way of bucket and shims operated by a pair of rockers, whilst the valve angle was narrowed from 40 to 30 degrees. Apart from the considerably higher 11.8:1 compression ratio, the superior power output of the liquid-cooled GSXR750 was derived from not only the weight saving of the pistons and connecting rods, but from revised inlet ports and a new 6.8 litre air box. Additionally, both the clutch and the gearbox, with totally new ratios for the latter, had been considerably strengthened.

... a smiling Chris Walker, he had some great races with Ducati mounted Neil Hodgson in both 1999 and 2000.

Clarion Suzuki GSXR750 rider Chris Walker with both wheels well clear of the ground at the BSB (British SuperBike) Cadwell Park round in 1999...

*GSXR600 (161) mounted Dyon Compton leading the field of SuperSport models at Mallory Park, at the Gary Walker Memorial meeting, 13th August 2000.*

For many years, it had been a major mystery why Suzuki had not followed up its hugely successful GSXR750 with a smaller version, for the booming SuperSport 600 class. Instead, it had clung grimly to the low-tech GSX 600F and later the RF600, neither of which made much impression, either on the race track or for that matter in the showroom.

*It was a mystery to many why it took Suzuki so long to build a smaller version of its hugely successful GSXR750, but finally, from the 1997 model year, they brought out the GSXR600. The machine illustrated is the 1998 GSXR600 British Championship winner on show at the NEC in November that year.*

Finally, for the 1997 model year, Suzuki succumbed to both inside and outside pressures and launched just such a bike, the GSXR600. Although this new 600 shared much of its frame, bodywork and engine components with its bigger brother, the newcomer had a character all of its own. For starters, the engine needed revving hard to get the best out of it, so, compared with, for example, the Honda CBR 600 was more suited to the circuit than the public highway. In addition, although cost cutting was evident in the suspension department - the 750 having inverted forks, the 600 conventional telescopic ones - the steering response was just as sharp, with plenty of feel. The braking, although not in the Yamaha class, was more than adequate. The aluminium frame was identical to the 750, although the swinging arm lacked its larger brother's bracing, and the 600 ran a slightly narrower rear wheel and a 180/55 17-inch tyre (the 750 a 190 section).

From the 1998 model year the engine was modified to deliver more mid-range torque and top-end power with new cam timing for greater valve lift, improved engine airflow and a larger exhaust collector box. Finally, for 2001 the GSXR600 was extensively re-engineered. Compared to the 'old' engine, the 2001 unit had shorter stroke dimensions of 67 x 42.5mm - as against the original 65.5 x 44.5mm measurements - to

*The 1998 World SuperSport Champion Fabrizio Pirovano with his GSXR600.*

reduce mechanical losses at high rpm. In this 'new' GSXR600, the valves were set at a narrower included angle (28 instead of 30 degrees), making the combustion chamber more compact and increasing the compression ratio from 12:1 to 12.2:1. The inlet valves were positioned 13 degrees and the exhaust valves 15 degrees from the cylinder centre line, versus the previous bikes 16 and 16 degrees respectively. The down draught angle of the inlet ports was steeper, 44 degrees from the horizontal instead of 41.5 degrees. The inlet valves were of a larger 27.2mm diameter compared to 26.5mm, whilst the stem diameter of the exhaust valves had been decreased from 4.5mm to 4mm. The remainder of the valve gear had also been modified. The cylinder-head casting was also changed and weighed less. The crankshaft, bearings, connecting rods, gudgeon pins, pistons, clutch assembly, and most of the transmission gears were also new.

And it wasn't just the power unit which had been heavily redesigned, but other new components included the frame, swinging arm, front forks, rear shock, wheels, brake calipers, and final drive chain. The bodywork had improved aerodynamics; dry weight 359lb (163kg) and a maximum speed of around 160mph.

*Novice rider Paul Haigh with his GSXR600 at Cadwell Park, 29th June 2002.*

*Djon Compton GSXR600 taking part in the British Junior Super Stock race at Silverstone, 16th April 2001. He was later to crash out, due to oil on the track.*

*Guido Metzeler, one of the three partners who make up the BMR Super Mono team. The dohc conversion of the Suzuki DR800 single is the work of the Austrian engineer, Applebeck.*

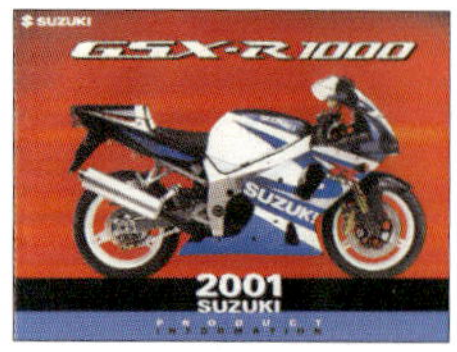


The GSXR750 WN was also a more comfortable machine than its forerunners - and had a lower seat height (780mm).

As before, it took Suzuki until the 1993 model year to introduce a liquid-cooled version of its 1100 - the WP. This was also a considerable improvement over the bike it replaced. Not only was there water-cooling, but new 6-pot calipers up front and a reduction in displacement from 1127 to 1074cc. Even with the latter change, this didn't prevent a 10bhp increase in power output - to 153bhp in unrestricted form.

For 1994 Suzuki introduced the GSXR750 WR. This had an additional 2bhp whilst weight decreased to 438.7lb (199kg). This also benefited from the 6-piston calipers found on the 1100 and an increase in front fork stanchion tube diameter from 41 to 43mm. There were also changes to the swinging arm and tyre sizes.

The next major update, a new bike in fact, used the same styling as the brand new GSXR600. Technically, there was a new engine, making the 750T the lightest and most compact machine in the 750 SuperSport category. With forced air induction, 128bhp and 394lb (179kg) - plus an equally new twin-spar chassis (still aluminium) and based on the factory's RGV Gamma GP 500, the GSXR shot back to lead its class once again. Although the 1997 (V) was unchanged, the following year saw the 750W. Developments included fuel injection, a 50 per cent larger air box, small engine modifications putting power up to 135bhp, and a closer ratio gearbox.

The next revision came with the Y model for the year 2000. This featured a more compact and lighter engine and yet another new frame. Overall dry weight had been reduced still further, to 366lb (166kg). The gearbox now employed staggered input and output shafts (thus reducing engine length) and the fuel injection was given two butterflies to improve emissions and throttle response.

As explained elsewhere, Suzuki was late developing a truly competitive 600 SuperSports bike, which didn't appear until the mid-1990s - almost a decade after Kawasaki, Honda and Yamaha.

*A works GSXR750 being ridden in the British round of the World SuperBike series at Brands Hatch in 1998 by James Witham.*

*The GSX1000 arrived for 2001 and quickly took over the mantle formerly held by Yamaha's R1.*

And although the GSXR1100 was a quick motorcycle it was largely left to the long-running GSXR750 to fly the flag in various racing events up to and including the World SuperBike (WSB) series which had begun back in 1988. However, the introduction of the new GSXR1000 for the 2001 model year put Suzuki back at the head of the field in unlimited class racing. In the process it effectively replaced the previously dominant Yamaha R1 which had been introduced some three years earlier.

With the main emphasis now going into the 600 class, apart from the still hugely popular SuperBike series at both national and world level, Suzuki have at last got competitive bikes in all three sectors of four-stroke racing: 600, 750 and 1000cc. And when one considers the huge developments already seen by the GSXR's family since the first model appeared in the mid-1980s. We can only imagine what is to come.

*James McBride (second left) 2002 New Era 600 SuperSport Club Champion. His Suzuki GSXR600, and other members of his team, known as JV Racing for 2003.*

# Tohatsu

# 8

*Tony Godfrey's Tohatsu 125 air-cooled twin-cylinder production racer, Snetterton, May 1963.*

The history of this little-known marque can be traced back to 1922, when the Takata Motor Institute began carrying out research into various forms of internal combustion engines. In 1932, the company, now trading as Takata Motor Manufacturing Ltd, was largely dependent upon the revenue earned from its thriving petrol-engined generator sales.

The business continued to expand, and in May 1939 was once again renamed, this time as Tokyo Hatsudoki Co. Ltd. By December 1941, when Japan entered World War 2, it had become one of the most important manufacturers in its field, and during the war years found its products in great demand, supplying thousands of generator sets to the Japanese armed forces.

Tokyo Hatsudoki survived the conflict with its production facilities intact. Nonetheless, the factory's management had a major problem because with the ending of the war, its biggest customer, the Japanese military, was all but disbanded. So production was switched at both the Tokyo and Osaka works to the manufacture of fire pumps and motorcycles.

Into the early 1950s, Tokyo Hatsudoki's production expanded rapidly, and the company found it necessary to open another Tokyo factory to cope with extra demand - particularly for its two-wheelers. At the same time, the motorcycle division's products began to be marketed under the Tohatsu name. By 1957, there was a four-model line-up of production roadsters with engine capacities of 86.7, 123, and 199cc, all single-cylinder two-strokes with piston-port induction.

## 1962 Runpet CR50

| | |
|---|---|
| Engine | Air-cooled single cylinder 2-stroke, with piston-port induction |
| Capacity | 49cc |
| Bore | 41mm |
| Stroke | 37.5mm |
| Comp ratio | 18:1 |
| Carburation | N/A |
| Ignition | magneto |
| Gearbox | Four speeds |
| Clutch | Wet, multi-plate |
| Frame | Steel, beam type construction |
| Suspension | Front: telescopic fork<br>Rear: swinging arm, twin shock |
| Brakes | Full-width drums, front and rear |
| Tyres | 18-inch front and rear |
| Dry weight | 111lb (50kg) |
| Max power | 6.8bhp @ 12,000rpm |
| Max speed | 84mph |

*Dual drum front stopper of the Tohatsu 50. Actually the chassis, suspension and brakes were probably the best of any comparable machine on sale to the general public at that time.*

*Mike Simmonds (Dave's older brother) during his winning ride on his 50cc Tohatsu at Castle Combe national road races, 20th April 1963. Behind, with his head well down is Graham Votier on an Italian Itom.*

The twin carb Tohatsu 124cc (43 x 43mm) air-cooled, piston-port twin cylinder engine.

By 1961, Tohatsu had risen to take some 3 per cent of the Japanese motorcycle market. With its success on the production front had come the realisation that to progress further, it would need to follow the bigger producers, notably Honda, and build competition machines.

The Tokyo Show, held in October that year, saw the first of Tohatsu's efforts - a couple of motocrossers (125 and 250cc) and a brand-new racing 'fifty', the Runpet CR50. The heaviest of the 50s exhibited, it weighed in at 111lb (50 kg). Its engine was a single-cylinder two-stroke, with slightly over-square dimensions and the astronomic compression ratio of 18:1. Maximum power was 6.8bhp at 12,000rpm. Other details included a close-ratio, four-speed gearbox, and a beam-type frame with telescopic forks and swinging-arm rear suspension.

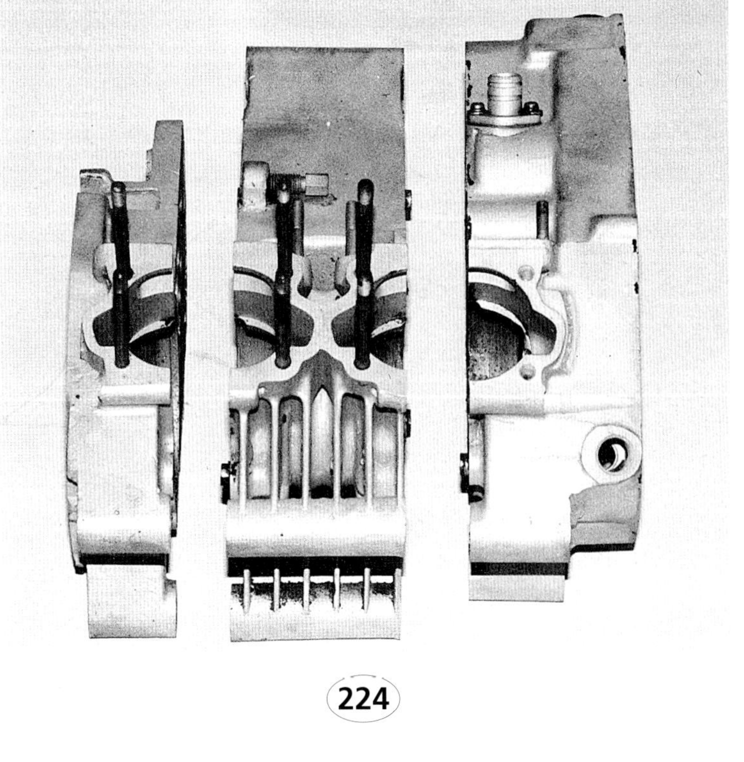

An unusual feature of the 125 Tohatsu was its 3-piece, vertically split crankcase. This allowed owners to strip and rebuild the engine with a minimum of specialised tools.

## 1963 125 Twin

| | |
|---|---|
| Engine | Air-cooled, parallel twin, two-stroke with piston-port induction and 3-piece, vertically split crankcases |
| Capacity | 124cc |
| Bore | 43mm |
| Stroke | 43mm |
| Comp ratio | 14 - 16:1 |
| Carburation | 2 x Amal 22mm |
| Ignition | Magneto<br>(later models 12 volt battery/coil) |
| Gearbox | Five-speeds |
| Clutch | Dry, multi-plate |
| Frame | Steel, twin duplex construction |
| Suspension | Front: telescopic fork<br>Rear: swinging arm, twin shock |
| Brakes | Front: twin 5LS drum, full-width hub<br>Rear: single 5LS drum, full-width hub |
| Tyres | 18-inch front and rear |
| Dry weight | N/A |
| Max power | 25bhp @ 12,000rpm |
| Max speed | 115mph |

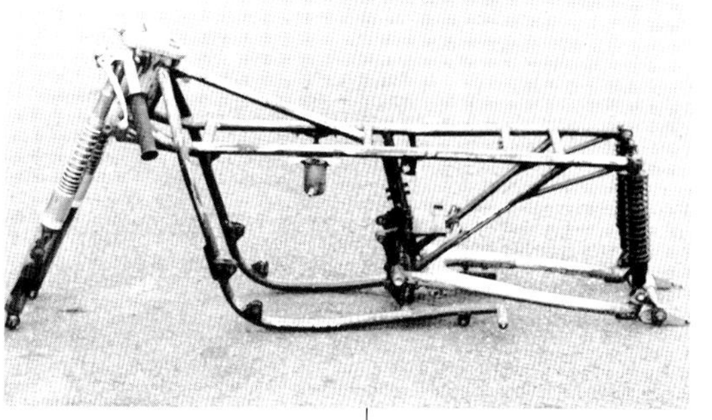

*Frame assembly of the 125 Tohatsu, full duplex with considerable bracing around the steering head. Its layout owed much to the Featherbed Norton.*

*The 125 twin's crankshaft was actually two assemblies, the offside one being assembled into the offside crankcase and the nearside crank, with the centre case attached, was pushed by hand into the size-fit spline of the offside crankshaft. The nearside crank was then fitted to complete the simple, but very effective assembly.*

*The 125cc Tohatsu twin was in many ways a scaled-up version of the company's 50cc. Like its smaller brother, it had truly exceptional cycle parts. It was also an attractive little bike.*

*Tohatsu 125 twin in the Brands Hatch paddock, the full width SLS rear drum brake, battery, ignition coil, swinging arm, rear shocks and Dunlop KR 'triangular' rear tyre.*



The company had also been busily developing a twin-cylinder model for 125cc events. Both this and the smaller model made their international debut at the US Grand Prix, held at Daytona in early February 1962. This came after several successes at home with prototypes during the previous year.

For Daytona, six riders were entered, two Americans and four Japanese. In the 50cc event, Tomada was placed third with Hanazawa fourth. In the 125cc race, Tohatsu entrants came in fourth, seventh, eighth and ninth.

Besides these works bikes, the same period also saw the production 125 Sport Road Racer offered to private customers. Although still a twin, this was clearly based on the Arrow touring model. Coded LB3, the Sport had a capacity of 124cc with square 43 x 43mm dimensions. The gearbox was a five-speeder, and the machine developed 17bhp at 8500rpm in top. Its specification even included an electric starter! Maximum speed with a racing kit was almost 90mph.

However, compared to its two-stroke rivals Suzuki and Yamaha, let alone the all-conquering four-stroke Hondas, none of the Tohatsus weretruly competitive. This led to the design and development of the definitive racing Tohatsus during 1962. Not only was there a completely revamped 125, but a brand-new six-speed 49.81cc twin. Coded CA, thiswas destined to become the only twin-cylinder 50cc racer offered to Joe Public. Its tiny cylinders had a bore and stroke of 31 x 33mm. Both machines were exhibited for the first time at the Tokyo Show in October 1962.

The new Tohatsu twins were extremely advanced for their time. The larger model was notable because of its three-piece, vertically-split crankcases, which allowed owners to strip and rebuild the engine with a minimum of special tools. The crankshaft was built as two 62cc singles and coupled with a size-fit spline which, although similar to early Yamaha practice, could be separated without resorting to a hydraulic press. The crankshaft, equipped with four ball-roller main bearings and four conventional neoprene oil seals, had full-circle flywheels and conventional caged roller bearing big-ends. The con-rods, however, were neither oval nor I-section. Instead, they were rectangular and fitted with bronze-bushed small-ends, unusual for a 12,000rpm two-stroke.

The Achilles heel of the engine was its pistons. These were prone to seizing and cracking around the gudgeon-pin bosses, and it was not until much later (1968) that a full solution was to be found, when a batch of replacement pistons were manufactured by the West German specialists Mahle.

The close-ratio, five-speed gearbox proved reliable, but not so the small air-cooled clutch. With an extremely high first gear, the punishment needed to get the machine off the line often led to all sorts of bearing and clutch-associated failures.

The cylinder barrels were of alloy construction with cast-iron liners. These were conventional in so far as they were three-port loop scavenged, but unconventional due to their extremely exaggerated spigot length. The Tohatsu had inlet ports cast into the crankcases, making the long cylinder spigot necessary to support the notoriously unreliable piston. The wide, unbridged inlet port did contain a small lip on its upper edge to prevent the piston rings opening into the port. However, the scuffing and cracking of failed pistons suggests that it would have been better if this lip had been extended into a full bridge. This would have helped support the rear of the piston which, because of the original Tohatsu design, was allowed to tilt and catch the base of this over-wide port. The cylinders were held down by four 8mm through studs but, due to the generous proportions of the liner, did not suffer any of the local seizing problems caused by heat distortion, often associated with this type of layout.

The central-plug head, looking extremely similar to an early Yamaha type, had a wide squish band and a deep tapering combustion chamber. The combustion volume was in the region of 14-16:1, an extremely high figure for an air-cooled engine and obviously a contributory factor to high piston temperatures and consequent failures.

The strange and violent distortion of the inlet port did nothing for the engine's output and, due to the low-set inlet ports, it was necessary to clear the 22mm Amal carburettors from the top of the vertically-split crankcases. Several owners changed these instruments for Italian Dell'Ortos of the same size.

The ignition, looked after by a crank-end-mounted contact breaker assembly, was fed from a frame-mounted 12-volt battery - although the earliest examples were equipped with a magneto.

The construction of the three-section crankcase was one of the more fascinating elements of the design. The offside crankshaft was first assembled into the offside crankcase. With the centre case attached, the nearside crankshaft was then pushed by hand into the size-fit spline of the offside crank. The nearside crankcase was then fitted to complete the simple, but very effective, assembly.

The engine's unique construction was matched by the innovative chassis. While other Japanese manufacturers, such as Suzuki and Yamaha, concentrated their efforts on simple top-tube frames, Tohatsu engineers designed a neatly crafted twin duplex affair which provided superb roadholding. In fact, for many years after the original engine was no longer competitive, Tohatsu cycle parts were used to house other power units. This trend continued until the mid 1970s.

*Dave Simmonds receiving the garlands of victory from the Brands Hatch steward in 1963, the year he won the 125cc ACU Star (British Championship) series.*

# 1963 CA50 Twin

| | |
|---|---|
| Engine | Air-cooled, parallel twin, two-stroke, with piston-port induction |
| Capacity | 49cc |
| Bore | 31mm |
| Stroke | 33mm |
| Comp ratio | 14 - 16:1 |
| Carburation | N/A |
| Ignition | Magneto |
| Gearbox | Five speeds |
| Clutch | Dry, multi-plate |
| Frame | Steel, twin duplex construction |
| Suspension | Front: telescopic fork<br>Rear: swinging arm, twin shock |
| Brakes | Front: twin SLS drum, full-width hub<br>Rear: single SLS drum, full-width hub |
| Tyres | 18-inch front and rear |
| Dry weight | N/A |
| Max power | 10bhp @ 16,000rpm |
| Max speed | 90mph |

*The Lex Mond Museum in Holland is currently rebuilding an extremely rare, Tohatsu 50cc twin. Many parts have to be specially made for the restoration.*

*The Tohatsu 49cc twin was the only one of its type ever to reach production. However, keeping it running was a problem due to frequent piston failures.*

The same applied to items such as the forks and brakes. Whereas these components could also be found on Suzuki, Honda and Yamaha machines of the period, this applied only to factory prepared works specials, while Tohatsu fitted them as standard to their over-the-counter racers.

Resembling its larger brother, the Tohatsu 50 was the only twin-cylinder machine of its capacity ever to be offered to private buyers, but it was afflicted by two serious problems. The first centred around its far from perfect handling, the other was its marginal engine reliability. The 31mm diameter pistons caused some problems, but it was the crankshaft which proved the really weak link.

Super-short big-end life - around 50 miles - was only part of the story. The rest was that when faced with the class-leading Honda CR110, the little twin was often revved in excess of 16,000rpm to keep in touch. This resulted in a spate of broken con-rods and the need for expensive items such as replacement crankcases and cylinder barrels to make good the ensuing carnage.

However, even though neither the 50 nor 125cc Tohatsu twins could be called the model of reliability, they were still more than fit for their intended purpose, that of winning races.

One man stood head and shoulders above the rest of the Tohatsu riders. This was the Englishman Dave Simmonds, from Stanwell, Middlesex. Quietly spoken Dave had started motorcycling on a 197cc Zundapp and began racing in 1960 on a 50cc Itom. For 1962, his father, a steward with BOAC (long since merged with British Airways), managed to buy a 50cc Tohatsu Runpet air-cooled single-cylinder engine in Tokyo, and it was using this powerplant that Dave started to go places. Tohatsu were impressed and in 1963, they supplied the Simmonds equipe (which also included elder brother Mike) with a pair of the then new twin-cylinder 50 and 125 cc racing machines free of charge - although the brothers had to pay a considerable amount themselves for freight and import fees.

*Ian Speller working on his Tohatsu 125 twin, again, at Brands Hatch. Note the Austin Mini in the background, mid 1960s.*

The larger machine arrived first, with the 50cc Tohatsu twin delivered after the TT that year - in which their own home-brewed Tohatsu engined single blew up in a big way.

Mid July saw the Simmonds brothers win both the 50 and 125cc events and set new lap records at Castle Coombe. This was quickly followed by a whole host of similar achievements throughout Britain that summer, perhaps the highlight being in October when Dave beat the works Honda star Tommy Robb in the 125cc race.

A month later, at the Japanese Grand Prix, the company announced that it was considering the sponsorship of a factory team for the 1964 European Grand Prix season. If they did, Tohatsu stated, it was likely that the team would be headed by Dave Simmonds with another English rider, Tony Godfrey, plus one or two Japanese.

Unfortunately, the idea was to remain but a dream, for in the subsequent months Tohatsu struggled from one financial crisis to another, until finally, in February 1964, the company was declared bankrupt. All the remaining racers, including spares, jigs and tools, were purchased by John Honda (no relation to the other Mr Honda), who then set up Japan Racing Motor Cycles.

Manufacture of the Tohatsu standard production roadsters was never resumed, even though there were strong rumours that the rights to produce the 1964 model line were to be sold to the Nationalist Chinese government in Formosa (now Taiwan).

Meanwhile, Dave Simmonds, assisted by his brother and father, continued to campaign the existing twins with a great level of success. Not only did he win the 125cc ACU Star (British Championship) in 1963, but he also went on to win the 125cc British Championship at Oulton Park twice - the only other rider to match this performance was a certain Mike Hailwood. Simmonds also won three TT Replicas on Tohatsu machinery. Later, Dave Simmonds became a works rider for Kawasaki (from 1967 onwards) - and a world champion.

*A well-patched 125 twin in the Snetterton paddock, 1964. It is still largely original, but showing signs of a hard life.*

*Dave Simmonds in his last year of racing the 125 Tohatsu before becoming a works Kawasaki rider in 1967. He is seen here en route to victory at Castle Combe's Quarry Bends, 10th September 1966.*

Meanwhile, after the bankruptcy, almost all the engineers formally employed by Tohatsu moved to the Bridgestone Motor Company (see Chapter 1). The Tohatsu 50cc racing-twin design was also used by Bridgestone as a basis for their very similar EJR-2 model, but this benefited from the use of water-cooling.

As late as 1966, Tohatsu was still in the news. Not only was Dave Simmonds having his final season prior to signing for Kawasaki, but a small number of new 50 and 125cc racers reached Britain from Japan Racing Motor Cycles. Essentially 1964-type bikes, these were imported by Wallingford dealer Jim Pink. They were mainly 125s (which sold for £550), but a few 50s also arrived. These were sold on to a Dutch company, as by then the 50cc racing class was almost dead in Britain.

Back in Japan, the new Fisco circuit, where the 1966 Japanese Grand Prix was due to be staged later that year, was opened on Sunday 13th March with a meeting split into five classes: 50, 90, 125, 250 and 350cc. With several works entries on the latest machinery, it was quite a surprise that Tohatsu riders finished first and second in the 125cc event. From then on, however, machines such as the five-cylinder Honda and four-cylinder Yamaha took total control of the eighth-litre class and the Tohatsu was finally vanquished.

*Mick Conlin was still successfully racing a 125 Tohatsu into the early 1970s. He is seen here at Thruxton, Summer 1971. By this time, the piston troubles had largely disappeared thanks to a batch of German-made Mahle components.*

# Yamaha - the classic years

# 9

*The TZ250C arrived for 1974, its 247c (54 x 54mm) engine ran on a 7.6:1 compression ratio and produced 48bhp at 10,000rpm.*

The Yamaha production-based racer was originally intended largely for the American market. As revealed in the companion volume *Japanese Grand Prix Racing Motorcycles*, the company sent its rider Fumio Ito to take part at the Catalina races during the summer of 1958. Catalina Island, a holiday resort off the coast of Los Angeles, was more used to hosting the rich and powerful than staging motorcycle racing. Unlike the American racing scene of today, in the 1950s racing Stateside usually meant poor attendances and awful road surfaces. Catalina was no exception. Its six-mile circuit was little more than a gravel track, and the event was more like motocross than road racing.

The machine which Ito used to secure sixth place was the short-stroke (56 x 50mm) twin YD-B, which had performed so well at Asama the year before. There were two machines, in fact, both being modified for Catalina. The most notable changes were raised pipes and a smaller-capacity tank.

In July 1959, the lessons gained by Yamaha's racing experience were offered for public consumption in the form of the YDS1 sports roadster, which was available with optional off-road or race kits. The latter comprised new cylinders, heads, ignition system, carbs and expansion chambers, plus certain cycle parts. The race-kitted YDS1, called the Asama, generated a useful 25bhp at 9000rpm and provided its rider with a maximum speed of around 95mph on optimum gearing.

The majority of the kit-type YDS I s went to the United States, as they fitted in well with the AMA's production based racing regulations. Some examples were also exported to

*Yamaha YL1 (built from 1966 to 1971). The 89cc (36.5 x 43mm) twin was offered not only as a series production roadster, but (as shown here) as a race kitted competitor in Japanese 90cc clubmans races. A few were raced in Europe and the USA.*

*Yamaha's first motorcycle the YA1 single cylinder 2-stroke was clearly based on the German DKN RT125. Its success was helped considerably by its class domination of the Mount Fuji and Asama races in 1955.*

Australia. None went to Europe, however - well, at least not directly. The one known example made a fleeting visit to Britain in the summer of 1960. This was the race-kitted YDS1 of Californian dealer Sonny Angel. En route for the TT, Angel took in the international *Motor Cycling* Silverstone Saturday meeting, held in late May at the famous Northamptonshire circuit. This resulted in a finish, albeit near the end of the field and after being lapped three times by race-winner Hailwood's Ducati desmo twin. For his European foray, Angel's Yamaha had been fitted with a dolphin fairing and a front brake from a Manx Norton, otherwise it was standard.

What wasn't generally known at the time was that Angel's machine had seized at Silverstone, and although he had cabled Japan asking for replacements, none arrived in time for him to compete in the Lightweight TT. This piston trouble was not confined to the Californian's machine, for virtually all the early race-kitted YDS1s suffered in a similar manner. This was finally solved by increasing the silicon content of the pistons and designing new, all aluminium cylinders with anodised walls. A change was

*Brian Warburton during practice for the Lightweight (250cc) Manx Grand Prix in 1965. Warburton finished 2nd after being slowed by a split fuel tank. The race was won by Greeves rider Dennis Craine at record speed.*

## 1963 TDIA

| | |
|---|---|
| Engine | Air-cooled, twin cylinder, 2-stroke with piston-port induction |
| Capacity | 247cc |
| Bore | 56mm |
| Stroke | 50mm |
| Comp ratio | 9:1 |
| Carburation | 2 x Mikuni VM20H |
| Ignition | magneto |
| Gearbox | Five-speeds |
| Clutch | Wet, multi-plate |
| Frame | Steel, duplex tubular construction |
| Suspension | Front: telescopic fork<br>Rear: swinging arm, twin shock |
| Brakes | Front: SLS drum, full-width<br>Rear: SLS drum, full-width |
| Tyres | 2.50 x 18 front; 2.75 x 18 rear |
| Dry weight | 212Ib(96kg) |
| Max power | 32bhp @ 9,500rpm |
| Max speed | 118mph |

*FK Wong with one of the very first TD1s built in 1962, riding at the Sembawang circuit, Malaysia, that year. This fairing off shot shows the short, bulbous exhaust expansion chambers.*

*Billie Nelson with the Doncaster Yamaha at Silverstone, 1965. Essentially this was a successful marriage of a TD1A power unit with a Ducati 125 Grand Prix chassis. It inspired a number of similar devices, using either the Ducati or Spanish Bultaco TSS frame. This was in response to the Yamaha's weight/handling deficiencies.*

*Privateer Mick Chatterton riding his own TD1C was the first Yamaha home in the 1969 Lightweight TT. It is worth pointing out that 1969 had seen the arrival of the new TD2. Chatterton's average speed for the 6-lap, 226.38 mile race was 91.16mph.*

also made from two piston rings to one. These changes were needed to cope with the higher engine speeds.

By 1961, the machines were beginning to show greater reliability, but were still prone to letting the rider down far too often.

In Spring 1962, an improved model, the YDS2, appeared. In standard road-going trim, Yamaha claimed it turned out 25bhp, and with the race kit fitted, a respectable 32bhp. Unfortunately, in reality, these figures were lower - 22 and 27bhp respectively.

The YDS2 kit comprised special cylinders, pistons, expansion chambers and racing carburettors, but very quickly the Yamaha management began to question the policy of marketing such a kit, for the factory had no control over how it was fitted and set up. Therefore, it was decided that in future the work would be done in-house. This, of course, led to a more specialised machine, which was designed and built as one unit - the TD1 was born.

A small batch of TD1 machines was built, but it was soon out-classed by a further improved machine. Coded TD1A, this entered production in October 1962, and one of the first examples was displayed at the Tokyo Show later that month, where it aroused considerable interest - not just from America and Australia where the TD1 kit bikes had been sold, but from new markets all around the world. The most important of these new outlets was Europe. With the well-known partnership of Geoff Monty and Allen Dudley Ward, of Twickenham, Middlesex, being confirmed as British concessionaires shortly afterwards, the Yamaha production racer concept was given a considerable boost.

# 1967 TDIC

| | |
|---|---|
| Engine | Air-cooled, twin cylinder, 2-stroke with piston-port induction |
| Capacity | 247cc |
| Bore | 56mm |
| Stroke | 50mm |
| Comp ratio | 8.1:1 |
| Carburation | 2 x Mikuni VM30SC |
| Ignition | magneto |
| Gearbox | Five-speeds |
| Clutch | Wet, multi-plate |
| Frame | Steel, duplex tubular construction |
| Suspension | Front: telescopic fork<br>Rear: swinging arm, twin shock |
| Brakes | Front: 2LS drum, full-width<br>Rear: 5LS drum, full-width |
| Tyres | 2.75 x 18 front; 3.00 x 18 rear |
| Dry weight | 229Ib(104kg) |
| Max power | 36bhp @ 10,000rpm |
| Max speed | 128mph |

*TD1C top end, with heads, cylinders and carburettors.*

*The TD1C arrived for the 1967 season and offered a considerable leap forward in the evolution of Yamaha's 250 over-the-counter racer.*

*1967/68 TD1C fairing off shot showing engine, frame, suspension and wheels.*

*Front (two-leading-shoe)...*

However, concept and results do not always go hand in hand, and so it was with the TD1A. Although it looked every inch a race winner, unfortunately it did not perform like one, even though Yamaha had made a considerable effort to transform the YDS2 roadster into the TD1A racer. The differences were numerous. The engine had new cylinders, heads, pistons, ignition and carbs, together with revised porting and closer internal gear ratios. A major difference between the TD1 and TD1A was in the exhaust system, the expansion chambers being reworked to provide a more usable power output.

*... and rear (single-leading-shoe) full width drum brakes of the TD1C.*

*Stuart Graham (standing with leathers and white helmet) about to take charge of the Padgett TD2 he rode to second place at Cadwell Park, May 1969. Behind is local specialist Derek Chatterton. Graham later won the 1000cc race on a Padgett TR2 350.*

The frame on the racer was constructed in a lighter gauge steel than the roadster, while the brakes and forks were completely redesigned to provide superior handling and greater stopping efficiency. The seat and tank were copied from the works RD48. Again, Yamaha claimed 32bhp. On paper, this should have provided a competitive machine for AMA class racing in the States, where the main opposition were Ducati and Parilla four-stroke singles, which could turn out around 30 bhp at best. However, the Italian bikes had two major advantages, reliability and leech-like roadholding.

Unfortunately for Yamaha and its buyers, the TD1A was not quite fully developed; its biggest failing was that its crankshaft-mounted clutch was not really up to the rigours of racing, so when Yamaha engineers conceived the close-ratio gearbox, they were forced to retain the standard low bottom gear of the roadster (so the clutch would stand more chance of surviving!). This meant a huge gap between first and second, which didn't help in obtaining decent lap times. It also meant that a missed gear could create havoc, as the engine speed clutch would often snap the crankshaft, leaving the unfortunate owner with an expensive repair bill.

*The works Yamaha 350 (112) which Mike Duff rode at Daytona in 1967. It acted as a prototype for the later TD2/TR2 series.*

Of the three TD1As imported into Britain during 1963, the most notable performances were gained by the bike ridden by the then unknown Bill Ivy, who was later to become a Yamaha works rider and world champion (see Chapter 9). Ivy was Monty's 'official' pilot, and his undoubted ability made up for the TD1A's shortcomings. In any case, at this time, Yamaha's main interest centred on the American racing scene; neither Europe nor other markets took priority in 1963.

*A 1969 TR2 347.4cc (64 x 54mm) with the fairing removed. Note inclined cylinders, full duplex frame and massive expansion chambers with long thin tail pipes. That year, it was the most competitive 350cc racing motorcycle money could buy.*

As early as January 1963, the leading American journal, *Cycle World*, had carried out a track test of the TD1A (alongside the YDS2 roadster), but unfortunately, as was the policy those days, none of its faults were mentioned. Even its maximum speed of 102mph was 'excused' by saying that the machine was set up for the Isle of Man race and was drastically over-geared for Riverside (a circuit in California). As the bikes were built for America, rather than Europe, this seems strange! Yamaha also sold the Ascot Scrambler in the States.

The Ascot was something of a 'halfway house' between the YDS2 and TD1A and was used for half-mile dirt tracks, rather than European-type motocross events.

With the debut of the improved YDS3, in the summer of 1964, the production racer department had the opportunity of getting rid of some of the inherent weaknesses in the TD1A. They were also fortunate to receive detailed information regarding the various failures experienced by the TD1A racers in America, where the importers, Yamaha International Corporation, based in Los Angeles, had carefully logged all the problems and fed them back to Japan.

With the TD1B, Yamaha made a massive effort to improve reliability and track performance. Once again, new cylinders, pistons, heads, ignition and carbs were the order of the day These modifications brought an extra 4 bhp. Additionally, the gearbox internals had been strengthened, front fork damping improved and new rear suspension units fitted. Sixteen were imported into Britain during 1964 and sold at a price of £520 each.

*The massive 220mm 4 leading shoe front anchor, as specified for the TD2/TR2 series.*

Like other over-the-counter Yamaha production-based racers, fully detailed specifications are contained in this and the following chapter. Ultimately, Yamaha were to challenge the mighty overhead cam Norton as the greatest in the sport - at least for the privateer.

However, success was not to come straight away, and even though improved, the TD1B was still not truly competitive. One of its main drawbacks still centred around its handling and roadholding. Many competitors sought a radical cure, mounting the Yamaha engine in a totally new set of running clothes. Probably the first such example was the Doncaster

# YAS1 and YAS3 twins

*The Kirkby brothers Roy (mechanic) and John (rider, right), with their home brewed YAS1. This employed a Honda CB160 frame and forks, Oldani front brake and Girling rear shocks; East Kirkby Airfield Lincolnshire, 1970.*

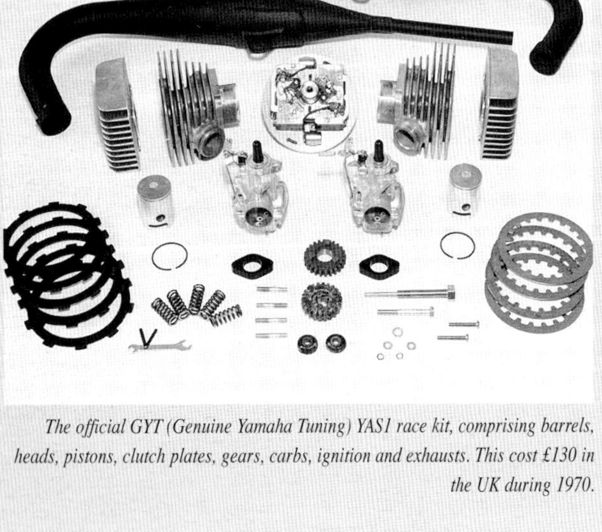

*The official GYT (Genuine Yamaha Tuning) YAS1 race kit, comprising barrels, heads, pistons, clutch plates, gears, carbs, ignition and exhausts. This cost £130 in the UK during 1970.*

*Neil Tuxworth with his Tex-Yam at Cadwell Park International, September 1970. Neil was later team manager for the Castrol-Honda World SuperBike squad.*

*Another leading 125 Yamaha rider of the era was the late Steve Machin seen here at his local Cadwell Park circuit in 1970. His brother Jack also raced the tiny Yamahas and the brothers even produced their own frame kit.*

*1973 Sumac, based on the YAS3 and built by Jack Machin. This machine won 27 of the 29 races it contested that year. Note the water-cooling, Italian Fontana double sided front brake and slim lines.*

The YAS1 air-cooled 124cc (43x43mm) twin arrived at the end of 1968 and was clearly derived from the earlier 97cc YL1. As it boasted 15 bhp at 8500 rpm and a 5-speed gearbox, it quickly became apparent that it had considerable racing potential. Very soon Yamaha were to offer the GYT (Genuine Yamaha Tuning) kit, which was not only comprehensive, but also expensive (costing £130 in the UK during 1970). Yamaha sources quoted 23 bhp at 14,000 rpm.

In Britain the first YAS1 to go racing was the Granby supported model. Tuned by Terry Beckett, this proved a winner in the hands of Austin Hockley almost overnight , and started a trend that others were soon to follow. Also instantly, the pukka racers such as the Honda CR93 and Bultaco TSS were being beaten into the ground by these road-based bikes. The biggest failings of the YAS1 were its marginal engine reliability and its chassis. The latter was largely cured once the special builders got to work.

The YAS1 was replaced by the 2 (only sold in Japan) for 1970 and by the improved 3 from late 1971. Horizontally ribbed cylinder heads were a hallmark of the later engine. And the standard engine, the '3' was also beefed up with improved piston/ring design, a sturdier clutch and a stronger gearbox. In standard guise all three engines were air-cooled. However, many converted them to water-cooling either by homespun cylinders or professionally designed and marketed racing aftermarket components.

This set of photographs shows just a selection of the huge number of YAS1 and 3 machines converted for track use.

*1974 125cc TT. Left to right; 2nd Ivan Hodgkinson (12), 1st Clive Horton (8) and 3rd Tom Herron (3), all mounted on race kitted Yamaha AS3s.*

*Charlie Williams (1) with the Derek Johnson water-cooled AS3 racer, Isle of Man TT 1974.*

## 1969 TR2

| | |
|---|---|
| Engine | Air-cooled, twin cylinder, 2-stroke with piston-port induction |
| Capacity | 348cc |
| Bore | 61mm |
| Stroke | 59.6mm |
| Comp ratio | 6.5:1 |
| Carburation | 2 x Mikuni VM34SC |
| Ignition | Magneto |
| Gearbox | Five-speeds |
| Clutch | Wet, multi-plate |
| Frame | Steel, duplex tubular construction |
| Suspension | Front: telescopic fork<br>Rear: swinging arm, twin shock |
| Brakes | Front: double sided LS drum full-width<br>Rear: 5LS drum |
| Tyres | 3.00 x 18 front and rear |
| Dry weight | 244lb(111kg) |
| Max power | 54bhp at 9,500rpm |
| Max speed | 145mph |

*Three stars at the Cadwell Park International in September 1969. Terry Grotefeld...*

*...Phil Read...*

*... and local hero Derek Chatterton. All are essentially stock 'out-of-the-crate' examples of either TD2 or TR2s, with the exception of Read's machine which has Italian Ceriani front forks and British Girling rear shocks.*

*Another TD2 with Ceriani forks and Girling rear shocks this one is owned by the Italian Giuseppe Visenzi and ridden by Chas Mortimer (open jacket, centre).*

*Derek Chatterton (kneeling between bikes) and his mechanic at Brands Hatch, circa 1970.*

Yamaha, a TD1A power unit in a set of cycle parts which had previously housed a 125 single-cylinder Ducati Grand Prix engine. Ridden by Billie Nelson, this machine, which made its debut at the end of 1964, was an immediate success. Others followed, using either Ducati or Bultaco frames. The most well known were no doubt those campaigned by Derek Chatterton (Ducati-TD1B) and Rod Gould (Bultaco-TD1C).

The TD1B got off to a good start across the Atlantic where, during 1964, Dick Mann and Gary Nixon chalked up a number of impressive race victories between them. Back in Europe, Roy Boughey finished fifth in the 250cc TT that year on another TD1B. On the British short circuits, Reg Everett finished second in the 1965 ACU Star Championship (the last year before it was renamed the British Championship), riding Ilford dealer Ted Broad's TD1B.

*The Swiss special builder and racer Marly Drixl with his TR2-powered 350 Drixton in 1970. The frame was extremely rigid and offered a lower riding position than a stock TR2. Forks and brakes are of Italian origin.*

Everett had previously ridden Greeves machinery and made his Yamaha debut at Snetterton on 10th May 1964. This was the start of a long-running association with Ted Broad, which was to last until the end of 1967, when Reg announced his retirement. During this period, he was twice more runner-up in the 250cc British Championship series (1966 and 1967), earning the title 'Mr Hard Luck'. Everett also rode various overbored 250 Broad Yamahas in the 350cc class (the first person to do so) with considerable success. It was on one such machine that he almost beat the great Mike Hailwood and the 350 four-cylinder factory Honda at Mallory Park. With a lap to go, Everett led by 200 yards, but rainwater got into the works and stopped him with victory almost in his grasp.

In 1965, the TD1B was given something of a mechanical face-lift. The most noticeable change was a redesigned exhaust system, with fatter expansion boxes and longer, narrower tail pipes, to provide more top-end power. Less obvious improvements included shorter pistons (giving different port timing), larger-diameter small-ends and modified internal porting. Also, in an attempt to cure crankshaft breakages associated with the inertia of the clutch basket, this portion of the crankshaft was almost doubled in diameter.

Only five of the new improved models reached Britain that year, the vast majority going to the States once more, where they were at last beginning to dominate the quarter-litre racing category.

However, Brian Warburton managed to finish second in the Manx Grand Prix during September 1965, even though he was slowed by a split fuel tank, in a race won at record speed by Greeves rider Dennis Craine. Generally, however, the TD1B was still not quick enough or reliable enough to see off the various singles, such as Greeves, Cotton, DMW, Bultaco, Ducati and Aermacchi on the British circuits - even though they had begun to come out on top across the Atlantic.

*Tony Rutter, later a four-time World F2 Champion in the 1980s aboard Ducati V-twins, with his TR2 during a wet race at Castle Combe, 21st April 1970.*

*Kel Curruthers after winning the 100 mile 250cc race at Daytona on the Don Vesco (with glasses) entered TD2B in March 1971.*

*Bob Heath looking happy even though his hands (and leathers) are somewhat dirty thanks to carrying out a strip-down on his TD2.*

The year 1966 saw more attention paid to Europe, with Britain coming out on top with 20 machines imported. By now, several of the top Yamaha dealers were entering bikes, including Ted Broad, Padgett's, Pearce and Nichols, Chattertons and Dugdales, and it was these dealer-entered machines which were the most successful. Typical of these was the Padgett's of Batley TD1B. Ridden by Don Padgett, this featured additional tuning, including a compression ratio raised from 9:1 to 10:1. The pistons themselves were modified to improve gas flow through the ports, and while the shape of the ports was unaltered, all passages were polished. The inlet tracts were reshaped, but the carburettor size (30mm) was unaltered. The factory expansion-chamber system was used, but with 2 inches removed from the length of the tail pipe.

*Yorkshireman Mick Grant first sprang to fame riding a Velocette then Yamaha powered specials for Jim Lee. Grant is seen here in the 1971 Junior TT, in which he finished 7th.*

A change that year in the factory specification was the fitting of stronger front fork springs. Another was a new, slimmer, longer tank, which was fitted in place of the old RD48-style component.

In service, the 1966 model TD1B still tended to be fragile, an additional clutch plate and the afore-mentioned increase in diameter not completely curing the problems in this direction. Small-end life, or lack of it, was another problem. For example, Padgett's recommended that their customers change the needle-roller small-ends every 150-200 miles - the equivalent of three short-circuit meetings.

In truth, it was not until the introduction of the TDIC the following year (1967) that at last the TD racing twins began to achieve real results and hang together for a longer period.

Once again, the production racer programme benefited from the introduction of a new roadster, this time the YDS5, launched in February 1967.

*The secret of the Lee-framed Yamaha TR2B was its excellent power to weight ratio and low centre of gravity.*

Like so many of the improvements in the past, those incorporated by the factory when designing the TD1C had come via the complaints department at the Stateside Yamaha International organisation. In this case, it was not so much a complaint, but rather the Japanese marketing something American tuners had conceived - the five-port cylinder. This was not the now accepted four transfer ports feeding directly from the crankcases, but two conventional transfer

*John Cooper surveying the component parts from a TR3, circa 1972.*

ports with two additional 10mm wide slits fed by holes in the piston wall. With gas now passing under the piston crown and over the small-end, it killed several birds with one stone. This resulted in more speed and greater reliability over its temperamental predecessor, the TD1B.

Another important bug, which was dispensed with on the TD1C, was the awful crankshaft-mounted clutch. On the new engine, the problems this caused were finally resolved by moving the clutch back to the primary gear shaft. With the benefit of hindsight, the question is, why wasn't it done long before?

The primary drive was by straight-cut gears on the left of the engine which, in turn, drove the five-speed cross-over gearbox.

*1971 Lightweight TT, Isle of Man, awaiting the start. Number 8 is Rod Gould, with a factory-supported machine, and number 2 is Kent Andersson on a sister bike. These works models quite often piloted developments incorporated into the production models the following year.*

*The Isle of Man TT circuit with a couple of TR2s screaming past the camera.*

Another problem that had not been cured was the less than reliable Yamaha magneto, which was a cause of many engine failures through the ease by which it lost the correct timing settings. The Amal-type Mikuni carbs also caused difficulties. They still suffered flooding, sticking slides and perpetual fuel surge. One can only presume that, at the time, these components were just not far enough advanced technologically to provide reliable service.

Even if it was still less than perfect, the TD1C was good enough to establish Yamaha as class leaders in road racing events around the world in 1967 - all bar a full Grand Prix event. From Daytona to Brands Hatch, the TD1C was king, and the various singles were at last totally outclassed.

The final version of the TD1B had given a reputed 33bhp at 10,500 rpm in 1966; the 1967 TD1C provided a more than healthy 36bhp.

Two of the quickest TD1Cs in Europe that year were Rod Gould's super-tuned, Bultaco-framed special, and the Ulf Svensson-tuned 'standard' model with six-speed box belonging to Sweden's Kent Andersson.

*During the early years of the Yamaha twin cylinder 2-stroke production racers, the Oriental strokers often had power in abundance, while their handling left room for improvement. European frame builders were quick to step in, and in Britain Colin Seeley found a steady market for his superbly engineered Yamsel machines. One of the first to be delivered went to John Cooper seen here leading Pat Mahoney in 1971.*

*Opposite: Phil Read awaiting the start of the 1971 Lightweight TT, which he won at an average speed of 98.02mph. He also set the fastest lap at 100.08mph. His machine featured an Eric Cheney frame and Helmut Fath-tuned engine.*

6
CHAMPION

*British company Hi-Tac beat Yamaha to putting a water-cooled conversion kit on the market for the 1972 season, for the TD2 (shown) and TR series.*

That same year, in March, Mike Duff debuted a totally new Yamaha in the 200-miler at Daytona. This was the prototype of the TR2 350 which was destined to enter production in time for the 1969 season. This prototype employed a four-speed gearbox, as AMA rules forbade the use of five-speeders. Despite the fact that he was giving away 150cc to the Triumphs and BSAs, and 400cc to the Harley Davidsons, Duff qualified in eighth place at 132mph, proving that this new piston-ported Yamaha was a force to be reckoned with.

Mick Chatterton (no relation to Derek) finished sixth in the 1967 250cc TT, whilst the following year, both Kent Andersson and Rod Gould achieved some excellent Grand Prix placings with their privately entered TD1Cs. Gould finished fourth that season in the final Grand Prix championship table - He finished third three times (in Belgium, Finland and Ulster), an outstanding achievement. Andersson had also finished third at the Nürburgring's season opener in West Germany, in front of Gould, who had taken fourth. At long last, the production-based, piston-ported

*The Hi-Tac liquid-cooled conversion fitted into a chassis. Almost looks neat enough to be a works job. Hi-Tac also produced a similar kit for the T500 Suzuki.*

# 1972 TD3

| | |
|---|---|
| Engine | Air-cooled, twin cylinder, 2-stroke with piston-port induction |
| Capacity | 247cc |
| Bore | 56mm |
| Stroke | 50mm |
| Comp ratio | 7.6:1 |
| Carburation | 2 x Mikuni VM34SC |
| Ignition | CD1 |
| Gearbox | Six-speeds |
| Clutch | Dry, multi-plate |
| Frame | Steel, duplex tubular construction |
| Suspension | Front: telescopic fork<br>Rear: swinging arm, twin shock |
| Brakes | Front: double 2LS drum, full-width<br>Rear: 5LS drum, full-width |
| Tyres | 2.75 x 18 front; 3.00 x 18 rear |
| Dry weight | 231.5lb(105kg) |
| Max power | 49bhp at 9,500rpm |
| Max speed | 138mph |

*A pair of brand new TD3/TR3 machines belonging to Jim Lee and ridden by Mick Grant, at Brands Hatch, spring 1972.*

*Newcomer Roger Marshall (later multi British champion and works rider for Honda and Suzuki) in the early days of his career giving the ex Mike Hailwood/Steve Machin TR3 a run at Silverstone in the mid 1970s.*

## TD/TR evolution

| | |
|---|---|
| 1969 | TD2 Air-cooled parallel twin 247cc (56 x 50mm) magneto ignition, Mikuni VM30SC carbs, 5-speed gearbox, 18-inch wheels, drum brakes, twin shock rear suspension, 44bhp at 10,500pm. |
| | TR2 as above but 348cc (61 x 59.6mm) Mikuni VM34SC carbs, 54bhp at 9,500rpm |
| 1970 | Unchanged |
| 1971 | TD2B 47bhp at 11,000rpm. Cylinder parts modified, revised small end bush, revised exhaust. Raised gearing (250 only). Fuel filler cap moved from right to left. |
| | TR2B 56bhp at 10,000rpm as above but with shorter skirt pistons on inlet side, thinner head gasket to raise compression ratio |
| 1972 | TD3 Revised bore and stroke dimensions of 54 x 54mm, 49bhp at 10,500rpm. Revised gear ratios. Wheelbase shortened from 1315 to 1300mm. CDI ignition, 6-speeds. |
| | TR3 Revised bore and stroke dimensions of 64 x 54mm, giving new capacity of 347cc, 58bhp at 9,500rpm. Revised gear ratios. Wheelbase increased from 1316 to 1331mm. CDI ignition, 6-speeds. |

Yamahas were good enough to get on the leaderboard at a European classic. Another factor, of course, was that both Honda and Suzuki had retired their works teams at the end of the previous season.

Duff had spent most of 1968 racing the new TR2 in North America. A disadvantage was the four-speed gearbox, which the AMA demanded for race machines over 250 cc (a clear ploy to assist Harley Davidson). For 1969, however, the rules were changed to allow five-speeds, which obviously benefited the Yamaha design.

Duff commented at the time, 'I reckon the 350 is faster than the old 250cc RD56 disc-valve works twin, and as fast as the 1965 three-cylinder 350cc MV. Acceleration is not as good as the MV's, but the new five-speed gearbox will do the trick.'

*Don Emde's 1972 Daytona 200 TR3 race winner with...*

# Don Emde's 1972 Daytona victory

Don Emde's 1972 Daytona 200 victory must count as one of the biggest upsets ever for this American classic. For starters Emde, whose father Floyd had been the winner of the 1948 Daytona 200, was riding a production 350 TR3 (the last of the air-cooled Yamahas) and faced enormous odds not only from a host of works entries, but the majority on much bigger displacement machines.

In addition to factory 750s from Norton and Honda, both Kawasaki and Suzuki fielded new, large capacity water-cooled two-stroke triples, whilst the talented New Zealander Geoff Parry rode a year-old TR500 Suzuki twin. All were up against the Bob Hanson-managed Kawasaki team of 750s ridden by the likes of Paul Smart, Yvon DuHamel and Gary Nixon.

Emde started the race tenth, but continued to progress steadily while mechanical troubles thinned the field of big bikes ahead. However Emde's TR3 seized early in the race, but restarted as Don headed for the pits, so he re-entered the race and went on to record a sensational win.

Don and his tuner Mel Dineson set two records at Daytona with their TR3: the first two-stroke victory as well as the smallest displacement bike ever to win the Daytona 200. Remarkably, three other TR3s finished behind Emde in second, third and fifth places. This victory began a 13-year run of wins by two-stroke motorcycles, all of which were Yamahas.

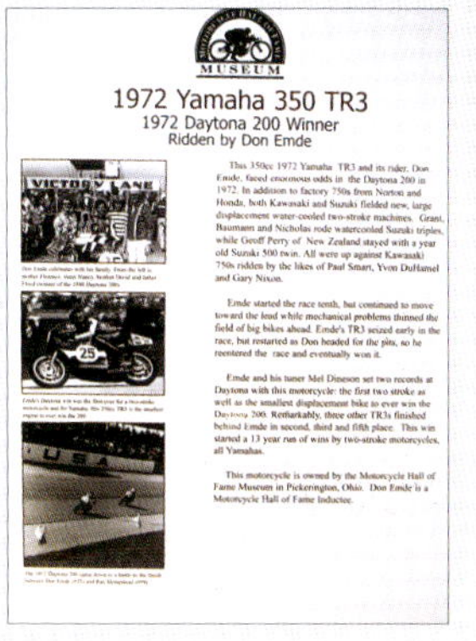

MUSEUM

1972 Yamaha 350 TR3
1972 Daytona 200 Winner
Ridden by Don Emde

This 350cc 1972 Yamaha TR3 and its rider, Don Emde, faced enormous odds in the Daytona 200 in 1972. In addition to factory 750s from Norton and Honda, both Kawasaki and Suzuki fielded new, large displacement water-cooled two-stroke machines. Grant, Baumann and Nicholas rode watercooled Suzuki triples, while Geoff Perry of New Zealand stayed with a year old Suzuki 500 twin. All were up against Kawasaki 750s ridden by the likes of Paul Smart, Yvon DuHamel and Gary Nixon.

Emde started the race tenth, but continued to move toward the lead while mechanical problems thinned the field of big bikes ahead. Emde's TR3 seized early in the race, but restarted as Don headed for the pits, so he reentered the race and eventually won it.

Emde and his tuner Mel Dineson set two records at Daytona with this motorcycle: the first two stroke as well as the smallest displacement bike to ever win the Daytona 200. Remarkably, three other TR3s finished behind Emde in second, third and fifth place. This win started a 13 year run of wins by two-stroke motorcycles, all Yamahas.

This motorcycle is owned by the Motorcycle Hall of Fame Museum in Pickerington, Ohio. Don Emde is a Motorcycle Hall of Fame Inductee.

Today Emde's 1972 Daytona 200 race-winning machine is owned by the Motorcycle Hall of Fame Museum in Pickerington, Ohio.

*... and without its fairing.*

# 1973 TZ250 A

| | |
|---|---|
| Engine | Liquid-cooled, twin cylinder, 2-stroke with piston-port induction |
| Capacity | 247cc |
| Bore | 54mm |
| Stroke | 54mm |
| Comp ratio | 7.6:1 |
| Carburation | 2 x Mikuni VM34 SC |
| Ignition | CD1 |
| Gearbox | Six-speed |
| Clutch | Dry, multi-plate |
| Frame | Steel, duplex tubular construction |
| Suspension | Front: telescopic fork<br>Rear: swinging arm, twin shock |
| Brakes | Front: double sided 2LS drum, full-width<br>Rear: 5LS drum, full-width |
| Tyres | 2.75 x 18 front; 3.00 x 18 rear |
| Dry weight | 228lb (110kg) |
| Max power | 51bhp at 10,500rpm |
| Max speed | 140mph |

*Water-cooling arrived for the Yamaha twins in the shape of the TZ350A (shown) and TZ250A. Basically, these original TZs used TR3/TD3 cycle parts with the liquid-cooled engine.*

*Pilot's eye view of the TZ250/350A series showing tank filler cap breather pipe, 14,000rpm tachometer and temperature gauge.*

*Derek Chatterton's career lasted from the early 1960s until late 1970s. he is pictured here on his TZ250 at Cadwell Park in March 1979.*

## 1976 TZ250 C

| | |
|---|---|
| Engine | Liquid-cooled, twin cylinder, 2-stroke with piston-port induction |
| Capacity | 247cc |
| Bore | 54mm |
| Stroke | 54mm |
| Comp ratio | 7.85:1 |
| Carburation | 2 x Mikuni VM34 SC |
| Ignition | CD1 |
| Gearbox | Six-speed |
| Clutch | Dry, multi-plate |
| Frame | Steel, duplex tubular construction |
| Suspension | Front: telescopic fork<br>Rear: mono-shock |
| Brakes | Front and rear hydraulically operated single discs with 2-piston calipers |
| Tyres | 2.75 x 18 front; 3.00 x 18 rear |
| Dry weight | 240lb (118kg) |
| Max power | 52bhp at 10,500rpm |
| Max speed | 141mph |

*Ulsterman Tommy Robb with his TZ250A in the 1970s...*

Because of the AMA's four-speed ruling, Yamaha engineers had been forced to concentrate on giving the 347.4cc (64 x 54mm) engine a wide powerband. They succeeded in providing usable power from 6000rpm. At 7500rpm, the horses were really storming. The redline was at 9500rpm, although they would, with reduced reliability, run up to 10,500rpm.

When it was announced in March 1969 that the company was to offer the TR2 and its smaller brother, the TD2, for general sale, more details emerged. Both machines were set to be winners 'straight from the crate'. The 250cc model, which replaced the TD1C, showed a power increase from the 39bhp of the 1968 TDIC to 44bhp at 10,000rpm, with a factory-quoted maximum speed of 133mph. Effective compression ratio from the closing of the exhaust port was 7.6:1. In place of the 56 x 50mm dimensions of the TD1C, the TD2 had square 54 x 54mm bore and stroke dimensions, giving 247.3cc.

*The hydraulically operated disc rear brake from the 1977 TZ250D. Note also swinging arm design and wire wheels.*

Like the 350, the gearbox was a five-speeder, and the bike tipped the scales at 110kg (243lb). Ignition was by Hitachi magneto, and automatic oil injection provided the lubrication ,a new feature on Yamaha over-the-counter racers.

The bigger model - the first 350cc racing Yamaha ever built for sale - was virtually a replica of the prototype used by Duff, but with five-speeds. Like the smaller unit, the TR2 used a development of the roadster unit and gave 54bhp at 9500rpm. Using the vast majority of the components from the TD2, the 350 had a dry weight of 115kg (253lb), with Yamaha claiming a top speed of 139mph.

*... and three decades later at Scarborough, Parade of Legends, 22nd September 2001.*

*TZ350A without its fairing. 54bhp at 9,500rpm and a dry weight of 253.5lb (115kg).*

The frames of the two machines were identical and were of the double full-loop type, previously only used for the works models. Likewise, the Ceriani style forks and massive double-sided twin-leading-shoe front brakes were developments of the type used by works riders Phil Read and Bill Ivy during the previous season.

The first four of each machine for the British market were allocated to Padgett's, Ted Broad, Hector Dugdale and Derek Chatterton. A similar situation applied for the first few months of the TD2/TR2 production; only 'selected' customers were allowed to buy! This meant that in 1969, only the world's top riders got the new models (or people with the right contacts and/or money!).

*The TZ350A in the colours of Irish importers Danfay. Note forward extension for the seat - denoting its use by a jockey-size rider.*

*TZ350B engine, showing air-cooled multi-plate clutch, radiator and hoses, cylinders, heads and carburettors.*

What the buyer got for his money is best summed up by the following extract from a track test carried out for *Motorcyclist Illustrated* by road-racer Alan Peck. 'A proper racing bike. I found no vices at all. Winding up from Druids (Brands Hatch) flat out in bottom to second, produced a tremendous sensation. The front end went airy, and the rear really kicked me in the pants. Wow! Manx Nortons were never like this.'

Among the purchasers was Phil Read, the 1968 125 and 250cc class champion. In addition, a handful of riders, including Rod Gould and Kent Andersson, received official semi-works rides on the new machines - plus a new 125cc twin (which didn't go on general sale at the time). These three riders got the best results in the first year, Andersson won two Grands Prix in the 250cc class (West Germany and Finland), while Read won one in the 250cc (Italy) and scored another in the 350cc class (Italy again). Andersson didn't really shine in the 125cc class, and the Frenchman Aureal's victory in his home Grand Prix was very much a one-off affair.

*The C series of TZ models introduced front and rear disc brakes, monoshock rear suspension and revised power units (350 shown).*

*The top three finishers in the 1974 Isle of Man Junior TT; Tony Rutter 1st (centre), Mick Grant 2nd (right) and Paul Cott 3rd (left). All rode TZ350s, Grant's with a Jim Lee chassis.*

1969 was the last year when machines with more than two cylinders and six-speeds were allowed, and that year's champion bike, the Benelli four, was not allowed to contest the 1970 250cc title race. This effectively let in the TD2, particularly after the gallant Ossa rider, Santiago Herrero, was killed in the Isle of Man. With the exception of the Spanish rider's victory in Yugoslavia before his fatal accident, the Yamaha production racer won every round. Rod Gould was an easy winner of the world title, coming first in six of the 12 rounds. Aussie, Kel Carruthers took four, and Andersson one. Other riders of TD2s who scored championship points that year were Huber, Mortimer, Sommer, Rosenbuch, Granath, Jansson, Lansivuori, George, Rutter, Van Dongan, Marsovsky, Bult, Smart, Turner, Olsson, Vincenzi, Molloy, Grassetti and the Belgian Memola - plus a certain Finnish newcomer, Jarno Saarinen. With this sort of domination, Yamaha took the first seven places in the title race.

*Tony Rutter negotiates Ballacraine during his victorious ride in the 1974 Junior TT.*

The 1977 TZ350 looked like this, with bulbous top to the fairing, cantilever suspension and discs front and rear .

# 1979 TZ350 F

| | |
|---|---|
| Engine | Liquid-cooled, twin cylinder, 2-stroke with piston-port induction and 6-port cylinders |
| Capacity | 347cc |
| Bore | 64mm |
| Stroke | 54mm |
| Comp ratio | 6.9:1 |
| Carburation | 2 x Mikuni VM38 SS with power jet |
| Ignition | CD1 |
| Gearbox | Six-speed |
| Clutch | Dry, multi-plate |
| Frame | Steel, duplex tubular construction |
| Suspension | Front: telescopic fork<br>Rear: aluminium swinging arm, mono-shock |
| Brakes | Front and rear hydraulically-operated single discs with 2-piston calipers |
| Tyres | 3.00 x 18 front; 3.50 x 18 rear |
| Dry weight | (108kg) |
| Max power | 72bhp at 11,000rpm |
| Max speed | 155mph |

Charlie Williams won his first Junior TT in 1975, he also contested the Senior on this 354cc Maxton framed TZ, entered by Dugdale Motors.

Yorkshire dealer/racer Tony Jefferies working on his TZ350, 1973.

# One man's TZ250D

Lewis (Lew) James Batty was born on the 18th December 1946 at Hambrook, a village near Bristol, but was raised in Yorkshire.

Lew began his racing career at the Cumbrian Silloth airfield circuit on a twin cylinder Norton Dominator in 1968. After a couple of seasons on the Domiracer he progressed to a Rickman Commando. It was aboard this machine that Lew was first to taste victory. This was followed by many wins and lap records on the short 1.5mile Cadwell Park club circuit.

Then in 1974 in an attempt to stay competitive he rode an ex Dudley Robinson, Padgett Yamaha TR2B, his best result that year was runner-up in the Bulmers Trophy at Croft.

An engineer by trade and with the help of Eric Stanbra he decided to build his own chassis to house a TR3 engine purchased from John Cooper in 1975, going on to win a Cadwell Park 350 National Race from the late Mick Patrick, Butch Hobbs and Paul Cott - all on TZs. There were several other other top six finishes at national and international level that season.

Then came a spell riding Frank Godfrey's TZ in 1976, which included racing in the Southern 100 and the Manx Grand Prix, Lightweight race in which he retired.

In late 1977 Manx resident and enthusiast Arthur Roney bought a brand new TZ250D from Blackpool racer/dealer Vin Duckett for Lew to ride both on the mainland short circuits and the 1978 Manx Grand Prix.

This partnership was the begining of a relationship with the bike that was to last a quarter of a century. Besides winning the Bulmers Trophy at Cadwell Park after a very wet (and close) race with Dave Housley, a highlight was the 1978

*The Batty pit crew, Scarborough, 12th July 2002. Left; Eric Stanbra (ex Mick Grant spannerman) and right; Lew's original mechanic Chris Moore.*

*Lew Batty during his ride to 9th and a silver replica on the Arthur Roney 1977 TZ250D Manx Grand Prix, 1978.*

*Comeback ride in the Post TT at Mallory Park on Sunday 9th June 2002 resulted in a 12th overall and 5th 250cc class, Forgotten Era race.*

Lightweight Manx Grand Prix.

After getting himself and the TZ on the leaderboard during the practice week, the clutch expired (a clutch plate broke) during the pre-race warm-up and Lew had to get permission from the clerk of the course to start last on the road, losing any chance of victory. However he pressed on finishing 9th and gained a silver replica.

But in 1979 a heavy fall at Cadwell Park when a piston seized at Park Corner, saw him high sided off the TZ, resulting in a serious head injury, the 'end of part 1' of Lew Batty's racing career.

Fast forward to May 2002, twenty three years on and that same TZ250D had been rebuilt, from what Lew describes as 'a very rusty state' and not having ridden a motorcycle for 23years he took it to Mallory Park practice session, prior to racing the TZ at the same circuit in a CRMC meeting. 12th overall and 6th in the 'A' group (the only 250 in the race) of the Post Classic class saw Lew a happy man.

Then at the Post TT at Mallory on the 9th June 2002 came another 12th place, followed a few weeks later by an outing at the new Rockingham circuit and 11th place.

For Lew, 'Scarborough's Cock of the North meeting was what all the rebuild and comeback was leading up to. He was rewarded by a pair of 8th places. For 2003 the bike was upgraded to 350G specification - to make it competitive against the rest of the field, but if interest in the 250 class grows, the original 250D engine will be ready to take off the shelf.

*Only change from original 1977 TZ250D specification on the Batty machine was the fitment of a Lockheed caliper at the front - a popular modification to improve stopping power.*

# Austin Hockley

*Austin Hockley seated on the original YAS1 125 twin in 1969, with his ex Chris Conn TD1A 250 in the background. Many thought the tiny Yamaha was something of a joke - until it began winning!*

Double British Champion Austin Hockley began racing in 1967 with a Triumph/Norton 650cc sidecar outfit. He described his 3-wheel career, 'I entered about five meetings but failed to finish due to engine failures and running out of passengers so I decided sidecars were not for me.' Then in early 1968, he was awarded £221 compensation from a road accident, and so, armed with this wind-fall and the money from the sidecar outfit, purchased an ex Chris Conn Yamaha TD1A.

However, some considerable expense was incurred sorting out the TD1A , and it was not until the 28th August 1968 that he was to record his first ever race victory, at Cadwell Park. Spurred on by this acheivement, Austin plucked up the courage to go and see Jack Glover who had recently opened Granby Motors a dealership in Ilkeston, Derbyshire.

Initially Jack agreed to help by paying the entry fees. Then with the arrival in the UK of the new Yamaha YAS1 125cc air-cooled twin cylinder roadster, Austin and Jack decided that besides the TD1A, they would convert one of the new 125s into a racer. As Austin recalls, 'This was a pretty ambitious move, and we were in fact about to start a trend that many other riders would follow.'

Jack Glover prepared most of the cycle parts, whilst Austin took the engine to local tuner Terry Beckett. Terry also supplied the dimensions for the exhaust system and these were fabricated by a local sheet metal company.

The first outing for the new machine came on the 22nd March 1969, again at Cadwell Park, with the YAS1-powered racer causing considerable interest - and as Austin says 'a fair amount of ridicule, in the paddock prior to racing getting under way'. Austin remembers, 'I would not admit it then, but with its spindly front forks and modified Honda front brake it did look like a converted roadster compared to the production racers of the day, the beautifully engineered Honda CR93 and the Bultaco TSS.' But after a 3rd his amusement changed to respect. At the end of the final race the following weekend (also at Cadwell Park), the little Yamaha had gained its first victory and the respect turned to envy. That year Austin had 10 wins with the 125 and 8 victories with the 250.

But this was only half the story. The Granby 125 was capable of winning, but it was also capable of breaking down, with a healthy appetite for big-ends. In addition, Austin's YAS1 didn't benefit from the Yamaha race kit - the latter not only giving more performance, but increased reliability too.

The highlight of 1970 was a Bronze Replica in the 125 Ultra Lightweight (125) TT. Then in 1971 a serious accident at the TT resulted in Austin being sidelined with a broken back and other injuries - leaving him unconscious for several days.

Into 1972 and the TT crash meant that Austin 'just couldn't get going'. So he decided to sell his 250. which by now was a TD2 (the TD1A having long ago been replaced by a TD1B), and got married.

*Winning the 1974 250cc Ulster Grand Prix, with his Granby TZ250B.*

*Austin Hockley (7) with his Granby YAS3 water-cooled model. Also in the picture is Charlie Williams (standing next to Austin) and Clive Horton on another YAS3 derived racer (3), 1974 Isle of Man TT.*

1973 saw a return to form. The 125, in YAS3 guise, had been water-cooled thanks to home-brewed cylinders. In the British Championship series, Austin and the late Steve Machin were equal in points going into the final round at Snetterton. On the last corner of the final lap, Austin outbraked Steve to take the title. The following year, 1974, saw the 125 uprated with Cees Van Dongan aluminium barrels and a new TZ250A from Granby Motors. This confidence was to be repaid by Austin finishing runner-up in the British 125 title race, and taking the 250cc championship, to add to the 125cc crown from the previous season.

For the first part of the 1975, now armed with 125, 250 and 350cc Yamahas, everything went well with several international events. However another bad accident, at Zandvoort in Holland, finally brought his season to a premature end.

Although Austin raced in 1976, it wasn't until 1977 that he started to get back into the groove, but now the 125 had been dropped and he was concentrating on the TZ twins. But his only Grand Prix points (except the TT) came in 1977 at Silverstone, when he finished 10th in the 350cc event. In the spring of 1978 Austin scored double national victories in the 250 and 350cc races at Donington Park's new circuit.

But then on the 8th September 1978 at the international Gold Cup meeting at Scarborough, Austin got a poor start on his TZ250, but by hard riding was up to 3rd before a broken brake anchor arm caused him to crash at the exit of the Esses section. This time his wife said 'enough is enough' and Austin quit after a decade in the sport which had seen him emerge as one of Great Britain's top Yamaha names.

During the 1990s Austin Hockley made something of a comeback, when he took part in a trio of Pastmasters events (on the Hinkley Triumph) at Mallory Park Post TT meetings. And he certainly showed he had lost none of his track skills with some excellent performances with a 5th, 3rd and a 2nd.

Austin's original air-cooled Granby YAS1 racer has survived and is now owned by former racer Lou Riley.

*Austin Hockley (left) and the bike's current owner Lou Riley reunited at a classic show during the late 1990s*

*The Broad Motors race team bikes in 1974. Left, a brand new TZ700 four, and right, the home-brewed 471cc 3-cylinder special, constructed by the Ilford-based dealership.*

In the 350cc class, things were somewhat different, with the FIM's new rules not applying to the larger class. This meant that the four-strokes were still very much in contention, with MV Agusta and Benelli doing well. However, Carruthers still took his TR2 into second place in the championship, but this was a somewhat hollow success, as the 1969 250cc champion's early season's success had been aboard Benelli machinery.

The 1971 season was even better for Yamaha, with Gould contesting both the 250 and 350cc categories. The company also offered limited backing to Charles Mortimer's 125 cc and to Jarno Saarinen's 250 and 350cc efforts. Gould did not win the 250cc class again, but Read on a private TD2 beat him by only a few points. Read's machine had several non-standard features, including a British (Cheney) frame and German (Fath) tuned engine.

Yamaha failed to win the 350cc class championship title that year (Agostini and MV scoring yet again), the next nine riders were all TR2 mounted!

Although Mortimer had high hopes of taking the 125cc Yamaha to championship glory, so it was something of a disappointment to all concerned that he could only finish fifth in the title stakes. However, he did have the satisfaction of winning the TT and finishing second in the Spanish Grand Prix. The best his team-mate, Andersson, could do was a couple of third places in West Germany and Sweden.

The 1971 production racers were coded TD2B and TR2B, but the changes were minimal, except for increases in power output: 250, 47bhp at 11,000rpm; 350, 56bhp at 10,000rpm.

Besides those already mentioned, two other riders were particularly successful - John Cooper and Mick Grant. Cooper used a Seeley-framed model (the Yamsel), while Grant campaigned a Jim Lee-framed device.

*Harris Engineering of Hertford, England built this special for Mike Trimby to ride at Daytona during the mid 1970s. Steve Bayford and Steve Harris (sitting on the bike) pictured at the American circuit.*

*TZ700 fairing off view from the left (nearside) showing engine, frame and the tortuous route of the exhaust system.*

For 1972, Yamaha introduced the TD3 and TR3. Their most notable innovation was the six-speed transmission. In addition, once again, there were power increases, with the 250 pumping out 49bhp at 10,500rpm, while the TR3 gave 58bhp at 9,500rpm. With the lower peak engine speed and the additional gear ratio, reliability was improved. This might not have mattered to a sponsored rider when someone else was picking up the bills, but it was of considerable benefit to the true privateer on a budget.

One of the most unusual and exciting projects undertaken by a private tuner with the new breed of Yamahas was carried out by Ilford dealer/sponsor Ted Broad, who built a three-cylinder version in 1972. The engine consisted of two TR3 cylinders from the 350, plus one from the TD2 250, giving a total capacity of 471cc. The mating of the extra cylinder was made easier because the dimensions of the two racing engines were identical, except for the cylinder bores.

Broad explained, 'We have coupled three standard cranks and have attached a special one-off crankcase on the nearside of a normal crankcase. Because the bottom halves of the 250 and 350cc engines are the same, it means we can run this engine either as a 471cc or, by replacing the 250cc cylinder and piston with one from a 350 engine, we can increase the capacity to 521cc and use the machine in superbike races.'

*This TZ700 was raced in the 1975 French Bol d'Or Endurance 24 Hour race, the twin headlamps needed for the night section of the event, were powered by batteries contained in the specially constructed seat hump.*

A TZ700 engine fully stripped for examination. Note how the cylinder barrel and heads are in pairs.

To reduce the possibility of the differing power outputs of the cylinders tending to twist the crankshaft, the middle cylinder was fitted with the smaller piston and barrel when the engine was run as a 471cc. To avoid possible balance problems, the weights of the 350 pistons were reduced to that of the 250.

Rider Barry Ditchburn was enthusiastic after the first test session at Snetterton, 'I was very impressed and found beefy torque from 7,000rpm - enough to get the front wheel well up if I got the power on too quickly coming out of the turns.'

Broad's three-cylinder engine was not the first such device, as Californian tuner Doug Schwerma had built a similar unit using TR2 components back in 1969.

In the World Championships, 1972 had seen Jarno Saarinen emerge as the new Yamaha star when he became 250cc champion and runner-up in the 350cc series. Furthermore, although Agostini retained his 350cc crown, he was pushed all the way.

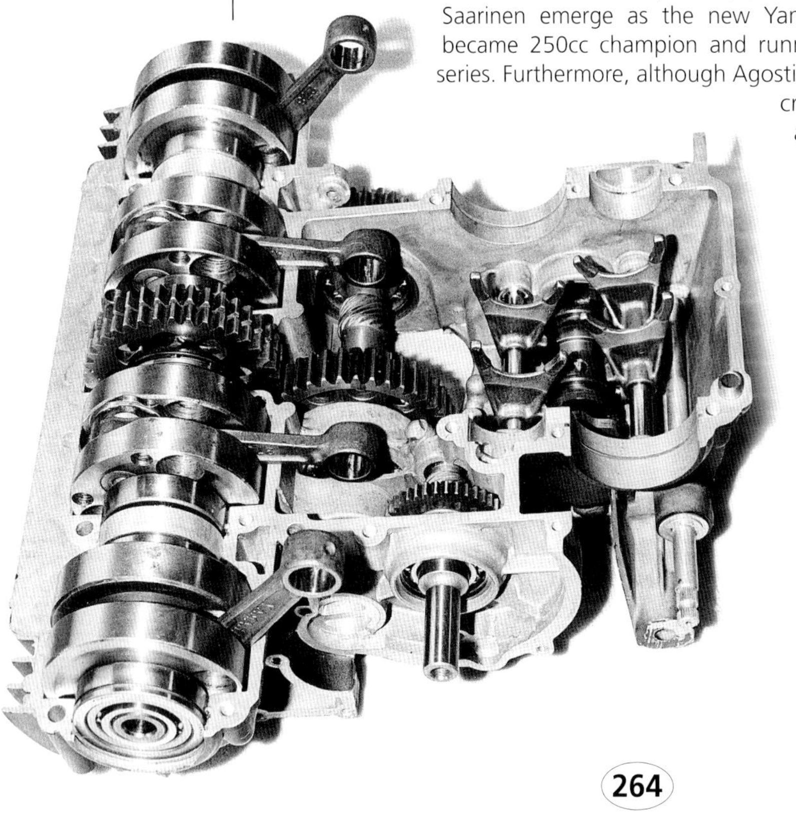

Bottom end of the TZ700, showing the horizontally split crankcases, crankshaft central geared drive, selector forks and drum.

*The young American Randy Mamola made a big impact when he arrived in Europe in 1979. He is seen here on his Yamaha during the Transatlantic Match Race Series at Brands Hatch held over Easter weekend that year.*

In fact, 1972 was a big year for the production based Yamahas, with four official riders, Saarinen and Gould in the bigger classes, and Mortimer and Andersson in the 125cc. There is no doubt, too, compared to previous seasons, that the biggest improvement came from the smallest twin, which won four Grands Prix (Andersson - Yugoslavia, Finland and Spain; Mortimer - Isle of Man).

All three capacities of 'works'-prepared twins acted as prototypes for the following year's production models - TA125 and TZ 250/350. When they appeared, however, the smaller bike was very much the poor relation, owing more to the air-cooled roadgoing 124cc (43 x 43mm) AS3 than the watercooled machines which Mortimer and Andersson had used. The production racer produced 24bhp at 12,500rpm and had only five speeds (the works models pumped out well over 30bhp and had six ratios). But if customers didn't get the full treatment with the smaller bike, they certainly did with the new 1973 250 and 350 over-the-counter racers. The six-speed water-cooled models offered the following output figures: 250cc, 50bhp at 10,500rpm, and 350cc, 60bhp at 10,000rpm. This represented maximum road speeds of 139mph and 149mph respectively.

*Hailwood with his TZ500 4-cylinder Yamaha 2-stroke at Governors Bridge, 1978 Senior TT. But he was not to repeat his famous Ducati victory of a few days before, after he was slowed when his steering damper broke on the 2nd lap.*

*The legendary Mike Hailwood about to bump start the Team Martini TZ500 in the 1978 Senior TT.*

*This team with their TZ700 created a new 1-Hour World Speed record at Daytona International Speedway in spring 1974. Left to right; Pete Schrick (team manager), Kel Carruthers (prepared bike) and rider Gene Romero.*

Saarinen made a huge impact at the beginning of the 1973 season, winning the Daytona 200 on a TZ350 and following this up with three straight wins in the 250cc World Championship series (France, Austria and West Germany). In addition, a brand new YZ500 four was wheeled out for the 500cc French Grand Prix at Le Castellet - which he duly won, beating Phil Read's four-cylinder MV Agusta. Proving this was no fluke, the 'Flying Finn' did the same again at the next Grand Prix at Hockenheim, West Germany. Perhaps the most exciting event in those heady days of Spring 1973, came when Saarinen rode a TZ350 twin to victory in the Imola 200-miler, against the cream of European superbikes.

The success of the TZ 250/350 models, even at the very highest level proved that Yamaha's production racers were a match for anything then available - even including factory works specials from other manufacturers.

Yamaha was also hard at work developing a larger four-cylinder model, the 694cc (64 x 54mm) TZ700, a machine which had been conceived exclusively to challenge Suzuki and Kawasaki in the Superbike category. The '700' had been secretly tested back in Japan on the company's own circuit by Yamaha's chief tester, Hideo Kanaya.

Yamaha had also signed up another Finn, 'Tepi' Lansivuori. This was largely because it was felt that Saarinen should concentrate on the 250, 500 and 700 (when ready), with Lansivuori backing up on the 250 and acting as number-one string on the 350. Both received support from the Japanese rider Kanaya. However, all this planning was turned on its head when Saarinen was tragically killed in the 250cc Italian Grand Prix at Monza in mid May. The season was to end with MV retaining their 350 and 500cc crowns, and Yamaha taking the 250cc (Dieter Braun) and 125cc (Kent Andersson).

So the new four-cylinder TZ500 and 700 machines were set back in their quest for honours - had Saarinen not been killed, there might well have been a very different result in both the 500 and F750 world championships.

As it was, race-goers had to wait until the following year for a new Yamaha challenger to appear. This was in the shape of Italian star Giacomo Agostini who, disillusioned by MV Agusta's lack of ability to develop a suitable F750 bike, had decided to defect to the Japanese marque.

*Johnny Cecotto after winning the 1976 Daytona 200 classic on a TZ750. He covered 52 laps of the 3.87 mile circuit (a distance of 201.24 miles) in 1 hour 51 minutes 48 seconds, an average speed of 108.77mph.*

*Early type TZ750 engine featured vertical instead of 5 degree inclined spark plugs.*

Thus, 1974 offered the possibility of the most exciting clash for years, as 'Ago' and Read rushed headlong into combat - personal and national rivalry, England vs Italy, Europe vs Japan, two-stroke vs four-stroke. This also offered Yamaha the possibility of pulling off world championship wins in all four solo classes, except the 50s, a feat never attempted since Honda's final fling in 1967.

Not content with this, Yamaha had gone a step further - if two 250s made an ultra-competitive 500, wouldn't two 350s make a 700 that flew? Agostini showed just how quick the bike was by winning the all-important Daytona 200 in March 1974 on a TZ700. The same rider also won the 350cc world title. Yamaha took the 125cc championship as well, thanks to Andersson. In the 250 and 500cc series, however, they were out of luck, Walter Villa (Harley Davidson) and Phil Read (MV) finishing the season as champions.

1975 saw Venezuelan star Johnny Cecotto take his 'works' TZ350 to a popular world title, and Agostini finally broke MV's hold on the Blue Riband 500cc crown.

At the end of 1975, Yamaha announced that it could only supply very limited support for its official riders in 1976, and would instead be offering improved production racers. This decision had largely come about because it needed all of its technicians to develop a new range of roadsters which could pass the very stringent exhaust emission rules that the Americans were insisting on - strange how smog over Los Angeles could halt a racing programme half way around the world.

*Monoshock, cantilever-framed version of the TZ750.*

When the new machines were duly announced in February 1976, it was seen that both the TZ250 and TZ350 had an additional 4bhp. Other improvements over the previous year's models included externally adjustable monoshock rear suspension and hydraulically-operated front and rear disc brakes with twin-piston calipers.

*Veteran racer and former Triumph tester Percy Tait rode this 4-cylinder TZ to runner-up spot in the 1975 Classic (1000cc) Isle of Man TT.*

Meanwhile, Yamaha's muscle machine, the TZ700, had become the TZ750, by way of an increase in capacity bv 48cc. The extra displacement had boosted the TZ750 to 100 bhp and allowed it a top speed of 167mph. However, this retained twin-shock rear suspension.

The new machine allowed Yamaha once again to challenge for honours at Daytona, and it was Cecotto who took the flag first, his TZ750 setting new race and lap records.

At the end of 1976, Yamaha proved once more that it had not been standing still on production racer development when it announced the mind-blowing works replica OW31. The cost in Britain was a cool £6571.63, making it the most expensive motorcycle ever offered on the British market up to that time. The importers, Mitsui, announced that the UK allocation was five machines A large spares kit, valued at around £800, was included in the price.

The quotas of the smaller twin-cylinder Yamaha racers were 48 TZ350s and 40 TZ250s. Prices would be £2884.26 for the larger capacity machine, and £2709.24 for the 250cc model.

*Percy Tait entering Ramsey during his ride to a brilliant runner-up position in the 1975 Isle of Man Classic (1000cc) TT. Classic didn't mean 'classic bike', but was for pukka race bikes up to 1000cc.*

*Roger Marshall riding Percy Tait's OW31 TZ750 with Spondon frame and cantilever rear suspension, circa 1976. Spondon Engineering of Derby built a number of frames for the TZ700/750 series, as many riders found the standard frame not to their liking.*

The 750 OW31 had bore and stroke dimensions of 66 x 54mm and offered a massive 140bhp at 10,700rpm. The works-entered versions, ridden by the likes of Cecotto, Roberts, Romero and the 1976 FIM F750 Champion, Victor Palomo, were timed at almost 185mph!

The competition, in the shape of Honda, Suzuki and Kawasaki, was stunned and were forced to retreat to their drawing boards. All three 'official' 750cc world championship titles went to Yamaha riders, (Steve Baker, 1977, Johnny Cecotto, 1978, and Patrick Pons, 1979). Yamaha also dominated the sidecar class after the demise of Konig dominance in 1976, with drivers such as George O'Dell, Rolf Biland and Jock Taylor.

Last, but not least, at the end of the 1970s, the company still continued to offer the finest 250 and 350 over-the-counter racers that money could buy. (The TZ series development history is contained in the following Chapter.)

All this racing expertise established Yamaha's reputation as being Japan's sporting manufacturer par excellence as it entered the uncertain decade of the 1980s.

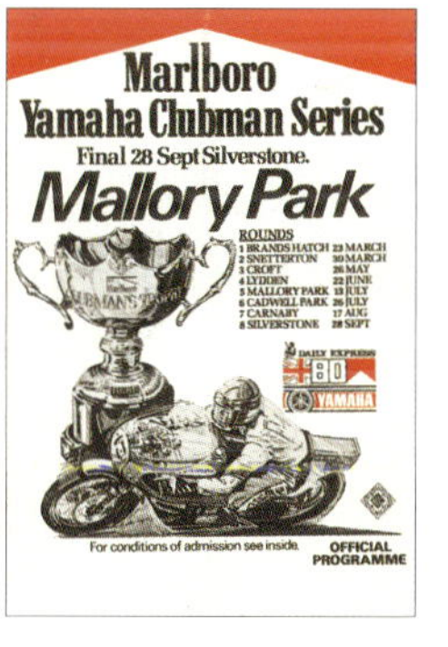

*Mark Middleton with the ex Ron Haslam 1977 TZ750, which he had owned since 1980, after purchasing it directly from Mal Carter. Stuart Hall who rode the bike in Forgotten Era events during the late 1990s, is crouching next to the bike.*

# The Birth of the YAMAHA Production Racer

In all of the books and articles written about the early bikes, little has been documented about the very first 'over the counter' racers to bear the Yamaha name. The initial evolution of the production racer seems to have been forgotten or maybe simply not explained by mainstream journalists. I hope to fill that gap by revealing the history behind my own TD1 Yamaha Production Racer.

In the past, it has been written that the early TD1s were 'hopelessly slow and unreliable' and some people even claimed that the TD1 was not even a real model. But the facts speak for themselves; it certainly was a true model and it was definitely no bad-handling slouch.

The availability of 'over the counter' racing machines in the early sixties gave the good privateer a real chance of mixing in with the factory teams. It also gave rise to a new breed of tuners and race developers, who soon learnt how to get the most from these simple two stroke engines. Men like Frank Sheene, Ted Broad, Geoff Monty and the Padgett's really put Yamaha on the map throughout the country, as well as making names for themselves.

By 1973 the air-cooled two stroke TD twins had evolved into the all-conquering water-cooled TZ series.

# The Asama and Kit Part Racers

July 1959 saw the birth of Yamaha's first sports bike, the 250cc YDS1. A 20hp twin cylinder stroke engine powered the steel tubed, duplex-framed machine. Featuring a five-speed gearbox, twin carburettors (both firsts in the Japanese markets), flat handlebars, combined speedo/tacho, fly screen, metallic gold paint and a top speed of around 85mph, it was really quite a refined sports bike in its day.

The YDS1 or 250S as it was also known, was loosely based on Yamaha's 1957 250cc works YD racers. These (the YD-A & YD-B) were highly successful 'knobbly tyred', high handlebar scramblers. They were built specifically for racing on the volcanic ash circuits in Japan, such as Mount Asama. These works machines looked incredibly similar to the German, Adler RS250 race machines of a few years earlier. Although given the freedom to design their own machine, the Yamaha engineers unsurprisingly choose to study the Adler MB250 for their first road 250cc, the YD1, built also in 1957. The crankcase design was the only part that was really copied.

At this time, Yamaha was the race leader in Japan. Like most other manufacturers of the era, Yamaha saw that victory on the racetrack created popularity amongst the motorcycle buying public. Race winning machines sold road-going motorcycles. And so, the YDS1 and its less sporting cousin and predecessor, the YD2 sold. In 1961 Yamaha actually started advertising these two models in British magazines such as *The MotorCycle* and *Motorcycle Mechanics*. The YDS1 was even shown in road or race trim. This was long before they actually imported any machines.

For budding racers of the day, and those wishing to copy the victorious volcano racers, Yamaha produced a set of tuning parts or 'Kit Parts' as they called them, to turn the YDS1 into a Clubmans racer. Kits were also available to make a full Scrambler version. Actually, bikes became available pre-kitted from the factory at one point. The race spec. engine was the factory designated YX24.

The Kits Parts YDS1 became known as the YDS1R, and later adopted the tag 'Asama Racer' in recognition of its previous history at the volcano circuit.

The basic Race Kit itself consisted of: -

A huge 6-gallon fuel tank, painted a dull brown-red, almost like red oxide.

Solo seat, coloured reddish - pink!

Clip on handlebars

Tuned barrels (initially iron, later alloy)

High compression cylinder heads

Special pistons

Chromed expansion chambers

Magneto ignition - Hitachi MC-2RY

Mikuni - Amal 276 28mm carburettors, with remote float chambers that attached to the rear frame down tubes.

Speedo/tacho bracket

Racing tyres

Other optional parts were also available: -

Rear set foot pegs

Rear set gear linkages and brake lever

Fly screen

Full fairing

Racing tachometer

With this fitment, the YDS1R was now a 30hp, 100mph road racer. It was though, unreliable and too heavy to be a winner in the western world of motorcycle racing. The first alloy barrels had chrome linings, which were by no means perfect. The plating would lift off from around the ports, causing seizures. The iron barrels were also used on many Asamas, before or perhaps while alloy ones were not available, or indeed as an aid to stop the seizures!

The bike also suffered from poor handling, as if a seizing engine wasn't enough to contend with! This was primarily caused by the weight of the bike and retaining the standard suspension units that were only just adequate on the sports

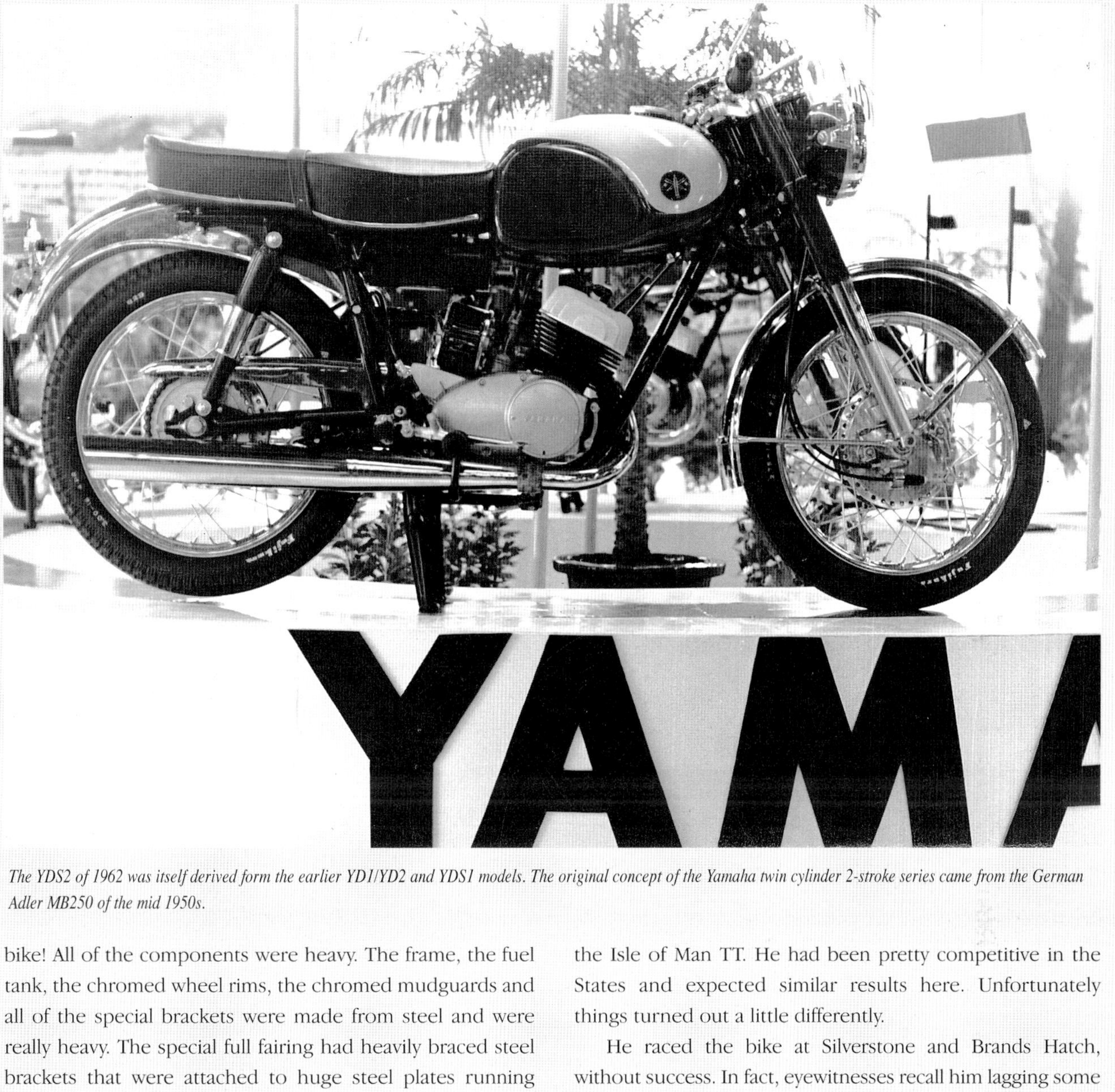


*The YDS2 of 1962 was itself derived form the earlier YD1/YD2 and YDS1 models. The original concept of the Yamaha twin cylinder 2-stroke series came from the German Adler MB250 of the mid 1950s.*

bike! All of the components were heavy. The frame, the fuel tank, the chromed wheel rims, the chromed mudguards and all of the special brackets were made from steel and were really heavy. The special full fairing had heavily braced steel brackets that were attached to huge steel plates running down the inside of the fairing. I seriously doubt whether the aerodynamic gains would have had any effect over the weight of the fairing itself!

As a matter of fact, the pressed steel framed YD2 tourer I mentioned earlier, did in fact see the race circuits, believe it or not! This would have been in a Flat Track or West Coast TT event. The tame 14.5bhp motors were 'tuned' and all of the non-essential steel and bodywork removed. A set of cowhorn bars replaced the flats, and the electrics were reduced to a direct loss system. It would have made a reasonably good introduction to two-stroke racing in the junior events, but not a winning combination. In 1960 the UK got its first visit from a Yamaha. Californian, Sonny Angel brought over a YDS1R to compete in a few mainland short circuit events and the Isle of Man TT. He had been pretty competitive in the States and expected similar results here. Unfortunately things turned out a little differently.

He raced the bike at Silverstone and Brands Hatch, without success. In fact, eyewitnesses recall him lagging some way down the field. His entry in the TT was also somewhat of a disappointment, actually running out of spare pistons before reaching the Island. He had to resort to matching the original pistons with another make, which turned out to be from an MV scooter! They were somewhat modified to fit, but appeared to work, as the bike gave a top speed of around 116mph on one section of the gruelling mountain circuit.

Sonny's YDS1 R was pretty well modified by the time n came over to the UK. He had fitted a Norton front brake, a different seat, home made rearsets and a fairing, in an attempt to improve handling and 'ridability'. It still retained its muddy brown-red fuel tank though!

Elsewhere the first Englishman to race a Yamaha in the Far East, after his time as a Tank Landing Craft Officer posted in Singapore, was Ken Roberts whodecided to live out there for a while. He was keen on motorcycling, so bought himself a bike, a race-ready YDS1 R Asama. Ken, now living in Leicester, recalls his first Yamaha racing experience the bike was an absolute pig! The pistons were the main problem; if you spent time lapping them in to the correct tolerance as described in the manual, the bike wouldn't run when it got hot and if you didn't lap them in, the bike would seize instantly!' The problem was that Yamaha hadn't got the silicon content right in the pistons, to control the expansion of the alloy. Ken continued 'I bought the bike from a Chinese dealer, it was second-hand, but was a fully kitted bike. I used to race it at the Gap Hillclimb, run by the Singapore Motor Club. I also raced it in the Singapore and the Indonesian Grand Prix (both the same place though, as the country went into independence, and changed its name). The circuit was really just a barriered-off section of a runway. We were taken across to the Island, with the bikes lashed onto the decks of a local fishing boat! That makes the annual pilgrimage with the IOM Steam Packet Company seem like a luxury cruise!'

Ken described some of the opposition at these races, 'I remember an English RAF officer posted over there who was given a Works Honda 4 to race, a chap called Chris Profit-White. Like many of the Servicemen over there, he got involved with the local race clubs, most of which were run by rich ex-pats who owned tea or rubber plantations. The Officer's Club had a large representation at the racing clubs.'

The Gap Hillclimb was a major event in the area and was for both two and four wheelers.The ex-pats tuned up their Jags and Bentleys, while the local Chinese rode their modified road going bikes.

'I remember I was at the 1961 Singapore Grand Prix when Yamaha turned up with their small black van.They wheeled out two race bikes also painted black, which were the works RD48 250 twins. Both machines never actually finished the race, breaking down with mechanical problems. Honda were also there, but no sign of any Suzukis.'

'I had a REME Engineer to help as my mechanic,' Ken recalled. 'After several seizures, we soon learnt to fit a different type of piston to avoid it! It seemed to work much better after that!'

Ken still owns an Asama racer, amongst other early Yamahas and is still active in the racing scene today. The YDS1 had a crankshaft mounted clutch; which many consider was the Achilles heel of the early Yamahas. Running at about 7500 rpm with a mere 20bhp going through it (as the standard 250S did), it was perfectly adequate. But, when speeds of over 9500 rpm were produced and over 30hp was being transmitted, things tended to work ...how shall we say...less smoothly!

The centrifugal forces acting on the clutch running at engine speed, obviously increases as the revs increase. This made the clutch less efficient at separating the plates. The clutch plates were effectively forced outwards, restricting sideways movement thus not allowing the plates from opening when the clutch lever was pulled. The ultimate effect of this was that the gearbox would not slow down enough to allow smooth gear changes. This created a clonk when changing gear, At race speeds however, this was further exacerbated. A forced, rushed gear change could turn the harsh clonk into a crankshaft failure or disintegrating clutch basket! It has been rumoured by a racer of the day that an American company produced a metal band, which wrapped around the clutch basket to try to avoid these exploding clutch catastrophes. But, I am unable to find any evidence of them (yet!). These clutches though, could be set up to work very smoothly indeed. It took careful preparation to get it bang on, but the better mechanics and tuners soon found out the tricks of the trade by carefully selecting and balancing out every single component.

# Second Generation

The YDS1 was produced up until early 1962. Yamaha had in its now typical way, studied its product, listened to feedback from customers and tackled the reported problem areas. During 1961 development took place on the new model, the YDS2 which was officially launched in March 1962.

In the same way that the Asama was available as a Kit Parts Racer, it continued to produce a Kit Parts model known as the YDS2R, and separate kits were also still available. The main improvements on the new model were in the engine and the brakes. The YDS1 looked good for its day and was a best seller, so the styling remained very much similar on the new machine. The brakes were bigger, the rear mudguard was beefed up a bit, the fuel tank knee grips grew, the chain guard tidied up and the battery box was put into a more conventional position, but apart from that the bike looked very similar. The colour scheme was also widened, with a choice of metallic colours instead of just gold. The fuel tank was now endowed with Yamaha's round 'tuning fork' logo, a corporate identity which has made a comeback on the 750cc road legal racer, the R7 or OW02.

The engine gained 5bhp, mainly due to improved porting and combustion chamber. It also had a new 'labyrinth' seal fitted between the 180 degree out of phase cranks. The actual crankshaft initially remained similar, although con-rods were modified on the later YDS2s. The bore and stroke remained the same at 56 x 50mm. Crankcases were modified slightly to allow an improved gear ratio, and modifications were made to the big ends.

The clutch remained the same, alhough weaker clutch springs were fitted and the primary drive was also slightly altered to slow the gearbox speed down to aid smoother gear changes. Initially carburettors remained the same as on the YDS1, Amal-Mikuni VM20H with 'ticklers'. But from August 1962, newer Mikuni VM20SH carbs were used, which had lever operated 'cold starter' chokes and were more effcient.

The full width wheel hubs were improved with water and dust-proofing grooves, and the front wheel gained a twin leading shoe brake. Both hubs were now polished and lacquered to enhance appearance.

The YDS2 has a really significant interest in the UK, as it was the first Yamaha to be imported into the country, alongside the YA5 125 single. It was the YDS2 though, that really put Yamaha on the map in Britain. It was better than any British-made 250cc of the day! Far more sophisticated than the contemporary British lightweights, it had flashy paintwork, a 5-speed 'box, reliable electrics, sporty looks, combined speedo/tacho, steering damper, optional fly screen, a smooth and lively 25bhp engine and a genuine 90mph plus top end, as fast as many of the 500s. Contrary to popular belief though, Japanese bikes were not cheap copies of 'British' bikes. At £266 the YDS2 was expensive. Comparable machines of the era included;-

Royal Enfield Continental £239
Ariel Arrow £187
Panther 250cc £189
Jawa 250cc £119
Matchless G2CSR £234
Norton Jubilee £243
Honda CB72 £259

Unfortunately though, the worst features of the YDS1 stayed. It still retained the crank mounted clutch and the unadjustable rear suspension units.

The advertised top speed for the YDS2 was 91mph. This was no idle boast, it really was that quick, although the claim 'twin cylinder, as smooth as a four!' was dubious. Apart from the Ariel Square four, what other four cylinder bikes were around to compare? I'm sure riders of the era would not have ridden many others. I guess it is fair to say though, that the bikes were very smooth, there was no distinct power band as a modern two stroke has. I suspect that the smoothness was due to having two carburettors feeding a fairly low state of tune engine.

Yamaha didn't really sell that many YDS2s in the UK. but it did make a big impression on all who rode them. The motorcycling press all gave the YDS2 a really good write up, whenever it was tested. A typical comment being 'startling performance, excellent quality' and 'general reliability' amongst other things.

It is unknown how many of the 30hp YDS2R racers or kits were sold. A few made it into Australia and America and there are unsubstantiated rumours of a few making it into the UK, but it was certainly advertised. There is a YDS2R full specification and set-up guide in the road going YDS2's service manual. The running-in procedure includes careful lapping-in of the pistons, how to check ignition timing, checking crank accuracy, plug selection, carb adjustments and all the necessities to prevent the bike from seizing up. I wonder just how many engine failures were due to not carrying them out. As well as the road going YDS2 and the YDS2Rs, the model was also available in scrambles guise, as YDS2CM and a fully kitted out US only Flat track Racer known as the YDS2M 'Ascot' Scrambler. This bike was factory designated YX74, and was only produced in limited numbers, so much so, that in fact when *Cycle World* magazine wanted to test one, in 1963 they struggled to find one! The Ascot was reminiscent of the earlier volcano racers, with high bars, undershot expansion pipes and a short solo seat. They were painted bright red with a white flash on the fuel tank and featured many of the special parts fitted to the YDS2 R and Scrambler. The frame was basically a standard YDS2 frame, although some claim it was made of a lighter gauge steel, which I think is not the case. The welding though, appears to be much tougher than on the standard bikes. Perhaps this was to make the bike that bit more rugged for the rigours of the West Coast TTs and quarter mile tracks at Daytona and indeed Ascot Raceway.

The special components consisted of :-

Twin cock fuel tank
Mikuni VM24 mono-block type carburettor.
Rigid footpegs (flip -up on the later bikes)
Solo seat (allowing rider to move around body weight)
Alloy rims
High bars
Racing tachometer
Number plate & tacho brackets
Race spec engine
Magneto ignition
Expansion pipes

These Ascots were immensely successful and popular. Nearly all though were destroyed in the caurse of the sport. Around 90% received serious modifications by the time they even hit the cinders. Rear suspension was the first to go, with steel struts replacing the units. Front brakes were disconnected and rear brake modified to be controlled by the front brake lever on the handlebars.

## Production Racers Trials

Up until 1961 Yamaha had been selling these race kitted or converted road models. They decided that a true, thoroughbred race ready machine should be available to the bike buying public, instead of them having to buy a road bike only to bin half the pieces. Yamaha really did listen to their customers. The first development along this line started late in 1960. With the idea of keeping the new bike reasonably affordable, they utilised the already available YX24 (YDS1 R) motor. They fitted one of these over the counter engines into one of the works YX47 (RD481) chassis. With several other minor modifications, such as a single-sided twin leading shoe front brake and making the rear wheel accept the right hand drive transmission chain, the bike was ready for trial. In fact, the factory entered two of these machines in an event at Daytona on the 12th February 1961. Yoshi Sunako and Fumio Ito again piloted the bikes, finishing fifth and eighth on the red painted machines. According to eye witnesses, the machines both had the words 'production road racer' sign written across the rear of the seat unit. The factory christened the machine the RR250.

A batch of 10 or so of these RR250s were produced for sale in the US, as an interim model. The factory had not yet finished designing the 'full' specification racer they had initially envisaged, so numbers were strictly limited. The bikes were sold at a few key outlets. On the East Coast, the franchise went to adistributor George Caswell based at Broomall, Pennsylvania and Frank Cooper in Los Angeles became the official Yamaha Motors main agent. At this point, Yamaha themselves had not actually started up their own headquarters within the USA.

The first bike to arrive at George Caswell's, was delivered in April 1961. It came as a surprise for Caswell, and he had no knowledge of the price or future availability. He kept this first machine and sponsored Harold McMullen, also of Pennsylvania to ride it in four races. The first race was at the Vinelands raceway, New Jersey on 14th May 1961. McMullen finished a rather promising third in the Amateur event. He also later raced the bike at the Laconia circuit.

In June a second racer turned up at the Broomall dealers. This machine was sold to Jim Munz who entered it in an event at the Indianapolis Raceway that same month. A few more were seen about the circuits on both the West and East coast circuits.

The US RR250s were all painted bright yellow, a paint scheme that was to stay with the American Yamaha race bikes for many years! It was said that this colour was chosen because it was Frank Cooper's favourite colour, and he was given the choice by the factory as to what colour they should be painted! The front forks, triple clamps (or yokes), front fender, fuel tank and seat hump were all painted yellow with the frame and swing arm black. Some of the machines came pre-fitted with a fairing and some with just a number plate. The front forks and unadjustable, rear suspension units were unique to the machine. A small racing tachometer was also fitted to the top pressed steel, triple clamp.

There was no provision for a rear mudguard or splashguard. Consequently, oil and petrol would be blown back by the carburettors onto the rear tyre! Because of this, most of the bikes were later fitted with splash guards held on with wire. Because of the distinctive colour scheme, these bikes became affectionately known as 'Yellow Tankers' or 'Yellow Road Racers'.

The performance of the Yellow Tankers was much better than the pre-kitted bikes. Weight loss, handling and braking were the biggest improvements over the Asama racers. At least one of these RR250s saw British soil, although not in the yellow colour scheme. A black machine was pictured in an old ACU archive and believed to have come into England as a personal import.

The RR250 was without doubt, the direct link between the works and production racers. By the end of the 1961 season, development of the 'full' production racer was completed. With its engine based upon the new and improved road models, the TD1 was born. Both were ready to be launched early the following season.

## The TD1

There is a strong belief throughout the Yamaha enthusiast's community that the early production racers evolved from one model to another. This appears to be true on the whole, as the early TD1s look very similar to the RR250s or Yellow Tankers. In fact, sales brochures of the day even show bikes that appear to be RR250s labelled as TD1s as late as 1964! Even the engine numbers on some of the Yellow Tankers share the same prefix. The new TD1s though, had several 'improvements' over the previous model. Firstly the frame had brackets tacked on the rear down tubes, to allow a small fibreglass rear splashguard to be fitted. The Kayaba forks were improved, the brakes gained meshing over the air inlets and the expansion pipes attached onto the frame differently. A new type of tacho was also fitted, made by Yazaki. One or two of these, destined for the Western World were actually calibrated in letters, from A to G. The machine also came with a full Grand Prix style fairing as standard. The basic rolling chassis though remained similar to the RD48. The majority of the TD1s were painted in the new factory race colours, with bright orange fuel tanks and a white seat hump. The rest of the machine was painted metallic bronze grey. The fuel tank had 'Yamaha'. in white lettering along its side. However, some machines were sold in the old works colours of gloss black throughout.

The newer TD1's fuel tank had its filler cap moved from the centre, nearer to the front and slightly to the left. This allowed the rider to lay flat across the tank without being poked in the ribs! It now also had a screw cap and not a Monza type. In fact, Yamaha were guilty of fitting whatever parts they had available in the factory at the time to whatever bike they needed to finish. If a bike needed a part, they fitted anything they happen to have.

The engine of the TD1 retained the Hitachi magneto (with red HT leads) and the 28mm Mikuni 276 carburettors. Improved 'low expansion' pistons were fitted and the barrels were now anodised. It was the pistons that now had to be carefully run in, as the bores were not easily re-boreable. The gearbox received an improved ratio and the clutch was the same as the standard YDS2, but with stiffer springs. The kick-start was removed, and a blanking plate fitted into the outer crankcase. The new racer was extremely expensive. In the UK it cost £494, nearly twice the price of the already expensive, top of the range YDS2. In today's money that would probably equate to somewhere around £15,000!

In some markets, to qualify as a road racer, the machine had to be road legal, with lights and silencers. The TD1 was no exception. It was advertised, displayed and available with electrics, front and rear mudguards, full length silencers and indicators!

The TD1 was advertised alongside the YDS2 and strangely enough the YDS2R Asama. The trio took centre stage on Yamahas' display at the 1962 Tokyo Motorcycle Show.

The American magazine *Cycle World* published their test a TD1 alongside a YDS2, in January 1963. The test riders were really impressed with it. They even entered the machine in a sprint race, and won. The only criticism given was that it was 'a trifle crowded for an over six foot rider' and the gear ratios 'felt a little widely spaced'. Yamaha gained a lot of respect from these test riders, who gave their bikes so much praise. It was praise they certainly needed in the new critical market of North America.

The constructive criticism was exactly what the Yamaha engineers wanted. It was something they could work on to improve their product. The basis of the machine though was exactly what people wanted, a fast, quality machine that had the potential to beat the traditional regular winners.

The actual racing department at Yamaha was only a very small part of the huge company. This meant that many of the components for the race bikes had to be built by sub-contractors. Designs were sent out to several companies, often to produce the same components, this led to slight variations. The race shop, unlike the rest of the factory, was staffed only with qualified engineers. As a matter of interest, the road bikes' assembly line was mostly staffed by women.

Nearly all of the aluminium components on the TD1 were sand cast items. The frames were all hand welded, high tensile light gauge steel. Many people had in the past thought that the frame was identical to the road frame, except that it was made from a lighter gauge steel. This is not the case. At first glance it does look similar, but there are a few major differences, the rear section around the shock absorber mounts, the headstock, and the pressed steel plate footrest hangers. The earliest TD1 frames had tubular fittings that mount the steering damper assembly and fuel tank. The later bikes had a domed stud to attach the fuel tank and a welded stud to locate the steering damper stay.

I mentioned earlier that the bikes were fitted with a single sided version of the works type brake. The front hub itself had an eight inch diameter brake, with an oblong air scoop cast into the front .Opposite the brake-plate, the hub had six holes bored into it to allow the hot air to escape and the hub itself was heavily finned. Both front and rear wheels were fitted with WM1 x 18inch alloy rims, made by DID, with the model name TD1 stamped into the flange. The front wheel was equipped with a 2.50 tyre and rear had a 2.75 section fitted as standard.

The actual engine of the TD1, as previously mentioned, was based upon the YDS2. The inner crankcases had parts of the casing milled off to make room for the bigger remote float carburettors and to allow easy access to the front sprocket. The crank itself was common to the YDS2, although it was set more accurately. The two forged pistons were connected to the crank via conrods with extra oil slots milled into the big ends.

The carburettor remote floats were attached to the rear of the engine by a steel bracket with each bowl held in place via a foam rubber mounting. This was rather an unsuccessful attempt to stop the fuel frothing up. Apart from the kick-start being blanked off, the clutch side outer casing remained the same. I have come across clutch adjuster covers made out of lightweight sand cast alloy, instead of the usual road bikes' die cast heavy zinc-alloy. Also some machines had a larger 'Yamaha' lettering cast into them. Some of the earlier Asamas were even supplied with a tiny steel plate covering just the adjuster. The magneto cover also saw some differences. On some machines, it was identical to the road going bike, but on the majority, the rear section covering the front sprocket was machined off, only to cover the magneto itself.

The claimed output from the TD1 was 31bhp at 8500rpm. This was regarded as being pretty accurate by all those who rode the bike. It weighted only 95kg, and was indeed as quick as many 500s. It was destined to start proving its worth.

The controls of the bike were fairly standard. The clutch and front brake levers were attached to clip-on handle bars, and had the cable adjusters built in. The tachometer was mounted onto the front fairing bracket, via rubber mounts. The tacho bracket itself went through several stages of evolution. On the early bikes, it was a mish-mash of angle steel and tubing, forming a horseshoe shape. The later bikes had this unit made neatly out of tubing only. Another difference between the earlier bikes, is that some were equipped with a change over option, that allowed the bikes to be set up for left foot braking and right foot gear change. A threaded tube was welded into the rear down-tubes to anchor the rear brake cable stay.

The new machine soon started to make a name for itself. The factory entered the works TD1s into an event at Karinosu near Kyoshu, Japan in July. They won the Clubmans race. Later in the year the team was entered into the first All Japan Grand Prix races at Suzuka. The factory entered teams in both the 250cc Novice and 350cc Novice classes. The bikes entered in the 350 were bored-out 255cc and renamed TE1s.

Minoru Mihashi won the 250cc race and Yoshimi Katayama came in second, both on TD1s. The 5th, 6th and 9th places were also taken by the TD1s. The hot favorites for the race were the CR72 Hondas which had slightly more power. But the wet conditions suited the Yamahas far better. As this was the novice class, the machines were not allowed to be equipped with full fairings, only a number plate was to be fixed on to the front.

Again the favourites in the 350cc events, the CR77 Hondas were beaten by the new Yamahas. TE1s took the 1st and 3rd places on the podium, Katayama taking the victory.

These works bikes were visually identical to the publicly available machines, except they were fitted with a more advanced type of expansion pipe. These were longer and more tapered, with a 1 inch diameter outlet. They were a successful experiment that would lead to the subsequent model having them fitted as standard.

Another high profile victory for the TD1 was in mid December, where one took the honours at the Indonesian Grand Prix in Djakata. *Motor Cycle News* reported that Geoff Monty would be entering a similar machine over here in the UK the following season.

The rumours that the TD1 production racer was slow, unreliable and had bad handling should now be proved otherwise! had it been that bad, they would surely have not have had these wins and Yamaha would have probably redesigned the machine completely.

## TD1s enter the UK

The first sighting of a TD1 in the UK was at the London Motorcycle Show in December 1962. Yamaha had a stand which displayed its entire range of road machines, along with the new production racer and a YDS2CM scrambler.

Geoff Monty of Monty and Ward Motorcycles, then of Twickenham, purchased the entire stand from Yamaha. They subsequently became the first offcial Main Dealers for Yamaha. Geoff Monty imported a further two TD1s, he kept the original example and sponsored riders to race it. Dave Degans rode the machine on several occasions and was scheduled to race the bike during the 1963 season, but the collaboration never took place. Bill Ivy was also one of the riders to get several races on the Yamaha, but he never succeeded in winning a race on it. His best result was on 22nd September at Brands Hatch, where he came second to Tommy Robb on a Honda CR72. For most of the rain sodden race, he was dicing with Joe Dunphy on a 27bhp Greeves Silverstone. There was though, another Yamaha in this race, ridden by a Canadian, G. Kellond. It is not known which model Yamaha this was, it may have been one of the other two Monty imported or it may well have been the previously mentioned RR250, or indeed another import, even a later TD1A.

Geoff Monty, being a special builder and tuner modified his TD1 a fair bit, to try and gain that extra bit of performance. He fitted better expansion pipes amongst other things, which allowed the engine to rev a bit higher than the recommended 9500rpm. Geoff also took some of the ideas that Yamaha had and fitted them into his own machines. Some even made it into production inside British two-strokes. Photos of Bill Ivy on the Monty TD1, at the Silverstone race, clearly show the longer expansion pipes, which led some people to think that this was actually a later TD1A. The UK's motorcycling press got their first test ride courtesy of Geoff Monty. Vic Willoughby of *Motor Cycle* tested the TD1 and again a YDS2, at Brands Hatch early in 1963. The report was issued on the 28th March 1963. The road bike got a very good write up, being labelled 'a dream', but the TD1 got a rave review, being classed 'a veritable vision!' Vic Willoughby stated, 'It's a little beauty, fits the rider like a glove and handles light as a feather. And, does it go!'

Two of the Geoff Monty TD1s were sold early on in the 1963 season. One went to John Field, who didn't have a lot of luck with the bike. He later switched to MV. At the end of the '63 season, Monty sold his remaining TD1 to Terry Springett.

Terry Springett had some success with his bike, winning a race at Brands Hatch in late July 1964. At that London Show back in 1962, the little Yamaha racer caught the eye of Robin Denny had been campaigning a Bill Lacey prepared ex-Mike

Hailwood Manx Norton, which was powered by an NSU Sportmax engine. He also owned a supercharged EMC 350cc Split Single, which he raced with the supercharger piston disconnected. Incidently, he was threatened with a ban from the ACU for entering a supercharged bike, even though it was not working!

Robin Denny was actually at Silverstone, when Sonny Angel made Yamaha's debut. He recalls seeing the brown bike 'plodding along at the back' and wasn't at all impressed. But, he recognised this bike to be something different. Anyhow, Robin was well impressed with the huge brake drums, and thought that if the bike warranted brakes like that, then it must be good! He enquired at Monty and Ward straight after the show, and placed an order for one in Mid-December. He received the bike on 30th May 1963.

When his TD1 finally turned up, he took it to his local circuit, Brands Hatch to run it in. Knowing how prone to seizure two-strokes were, he took meticulous care in mixing the Castrol R with the fuel. This seemed to pay off for Robin, as he never remembered having any major seizures. Perhaps the way he treated the bike helped as well, for he never exceeded the 9500rpm limit and he always kept a strict eye on the ignition timing.

It was in only his second race that Robin gained his first win on the bike. It was the British Motor Cycle Racing Club's 'Norwich Trophy' event at Snetterton, on the 30th June 1963. This made him the first Yamaha rider to win a race in the UK and indeed Europe! Although only a 'closed-to-club' meeting, it was still Yamaha's first European win, only one week before Ito and Sunako's famous 1-2 Grand Prix victory in Belgium.

That win was not his only victory on the bike. He gained several other good results up and down the country. His favourite circuit was Oliver's Mount in Scarborough, where he thought the Yamaha was ideally suited to the tight hairpin and narrow comers. He raced there in 1963 and 1964.

Robin still has fond memories of the bike. At one race he recalled overtaking a Honda with both tyres sliding! 'it still felt stable and under control.' he remarked. Indeed he thought the bike always handled well and felt stable at high speeds and throughout cornering. A bonus was that the TD1 was good in tight corners and hairpins. This was due to the very low first gear and not having a pronounced powerband, like the later machines.

Robin was lucky enough to gain backing from Mitsui, in the form of technical assistance from Frank Williams their UK chief. He kept Robin informed of all the necessary technical details such as ignition timing, plug selection and piston design. Mitsui also supplied Robin with a set of front forks after a spill at Charlie's Bend, Cadwell Park, late 1963. He came off and hence destroyed them! A similar fate awaited the fuel tank, as the dealer tried to blow out the dent with compressed air. This only caused the seams to split and the tank was ruined.

Because the spares were not available off the shelf, Robin wrote a letter to Mitsui explaining his predicament. They responded by flying him a complete new front end over from Japan, free of charge as he had been doing so well. Mitsui took a keen interest in Robin after that event. The forks he received were the new improved TD1A type. Because he could not get a genuine fuel tank, he fitted a fibreglass unit. This was to stay on the bike for the rest of its racing life! Whilst the bike was being rebuilt, the new fuel tank was painted orange and the frame received a coat of blue paint.

In the 1964 and 1965 seasons he also gained sponsorship from Reynolds chains and Girling shock absorbers. He said, 'The original unadjustable shocks were not completely worn out, but any free parts you could get were well worth having!'

In October 1965, Mitsui - Yamaha telephoned Robin and offered him the pick of the bunch from the first batch of 5 new TD1Bs. A new TD1B was duely added to the stable, which now consisted of the TD1, TD1B and an EMC 125 which he swapped with Joe Ehrlich for the 350 split single.

For the final few races of the 1965 season, the TD1 was entered as a 350cc, where it was still able to perform surprisingly well. Robin was competing in the 1965 Mallory Park, Race of the Year on the TD1, lying in second place behind John Cooper, when he suddenly lost power. He couldn't rev the bike more than about 7000rpm, so decided to retire. After the race, he took the bike along to Mitsui to investigate. At the time, Nick Nakamura was over from Japan to visit Yamaha and Mitsui's UK headquaders. Mr Nakamura cast his eye over the TD1 and soon found the problem to be slipped ignition timing. The TD1 was sold on during the winter of 1965 to finance the other bikes. But Robin never felt as comfortable on the later bike, and he didn't get on with it as well.

The following year he noticed his old bike at a meeting. He saw that the new owner had fitted bracing tubes across the frame. It was a modification that Robin never thought necessary, but it was all the rage at the time. Many frame makers such as Colin Seeley were making these type of frames and they were very successful, but not really necessary on a 95kg, 31hp machine.

Robin later switched to racing four wheels, driving for the works Simca team, in races such as Monza. Photographs of Robin's bike when it was new, show the bike to actually have the works type expansion pipes fitted. This coupled to the keen interest from Mitsui and several other subtle differences in cycle parts, suggest the bike was a works bike that was reconditioned and sold on as a new machine.

Yamaha at the time, were still under guidance from their Nippon Gakki parent company, and so were forced to sell whatever they could. Shots of the Suzuka bikes appear to be identical, and compared to the Geoff Monty TD1, the Denny bike shows many slight differences. The original Geoff Monty TD1 from the London Motor Cycle show was frame number T1-007. The Robin Denny bike had frame number T1-052, but there were many differences that suggest it was actually earlier than T1-007.

Historically, there has always been some confusion as to the total number of TD1s built, So all I can do is give the evidence available. Yamaha themselves did not keep any offficial records. They were only able to confirm that the TD1A was made from frame number T1-060 onwards, and hence some people believe that sixty TD1s were built. But, many people who were on the scene at the time think that only around a dozen were produced. Again, the theory about Yamaha fitting any parts they could, may account for this confusion, for there were several different TD1 variations. To add to the confusion it is also evident that some artificial number increasing took place...

But what is known, is that three were imported into the UK, a similar number went to Australia a few made it to the US and several were scattered around the far East and Japan.

The main confusion regarding numbers produced seems to stem from the constant improvements to the design of the machines. I would like to state here, that there were actually 2 distinct types of TD1, an early 'original' type and a later variant.

The first batch of TD1s consisted of 20 machines, at least

*British serviceman J Nightingale with his TD1 at Seletar airfield, 1963.*

10 must have been the works bikes as used at Suzuka. The second batch had the pressed steel plate type of footrest hangers replaced in favour of a steel tube type, which was used on all of the subsequent models. Still around now, frame number T1-034 from this batch has this type of hanger arrangement, as does frame number T1-059. T1-052 though, the Robin Denny bike, has the early plate type...

On this basis, I am pretty much convinced that Yamaha originally sold around 10 or 12 of the first batch bikes during 1962, and afterwards sold the second batch of bikes, of anywhere around 20 - 24. They then needed to supply outstanding orders, and sold on a small batch of the reconditioned works bikes, renumbered with later numbers. The later second batch of TD1s bore a resemblance to the early bikes bar the footpeg hangers, but were not yet to TD1A specification. They were also still fitted with the stubby Asama type pipes.

## TD1A Development

The feedback gained from the 1962 TD1 led Yamaha to make some alterations for a new improved model. The frame was the first thing to be beefed up. The headstock reinforcing webs were relocated to inside the frame down-tubes and the swinging arm mounting plates were now box sectioned. The footrest hangers were fabricated from steel tubing instead of the plate steel of the early TD1s. The steering damper assembly now located directly onto a welded stub under the headstock as per the YDS2. Also the reinforcing plates that ran down the front down-tubes were extended slightly and the rear splashguard mountings were now threaded into the frame. The fuel tank mounts also became round-headed studs on which to attach the rubber bands. The seat unit also mounted slightly differently to the earlier bike.

The front forks and yokes (triple clamps) also underwent a complete make over. The fork sliders lost a reinforcing band from around the mudguard stays. The stanchions gained a milled top edge that located into the top yolk, unlike the TD1s where the forks only butted up against it.

The front mudguard was made shorter and slightly wider and had two 'Y' shaped centre brackets. The TD1 had a one-piece steel centre bracket that also acted as a brace.

The expansion pipes were now of the works style but mounted slightly differently. Cosmetically the bike remained similar, with a red fuel tank and grey frame, although the 'Yamaha' lettering along the fuel tank, was now gold. The engine was still based upon the YDS2 and remained similar to the previous models. The pistons now though, were fitted with only one piston ring, in order to reduce friction. The magneto cover was a specially cast one-piece unit, instead of

*Royal Air Force serviceman Johnny Munn screams his TD1B off the line during a sprint in Singapore, mid 1960s. Malaysia and Singapore were important Yamaha outlets.*

a milled-off road unit and the gearbox ratios were once again altered, and the gears themselves were beefed up. The only other difference was that the engine gained a kickstart.

The new model's engine was claimed to give a further 4hp, giving 35hp. The TD1As were fast. In the 1963 Daytona Lightweight race, Al Gunter set a qualifying lap of 128mph around the 2 1/2 mile circuit. This speed was fast enough to qualify on the front row of the 750 class! The net result of performances like this, was that 'small' two-strokes became banned from the main Daytona classic. The AMA chose to ban them, because of their links and 'support' from the major influence of US motorcycling, Harley Davidson.

The first batch of 16 TD1As arrived in England during February 1964, at a cost of £520 each. Strangely enough though, unlike in the US the TD1As did not have the same immediate success. Many riders rated the engine, but just didn't like the frame. Billie Nelson was one such rider. He campaigned a TD1A engine, grafted into a Ducati rolling chassis; the Doncaster-Yamaha. Geoff Monty and Frank Sheene also bought TD1As and both had Bill Ivy race them on the odd occasion.

Ted Broad was another top tuner and developer who bought one of the first batch of TD1As. At around the same time, the up-and-coming Reg Everett was looking for a ride. Reg had heard that Ted Broad had bought one of these new Yamaha production racers and decided to track him down and ask him for a ride. This resulted in a test ride at Brands Hatch, where Reg put the Yamaha through its paces and impressed Ted enough for a 'You'd better race it then!' response.

The first few races saw the Broad-Everett team experiencing the trials of the early Yamaha racers, mainly in the form of the crank mounted clutch! Reg recalls about three or four crank failures due to this. This again was caused by the over revving effects caused by Ted's tuning. But Ted came up with the idea of making a heavy gauge crankwheel shaft and bigger main bearing to stop this happening. The new crankwheel was actually machined from a Jaguar car halfshaft! It seemed to work though, as after this modification the problem never occurred again. It was actually this kind of crank strengthening that Yamaha applied to the later TD1B and YDS3 bikes.

The first win came in July 1964 at Snetterton, followed by

several more top three places. 1965 saw Reg finish runner up position in the 250cc UK Championship. Also, taking the coveted 250cc King of Brands title, a race he dearly wanted to win. That year also saw him gaining a ride on one of the Works Yamaha RD56s, partnering Bill Ivy. Unfortunately though, the RD56 blew a small end bearing whilst laying in 2nd place behind his team mate! Bill's machine was to also suffer the same problem, slightly later in the race.

Between races, the factory teams works bikes were often stored in private workshops or motorcycle shops. It was due to this, that Ted Broad had the opportunity to 'study' the RD56s! This resulted in Reg's TD1A gaining a set of RD type expansion pipes. With the strengthened crank, Broad tuned motor, works expansion pipes and numerous other mods, the engine was now capable of revving to 12,000rpm. By the way, it was the original TD1A that was kept and uprated to keep the competetive edge, up until the 1967 season.

To get a bit more racing in, Ted Broad bought another Yamaha and bored in to 270cc, allowing entry to the 350cc class. That bike appeared to be a TD1B, but as I said previously, Ted kept on modifying the bikes. This extra machine gave Reg a bit more race action and valuable track time. The 270 gave the 350 Manxes a good run for their money, for Reg thought that they were heavy and sluggish compared to the lightweight Yamaha.

The 1966 season ended, gaining another runner up position in the 250 British Championship. Early 1967 started well, but turned out to be a disaster for the team. Ted had built a totally new bike, based on a TD1C engine and a home made frame. Other competitors of course, were using TD1Cs in various forms and were doing well with them. Reg's bike though was unreliable, ending up with DNFs in nearly all of the races. It wasn't until it was too late to win the title that the fault was found. Restricted airflow from a slimline fairing had caused the engine to overheat! The offending article was removed, and reliability restored. But, the damage had been done to Reg's confidence and his desire to race. He announced his plan to retire the following year. Reg again, came in as runner up in the British Championship in his final season's racing. He had one last race on a Ducati, partnering Paul Smart in an endurance race at Barcelona, finishing 2nd. Reg retired from racing in 1968, with 31 wins to his credit, making him one of the best privateers of the day and of course, the most successful UK rider of a Yamaha TD1A production racer.

*Early YDS3 shared fuel tank and paint work with the YDS2, but differed with side panels and Autolube. It arrived mid 1964.*

*A race kit was produced for the YDS3 consisting of engine, carb and exhaust components.*

# 1964 YDS3 Autolube and TD1B

As previously mentioned, Yamaha were continually trying to improve their products; and as a result the YDS2 sportster was to be fully redeveloped into a new machine.1964 saw the first 250cc to carry the 'Autolube' self-mixing oil system. The YDS3 was not just a YDS2 with a few refinements. It was a totally new bike, although it still retained the same styling. The main improvement to the engine was a stronger crankshaft, a direct result of feedback gained from racers like Reg Everett! Unfortunately though, the clutch remained on the crankshaft. This I find slightly odd. The very first Yamaha 250. the YD1 was fitted with its clutch on the gear shaft. All models up to this date had the clutch on the crankshaft, even though the feedback was all in favour of the clutch being mounted on the gear shaft. Still at least the crankshaft itself was less likely to snap!

The other main improvement to the engine was of course, the Autolube system. This utilised a mechanical oil pump driven via a gear on the gearbox shaft. It gave the YDS3 a distinctive bulge on the side of the crankcase. This form of oil pump drive though had its drawbacks:- if a throttle-happy boy racer sat at the lights with the bike in gear, clutch lever pulled in and revving the engine, the oil pump would not be driven. Should the lights change and the bike speed off, the oil-less engine would rapidly seize up causing an unecessary repair bill.

As the TD1A was based on the YDS2, the YDS3 lent its improvements to the TD1B. The first 1 Bs retained the 1As round orange-red fuel tank (known as the 'watermelon tank' in the USA), seat unit and general chassis. The rear shocks were improved with stiffer, adjustable bodies and the forks were again up-rated. The engine was of course now based upon YDS3 crankcases, with tuned, chrome lined alloy barrels, racing heads,1.5mm parkerised cast iron single ring pistons and racing crank. The bulge on the side of the crankcase, which housed the oil pump on the YDS3 was now empty, behind it was only a blanking off plate. The redundant

*Ilford Essex dealer and race entrant Ted Broad at work on a special 270cc version of the TD1B which his rider Reg Everett campaigned in the 350cc class at British short circuit during 1967.*

alloy of the oil pump housing was often removed by racers, trying to save that extra bit of weight. The clutch though was improved for the racer, it now was a special unit with spur gear primary drive, as opposed to the previous model's road derived helical cut gears.

The gearbox received improved ratios and the engine still retained its kickstart! The TD1B was again fitted with Amal 276 clone carburettors and initially, the floats stayed bolted onto a bracket at the rear of the engine. As mentioned earlier, the TD1B was to gain one of the major improvements Yamaha had been working on, a better expansion pipe. It was now much fatter, with a narrower 'pea shooter' end pipe. This allowed a higher revving engine, with more top end power and a distinctive power band. The pipes were still chromium plated. A newer type of magneto was fitted to the 1 B, this time it was a MF2-RY, differing only in a minor way.

The new model was an immediate success, gaining lap records and race wins on both sides of the Atlantic. Again though, the bikes were more popular and successful in the USA. During early 1965, the bike was cosmetically changed. It was given a long, pointy white fuel tank and a more squared-off seat unit. While the frame and chassis still remained the same metallic grey finish, the bike had a sleek modern look. The frame was actually modified to suit the new body-work. Another subtle improvement was the introduction of wider tyres. The front was now a 2.75 x 18, while the rear became a 3.00 x 18.

The carburettor float bowl bracket was relocated to try and stop the fuel frothing. It was mounted onto a bracket hanging down from the frame, under the fuel tank.

As with all of the Yamaha models, other variances appeared on the TD1B; a whole batch of identical bikes, would have been a miracle! The final variation of the 1 B ended with the addition of a new aluminium top yolk and improved rear suspension units. This model lasted until 1967 when, at last, the old style crank mounted clutch was ditched!

## The TD1C

The TD1C was without doubt the racing bike which made Yamaha's name in the UK. It was so effective at winning races and because of its new clutch layout, was a fast and reliable machine. The bike started winning big races and gaining lap records all over the country, and indeed the rest of the world. Don Vesco actually won the Daytona Grand Prix on his works TD1C, known as the YZ607. Yamahas' new 1967 sports model, the YDS5 was the basis for the engine. Apart from the engine/clutch differences, the basic machine was identical to the last of the TD1Bs.

The only real cosmetic differences were the expansion pipes; these were now painted silver, as opposed to chrome plated. Don Padgett ran a TD1C in the 1967 Manx Grand Prix. Brian Ball won the 250cc British Championship in 1968 on his. Charlie Williams won the 1971 Lightweight Manx Grand Prix on his TD1C, Marty Lunde took the Brands Indy circuit lap record on his 1C.

As tuners got more and more power from the engine, the weaknesses of the old frame began to show., it was essentially the same as the mid production TD1Bs of 1965. It was just about adequate back then, but the new motor had proven itself as a strong unit, and prime for tuning to the max. But the frame just could not handle the extra power or speed. This may seem reminiscent of Japanese road bikes of the early to mid seventies! The engines were developed to give top performance but the frame was not developed to match. The most a standard TD1C saw was a bracing strut welded between the headstock and swinging arm mount.

Dealers, Padgetts of Batley, West Yorkshire, (Peter and Don) also were not limited to road racing, with their machines. They sponsored Des Heckle to enter in sprints and World Record attempts. They loaned him a Padgett tuned TD1C engine, to power a new bike Des had built. In keeping with the Padgett race team, they insisted the bike be painted in the familiar Padgett's race colour. So, the whole frame was painted Yellow. Des was one of the top flight sprinters of the era, already having numerous National and World Records to his credit. His previous mount was a Villiers Starmaker-powered bike that had featured many times on the front cover of *Motorcycle Sport*.

Des raced the new machine several times taking several National Records, induding the Standing Start 1/4 mile, but the main achievement came in late September 1970, at the National Sprint Assodation's World Record meeting at Elvington Airfield organised by George Brown. Des broke 4 World Records that weekend, two on his 125 Yamaha and two on the TD1C. The 250 took the Standing Start 1km and the Standing Start 1mile, which remained a World Record for well over 10 years!

*Motor Cycle News* covered the event, with Des in action on the TD1C as the main photo subject. He took the Standing Start Kilometre Record to 22.83 Seconds, at 97.95mph, and the Standing Start 1 Mile to 33.26 Seconds, at 108.23mph. With the machine, he also ran the Standing Start 1/4 mile at 11.6 seconds.

Richard Tracey.

*The 1967 Daytona 100 mile 250cc race, with 4 Yamahas completing the first lap. Eventual race winner Gary Nixon (9) leads Mike Duff (10), Robert Winters (21) and Donald Twigg (31)*

# TZ700/750 series

The TZ750 was launched at the Tokyo Show in early 1973. Designated the TZ750A, it was actually a '700', 694cc - basically a pair of TZ350 twins side-by-side. Its bore and stroke were also identical to the 350cc at 64 x 54mm. But there were differences. For example, the squish band of the bigger bike was dropped 2mm on the TZ350 to 1mm. In addition the exhaust port differed from the 350, sitting 1.5mm lower in the cylinder barrel. This provided more mid-range, at the expense of top end, making the TZ four cylinder easier to ride.

Yamaha used 4-petal reed valves (developed from their successful motocross engines). At that time, the production TZ350 was only simple piston-port induction; and again more was aimed at broadening the power band. To accommodate the introduction of the reed valve assembly, the cylinder barrels were equipped with a fifth transfer port on the intake side, the pistons had a cut-out in their skirts. These modifications produced an extended inlet duration which allowed more complete filling of the crankcase.

Because Yamaha engineers were worried that piston reliability would be compromised, a few of the early TZ750s were supplied without the trimmed piston skirts.

A casual observer would have thought that the new Yamaha four, with its across-the-frame cylinder layout would have featured a single crankshaft. But in fact there were two assemblies sitting side-by-side in the horizontally-split magnesium crankcases.

On the inboard end of each crankshaft was a 10mm wide gear - this engaged a 20mm wide gear located at the rear of the cranks. The crankpins were set 180 degrees apart which provided a firing order of 1, 4, 2 and 3.

The countershaft transferred drive from the crankshafts to a huge 7-plate dry clutch assembly. Power was also supplied via a primary gear, to a magneto rotor, and to a transmission oil pump, and a water pump.

There was no two-stroke oil pump on the TZ four, lubrication being take care of by simple petroil mixture. A quartet of 34mm Mikuni carburettors were fitted. Yamaha's official figures gave the power output of 90bhp at 10,000rpm. This, combined with an all-up ready-to-race weight figure of 168kg (370lb), was pretty impressive for the time.

Chassis design comprised a tubular steel open loop frame with box-section rear swinging arm and twin shocks - very similar to the original YZR500 four raced by Jarno Saarinen in early 1973. Although the engine sat fairly high in the frame, ground clearance was still something of a problem. This was not due to engine width, but rather the exhaust touching down.

The four pipes were at first mounted beneath the engine, and to alleviate the grounding glitches, the two inside pipes were actually flattened in their mid-section - which from a performance point of view was a drawback. Another problem was that the pipes were prone to fracture and had to be strengthened.

Later models largely solved this problem by re-routing the left side outer pipe up and around the carburettors. This allowed more room for all the pipes to be the desired shape, whilst at the same time curing the fracturing problem.

A pair of 298mm (11.73in) brake discs was specified for the front wheel, with an equally large single disc at the rear. A drum rear brake had originally been considered but this was axed after testing. Giacomo Agostini took the new machine to two brilliant victories - the Daytona 200 and a few weeks later the Imola 200.

Towards the end of 1974 the TZ750B, as it was known, was introduced, the cylinder bore being increased to 66.4mm, giving a full 750cc. Along with the increase in engine displacement, specific components were upgraded - most notably the water pump and the rear tensioner, both of which had been considered not strong enough to cope with the additional 10bhp.

Towards the end of 1975 the production TZ750B became the TZ750C, which was virtually identical.

At Daytona in 1975, a trio of very special TZ750s had been provided for Kenny Roberts, Steve Baker and Giacomo Agostini. These bikes were effectively 750 engines shoehorned into the 500GP monoshock chassis. Kenny Roberts openly admitted that: the new suspension cured the twin shock model's tendency for high speed weaving and that the machine handled a lot better. However, as it happened none of the special monoshock bikes won; instead this honour went to Gene Romero on a Kel Carruthers tuned production twin shock bike.

It wasn't until 1976 that Yamaha produced its ultimate F750 four cylinder two-stroke, the highly esteemed OW31. Lightened by some 18kg (40lb) it also gave more power. Yamaha had again looked at the 500GP chassis for inspiration. Factory sources alleged Roberts was clocked at 182mph during qualifying for Daytona that year.

For 1977 Yamaha produced a production version of the previous year's OW31 factory racer. But it wasn't really a proper replica because the engine was virtually the previous year's production 'C' motor, whilst the chassis was made from heavier materials - so there was only a slight reduction in weight over the previous year's TZ.

In search of rigidity, the frame gained an additional tube underneath the power unit at the front and between the loops of the cradle itself. In addition some changes were necessary to accommodate the new monoshock rear suspension, employed for the first time on a production TZ750. Finally, new exhaust pipes complete with integral silencers were employed, needed to comply with the ever harsher FIM noise levels.

1977 marked Agostini's final season and besides finishing 3rd on an OW31 in the 750cc World Championships he posted his final victory in the last round of that year's championship, with a magnificent victory at Hockenheim. Without doubt 1977 was also the high point of the TZ750 series, and although the TZ750E and F models were built between 1978 and 1983 the model would never quite dominate the circuits as it had done.

In 1980 the FIM announced its decision to axe the F750 World Championship, which ultimately meant the death of the TZ750. In January 1983 the final TZ750F was sold, thus ending one of the most exciting chapters in modern motorcycle racing.

*The bigger and more powerful TZ750 arrived in 1975. The 748cc (66.4 x 54mm) sported CD1 ignition and produced 100bhp at 10,000 rpm. Maximum speed was 168mph.*

# Yamaha - the modern years

# 10

*British Championship round Olivers Mount, Scarborough 1981. The line-up is basically made- up of Japanese 500 Grand Prix 2-strokes from Suzuki and Yamaha.*

As Yamaha entered the 1980s, its series production street bikes and its racing effort was still centred around the two-stroke. This was in contrast to much of the rest of the industry which was firmly four-stroke, led by Honda. From an environmental viewpoint the four-stroke ruled supreme, but from a racing perspective the two-stroke was top dog. Even Honda had to switch to the dreaded 'ring-dings' to achieve 500 Grand Prix success (see Mick Walker's Japanese Grand Prix Racing Motorcycles, Redline Books).

*Some excellent results saw Alan Carter being given a works backed (via British importers Mitsui) TZ250 for 1983. He made history by becoming the youngest rider up to that time to win a Grand Prix, the 250cc French in May in 1983.*

Toward the end of the 1970s development of the TZ250/350 twins had taken something of a back seat due to the company's need to develop a new range of four-stroke roadsters and the arrival of the four-cylinder TZ500/700/750 racing series. But with the launch of the 'F' version of the TZ250/350 for the 1979 model year much needed improvements were introduced. Notable was a more compact (lower) frame. Perhaps unsurprisingly this was soon being referred to as the 'Lowboy' and was accompanied by an equally new aluminium box section swinging arm. A weight pruning exercise had also been carried out, which saw the introduction of aluminium brake calipers, in place of the former steel components. The rear disc diameter was decreased by 30mm - this being one of the first occasions when a manufacturer had employed the now universal larger front/smaller rear brake disc diameter set-ups found on today's machinery. But at the end of the 1970s the vast majority of road and racing bikes featured the same diameter front and rear.

*New for 1981 was the TZ125 single. It was never to catch on in the same way as its Honda counterpart, the MT and Later RS.*

At the same time Yamaha's TZ engineering team attempted to improve front end handling problems by redesigning the forks (new fork sliders and internal changes including damping pistons) and changing the caster from 27.5 to 26 degrees. The dry weight of the TZ250F was down by no less than 21.5lb(10kg) from the outgoing E series of the previous year.

*This 1982 TZ250G raced by Swiss rider Jacques Cornu, has an aluminium Dutch Nico Bakker frame, rising rate monoshock rear suspension and HH (Hans Humel) cylinders.*

Of the two engines, the bigger model had by far the lion's share of development that year. So the TZ350F featured 6 ports, instead of the E's four. This was achieved by placing a bridge in the centre of the main transfer port of the cylinder barrel. It worked on the following basis: the transfer port nearest to the exhaust port opened first, followed 0.1mm later by the middle port and, after another 0.1mm increment, the final port. The roofs of these ports were not the same as the smaller engine. The slower internal speeds of the TZ350 internals permitted the scavening stream of fresh charge to be directed marginally higher over the piston crown without it being lost via the exhaust. The inlet side of the TZ350's piston was set up accordingly - opening the port earlier and closing it later. Yamaha also found that they were having problems keeping the larger TZ twin's exhaust system within the FIM's rule book. This meant that both header pipes had to pass over each other where they passed at the base of the crankcase of the engine.

The power out of the TZ350F was 72bhp at 11,000rpm - compared to the E version's 64bhp at 10,500rpm. Some of this was due to the fitment of the larger Mikuni VM carburettors - up from 34 to 38mm. And for the first time on a production racer, Yamaha employed a power jet. This was placed in the inlet tract of both cylinders. The 'jet' provided additional fuel only when the engine's revolutions exceeded 7,500rpm, in effect giving a top end boost.

*New Era clubman Rob Pywell putting his 1995 TZ125 single through its paces at Snetterton, Saturday 6th July 2002.*

## 1981 TZ250 H

| | |
|---|---|
| Engine | Liquid-cooled, twin cylinder 2-stroke with reed-valve induction and mechanically-operated power valves. |
| Capacity | 249cc |
| Bore | 56mm |
| Stroke | 50.7mm |
| Comp ratio | 7.6:1 |
| Carburation | 2 x Mikuni VN36 with power jet |
| Ignition | CD1 |
| Gearbox | Six-speeds |
| Clutch | Dry, multi-plate |
| Frame | Steel, duplex tubular construction |
| Suspension | Front: telescopic fork; Rear: aluminium swinging arm, mono shock |
| Brakes | Front and rear hydraulically-operated single disc with 2-piston calipers |
| Tyres | 3.00 x 18 front; 3.75 x 18 rear |
| Dry weight | 234Ib(106kg) |
| Max power | 57bhp at 11,000rpm |
| Max speed | 145mph |

*The second major redesign of the TZ series came in 1981 with the 250H model. A spate of piston and to a lesser extent big-end failures on the G model saw the bore and stroke revert to 56 x 50mm, the crank pin diameter increased and the crank flywheels discs reduced in weight.*

*The chassis also received a makeover making the machine lower and giving the TZ250H superior handling over the outgoing G model.*

A Cadwell Park shot from 1984, showing Steve Chambers with his TZ250 negotiating Mansfield Corner.

For 1980 the TZ250/350 prefix was 'G'. But from now on the development cash went into the smaller bike. In fact the 350cc class was on the way out of the FIM's calendar - the final round of the 350cc world series taking place in September 1982 (at Hockenheim, Germany - and fittingly won by a privateer - Manfred Herweh - on a production TZ).

The last of the TZ350 series, the 'H' was in fact virtually identical to the 1980 G. Following the successful introduction of the Power Jet system on the TZ350F, the TZ250G of 1980 sported the same set-up. Again, this provided useful additional top end performance. To take advantage of this, the engineering team revamped the cylinders and pistons. However, although extracting a useful increase in power (around 3-4bhp depending on the engine) it also brought with it a notable decrease in the life of some engine components - notably the pistons and crankshafts. This had two results. The first one was the frequent use of aftermarket Hoeckle crankshafts and the need to carry out a full rebuild after each meeting (or a trio of short club-type events). The other was that it brought to an end the long running 247cc (54 x 54mm), piston-ported engine with its single cylinder block casting (making it more expensive when a replacement was needed). Compared with the outgoing TZ250G, the 1981 'H' cost £4,500 against £3.900. And this in a year which heralded a world-wide recession. However, Yamaha largely got away with it, due to the fact that the 'H' was a much superior bike to the 'G' - and much more reliable and thus less expensive to keep on the track.

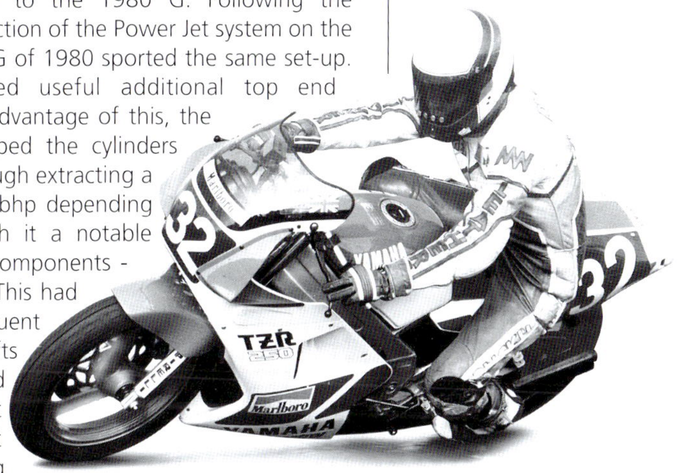


Yamaha International Cup, Vallelunga, near Rome, 18th October 1987. British rider Darren Dixon (also a highly successful sidecar driver) with the 250TZR he took to 2nd place.

The new for 1988 reverse cylinder TZ250 model.

# 1990 TZ250 A

| | |
|---|---|
| Engine | Liquid-cooled, twin cylinder 2-stroke with reverse cylinders with rear facing exhausts. Reed-valve induction directly into crankcase, 6-petal reeds. |
| Capacity | 249cc |
| Bore | 56mm |
| Stroke | 50.7mm |
| Comp ratio | 8.2:1 |
| Carburation | Front mounted |
| Ignition | CD1 |
| Gearbox | Six-speed |
| Clutch | Dry, multi-plate |
| Frame | Aluminium Delta-box construction |
| Suspension | Front: telescopic fork<br>Rear: aluminium swinging arm, rising rate single shock |
| Tyres | 3.5 x 17 front; 5.25 x 17 rear |
| Dry weight | 216Ib(98kg) |
| Max power | 70bhp at 11,000rpm |
| Max speed | 155mph |

*Frame, engine, carburettors, clutch and rear facing exhausts exiting from seat.*

*Details of the reverse cylinder TZ250 which ran from 1988 until 1990.*

*New reverse cylinder TZ250S at Oliver's Mount Scarborough, July 1988.*

## 1993 TZ250 E

| | |
|---|---|
| Engine | Liquid-cooled, 90 degree v-twin, 2-stroke, with single crankshaft, balancer shaft, guillotine exhaust valves and reed induction |
| Capacity | 249cc |
| Bore | 56mm |
| Stroke | 50.7mm |
| Comp ratio | 8.3:1 |
| Carburation | 2 x Mikuni TM38 |
| Ignition | CD1 |
| Gearbox | Six-speed |
| Clutch | Dry, multi-plate |
| Frame | Aluminium Delta-box construction |
| Suspension | Front: telescopic fork<br>Rear: aluminium swinging arm, rising rate single shock |
| Tyres | 3.75 front; 6.0 x 17 rear |
| Dry weight | 218Ib(99kg) |
| Max power | 77bhp at 12,000rpm |
| Max speed | 161mph |

*The first year of the new v-twin over-the-counter production model, was the TZ250B of 1991. Barry Utting in action at Croft Autodrome.*

*One of the TZ250 v-twins photographed at Brands Hatch in August 1994; British National Championships.*

## 1985 TZ250 N

| | |
|---|---|
| Engine | Liquid-cooled, twin cylinder 2-stroke with reed-valve induction directly into crankcase, 4-petal reeds |
| Capacity | 249cc |
| Bore | 56mm |
| Stroke | 50.7mm |
| Comp ratio | 8:1 |
| Carburation | 2 x Mikuni VM38 with power jet |
| Ignition | CD1 |
| Gearbox | Six-speed |
| Clutch | Dry, multi-plate |
| Frame | Steel, duplex tubular construction |
| Suspension | Front: telescopic fork<br>Rear: aluminium swinging arm, mono shock |
| Brakes | Front and rear hydraulically-operated discs; dual front; single rear |
| Tyres | 3.00 x 17 front; 3.75 x 18 rear |
| Dry weight | 227Ib(103kg) |
| Max power | 64bhp at 11,000rpm |
| Max speed | 150mph |

*Dean Johnson riding the 1995 Fowler's TZ250 crests the mountain at Cadwell Park during the British Championship round at the Lincolnshire circuit, August 1996.*

*Teenager Michael Hetzburg with his new 1998 TZ250 at Cadwell Park that year. The bike was very different from the earlier model.*

For the 1998 season Yamaha introduced an updated TZ250. It was a considerable improvement over the outgoing model but still struggled to get on terms with the best of the Aprilia and Honda machinery.

This was thanks to the hugh amount of time and money that the company had spent on the 500 factory bikes. This technology was employed in the redesign of the TZ250H engine. Make no mistake the H series onwards of the TZ250 was a new breed. Not only were there new 56 x 50.7mm dimensions, giving 249cc, but much else in the engine department was new too. For starters, the TZ250, cylinder castings were individual components, base-moulded to the crankcase. Another major change was that the engine now ran backwards. This innovation achieved vastly increased piston life - the power strokes of the motor now driving the skirt of the piston against a solid wall of cylinder beneath the exhaust port. This provided (unlike the 250G) real support and thus much longer life. Colin MacKellar in his book *Yamaha All Factory and Production Road-Racing Two-Strokes 1955 to 1993* (Crowood) sums things up nicely, saying, 'The wall of the TZ250G cylinder looked like a Swiss cheese'.

New era clubman Bruce Dunn with his 2002 TZ250 winning at Snetterton, Norfolk, 6th July 2002.

# TZ250 Evolution 1972 - 1993

*Ron Williams of Maxton Engineering won considerable credit and a degree of fame by producing a series of frames for Yamaha's TZ series. These examples are seen in the TT paddock, mid 1970s. they were ridden by the likes of Charlie Williams and Bernard Murray.*

1972 TZ250 — Pre-production model raced by works supported riders. Essentially the drum brake TD250, but with liquid-cooling and water pump in place of autolube system on air-cooled models.

1973 TZ250 A — Some production examples built spring 1973 54 x 54mm bore and stroke, horizontally split crankcases. Drum brakes 18-inch wheels, twin shock rear suspension 51bhp at 10,500rpm. DC1 ignition.

1974 TZ250 A — Main production batch of A model.

1975 TZ250 B — Largely unchanged.

1976 TZ250 C — Mono shock rear suspension, with 20 position shock adjustment. Shock absorber extended from steering head to swinging arm. Front and rear disc brakes. 52bhp at 10,500rpm. Alloy brake discs, steel 2-piston calipers.

1977 TZ250 D — Raised exhaust ports.

1978 TZ250 E — Same as D model.

1979 TZ250 F — 'Lowboy' chassis; aluminium swinging arm, aluminium brake calipers; smaller diameter rear disc; modified front forks, new connecting rod, new exhaust.

1980 TZ250 G — Stiffer front fork; Power jet system for carburettors, piston and cylinder revised. 55bhp at 11,500rpm.

1981 TZ250 H — Major redesign; separate cylinder castings, Power valve, 56 x 50mm bore and stroke, 2 crankshaft, new Mikuni carburettor design, lighter frame, 55bhp at 11,000rpm.

1982 TZ250 J — Only minor changes.

1983 TZ250 K — New cylinder heads, 38mm round slide Mikuni carbs, magnesium clutch cover, compact clutch, new exhausts, lighter frame, revised suspension; narrower fairing. 59bhp at 11,000rpm.

1984 TZ250 L — Engine fitted 250 K kit parts as standard, featuring electrically-operated Power valve as standard, new exhaust, re-jetted carbs and pistons with shorter skirt on the inlet side. Crankpin and con-rods strengthened. New piston design. Increased wheelbase, strengthened swinging arm revised castor, engine mounted slightly further forward. 60bhp at 11,000rpm.

*Scot Donnie McLeod a top runner in British and international events on his Dalmac Racing TZ250L, Cadwell Park, Easter 1984.*

1985 TZ250 N — Major engine revision, reed valve induction directly into crankcase, 4-petal reed, new exhaust and revised carburation, 17-inch front, 18 rear wheels.

1986 TZ250 S — 6-petal reeds, totally new chassis using aluminium Delta-box twin spar frame, rising rate mono shock rear suspension developed from type pioneered on YZ motocrossers. 3-spoke light alloy wheels.

*One of the brand new TZ250L models on display by Fowlers of Bristol at the Road & Racing show, Alexander Palace, North London, January 1984. It had been specially airfreighted to the show from Japan.*

1987 TZ250 T Flat-slide 38mm Mikuni TM carburettors. Wider (72mm) 6-petal reed valves, new exhausts.

1988 TZ250 U Reverse cylinders with rear facing (straight) exhausts and front mounted flat slide carbs. Cylinders tilted forward by 60 degrees. One-piece crankcase. Side-loading gearbox, revised cooling system, revised swinging arm, dual iron front brake discs with 4-piston calipers 17-inch wheels front and rear.

1989 TZ250 W New Nissin brake calipers on both wheels, revised exhaust. Power jet on carbs now wired up to an electronically driven solenoid which kept jet dormant until the engine reached 9,500rpm. Strengthened crankshaft, revised port timing. Front forks given damping adjustment, modified rear suspension.

1990 TZ250 A Last of parallel twin models. Smaller crankcases, revised water jackets around cylinders, more powerful water pump.

1991 TZ250 B New 90 degree v-twin engine with offset cylinders, single crankshaft, drive on offside end of crank, balancer shaft. Engine bolted directly to Delta-box frame. Guillotine exhaust valves and 38mm TM carbs retained. Totally new cooling system, revised port timing. Engine running forward. Gearbox revised by 'stacking' the two gear shafts. Engine now a full stress member of the frame, with revised swinging arm. Inverted front fork, detailed changes to rear suspension.

1992 TZ250 D Six-port cylinders from 1991 D kit. Frame modified in area of rear suspension. Upper mounting bracket.Sub-frame now merely seat support. New front forks, with increased adjustment facilities.

1993 TZ250 E Slight changes to transfer and auxiliary exhaust ports plus revised mapping sequences for digital ignition. 0.25 inches wider front wheel rim. Improved aerodynamics due to new fairing/seat.

# LC - One for the Boys

*One of the larger displacement 350LC in action at Donington Park, circa 1982.*

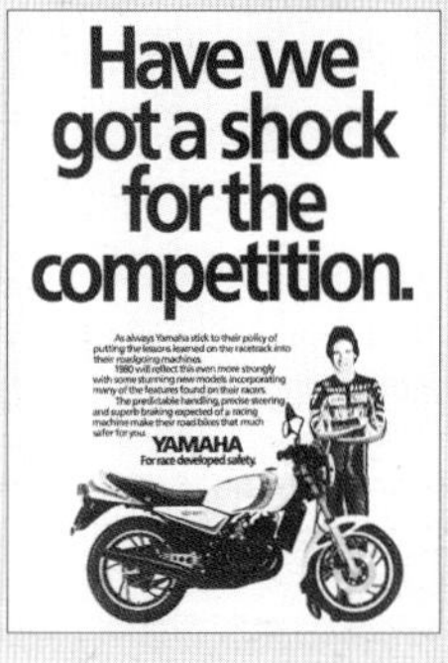


The world had its first glimpse of the new RD350 LC in October 1979, when in replacing the long running air-cooled RD series, it was the star attraction at the Paris Show.

That original 350 was the beginning of a whole family of machines: RD250 LC, RD125 LC, RD80 LC, 350 YPVS and finally the flagship RD500 LC four.

In launching the LC, Yamaha took several major technological steps, including introducing cantilever rear suspension and liquid cooling to bring riders a new dimension in two-stroke performance - at affordable prices.

The 250 and 350 LC models were aimed primarily at Europe and the sporting rider, and started to arrive in Spring 1980. These were bikes for the fast road rider or aspiring racer. Compared to earlier Yamaha series production two-strokes they contained all manner of innovations, much of the technology coming direct from their TZ brothers. The most obvious was liquid cooling (LC). Yamaha used a mixture of 50 per cent distilled water and 50 per cent ethylene glycol (anti-freeze), forced around the aluminium cylinder block by a crankshaft driven pump.

Commonality was a valuable feature of the LC series: 350 LC barrels fitted the 250 LC; the 250 and 350 LC barrels fitted the air-cooled RD; and TZ barrels (up to 250 G) fit the RD and LC. So it would be logical to presume that the LC power unit was directly developed from the TZ; wrong! Instead it owed more to the air-cooled roadster RD.

A common factor of both the RD and LC families was reed valve induction. And was largely responsible for the LC's ease of starting and lusty low-mid range power delivery in both 250 and 350 engine sizes.

Components such as the 6-speed gearbox and crankshaft were derived from the old RD models. Details may have varied but the basics were the same. Electrics was another area where much was as before. For example, the dependable crankshaft-mounted generator/ignition needed no development, as from the late 1970s it had provided a valuable boost to reliability.

*Cambridgeshire rider Rod Harwin in action with his 250LC at Cadwell Park, April 1984.*

So what was new? Well, the cantilever suspension found on the original 250/350 LCs was developed from the YZ motocrossers. It offered increased rigidity and much longer rear wheel movement compared with the previous pivoting fork of the RDs with their twin shocks. The single De Carbon-type rear suspension unit was tucked away under the frame and received little in the way of cooling air - and what it did get had already been warmed by the engine and radiator. So it is perhaps unsurprising that this was to prove one of the few weak points of the design; LCs suffering from, in extreme cases, total damper failure.

Another major development on the LC series was the anti-vibration engine mounting system. Again simple, but effective, the motor was pivoted at the rear and retained by high deflection rubber bushes at the front. The engine was simply bounced up and down; so noticeable was the effect that one could literally see the engine moving independently to the frame!

When first introduced, the 250/350 LCs gained a reputation for breaking exhaust pipes due to excessive engine movement. This was cured in 1981 when two additional rubber bushed tie-rods were added. These fixed to the underside of the crankcases and extended forward to the frame, allowing vertical but restricting lateral engine movement.

A common complaint on the outgoing air-cooled RD series had been crankshaft failure due to lack of oil. This was usually the result of neglecting to check the oil tank. Yamaha's response was to fit the 250/350 LC with a panel of warning lights, including one for the above purpose; but for racing many simply blanked off the oil pump and used straight petroil mixture.

In racing itself the LC pair immediately made an impact. The 250 LC won its class in the 1980 Isle of Man Production TT. The 350 was equally successful dominating the 500cc production category. Between them the two LCs won nearly everything in sight; from club championships to major international events. Attempting to list these successes would require a book in itself, but the simple fact is that an LC of either capacity: 247cc (54 x 54mm)/347cc (64 x 54mm), with a modest amount of tuning, produced the sort of performance that a few years previously would have been sufficient to win a national championship.

'Legal' modification tuners such as Stan Stephens and Gerry Pell were soon extracting around 46bhp at 9000rpm (250) and 54bhp at 9,500rpm (350).

Formula 2 category racing was completely different; with TZ type modifications allowed, the 350 LC engine put out around 75bhp and propelled the best bikes to well over 140mph.

Australian, Graeme McGregor won the 1984 Formula 2 TT at a record average speed of 108.78mph. His machine was an Arnold Fletcher tuned non-power valve 350 LC engine housed in a pukka TZ chassis.

The Pro-Am series of the early 1980s was a great success. Essentially a grid of 40 odd 350 LCs was provided by the British importers Mitsui. The riders taking part had to pick an ignition key to know which bike they would be racing that day. It was a great idea and effectively stopped any form of

*The Marlboro Clubmans series, Lydden Hill, Kent 1984 and a squadron of LC pilots. Dean Askin leading from Andy Muggleton, Stu Melen, Gerry Mobey and John Goldfinch.*

*Left to right: Iain Pero (2nd), Jean-Phillipe Ruggia (1st) and Graeme Muir (3rd) the three top men at the RD350 International Challenge Cup, Zandvoort, Holland, 17th and 18th August 1985.*

cheating. So everyone got an equal chance. No 'buy your rides' which so taints much of national type racing today. Pro-Am certainly delivered the goods by uncovering new talent. Riders such as Niall Mackenzie, Alan Carter and many others began their careers aboard the venerable LC.

As a lasting testament to the LC, many examples are still being campaigned today and for many years the LC class was the most hotly contested at any club event, earning the riders the dubious title of 'Headbangers'. But what you got was close, competitive racing, with scrapes all the way down the field. Almost every LC rider had to fight his own battle to gain a position higher up the leader board than his rival. What racing, what bikes!

*The Pro-Am series for 350LCs proved tremendously popular. Here Kurt Langen (11) leads Steve Chambers (3) into Mansfield Corner at Cadwell Park, Summer 1984.*

*The final round of the 1985 RD350 International Challenge Cup 28th October was held at Carole circuit, Paris. Here Englishman Kenny Irons (3) leads Swede Stefan Schoenburg (6) and Jean-Phillipe Ruggia (1) and a horde of other competitors.*

## 1983 RD350 LC

| | |
|---|---|
| Engine | Liquid-cooled, parallel twin, 2-stroke with reed-valve induction and YPVS; Autolube lubrication |
| Bore | 64mm |
| Stroke | 54mm |
| Capacity | 347cc |
| Comp ratio | 6:1 |
| Ignition | CD1 |
| Carburation | 2 x Mikuni VM 26mm |
| Gearbox | 6-speed |
| Clutch | Wet, multi-plate |
| Final Drive | Chain |
| Frame | Steel tubular construction, full cradle |
| Suspension | Front: telescopic forks<br>Rear: cantilever swinging, Yamaha mono cross |
| Wheels | 18-inch aluminium |
| Tyres | 90/90 51H 18 front; 110/80 58H 18 rear |
| Brakes | Front: 2 x 270mm discs with 2-piston calipers<br>Rear: single 260mm disc with 2-piston caliper |
| Dry weight | 320lb (145kg) |
| Max power | 59.1bhp at 9000rpm |
| Max speed | 120mph |

*The new-for-1983 Power Valve YPVS 350LC. The rider here is Gordon Allott on the Stan Stephens tuned Garozzo-backed model at Donington Park. He later became an international rider with Team Decorite.*

*Future Grand Prix star Alan Carter awaits the start of an LC race at Donington Park.*

*Ponderosa circuit, Flookburgh, Cumbria, 1982, riders awaiting their turn to get out on the tarmac, numbers 19, 12 and 30 are all LC Yamahas - the most popular production racer of its generation.*

*A TZ350H in action at Snetterton in 1982, rider Barry Utting.*

To achieve the reverse in rotation the development team placed a jackshaft to the rear and base of the crankshaft, thus reversing the rotation of the engine before it reached the transmission.

Yet another major alteration was to the crankshaft design. In fact there was now no longer a single unit. Instead the nearside (left) assembly came with a gear pressed on its inboard end, this operated the aforementioned jackshaft. The offside (right) crank was equipped with a smaller diameter gear pressed to its inboard extremity - this providing a spline-fit with teeth cut on the inner surface of the gear on the other crankshaft.

*TZ350 being raced during the early 1980s by Ian Pratt, with on-standard Dymag wheels.*

Coupled with a lower piston speed of the new shorter stroke dimensions, a redesigned stronger crankpin and lighter crankshaft flywheels conspired to reduce the crankshaft weaknesses with which the 250G had been blighted significantly.

The offside crank also drove the mechanical governor for another important innovation: the Power Valve mechanism - ultimately know as YPVS Yamaha Power Valve System. The operation of this is described in a separate boxed section within this chapter. After considerable thought the design team opted not to provide its TZ250 customers with the electrically-operated set-up from the TZ500. In its place they came up with an ingenious lay-out of ball bearings, curved cups

*The RD350 LC (YPVS) International Challenge Cup series held at Zandvoort, Holland over the weekend 17th and 18th August 1985. Jean-Phillipe Ruggia of France (5) leads the Australian pairing Graeme Muir (25) and Iain Pero (24).*

*The late Phil Mellor TZ350, winning the 350cc Isle of Man TT, 1983. Note fly-covered fairing! His average speed for the 226.38mile race was 109.71 mph.*

and spring which converted the movement of the ball bearings caused by the centrifugal action of the rotating crankshaft into vertical movement of the power valve linkage. This action caused the pair of valves, linked via an Oldhams coupling, to rotate in their housing within the respective cylinder. Below 8,750rpm, the power valves remained fully closed, venturing 6mm into the exhaust port. By 11,000rpm, the said port was fully exposed with the engine exiting spent gases via the exhaust port.

The carburation was another area of change for the H model. In place of the G's Mikuni VM34 SC instruments came new VM36s. These carbs, known as the 'ZC', featured a cylinder side cutaway of the cylindrical slide, which exposed the main jet to the crankcase vacuum. This modified carburettor type was Mikuni's response to the success garnered by the American Lectron. Produced by a small Michigan-based concern and the work of Norm Quantz, the Lectron was a flat-slide instrument which featured a single needle which controlled fuel flow throughout the range of engine revolutions. For five years Lectron offered a way of improving upon the Mikuni and thus found its way onto several TZs, including the works-supported mounts of Kenny Roberts.

*A youthful Alan Carter winning the 350cc race aboard his Pharaoh TZ350, Donington Park, October 1982.*

To show potential buyers that this was a complete rethink of the TZ formula, the cycle parts received attention too. Both the rake and trail were changed 28 degrees and 87mm (against the G's 26 degrees/92mm) . The wheelbase was also longer - up from 1935 to 1950mm. Not only was the frame 6.5lb(3kg) lighter, but the engine was repositioned forward by a small amount. Suspension wise, the main improvement was to make the aluminium single rear shock absorber more adjustable - with bump-stop adjustment being added to the existing rebound. It is also worth noting that some of the top privateers were able to obtain special kits so that they had electrically rather than mechanically operated power valves. With these the performance was improved, almost matching the works-only Kawasaki tandem twins.

A combination of circumstances meant that little work was carried out on the TZ250 the following year, so the 1982 'J' model was virtually unchanged except for modified front forks, alternative gear ratios and changes to the exhaust system. Yamaha was not only struggling with greatly reduced sales of the series production roadsters, caused by the economic downturn, but had to make considerable efforts in its attempt to get back on terms in the 500cc Grand Prix class at world level. But even with no real development and the distractions outlined, a virtually stock TZ250, ridden by Frenchman Jean-Louis Tournadre surprised everyone (including Yamaha) by beating all the full works bikes to take the 250cc world title - Yamah's first after eight years in this class.

*Barry Sheene, TZ500 with by now limited factory backing, at Donington Park on the 19th June 1982.*

# YPVS

*Mechanically controlled TZ250H Power Valve cylinder from the early 1980s.*

YPVS stood for Yamaha Power Valve System and was pioneered on the company's TZ250 H racer of 1980. From then on it was to become an integral part of racing and high performance SuperSports, including the RD350 LC and the RD500 LC. Whilst the latter was not widely used on the track, the former most certainly was. When the RD350 LC YPVS was unveiled to the public at the 1982 Cologne Show, many observers initially thought the newcomer was simply a restyled version of the existing 350 LC. But they were wrong. Actually, it was considerably different, with the YPVS producing 59.1bhp at 9000rpm - 12 more horses than its predecessor. This meant that its power output would have shamed any 350 circuit racer of only a few years earlier and here it was as a street legal roadster even though it could be raced successfully with the minimum of effort.

One of the most vital changes over the outgoing LC was the YPVS. Very simply, this was a valve which operated in the exhaust port window and was to transform two-stroke performance in future years. The timing on such an engine would exceed 200 degrees to obtain the necessary port area to handle the exhaust gas within the time available. This would produce, on a conventional 2-stroke engine, a power delivery far worse than on a less highly developed engine - say one of the company's RD400 air-cooled models; as well as poor response at low rpm, the power would arrive like a kick from a horse. The answer, Yamaha engineers found, was to change the exhaust port height whilst the engine was running, increasing the port height and area as the speed increased. The Yamaha Power Valve System afforded high gas-trapping capability at low speeds and provided the necessary port area for peak power at higher engine revolutions.

The valve control system of the series production LC 350 YPVS was electronic, but during development of the system on the TZ racer, a mechanical centrifugal type (similar to a contact breaker advance) was tested, as was a hydraulic system employing the engine's water pump. But the electrically driven system ultimately emerged a clear winner, consuming less power and having more accurate control over the valve than the other systems.

It worked on the following basis. The engine speed was first detected from the ignition via a simple frequency to a voltage convertor, the battery driving the 0 - 12 volt motor, which in turn rotated the power valve: 0 - 5000rpm equalling 0 volts (valve closed); 9000rpm equalling 12 volts (valve fully open).

Since Yamaha introduced the technology, the power valve theme has been taken up by several other manufacturers, notably Aprilia, Honda and Suzuki, who have all produced their own variations each having its own, patented, name title.

*The valve control system of the 350YPVS was electronic.*

*Mark Plato with the RD500 LC V4 2-stroke in the 6-Hour Endurance race at Snetterton in 1985.*

The works-supported TZs of Carlos Lavado and Martin Wimmer did however, have a real hand in what was to appear as the 1983 TZ250K. During 1982 they had in effect ridden prototypes, many features of which were incorporated in the following year's production model. These included new round slide 38mm carbs, a magnesium clutch cover, a more compact clutch assembly (with one less plate), new cylinder heads, a new exhaust system, revised suspension, lighter springs both front and rear, a lighter frame and a narrower fairing. Added to these changes was a decrease in weight by 6.5lb (3kg). However, few 250Ks were sold - a combination of the continuing economic climate and another rise in price (to £5,250 in the UK). Not only this but customers were still without the electric power valve set-up, which remained an expensive option but which was needed at the highest level to achieve results.

The 250L went on sale in February 1984. The engine now contained the 250K kit parts - so customers at long last got the electric power valves - plus new exhaust, re-jetted carburettors and revised pistons which featured shorter skirts on the inlet side. In addition the bottom end had been strengthened by the use of improved crankpin and con-rod assemblies to prevent connecting rod failure.

But again the 250L attracted few takers, as the price quite simply had reached an astronomical £7,500 (well over £20,000 at today's level).

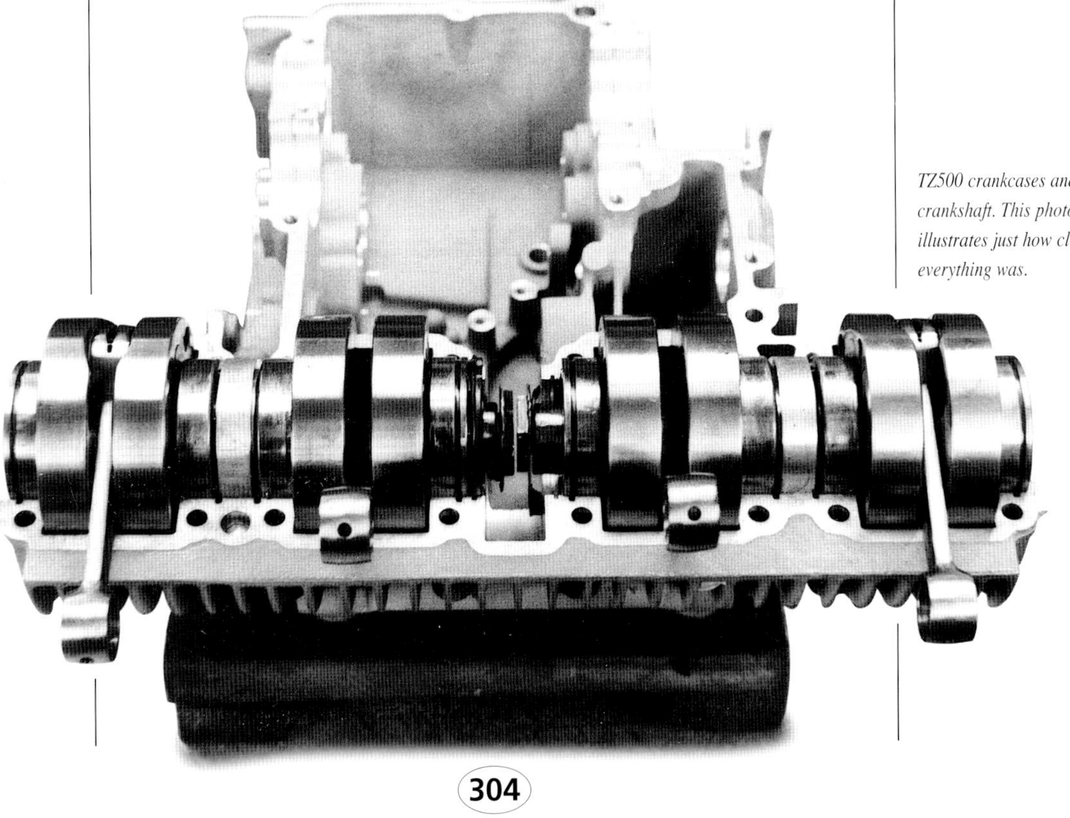

*TZ500 crankcases and crankshaft. This photograph illustrates just how close a fit everything was.*

*A 1980 TZ500, largely standard bike with exhaust valve mechanism. American Morris magnesium wheels.*

To rub salt into the wound Yamaha also produced yet more expensive special kits (these often cost at least half a new bike!). Consisting of revised cylinders (featuring wider exhaust ports) and heads (with almost no squish band) plus guillotine power valves; these special 'works' kits proved a real let-down. In fact the German works rider Martin Wimmer refused the kit he had been given, instead opting to pay himself for aftermarket cylinders from tuning wizard Hans Hummel! These proved so successful that by the middle of that year the majority of TZ owners were using Hummel components. A further blow to Yamaha's pride was that the Hummel cylinders did without any form of power valve!

In addition Kenny Roberts works supported TZ team riders opted to use the Austrian Harold Bartol, who had developed his own cylinders employing reed valves.

It is worth noting that Frenchman Christian Sarron won the 1984 world title using a 250L and Hummel cylinders.

The new TZ quarter-litre racer was the 250N which debuted late in Winter 1985 and featured a much-changed engine - Yamaha acting in response to the considerably poor publicity received with the 1983 K model. Even so, yet again they managed to get things horribly wrong. The basic idea was sound, using reed valve induction directly into the crankcase. Reed valve technology had already proved itself, first at Honda then at Yamaha (on factory 500s).

Both Yamaha and Honda - the latter with their brand new over-the-counter RS250 benefited from being able to sell reed valve 250s for the 1985 season. But sadly for Yamaha, only Honda got things righ. Why? Well the TZ250N employed a 4-petal reed block which was simply not big enough. But quite why Yamaha got itself in this mess is strange, as its factory - supported riders Wimmer and Lavado were given engines with 6-petal reeds from the beginning of that year. So did Yamaha simply not care, was it trying to save money or did it just make a mistake? I would favour the latter explanation. Although on paper the 250N had some worthwhile changes

*Barry Sheene became a Yamaha TZ500 privateer for 1980 and stayed with the model until almost the end of his career in 1984 when he returned to a Suzuki RG500. He received backing from Akai, AGV and Champion amongst others.*

*Steve Parrish on the latest version of the TZ500 with backing from British importers, Mitsui, 500 Gold Cup, Donington Park, 18th April 1982.*

*The view most other competitors got of TZ500 mounted Steve Parrish that day.*

*Mitsui-supported Steve Parrish at Quarter Bridge during the 1985 F1 TT.*

*March 1986, the British Yamaha importers Mitsui with their racing team in the shape of rider/manager Steve Parrish (left), Kenny Irons (centre) and Mitsui marketing boss Ray Ross (right). Sadly Irons was to suffer fatal injuries that year during a warm-up lap at Cadwell Park, ending a promising career.*

including modified cylinders, new exhaust pipes and reworked carburettors (still Mikuni VM38 instruments) the end result was a motorcycle which simply didn't perform. All this was highly embarrassing, as Honda was the new boy on the block with its RS250, where Yamaha could trace its involvement with over-the-counter 250-class production machinery back to the early 1960s.

When Yamaha introduced its next TZ250, the S in early Spring 1986, many expected it to be a v-twin. But instead the company opted to build an entirely new chassis. Not only was this in aluminium but it was of the 'Delta-box' layout with twin spars. Just as notable was the total redesign of the mono-shock rear suspension. The system Yamaha had used up to now, and introduced in the 1976 TZ 250/350C series was to have a giant shock absorber which ran from the steering head to the swinging arm. But compared to developments since Yamaha's innovative move, this was now not only long in the tooth, but agricultural by comparison. The best form of mono-shock had been found to be 'rising rate'; this was much more effective on all forms of road surface. So

The late Rob Vine during the 1985 Formula 1 Isle of Man TT on his FZ750.

Yamaha followed this new trend and even though dry weight remained at 103kg the 'S' was a neater, better handling bike than its predecessors. The swinging arm now had a hole through which the rear shock passed and was massively braced. The rising rate system employed a series of rocker arms to link up the shock with the frame and swinging arm.

For the first time on one of its TZ twin cylinder over-the-counter racers Yamaha gave the 1986 250S aluminium wheels; these featuring three spokes. Like the outgoing N model, these were 17-inch front and 18-inch rear. And although the new frame served its apprenticeship at Grand Prix level (making its debut in mid 1985), the same could not be said of the engine. Largely the TZ remained as before, whereas the factory entered machines debuted an all new 60 degree v-twin for 1986 (coded YZR 250).

Instead Yamaha opted to stick with its parallel twin layout for customer bikes, although the S did benefit from the employment of 6-petal reed blocks in place of the poor performing 4-petal reeds used the previous year. With the improvement outlined above the 1986 TZ250S was not a bad bike, in fact to be honest it was the best of its breed so far. The only problem was the Honda RS250, which was even better.

For 1987 - and long after Lecron had pioneered the use of flat slide carburettors - the TZ250T gained a pair of these instruments - 38mm TM Mikunis. Matched to wider (72mm) 6-petal reeds and a new set of exhausts the later TZ was ready for action. That said, the T was very much an interim bike, as two factions within Yamaha were battling over whether to remain with the long running parallel twin format or to claw back some of the development costs of the YZR v-twin, by offering a production version for sale.

åSteve Parrish, FZ750, 1985 Isle of Man TT.

The FZ750 arrived in early 1985 and was the first of the 5-valves-per-cylinder Genesis 4-cylinder models. This photograph of a fully prepared Superstock racer, taken in March that year, shows the slanting cylinders, anti-dive forks and monoshock rear suspension.

In the end the answer was a compromise, but in many ways a radical one. Controversially, the cylinders had been reversed, so that now the carburettors were at the front, the exhausts to the rear. This, Yamaha claimed, gave that the dead straight line of the pipes meant improved performance, whilst the inlet side benefited from cooler air; being mounted as they were very low and away from the radiator. The downside of this was that stones or other objects could be thrown into the carbs!

Besides the cylinders being canted forward by some 60 degrees - almost horizontal - the crankcase was no longer horizontally split, but in fact a brand new one-piece casting, with a side-loading gear cluster which had been pioneered on the works YZR250 v-twin.

Access to the gearbox was now much easier, but it was not of the full cassette type, as found on some competition machinery in the following decade.

Keith Heuwen awaits the start at Donington Park on his FZ750, Spring 1985.

FZ750 trio, Steve Parrish (6) David Griffiths (25) and Roy Swann sweep into Surtees Bend at Brands Hatch on the 5th April 1985.

*Works YZF750 circa 1986-88.*

Even though the cylinders had been reversed, the engine still ran backwards with power taken from the centre of the crankshaft via a countershaft to the clutch.

Also reversed was the flow direction of the cooling system. This saw the crankcase getting the coolant first, which then flowed through the cylinders and finally the heads before returning to an extra-large aluminium radiator. Previously, the cooling fluid had reached the heads first, resulting in them being overcooled; this also caused a drain in flame travel energy from the spark plugs.

Except for transferring the triangular tubing of the swinging arm from above to below - and thus helping decrease the centre of gravity, enlarging the area of aluminium box section between the twin frame spars - now with the top of the rear shock absorber bolted to it, the chassis was unchanged.

Finally, the 250U was the first TZ to employ double discs to the front wheel, both discs featuring 4-piston calipers. The rear retained a smaller single disc with a 2-piston caliper.

It is also worth noting that besides the works TZR models (now with the vee of the cylinders increased to 70 degrees), several factory-supported riders at various times rode the TZ250U. These bikes featured several special components, notably on electronically-controlled power jet in the inlet of the carburettors. Meanwhile, Martin Wimmer and Jean-Phillipe Ruggia made use of Hummel cylinders. It is worth noting that these latter components were raced both with and

*Left to right: Daron Dixon (England) 2nd, winner Ian Saunders (Australia) and Matthew Blair (Australia) 3rd. Yamaha TZR International Cup, Vallelunga, 18th October 1987.*

# YZF750 SP

For 1993 Yamaha introduced two new production 750s, the YZF750R for road use and the YZF750SP for racing. Both used much of the engine and chassis technology developed in the factory YZF750 race programme of the previous year.

The engine was a highly modified version of the OWO1 unit. The liquid-cooled, slant-block 20-valve four cylinder breathed through a quartet of 39mm Keihin flat slide carburettors featuring TPS (Throttle Position Sensor). This system allowed precise ignition timing depending on the throttle position.

The cylinder head of the 1993 YZF continued to use the 5-valves-per-cylinder pioneered on the FZ750 back in 1985, but the downdraft carbs of the YZF delivered the fuel/air mix to the head via reshaped inlet tracts that were straighter and narrower than the OWO1.

The inlet valve angle was changed for improved gas flow, whilst the compression ratio was reduced from that on the OWO1 (13.2:1). Valve sizes remained unchanged at 23mm inlet and 24.5mm exhaust. The cylinder head changes, combined with 10mm spark plugs, gave an improved combustion process.

The race kit for the SP included: teflon topped pistons, titanium connecting rods, special race ignition, fiercer cam profiles, 4-2-1 exhaust with carbon fibre muffler, carbon-fibre air box.

The aluminium Delta-box frame used on both the YZF750 R and 750 SP was a replica of the design used by the factory's 1992 race bikes. It featured a short wheelbase of only 1420mm - 30mm shorter than the OWO1, and 50mm shorter than the FZR1000 street bike. Rake angle was 24 degrees, which was 0.5 degrees less than the OWO1 and trail was 97mm, some 3mm less.

The best suspension for the machine was found to be the latest Swedish Öhlins 43mm inverted front fork, with a rear shock from the same source. The latter was used in conjunction with a well-braced, flex resistant factory swinging arm and kit version of the rising rate rear linkage.

Compared to its predecessor, the OWO1, the YZF750 SP had a lower front area, helped by a new style air-box which took its feed from a scoop in the top of the radiator which in turn improved the aerodynamics of the fairing; (on the OWO1 it was through fairing mounted inlets). The YZF750 SP came with a lightweight seat and a new, slimline 19-litre tank. With all the carbon-fibre goodies and Öhlins suspension, a fully race kitted machine weighed in at 165.5kg, just 0.5kg above the minimum FIM limit for ready-to-race SuperBike machines.

*British and World SuperBike star Chris Walker racing the Cadbury's Boost YZF750 at Donington Park, 1997.*

## 1993 YZF750 SP Factory race kit fitted

| | |
|---|---|
| Engine | Liquid-cooled, across-the-frame, dohc, 4-cylinder, with 20-valves |
| Capacity | 749cc |
| Bore | 72mm |
| Stroke | 46mm |
| Comp ratio | 13.2:1 |
| Ignition | TCI digita |
| Carburation | 4 x keihin FV KD 39.4 with TPS sensor |
| Gearbox | 6-speed |
| Clutch | Wet, multi-plate |
| Final Drive | Chain |
| Frame | Fabricated, lightweight alloy Deltabox |
| Suspension | Front; Öhlins 43mm inverted telescopic forks<br>Rear; Aluminium swinging arm with Öhlins single shock absorber |
| Wheels | Marchesini 3-spoke 17inch |
| Tyres | 310/4.80 R17 front; 185/55 R17 Rear |
| Brakes | Front; 2 x 320mm carbon-fibre discs with 6-pioston calipers.<br>Rear; single. |
| Dry weight | 346Ib(157kg) |
| Max power | 137bhp at 12,500rpm. |
| Max speed | 167mph. |

*Rob McElnea's Team Mitsui-Loctite YZF750SP on display after winning the British Championship title in 1993. By now the specification included inverted front forks, 4 piston brake calipers and other smaller changes.*

## 1998 YZFR1

| | |
|---|---|
| Engine | Liquid-cooled, across-the-frame, dohc 4-cylinder, with 20-valves and EXUP. |
| Capacity | 998cc |
| Bore | 74mm |
| Stroke | 58mm |
| Comp ratio | 11.2:1 |
| Ignition | Electronic |
| Carburation | 4 x Mikuni 32mm |
| Gearbox | 6-speed |
| Clutch | Wet, multiplate |
| Final Drive | Chain |
| Frame | Aluminium Delta-box 2 |
| Suspension | Front; Inverted telescopic fork<br>Rear; Braced swinging arm, with rising-rate single shock absorber. |
| Wheels | 17in. 3-spoke hollow aluminium. |
| Brakes | Front; 2 x 320mm discs with 4-piston calipers.<br>Rear; single 220mm disc with 2-piston caliper. |
| Dry weight | 390Ib (177kg) |
| Max power | 150bhp at 10,000rpm |
| Max speed | 173mph |

without the power valve system. The works specials were also considerably lighter than the customer bikes, making use as they did, of some titanium and carbon fibre bits.

The American John Kocinski made his European debut riding a very special TZ250U. This bike, featuring a British-built carbon composite frame, used the same geometry as the production Delta box component. But an unfortunate series of crashes saw the highly talented Kocinski return home, where he dominated the 250cc category aboard a TZ250 using a standard Delta box chassis.

Next came the TZ250W for the 1989 model year. This bike was very much a carefully detailed development of the U, rather than a major redesign. Changes included fuller and shorter exhausts, new Nissin brake calipers, modified Power jet system (now wired up to an electronically driven solenoid which brought in the jet action at 9,500rpm) and visually, bright red aluminium wheels (still 3-spoke affairs).

Internally, there were changes to the crankshaft, port sizes, piston skirt length and transfer duct shape.

Another alteration concerned the front forks, which now came with the ability for damping adjustment. An improved rear shock absorber and carbon fibre end cans for the exhaust completed the picture.

*Rob McElnea with his FZR750R(OWO1) Donington Park, 1990.*

*The 1989 FZR750R(OWO1). The machine was a limited production replica of the company's victorious YZR750R works racer and was produced in a high enough number for homologation in both F/M SuperBike and Formula 1 World Championships.*

And at long last the customer could pay his money and have a motorcycle capable of beating the Honda RS250 at everything except Grand Prix type events, where works specials dominated the proceedings.

For 1990 Yamaha built the last of its parallel twins, the TZ250A. This was not as may be supposed the 250W with minor changes. Instead the development team seemed intent on going out on a high; making the latest machine significantly different in several important respects. First the crankcases were reduced in size, being some 30mm narrower, there was a switch back to base mounted cylinders and a tighter water jacket around the cylinders, with a beefed-up water pump. Maybe these changes don't sound much, but collectively they created 'best in breed' - a fitting way for the parallel twin concept to bow out.

Welshman, Ian Lougher won a famous victory in the Isle of Man TT on a TZ250A, whilst in Europe future Grand Prix star Dutchman, Patrick van den Goorbergh brought his 250A home in third place in the European Championships - in fact van den Goorbergh finished with exactly the same number of points as the 1st and 2nd placed Aprilia riders, but with less victories.

With John Kocinski's 250cc world title aboard a factory TZR250 v-twin, Yamaha now considered the time right to switch to a v-twin for the TZ in 1990. This was also influenced by a buoyant Japanese domestic race scene - which saw a staggering 35,000 licence holders that year. Yamaha bosses reckoned that a replica of Kocinski's title winner would not only sell well, but it would also help spread some of the huge development costs that the v-twin had accrued during its developments.

Thus it was that when the 1991 TZ250B was launched, pundits were surprised to learn that the asking price was only slightly up on the figure asked a year earlier for the reverse cylinder TZ250A parallel twin. About the only people who were not happy were those who had forked out for the preceding model.

The 'B' was a giant step for the TZ series, even though Yamaha had used the v-twin layout for the last five years at Grand Prix level. The vee of the cylinders was 90 degrees - which most engineers agree is the format which provides the smoothest running. When the first factory YZRs were

## EXUP

EXUP (Exhaust Ultimate Power Valve) was in effect the company's way of doing to the four-stroke engine what it had done to the two-stroke.

Essentially EXUP was a special variable exhaust valve, but unlike on the two-stroke, this was fitted to the exhaust system (in the collector box), and was operated by a computer-controlled servo motor which performed according to the engine's rpm.

The valve effectively regulated exhaust pipe-end conditions, thereby controlling the exhaust gas pressure wave produced during inlet and exhaust valve overlap.

EXUP had the advantages of improving intake efficiency, reducing fuel consumption and allowing engineers to improve low-mid range torque without having to sacrifice peak rpm performance.

The first Yamaha production model to feature the system came in the spring of 1987, in the shape of the 'Japan-only' FZR400R. This motorcycle had a 399cc (56 x 40.5mm) Genesis-design, 16-valve, liquid-cooled, across-the-frame, 4-cylinder engine featuring narrow angle valves, straight inlet tracts and compact combustion chambers for optimum power output, while the block was inclined forward at 35 degrees.

The FZR400R not only featured EXUP, but many race-type components as standard. It also proved a top seller in Japan - for example in 1986 there were no fewer than 23,450 licensed racers lined up on the grid. Many of these chose to race either 250cc two-stroke or 400cc four-stroke production based bikes. And the FZR400R soon became the most popular four-stroke choice. This is easy to understand when one considers that most of the near 25,000 competitors were either in novice TT Formula or SP (Sport Production) classes.

In Europe, during the mid 1990s the FZR400 became the top choice of SuperSport 400 racers, the type winning club and national championships in Great Britain, France, Germany and Holland for example.

Sadly, however, in recent years the 400 class has gone into decline, whereas the 600s have taken over in club and national SuperSport competition.

built, separate crankshafts had been employed. However, by the time the production TZ250B arrived, only a single crank was used. Because of the large central main bearing (not found for example on the 90 degree Ducati v-twin) there was a fairly wide spacing between the cylinders for the piston/connecting rod assemblies. So to avoid the expected vibes, a second gear on the offside end of the crankshaft drove a balancer shaft to the rear of the engine.

The combustion of a 90 degree angle and balancer shaft meant that the Yamaha design team was able to mount the 250B power unit directly into the aluminium Delta box frame. And because of the engine's smoothness there were none of the problems associated with occasional frame breakages under poor road surface conditions as had been encountered with the parallel twin alloy-framed TZs.

*Launched in Japan in 1987, the FZR400R was a 399cc (54 x 40.5mm) dohc 16-valve 4 with liquid cooling and EXUP (Exhaust Ultimate Power Valve), a special variable exhaust valve fitted to the exhaust system's collector box.*

For the first time in a decade the engine ran forwards. The massive inlet port which had killed pistons in the TZ250G was now history. Crankcase reed valves had solved this particular problem - with a small series of transfer ports - meaning that the piston skirt was much better supported and thus had a less stressful life. Old features of the engine were the 56 x 50.7mm bore and stroke dimensions, the flat slide Mikuni TM 38mm carbs and the guillotine exhaust valves. Otherwise wherever one looked things were different. The engine of the v-twin was more compact than the old parallel model. Some of this was in the layout of the cylinders, some because the gearbox had been remodelled by 'stacking' the two gearbox main shafts.

Compared to the old parallel twin, the v-twin engine offered improved mid-range power - the actual top speed not being that different between the 1990 'A' and 1991 'B' machines. Not only was the port timing of the

*Peter Berwick FZR400RR taking part in the British Super Teen Championships, 1993.*

two engines noticeably different, but the differences between the power characteristics of the parallel twin and the v-twin formats meant that the new engine was far better equipped to offer drive out of corners - an important feature in a racing machine.

A major change in the chassis department concerned the frame, which no longer featured rails under the motor; instead the engine acted as a stressed member. Again this probably could not have been achieved with the parallel twin due to increased vibration levels as already explained. A new swinging arm was needed, if for no other reason than the routing of the exhaust system. Although the rear rising rate suspension only received minor attention the same could not have been said about the front end; here being a brand new inverted telescopic fork assembly. However, even though it looked the part, the 'B' model's performance that year left much to be desired, suffering from glitches and being difficult to fine tune.

From then on the v-twin TZ followed an evolution which saw steady, if unspectacular progress. In national racing the TZ often gave Honda's RS its only real competition. For example, in Great Britain during the early 1990s the national 250cc championship swayed from Honda to Yamaha and then back again. But after the mid 1990s the RS and of course the Italian Aprilia really took charge. A mini redesign towards the end of the 1990s at least put the TZ back in contention, but not noticeably better than its two rivals. In fact it seemed that Yamaha's TZ was marking time. Proof of this was the TZ125 - a rival to Honda's all conquering best selling RS125. The TZ appeared in 1992, but never really made the grade and by the middle of the decade was quietly axed.

Instead Yamaha seemed to put their real effort into the Grands Prix and World SuperBike racing, the latter through a series of 20-valve four cylinder engines.

*Mick Walker Racing teamster Darren Wnukoski taking his FZR400 to victory at Mallory Park, Spring 1997.*

# Yamaha Race School

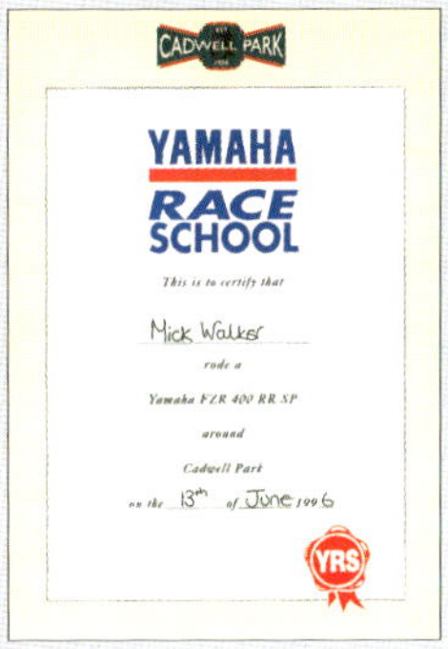
CADWELL PARK

YAMAHA RACE SCHOOL

This is to certify that

Mick Walker

rode a

Yamaha FZR 400 RR SP

around

Cadwell Park

on the 13th of June 1996

YRS

*Certificate awarded to those successfully taking part in the Yamaha Race School.*

For several years during the mid 1990s Mitsui, the British Yamaha importers based in Chessington, Surrey backed the Yamaha Race School run at Cadwell Park, Lincolnshire.

The school used a number of instructors including Chris Walker, Mark Phillips and Shaun Brown. As for motorcycles, these were FZR400RR SP (Road Race Sport Production), pretty much, in the author's opinion, the ideal bike for such a task.

The rights to run the school at Cadwell Park (and certain other British circuits) changed in 1998 to the Ducati Performance set-up, using 748 (and 996) V-twins.

But for many, the 400 Yamaha provided the first track experiences for budding road racers, in any era before track days became the norm.

*Mick Walker trying one of the Yamaha Race School's FZR400RR SP machines at Cadwell Park, summer 1996.*

Actually Yamaha engineers began work on what was to emerge as the FZ/FZR project as far back as 1977. And before 20-valves were chosen, extensive testing was carried out with both 6 and even 7 valves per cylinder! However, as the engineering team ultimately discovered, the best format was two exhaust valves and three inlets. The 5-valve-per-cylinder layout meant that enough gas flowed into the (theoretically superior) lens-shaped combustion chamber to provide the potential for a relatively higher output than conventional 2 or 4-valve heads. Using a single spark plug (as opposed to a twin plug layout on the 7-valve prototype engine) - the bi-convex chamber provided excellent flame propagation. In layman's terms, all the mixture shoved into the chamber is burnt quickly and efficiently. This provided the added advantage of allowing high compression ratios and a slightly dish-topped piston. A Yamaha engineer confided with the author that this set up provides an additional pent-roof chamber.

In 1982 the development team settled on a 5-valves-per-cylinder 750cc with four across-the-frame cylinders. Actually Yamaha had several teams of engineers working on the project - but without knowing what the others had come up with. The choice, when it came saw the teams' results pooled and a definitive design emerged.

The result was the FZ750, launched for the 1985 model year. Besides the 5-valve technology, the other radical (at least compared to other Japanese manufacturers' across-the-frame fours), was the 45 degrees forward slant of the cylinders. This lowered the centre of gravity and was influenced by the latest trends in automobile racing engine design.

The balance of the liquid-cooled dohc 749cc (68 x 51.6mm) engine displayed Yamaha's old obsessions with narrowness. The generator was located on top of the gearbox behind the cylinders and chain driven from the crankshaft. Not content with that, the electronic ignition trigger was on the nearside crank web and the sensors mounted on the crankcase halves. As a result the FZ's crankcases were as narrow as would have been achieved had the unit been a V4. The width across the barrels had been minimized by a hybrid wet/dry liner system which directly water-cooled the top section of the liners only.

# Ian Lougher

Mention Joey Dunlop or Philip McCallen in respect of recent Isle of Man TT performances and most enthusiasts will instantly recognise their names. However, there is a third natural roads man who deserves to be remembered; Ian Lougher. Ian has had a vast amount of success, not in the Island, but in Northern Ireland and the famous Oliver's Mount circuit, Scarborough.

In fact, in July 2002 Ian Lougher notched up his 50th victory at the Yorkshire seaside venue, something of a record in itself. Originally from South Wales, but now resident in Northern Ireland, Ian Lougher began racing at his local Llandow circuit on an RD400 Yamaha in 1982. His first visit to Oliver's Mount was in 1985, riding a Yamaha 350F2. He recalls, 'I didn't like the circuit at first, especially the last jumps, before the now introduced Farm Bends chicane. The circuit needs a lot of learning, but becomes very enjoyable once this has been achieved.'

Not only has Ian Lougher scored at Scarborough, but has also recorded 25 victories in the Southern 100 (held over the Billown circuit near Castletown, Isle of Man each July) and is second only to Joey Dunlop.

His first Isle of Man visit was in 1983 when he finished 3rd in the Newcomers race. The first TT was in 1985 when he returned on a Yamaha TZ250. Since then he has chalked up 6 TT wins and 3 lap records.

Other prominent results include 5 NorthWest 200 victories and 4 Ulster grand Prix wins.

Ian Lougher has also had some successes in British short circuit events, notably finishing 3rd in the British 125cc Championship series in 1989 and 2nd in 1998, in the latter he finished behind champion Chris Palmer by a mere 2 points, but achieved more wins than any other rider.

*Ian Lougher at his favourite circuit, Oliver's Mount, Scarborough.*

Ian Lougher wins at Oliver's Mount (up to July 2002)

| | | | | | |
|---|---|---|---|---|---|
| 1989 | Gold Cup Nat 125cc | 2 | 1998 | Spring National 125cc x 2 - Junior 175cc - 400cc | 3 |
| 1990 | Spring National 2 Nat 125cc-1 250cc | 3 | 1998 | Cock o' the North 2 x 125cc | 2 |
| 1991 | Cock o' the North 250cc | 1 | 1998 | Gold Cup 125cc | 1 |
| 1991 | Gold Cup 1 leg Phil Mellor Trophy | 1 | 1999 | Spring National 125cc | 1 |
| 1992 | Cock o' the North Junior 250cc | 1 | 1999 | Cock o' the North 3 x 125cc - 2 x 400cc | 5 |
| 1994 | Spring National 125cc-Junior 175cc-400cc | 2 | 2000 | Cock o' the North 400cc - Superbike - Cock o' the North | 3 |
| 1994 | Cock o' the North 250cc-400cc | 1 | 2000 | Gold Cup Lee Pullan and Phil Mellor Trophies | 2 |
| 1995 | Cock o' the North 125cc | 1 | 2001 | Spring National 125cc - Junior 400cc - 1300cc | 3 |
| 1995 | Gold Cup 1 leg Phil Mellor Trophy | 1 | 2001 | Cock o' the North 600cc - National Superbike | 2 |
| 1996 | Cock o' the North Junior 250cc | 1 | 2001 | Gold Cup 125cc x 2 - 600c - Lee Pullan | 4 |

1996 Gold Cup 125cc 1 leg Phil Mellor and Lee Pullan 3 2002 Cock o' the North 2 x 125cc - 2 x Junior 250cc - 400cc - 600cc - 2 x Superbike - Cock o' the North 8 1997 Spring National 125cc 2

1997 Cock o' the North 125cc - Junior 400 2 1997 Gold Cup Phil Mellor Trophy 1

*Phil Read Junior with his FZR600 accelerates out of Russell's Corner at Snetterton, May 1993.*

The only truly conservative engineering feature concerned the centrally mounted cam chain, which made things awkward when a replacement was needed.

The valve train saw a cam lobe for every valve - direct operation without rockers - and hollow chrome molybdenum camshafts. Valve adjustment was by bucket shims. The bucket and shim layout meant that load-bearing surfaces were larger than with conventional tappets. The valves themselves were each equipped with a single, oil-tempered, silicon-chrome spring, and had to cope with less severe lift than on a 4-valver due to superior gas flow.

This all added up to a very tough valve train. A 6-speed gearbox was specified. Much of the balance was pretty conventional - the frame being a box section affair, but unlike its rival, the Suzuki GSXR, the FZ750's frame was made of steel - even if the layout had been derived from Kenny Roberts' YZR500 GP racer. The front down tubes were detachable for easier engine removal, the swinging arm an aluminium affair, pivoted on needle roller bearings. Rear suspension was taken care of by a rising rate single shock, whilst up front, a pair of conventional telescopic forks (with 39mm stanchion) gave the four cylinder Yamaha a good degree of handling and road holding abilities.

A trio of opposed piston calipers and discs looked after the braking, with six-spoke cast alloy wheels with 16-inch and 18-inch front and rear tyres respectively.

In standard, untuned guise, the 1985 FZ750 put out 106bhp at 10,500rpm - but the most impressive figure was that of torque, 63ft/lb (8kg/m) at 8000rpm.

Next to the Suzuki's GXR-750 the Yamaha was a serious challenger - something which at that time neither Honda or Kawasaki could boast. And like Suzuki, Yamaha soon came up with a larger engined version. This arrived for 1987 and was called the FZR1000 Genesis.

*The 1989 FZR600 at last gave Yamaha a shot at the important SuperSport 600 class.*

# The Linsdell GTS/YZF project

*Steve Bond (sponsor) and Steve Linsdell with the newly completed GTS/YZF at the Isle of Man TT, 1994, directly before its first test was to come.*

The Yamaha GTS1000 was launched in 1993, but received less than enthusiastic reviews from the press. However racer/engineer Steve Linsdell of Flitwick Motorcycles, Bedfordshire thought differently and decided to convert one into a racer. Not only this but its debut came in no less an event than the Isle of Man F1 TT.

Steve Linsdell, one of Mitsui-Yamaha's main British dealers, specialises in FZ/FZR/YZF tuning. He is also a racer of considerable ability having previously competed in the Manx Grand Prix, North West 200 and the TT. Steve began racing with a Royal Enfield Bullet in the Vintage class during 1977. He continued to race Enfields, including a 700cc twin and a 500cc Seeley-Enfield until the end of 1981. He became Vintage Champion, and also finished runner-up in the 1981 Manx Grand Prix Newcomers Race on a 500 Enfield producing a mere 40bhp, behind a Yamaha TZ500 four and in front of a quartet of Suzuki RG500s. Steve married in 1982 and and built his own bungalow.

In 1985 he began a long association with Steve and Elaine Bond (who still sponsor him now) Riding a Yamaha FZ750, he finished third in the Manx Grand Prix.

1986 was his first year at the TT, finishing 3rd on an XJ600F in the Production 600 class. From then until 1992 he raced the FZ750 in, 'all sorts of races with some good results, but not always on the road circuits I loved.'

In 1993 Steve Bond bought a new YZF750, but, 'It wobbled so badly that it made me build the GTS!'

Hating that YZF, Steve then set out to build a GTS racer - using the YZF engine (because TT rules only allowed a 750). It was finished just in time to start practice in the 1994 TT. In fact the first time it turned a wheel was down Bray Hill.

Although a 'very big bike and still a heavyweight', Steve Linsdell says, 'I ended up in 8th place in the F1 TT.' It was the fifth fastest bike through the speed trap after the factory Honda V4s of Hislop, McCallum, Dunlop and Ward. (the GTS clocked 167mph, compared with McCallam's RC45 at 174mph).

After more development which included fitting a narrower front arm and lighter front wheel, with a PFM brake, the YZF/GTS finished 6th in the 1995 Formula 1 TT. As Steve Linsdell says, 'Not bad for a tourer with a few mods.'

Perhaps the most surprising aspect of the GTS racer was the way it handled. Steve recalls, 'It had fantastic stability (117mph laps with no steering damper fitted) had a good aerodynamics and worked the front tyre very gently. Its drawbacks were its size and weight.'

Steve then made a Mark 2 version which was much lighter and more compact. He was still using this bike in 2003.

*Rear disc relocated next to swinging arm pivot.*

# 1994 Linsdell Yamaha GTS/YZF

| | |
|---|---|
| Engine | Liquid-cooled YZF750SP dohc five-valves per-cylinder, across-the-frame four. |
| Capacity | 749cc |
| Bore | 72mm |
| Stroke | 46mm |
| Comp. ratio | 12:1 |
| Ignition | Electronic |
| Lubrication | Wet sump, oil pump |
| Carburation | 4 x Keihin 38mm |
| Gearbox | Close ratio, 6-speed |
| Clutch | Wet, multi-plate |
| Final drive | Chain |
| Frame | Standard GTS frame and swinging arm. |
| Suspension | Single shock front Öhlins and rear Proflex |
| Wheels | 17inch front and rear |
| Tyres | Front 120/70 x 17, rear 180/55 x 17 |
| Brakes | Front single 320mm disc<br>Rear single 220mm disc |
| Dry weight | 397Ib(180kg) |
| Max power | 122bhp @ 13,500rpm |
| Max speed | 174mph(280kph) |

*Front suspension unit.*

*YZF750 engine gave 122 bhp and used a quartet of 38mm flat-side Keihin carburettors.*

*Cooling radiator aft of the engine unit.*

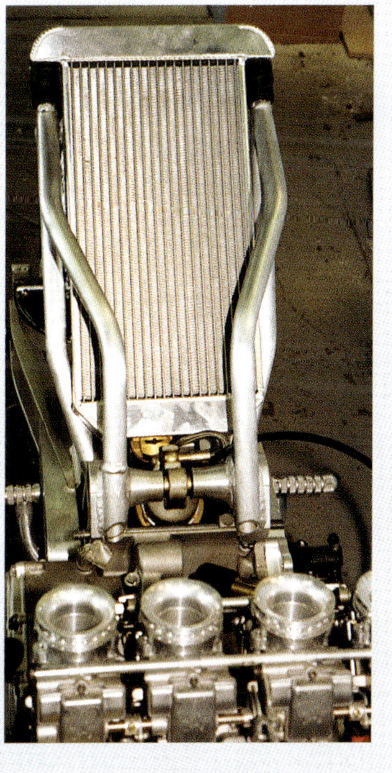

*A Mark 2 version was built mainly to reduce weight. Steve Linsdell was still racing the bike in 2003.*

*Junior TT, 7th June 2000, race winner David Jefferies with the V&M 600R6. His winning time was 1 hour 15 minutes 52.8 seconds, at an average speed of 119.33 mph. Sadly David was killed during practice for the 2003 TT.*

*The late David Jefferies signing autographs; Scarborough, September 2001.*

This time the frame was aluminium and together with the TZR250 2-stroke twin, was the first series production roadster-orientated Yamaha to make of this Grand Prix race developed frame technology.

The FZR1000 engine was essentially a bored and stroked 75 x 56mm FZ750, giving a new displacement of 989cc.

During development the larger engine had suffered from vibration. It was found that using special lightweight pistons and connecting rods was the only way of solving the problem. Despite the increased bore size, the FZR's block was no wider than the 750's. This was made possible by using parts of 'siamesed bores' - best described as a sort of figure '8' with two cast iron liners side by side.

Taking a leaf out of Suzuki's book, the FZR1000 employed under-piston oil-jet cooling besides its FZ - derived liquid cooling.

With 135bhp and 165mph the FZR was quick, making it a favourite for open class production events. Actually, Yamaha dominated the late 1980s unlimited production racer scene and thus was able to put one over the GSXR1100 Suzuki. But in the 750cc class the Suzuki ruled the roost.

There were three developments for the 1989 model year: an EXUP-equipped FZR750R (OWO1) and a brand new middle-weight, the FZR600. All three were important bikes.

Not only did the 1-litre bike get the EXUP system (see boxed section), but it also gained a revised Delta-box frame. Gone were the dual front down tubes of the previous model's frame. The engine now bolted directly to the frame at the cylinder head, at the top of the upper crankcase and, as before, at the rear. By making the engine a stressed member, overall frame rigidity and strength was increased.

This more compact design made it possible for a 10mm shorter wheelbase and a new 26 degree fork angle - thus giving quicker steering.

The fork stanchion tube diameter was increased from 41 to 43mm, whilst at the rear there was a modification to the linkage arms, increasing shock absorber strokes from 50 to 70mm.

There were also changes to the rear wheel diameter (from 4.50 x 18 to 5.50 x 17-inch); new 4-pot opposed piston calipers at the front with the

Ottringham, East Yorkshire rider Trevor Tanton (right) and his father/mechanic Alan with their 2000 model R6, Scarborough, Cock of the North, September 2002.

top piston larger than the bottom (33.96 and 30.23mm respectively); and new larger diameter, hollow wheel axles and swinging arm pivot.

The front axle diameter increased from 15 to 17mm, the rear from 17 to 20mm, and swinging arm pivot from 16 - 20mm - all these features coming directly from the works YZR racers.

Finally, the engine's displacement had risen to 1002cc (75.6 x 56mm) with a higher compression ratio (12:1), thinner piston rings (to reduce frictional losses) and a redesigned combustion chamber with straighter inlet ports, larger (38mm) carbs and of course EXUP. All this meant the 1989 FZR1000 was a rocket ship, being able to exceed 170mph in standard, untuned guise.

In 1987 and 1988, Yamaha won the prestigious Suzuka 8 Hours race; one of the toughest events for 4-strokes in the world. To take full advantage Yamaha decided to market a replica of the victorious YZF750. The result was the new FZR750 R (OWO1). Employing an ultra-short stroke 72 x 46mm, 749cc, Genesis-inspired engine, this was a pukka racer

Martin Appleyard with his V&MR6 cresting the famous 'Mountain' at Cadwell Park, New Era Superclub Championship 29/30th June 2002.

*Andrew Plumridge, with his fully kitted Yamaha R1, Pegasus Club races, Cadwell Park, Sunday 20th October 2002.*

When it was announced at the end of 1997, the R1 caused a massive stir, throughout the 1-litre motorcycle world, not least because it weighed in (in road trim) at an amazingly low 390lb (177kg) - less than the majority of SuperSport 600s!

The R1's project leader in Japan was Kunihito Miwa, who had decided back in 1995 to set about designing and building the fastest, lightest and best handling sports bike possible.

The R1 featured a compact version of Yamaha's familiar 20-valve four cylinder engine. Displacing 998cc (74 x 58mm), it was considerably smaller and lighter than its predessor, the YZF1000R (Thunderace), and employed a one-piece cylinder and crankcase assembly. A more sophisticated EXUP system took into account rpm, throttle position, and even the speed at which the throttle was being opened, and provided additional mid-range torque.

The R1's shorter, more compact engine sat well forward in the new aluminuim twin-beam Delta-box frame, allowing a longer swinging arm (also in aluminuim) to improve stability and traction. The wheelbase of the R1 was extremely short. at 1395mm (54.9in). The Honda CBR900R FireBlade's was 1405mm (55.3in).

Suspension was multi-adjustable, and the upside-down front forks featured additional rebound at the end of their travel to help keep the front wheel down under hard acceleration. Engineering chief Kunihito Miwa and his team also paid particular attention to components such as the wheels (a massive 6 inch rear, with a 190 section tyre) and brakes, which, although based on the YZR1000R, had been revamped to reduce weight.

Although largely conceived as a roadster, the R1 had in many ways been designed as a race bike with respect to its 'minimum weight' thesis. As an example of this the 4-piston front brake calipers had been lightened - to reduce unsprung weight, whilst the 3-spoke alloy wheels were hollow and considerably lighter than that of comparable machinery. Losing weight Miwa reasoned, assisted suspension performance.

Another feature of the R1, like other big-bore 5-valves-per-cylinder Yamaha four cylinder engines, is the engine's tractability, it being possible in standard, untuned form, to drive smoothly at 20mph in top gear, then, with little or no hesitation accelerate all the way up to the 11,500rpm red line, truly amazing !

Even though the original R1 was a brilliant bike (voted *Motor Cycle News* Machine of the Year in both 1998 and 1999), Yamaha still saw fit to update the R1 for the 2000 model year.

In total, the new generation R1 had more than 250 changes (most of them relatively minor). One of the most notable was an all new fairing which increased aerodynamic efficiency and at the same time helped reduce rider fatigue (important in long distance, endurance-type events). In addition, by fitting a range of special lightweight components - including a new titanium muffler - Miwa and his development team were able to shave 4.4lb (2kg) off the weight, taking it down to 385lb (175kg) in road legal guise.

The arrival of Suzuki's new GSXR1000 for the 2001 model year took Yamaha off the front line - certainly the R1 was no longer the dominant force it had been in Open Class racing events.

*Launched at the end of 1997 the YZFR1 made an equally good road or racing motorcycle. The 998cc (74 x 58mm) 20-valve dohc 4 could reach 178 mph in standard guise or 190 mph with the race kit. This 2000 model is seen here with rider Andy McPherson, New Era Super Club, Saturday 20th July, 2002.*

# The ultimate R1

*This 2000 model year R1 has just about every conceivable tuning and chassis upgrade possible to buy.*

This 2000 model year R1 has had the full treatment, with just about every conceivable tuning mod and chassis uprate possible.

The list includes:

Fully race tuned engine.

Ram air box.

Complete Akrapovic exhaust system, including carbon fibre muffler.

Promec offset front fork yokes.

Öhlins rear shock.

Katec front forks.

Full AP braking system, including 6-pot front calipers.

Marchini lightweight wheels.

Stretched and braced aluminium swinging-arm.

Öhlins hydralic steering damper, with Harris bracket.

Promac multi-adjustable rear set footrests.

Lap timer.

Extensive carbon-fibre components.

Larger radiator.

Braided brake and clutch hoses.

*Stretched and braced aluminium swinging arm, Promec multi-adjustable rear sets and Öhlins rear shocks.*

*Fully floating discs with AP 6-piston calipers and Katec front forks with Promec offset forks.*

*Drilled solid rear disc with a caliper at the rear.*

*A year after the R1 came its smaller brothers the R7 and 750. This race kitted World SuperSport model is on display at the Munich Show, September 1998. Besides the engine, other changes include Nissin 6-piston front brake calipers, fully floating discs, lightweight wheels, race bodywork, racing exhaust and slick tyres.*

capable of winning right up to international level. It was also Yamaha's way into the fast growing WSB (World SuperBike) competition, which had begun in 1988.

The shorter stroke effectively reduced piston speed so the engine could rev higher without the limiting factor of piston failure. The corresponding increase in bore meant a larger diameter combustion chamber, with space for longer valves.

Besides the bigger valves there were very light, immensely strong titanium-alloy connecting rods, plus lightweight pistons with only two rings (one compression, one oil control).

Other details of the OWO1's specification included flat slide carbs, digitally controlled electronic ignition, a 15mm lower cylinder block (due to the shorter stroke), which in turn allowed an alteration in the engine's inclination from 45 to 40 degrees and a 20mm shorter wheelbase which quickened up the steering. Racing demanded a closer ratio set of gears for the 6-speed box, a special wet clutch and the removal of the radiator cooling fan. In addition, the bike was upgraded with alterations to the Delta-box chassis, an Öhlin's racing rear shock, 17-inch hollow spoke wheels with low profile Michelin radial racing compound tyres. As if all this was not enough and demonstrating the increasing importance of big money in the results race, there was an extensive (and very expensive) factory race kit. This included forged pistons, an exhaust to be used with the existing EXUP system, and inlet camshaft and carburettor-setting parts to adjust the air/fuel mixture required for the increased power output.

The third newcomer for 1989 was the FZR600, which replaced the ageing air-cooled FZ600. With this newcomer Yamaha at last had a machine suitable for the fast growing SuperSport 600 racing class.

The FZR600 followed the 'Genesis concept' of inclined engines and Delta-box frames which had made the larger FZRs such a success. But like the smaller FZR400 didn't boast 5-valve heads. Displaying 599cc (59 x 54.8mm), this twin cam engine delivered a shade over 90bhp at 10,500rpm. The power was kept on the boil by way of a 6-speed gearbox in which 5th and 6th gears employed reverse-taped dogs (back-cut) for positive engagement and improved reliability.

Much of the technology came from the larger FZRs but in reduced sizes; 38mm fork stanchions, dual 298mm front discs with a single 245mm component at the rear and narrower rubber.

Since then Yamaha has attempted, not always successfully, to keep ahead of the opposition. Developments have included the FZR1000 with inverted forks (1991), the OWO1 replaced in 1993 by the YZF750 SP, whilst the 998cc (74 x 58mm) R1 arrived in 1998 and the 599cc R6 debuted the following year.

Except for the possible exception of the R1 none has succeeded in putting Yamaha at the top of the tree and with the arrival of Suzuki's GSXR1000 in 2001 even the R1's lead has been eroded if not surpassed. What next Mr Yamaha?

# Japanese motorcyle manufacturers

| | |
|---|---|
| Asahi | 1953 - 1965 |
| BIM | 1956 - 1961 |
| Bridgestone | 1952 - 1968 |
| Cabton | 1937 - 1961 |
| Center | 1952 - 1962 |
| Champion | 1960 - 1967 |
| DWB | 1957 - 1961 |
| Ebu-Star | 1952 - 1955 |
| Echo | 1957 - 1961 |
| Emuro | 1953 - 1959 |
| Fugi Kikai | 1961 |
| Gasuden (Fugi) | 1955 - 1961 |
| Giant | 1924 |
| Hirana | 1951 - 1961 |
| Hodaka | 1964 - 1978 |
| Honda | 1947 - |
| Hosk | 1955 - 1958 |
| Hurricane | 1956 - 1961 |
| IMC | 1956 - 1960 |
| International | 1952 - 1957 |
| Itagaki | 1954 - 1960 |
| Ito Imc | 1951 - 1961 |
| Kanto | 1957 - 1960 |
| Katakura | 1960 - 1967 |
| Katayama | 1956 |
| Kawasaki | 1961 - |
| Kitagawa | 1955 - 1959 |
| Lancer | 1957 - 1961 |
| Lilac | 1949 - 1967 |
| Martin | 1956 - 1961 |
| Meguro | 1937 - 1964 |
| Meihatsu | 1953 - 1961 |
| Mishima Nainenki | 1955 - 1959 |
| Miyata | 1909 - 1964 |
| Mizubo | (produced by Cabton) |
| Monark | 1955 - 1962 |
| Nissan | 1951 - 1956 |
| NMC | 1953 - 1961 |
| Omega | 1960 - 1966 |
| Pointer | 1946 - 1962 |
| Rabbit | 1946 - 1968 |
| Rikuo | 1935 - 1945 |
| | and 1953 - 1962 |
| Rocket | 1952 - 1967 |
| Rotary | 1953 - 1961 |
| Sanyo | 1958 - 1962 |
| Shin Meiwa | 1955 - 1964 |
| Showa | 1955 - 1962 |
| Silver Pidgeon | 1952 - 1965 |
| Silver Star | 1953 - 1958 |
| SJK | 1956 - 1962 |
| Sumita | 1951 - 1955 |
| Suzuki | 1952 - |
| Tohatsu | 1949 - 1964 |
| Toyomotor | 1957 - 1961 |
| Tsubasa | 1950 - 1960 |
| Yamaguchi | 1953 - 1964 |
| Yamaha | 1953 - |

# Index *figures in italics refer to captions*

# OTHER TITLES BY MICK WALKER

*Titles in bold published by Redline Books*

**Mick Walker's British Racing Motorcycles**
**Mick Walker's Italian Racing Motorcycles**
**Mick Walker's German Racing Motorcycles**
**Mick Walker's European Racing Motorcycles**
**Mick Walker's Japanese Grand Prix Racing Motorcycles**
**The Manx Norton**
**The AJS 7R**

Ducati Singles
Ducati Twins
Spanish Post-War Road & Racing Motorcycles
Moto Guzzi Twins
Moto Guzzi Singles
MV Agusta Production Machines
Greeves
Ducati Desmo – The Making of a Masterpiece
International Six Days Trial
Italian Motorcycles
Manx Norton
Ducati & Cagiva Buyers Guide
Mick Walker's Classic Italian Gallery – The Road Bikes
Mick Walker's Classic Italian Gallery – The Racing Bikes
BMW K-Series Motorcycles
Café Racers of the 60s
Superbike Specials of the 70s
Ducati Singles 2nd Edition
Ducati Twins 2nd Edition
German Motorcycles
Ducati Singles Restoration
Ducati Twins Restoration
BMW Twins Restoration
Moto Guzzi Twins Restoration
Aermacchi
Benelli
MZ
Morini
British Performance Two-Strokes
Ducati Buyers Guide
Moto Guzzi Buyers Guide
Ducati
Yamaha
Suzuki
Honda
Moto Guzzi
Kawasaki
Endurance Racing
Kawasaki Fours – The Complete Story
Classic British Racing Motorcycles
Classic Italian Racing Motorcycles
Classic German Racing Motorcycles
Classic European Racing Motorcycles
Classic Japanese Racing Motorcycles
Classic American Racing Motorcycles
BMW Twins – The Complete Story
Moto Guzzi V-twins – The Complete Story
Laverda Twins & Triples – The Complete Story
Ducati 4-Valve V-Twins – The Complete Story
Ducati 2-Valve V-Twins – The Complete Story
MV Agusta Fours – The Complete Story
Aprilia – The Complete Story
Gilera – The Complete Story
Classic Motorcycles
Performance Motorcycles
Miller's Classic Motorcycle Price Guide 1995
Miller's Classic Motorcycle Price Guide 1996
Miller's Classic Motorcycle Price Guide 1997
Miller's Classic Motorcycle Price Guide 1998
Miller's Classic Motorcycle Price Guide 1999
Miller's Classic Motorcycle Price Guide 2000
Miller's Classic Motorcycle Price Guide 2001
Miller's Classic Motorcycle Price Guide 2002
Miller's Classic Motorcycle Price Guide 2003
John Surtees Motorcycle Maestro
Ducati 2000 (exhibition catalogue)
Ducati. Taglioni and his World Beating Motorcycles
Encyclopaedia of Motorcycles
BMW Z Series (cars)
Royal Enfield - The Complete Story
Ducati The Racing Story
Norton The Racing Story
Ducati Buyers Guide 2nd Edition
Ducati Buyers Guide 3rd Edition
Moto Guzzi Buyers Guide 2nd Edition
Ariel - The complete Story
BMW - The Racing Story